# RELIGIOUS ORIGINS OF THE AMERICAN REVOLUTION

AMERICAN ACADEMY OF RELIGION
Aids for the Study of Religion Series

Series Editor:
Gerald J. Larson
Volume Editor:
Doug Adams

PAGE SMITH
is Professor Emeritus of American History at the University of
California at Santa Cruz. He is the author of numerous books,
including *Daughters of the Promised Land: Women in American
History,* and the Bancroft prize winning two volume work, *John
Adams.* His most recent publication is a two volume work on the
American Revolution.

Number 3
RELIGIOUS ORIGINS OF THE AMERICAN
REVOLUTION

by
Page Smith

SCHOLARS PRESS
Missoula, Montana

# RELIGIOUS ORIGINS OF THE AMERICAN REVOLUTION

Edited, with Introduction and Annotations

by

Page Smith

Published by

SCHOLARS PRESS

for

American Academy of Religion

Distributed by

SCHOLARS PRESS
University of Montana
Missoula, Montana 59812

# RELIGIOUS ORIGINS OF THE AMERICAN REVOLUTION

by

Page Smith

Material from *Calvin: Institutes of the Christian Religion*, The Library of Christian Classics, edited by John T. McNeill and translated by Ford Lewis Battles. Published simultaneously in the U.S.A. by The Westminster Press, Philadelphia, and in Great Britain by S.C.M. Press, Ltd., London. Copyright © 1960, by W. L. Jenkins. Used by permission.

Materials from *Christian Realism and Political Problems* by Reinhold Niebuhr, published in the U.S.A. by Charles Scribner's Sons, 1953. Copyright © 1953 by Reinhold Niebuhr. Used by permission.

Library of Congress Cataloging in Publication Data

    Main entry under title:

    Religious origins of the American Revolution.

      (American Academy of Religion aids for the study of religion ; no. 3)
      1. United States—History—Revolution, 1775-1783—Religious aspects—Addresses, essays, lectures.
    2. Theology, Protestant—Addresses, essays, lectures.
    I. Smith, Page. II. Adams, Doug. III. American Academy of Religion. American Academy of Religion aids for the study of religion ; no. 3.
    E209.R38    973.3    76-13157
    ISBN 0-89130-121-6

Printed in the United States of America

Printing Department
University of Montana
Missoula, Montana 59812

# TABLE OF CONTENTS

v

# Introduction

It has become a commonplace to state that Christianity is (or was) a radical religion: that in comparison with the other world religions it contained a principle or a set of dogmas and doctrines which were intended to work a radical change in the world. That it contained other doctrines that worked to quite different ends is also clear enough. But through much of the last two thousand years the Christian doctrines tending to produce change have predominated over those tending to preserve the status quo.

Moreover, Christianity evidenced a striking capacity for renewal and regeneration so that when the institutional church showed signs of rigidity and calcification reform movements took place that stimulated change in the church itself. The Protestant Reformation was such a movement of reform within the Christian Church. It proved to be the most radical re-forming of the church in its long history.

Arnold Toynbee has written that the American Revolution was made possible by American Protestantism. That, very simply, is the assumption on which this anthology is based. The assumption is perhaps best stated as proposition. The Protestant Reformation produced a new kind of consciousness and a new kind of man. The English colonies of America, in turn, produced a new and unique strain of that new consciousness. It thus follows that it is impossible to understand the intellectual and moral forces behind the American Revolution without understanding the role that Protestant Christianity played in shaping the ideals, principles and institutions of colonial America.

The American Revolution might thus be said to have started, in a sense, when Martin Luther nailed his 95 theses to the church door at Wittenburg. It received a substantial part of its theological and philosophical underpinnings from John Calvin's *Institutes of the Christian Religion* and much of its social theory from the Puritan Revolution of 1640-1660, and, perhaps less obviously, from the Glorious Revolution of 1689.

Put another way, the American Revolution is inconceivable in the absence of that context of ideas which have constituted radial Christianity. The leaders of the Revolution in every colony were imbued with the precepts of the Reformed faith. Even though in many specific instances Christian orthodoxy was modified by Enlightenment ideas, there was a kind of irreducible stratum of Christian doctrines or none at all.

When Luther made his dramatic gesture of defiance in 1517 he did more than attack specific abuses in the Roman church; he struck at some of its basic dogmas. He insisted, for instance, that a man or woman could find salvation only through faith. And, perhaps most significant in its effect on the settlers of the New World, Luther held that the individual was wholly responsible for his own salvation.

If Luther was the originator of the Reformation, John Calvin was its most formidable theorist. In his *Institutes*, Calvin presented the doctrinal basis of the branch of the Reformation that, as Calvinism, became the foundation of American Puritanism. The *Institutes* was, in effect, the charter for a new kind of consciousness, a new way of looking at the world and one's fellows, as well as a new way of understanding the relationship of the individual to the Divine.

Before the Reformation, people had belonged, most typically, to orders; to social groups and classes, to communes and communities — estates — by which they were defined and which set the boundaries of their worlds and established their identities; they were clerks, aristocrats, priests, artisans, members of guilds, of burghs. No one had to live in doubt or uncertainty about his or her place in the world. That place was defined and codified; represented practically and symbolically in a hundred different ways. If such individuals understood the general principles that governed their places in the earthly order of things, they also had reference to an equally specific set of rules regarding their place in the heavenly kingdom. They were incorporated; part of a social body. It followed that Medieval man did not think of himself as an "individual;" he thought of himself as a member of one of the clearly established orders of society. These traditional orders did not so much submerge him as define and protect him. Above all, they contained him.

Luther and Calvin, by postulating a single "individual" soul responsible for itself, plucked a new human type out of this traditional "order" and put him down naked, a re-formed individual in a re-formed world.

The doctrine of a "priesthood of believers" with each person responsible directly to God for his or her own spiritual state brought new burdens for the individual psyche; but it brought remarkable new opportunities as well. The individuals who formed the new congregations established their own churches, chose their own ministers, and managed their own affairs without reference to an ecclesiastical hierarchy. Thus there appeared modern man (or his essential integument), an introspective, aggressive individual who was able to function remarkably well outside these older structures that had defined people's roles and given them whatever power they possessed.

What this transformation meant was an almost incalculable release of new human energy into the stream of history. Put another way, Luther and Calvin invented the individual; and these individuals, at least relatively secure in their relationship to God and confident of their own powers, worked remarkable changes in the world. This new individual proved almost equally adept at founding new sects and denominations as well as new financial enterprises, and, indeed, entire new communities. One of the obvious by-products was the notion of a contract entered into by two people or by the members of a community amongst themselves that needed no legal sanctions to make it binding. This concept of the Reformers made possible the formation of contractual or, as the Puritans called them, "covenanted" groups formed by individuals who signed a covenant or agreement to found a community. The most famous of these covenants was the Mayflower Compact. In it the Pilgrims formed a "civil body politic", and promised to obey the laws their own government might pass. In short, the individual Pilgrim invented on the spot a new community, one that would be ruled by laws of its making.

The Reformers maintained that the Roman Catholic Church, by reserving to itself — to its priests and functionaries — all the doctrines and teachings of the Church, had kept people locked up in rituals and ceremonies, which, as Calvin put it, condemned "the miserable multitude" of believers to "the grossest ignorance." "Faith," Calvin went on, "consists not in ignorance, but in knowledge . . . " The faithful must know at first hand the word of God. The only infallible way of knowing God's word was to read and study it as it appeared in the Holy Scripture. It followed that knowledge rather than authority was essential to an enlightened faith. The importance of the Reformers' emphasis on the literacy of all the faithful was recognized by Massachusetts lawyer-patriot John Adams. "They (the Reformers) were convinced from history and their own experience," he wrote, "that nothing could preserve their posterity from encroachments of the two systems of tyranny, the Roman Church and the English monarch . . . but knowledge diffused generally through the whole body of the people. Their civil and religious principles, therefore, conspired to prompt them to use every measure and take every precaution in their power to propagate and perpetuate knowledge. For this purpose they laid very early the foundations of colleges . . . and it is remarkable that they have left among their posterity so universal an affection and veneration for those seminaries, and for liberal education, that the meanest of the people contribute cheerfully to the support and maintenance of them every year . . . so that the education of all ranks of people was made the care and expense of the public in a manner that I believe has been unknown to any other people ancient or modern."

One of the most fundamental changes wrought by the Reformation was to give the family unit an importance that it had never enjoyed before. In the new, re-formed family the father assumed the priestly duties once performed by the church. He usually led family prayers, read the Bible aloud in the vernacular, and even assumed certain teaching responsibilities. The family, as the essential unit and center of Christian life, took on a new dignity and power; it was as though the power of the institutional church had been divided up among the reconstituted familes of the Protesting faith.

This change in in the family also promoted the freedom of the individual. In doing so it served to release new energies in society, to create new enterprises and new wealth. In traditional European societies, sons characteristically expressed their loyalty to their fathers by following the same trade or calling. However, since the son in the new family learned the most crucial truths — those necessary for the salvation of the soul — from his father, he was relieved of the burden of loyalty in other spheres, becoming free to go beyond his father in terms of his own worldly ambition. If his father was a carpenter or farmer, the son might aspire to be a lawyer or a merchant without feeling that he was rejecting his father. On the contrary, the son might best express his gratitude for his father's guidance by going beyond what his father had achieved. The result was a great increase in what we have come to call social mobility.

The impetus to get ahead in the world grew out of the new faith. Calvin placed great emphasis on the work a man did as a way of serving and pleasing God. Work was not a sure road to salvation, for Calvin was a strict predestinarian — that is, he believed salvation was bestowed by God according to His inscrutable plan and could not be earned by either faith or works. But to work conscientiously and well at any task, however menial, was to praise and bear witness to the goodness of the Lord. The consequences are familiar. Protestant countries, and perhaps most characteristically America as the most Protestant of all countries, have been work-oriented. Work has been the major American preoccupation or indeed obsession, an avenue to secular salvation, a vindication of the individual and of individualism itself.

Closely related to the ethic of work was Calvin's view of time. Time was seen as an arena in which one worked out so far as possible one's own salvation. All time was impregnated with the Divine Spirit. Everything done in time and with time came under God's scrutiny. None of it was private, or neutral or unobserved. Time must, therefore, be used carefully, prudently, profitably, devoutly, every hour and every minute of it accounted for and none wasted. Benjamin Franklin produced dozens of aphorisms exalting this concept: "early to bed and early to rise," "the Devil makes work for idle hands." Indeed, Americans like Franklin often seemed to feel that work (and its hoped-for concomitant, money) was a surer path to salvation than piety.

This typically American attitude toward time had important ramifications and consequences. The notion of time as God's time — time that had to be filled up with useful activity and regularly accounted for to God — created a vast new source of human energy. In America it resulted in an "energy pool" that made possible the domesticating of a wilderness in a remarkably brief time. Perhaps above all, it robbed the future of its menace. Future time, because it was God's time, was not threatening, not full of danger and uncertainty, but full of promise, full of the expectation of the revealing of God's plan for man, and of man's faithful response. The Federal Constitution was in this sense a monument to the reformed consciousness. This new sense of time as potentiality was a vital element in the new consciousness that was to make a revolution and, what was a good deal more difficult, form a new nation.

Austerity, reserve, self-denial were also demanded by Calvin. The Reformer took thought for the morrow; he laid something by to care for himself and his less fortunate fellows. He enjoyed the good gifts of God but with restraint. In Calvin's words, good Christians "should indulge themselves as little as possible . . . they should perpetually and resolutely exert themselves to retrench all superfluities and to restrain luxury; and they should diligently beware lest they pervert into impediments things which were given for their assistance." Calvin did not require excessive austerity; this would have been a denial of the bounty and generosity of the Maker. But license was a sinful perversion of means into ends.

Such preoccupations led, quite naturally, to an extreme degree of self-consciousness and introspection. Those present-day Americans who are constantly examining the state of their psyches are, in this respect at least, descendants of the Puritans. The faithful Reformer spent an inordinate amount of time in a painstaking audit of his state of grace or gracelessness. He frequently kept a diary or journal in which he recorded every step forward and every dismal backsliding, a ledger of moral debits and credits, often written in cipher to preserve its secrets from prying mortal eyes. Even Cotton Mather, one of the greatest of the late Puritan leaders, confessed to his diary that he was tempted to "self-pollution," suicide and blasphemy, was full of doubts and on occasion uncertain of the existence of God and of his own salvation.

We might thus say that the Reformer set out on the lonely and difficult task of learning and doing God's will. "Not my will, but Thy will, O Lord, be done," he prayed. If he did not always understand God's will or was not able to conform to it, he learned to live, to a remarkable and perhaps unprecedented degree, by his own will. This self-willed struggle proved to be an unusually demanding, endlessly challenging and often exciting enterprise.

The Reformation left its mark on every aspect of the personal and social life of the faithful. In the family, in education, in business activity, in work, in community and, ultimately, in politics, the consequences of the Reformation were determinative for American history. The "faithful" were, to be sure, most prominently located in the New England colonies; but they were by no means confined to that region. The Congregationalists were the classic Puritans in doctrine and church polity; but their Presbyterian neighbors were just as surely Calvinists. Quakers might differ in matters of theology; but they were perfect examples of the new consciousness produced by the Reformation, in some matters more Puritan than the Puritans. The Baptists' rejection of infant Baptism was anathema to other denominations; the Methodists were more rigorous about the indulgence of the senses; the Anglicans more tolerant (or less pious depending on the point of view). The German Lutherans in Pennsylvania, like their master, eschewed the world as did the other pietist sects (most of them German in origin) the Mennonites, Dunkards, Moravians. From the austerest Quaker to the most profligate Anglican was an extended social and theological journey to be sure. But all along that spectrum of Reformed Christianity one could find common denominators more important than all the differences. All partook of the re-formed consciousness.

Today we are perhaps most aware of the negative aspects of that consciousness or character-type that we understand to be our heritage from the Reformation. It is depicted as sour, austere, repressive, materialistic, competitive, anxious, arrogant, authoritarian, both defensive and aggressive, inhibited, excessively individualistic. And it may well be that the creative potentialities in that consciousness have been mined out, that what we presently experience in such a negative way are the unattractive residues that remained when the Puritans' zealous faith and passionate desire to redeem the world for the glory of God had dwindled away.

Remote or repugnant as Puritanism may be to us today, it is essential that we understand that the Reformation in its full power was one of the great emancipations of history. Those who drew together under the new revelation unquestionably felt themselves filled with the grace of God and experienced the joy of creation in its deepest sense. Those who embraced the Reformed faith were, or at least felt themselves to be, truly liberated; they entered into a genuinely new world of the spirit and received in consequence the power to establish a geographically new world. The Reformers were not simply men and women who subscribed to a set of theological propositions, most of which seem thoroughly uncongenial or obscure to us today. They were men and women, individuals in a quite new sense, with a transcendent vision and the passionate determination to transform the world in accordance with that vision.

The political   consequences of the social attitudes engendered by the Reformation can be clearly seen in the English Civil War. The resistance of the radical Protestant elements in the British Parliament led to the Long Parliament, the overthrow of the Court party and, eventually, the beheading of the King and the dictatorship of Cromwell. In this strange and bloody episode all the radical political propensities of the Reformed faith welled to the surface. The Presbyterian and Puritan leaders in Parliament were comparatively mild in their doctrines when compared with the Diggers, Levelers, and Fifth Monarchy men. The Diggers asserted: "*England* is not a Free People, till the Poor that have no land, have a free allowance to dig and labour on the Commons," i.e. the public land; and Jerrard Winstanly argued that the earth was a "common treasury of livelihood to whole mankind, without respect of persons." "The Community of Mankind" was the first community composed of all those joined in "the unity of spirit of Love, which is called Christ in you, or the Law written in the heart, leading mankind into all truth, and to be of one heart and of one mind." The second was the "Community of the Earth, for the quiet livelihood in food and raiment without using force, or restraining one another. These two Communities . . . is the true Levelling which Christ will work at his more glorious appearance; for Jesus Christ the Saviour of all men, is the greatest, first and truest Leveller that ever was spoke of in the world."

The doctrines of the Levelers, discredited and ignored for more than a hundred years, found expression in the classic phrase of the Declaration of Independence — "all men are created equal. . ." The right of resistance to unlawful authority, so clearly enunciated by the Parliamentary leaders and confirmed by the Glorious Revolution of 1689 was the basis on which the Americans opposed the unlimited authority of Parliament over the British colonies.

There was another important respect in which Reformed Christianity manifested itself in the political sphere. It brought with it a revival of the discussion of law — the laws of nature, natural law, celestial law and municipal or man-made law. This was a heritage that reached back to the ancients and that received its classic Christian formulation in the works of Saint Thomas Aquinas. However, the Reformation aroused a new interest in the nature and sanction of law, especially on the part of theologians of the Anglican Church. It was Richard Hooker, an Anglican divine, who wrote in his *Ecclesiastical Polity* the line dangerous to kings and tyrants: "Laws they are not which public approbation hath not made so." Protestant theologians and theorists incorporated into the political thought of the Reformation the great principles of natural law which were to play such an important role in developing the theoretical foundations of colonial resistance to Parliament and of the Federal Constitution itself.

The problem, as Richard Shaull suggests, that remains at the center of all questions about the relation of human beings to the Divine might be termed the problem of original sin versus Christian Utopianism. Original sin involves the notion of an unchanging element in human nature, qualities or characteristics "original" and continuing.

Christian Utopianism, on the other hand, might be said to be grounded in the injunction: "Love thy neighbor as thyself," and similar "impossible" demands. Christian theology has always been, in essence, a balancing of these claims. In no period of our history as a people have they been more precisely weighed than in the era of the American Revolution. The Founding Fathers, believing for the most part in some form of the notion of original sin, nonetheless dared to believe also in a new and better age for all mankind. Thus the Reverend Samuel Thacher could declare, "Liberty is a pure, original emanation from the great source of life which animates the universe. . . " and assert confidently that the benefits of the American Revolution could not "be compressed within the compass of a few pages. Its effects are not confined to one age or country. The human mind has received a stimulus and attained an expansion which will extend its influence beyond calculation." Americans have, in short, begun the "emancipation of a world."

The Federal Constitution was, in effect, an effort to reconcile on the practical political level original sin and Christian Utopianism. In this context the Declaration of Independence appears as the classic political credo of a utopianism whose Christian antecedents are plainly discernible.

The American Revolutionary tradition was soon reduced to a reiteration of "freedom, equality, and liberty." Abstracted from revolutionary politics, these became, in time, merely pious utterances. Today the challenge of the Bicentennial Era is, as the Founding Fathers most commonly put it, to return to *first principles*. For the Christian, the most important of these principles is that God rules the world, and that all human orders are merely efforts to emulate the Divine order.

It thus follows that the task of the Christian is always to be *radical* to the existing establishment and *conservative* to secular revolutionaries who, as Reinhold Niebuhr reminded us, are constantly attempting to make their ideals into the ultimate goals of history. For the Christian, this is heresy.

The importance of Christianity is as an incommensurable, inexhaustable, (I suspect) irreplaceable, "re-adjuster" — that which *must* survive every social upheaval, every revolution, every war. It is coterminus with history itself or else it is nothing but a system of consolation, another "world religion."

In Richard Shaull's words "the end / in this case the end of the old order of king and Parliament / is the occasion for a new beginning, and men are free to allow the old to die in trust that out of that death, the new will emerge." This is faith in the future as governed by God's will which, even if men cannot discern it, is there; this is the primary, original source of all "utopian" thinking: the future will be better than the past.

The Bicentennial Era which has so discomforted academic historians poses equally difficult questions for the Christian community. If the American

Revolution is indeed inconceivable without the imperatives of radical Christianity, what does this fact suggest about the Church (or churches) today? How is the complacent and conservative body of Christians to be roused from its lethargy and made the active agent of The New Age?

It is probably safe to say that most anthologies are based on assumptions generally accepted by scholars in the field. Thus, an anthology of writings of black Americans is based on the widely held view that the attitudes and opinions of blacks, however sorely neglected they may have been in the past, are important to a proper understanding of our history. Similarly, a collection of political documents having to do with American constitutional history would contain a reasonably clearly defined sort of documents, including among other things, the Federal Constitution and certain key decisions of the Supreme Court.

The case is somewhat different here. There has been no general acceptance by academic scholars of the centrality of Protestant Christianity to an understanding of the American Revolution. This theme has, at best, been dealt with by most scholars as a peripheral issue, alluded to in passing where it is mentioned at all. Therefore the selection of materials in this anthology has been made in order to argue a case that has not yet been adequately argued. It might thus be called a "didactic anthology," a work which presents a case not in the typical monographic style of analysis and exposition but rather as a lawyer presents a brief — by presenting to the reader the documents upon which the argument rests. We might say that the case of *The Primacy of Protestant Christianity in Understanding the Origins and Nature of the American Revolution* versus *Academic Historians* rests on the arguments herewith presented to the court of public opinion. I am, of course, well aware of the problems and dangers attendant upon such a method; but I risk them gladly since at the least they may open a debate on this largely neglected question.

# 1

---

[The texts may be consulted in any translation; but the most popular translation in New England was the Geneva Bible (1560), translated by English exiles in Geneva who reflected John Calvin's thought.]

## Ezekiel and Micah

It is easy in reading the political tracts and newspaper editorials turned out by the leaders of colonial opposition to the arbitrary rule of Parliament to overlook the fact that there was in the stubborn resistance of the ordinary men and women of the colonies a substantial admixture of passionate devotion to what they conceived to be their God-given liberties (ratified, so to speak, by the British constitution), along with a visionary idealism, even fanaticism, that is perhaps best represented by the Book of the Prophet Ezekiel. Ezekiel, with its torrent of exotic images, its wheels within wheels, its strange apocalyptic beasts and undecipherable mysteries is one of the most imponderable books of the Old Testament. If we are inclined to think of the American Revolution as a sober, restrained, rational and orderly political movement, the Book of the Prophet Ezekiel should help to disabuse us of such a notion. Revolutions are "profound and passionate" events emanating from the deepest emotional resources of a people.

As the Revolutionary crisis developed, the colonists of Whig persuasion identified the Mother Country with the dark indictments of the prophet: "Because ye multiplied more than the nations that are round about you and have not walked in my statutes, neither have kept my judgments . . . therefore . . . saith the Lord God . . . even I am against thee, and will execute judgments in the midst of thee, in the sight of the nations." In short, they felt confident that God was on their side. Equally, in the images of destruction and resurrection they could read the hope of a redeemed humanity, led out of the land of Egypt by a people chosen of the Lord.

The Book of the Prophet Micah, among the shortest books of the Old Testament, shared with the Book of the Prophet Ezekiel, a special place in the religious affections of the English colonists. It was from Micah that John Winthrop, who wrote his *Model of Christian Charitie* as the spiritual charter for the Puritan settlers on board the *Arabella* on the way to the Massachusetts Bay Colony, quoted the sixth chapter, eighth verse: "for what doth the Lord require of thee, but to do justly, and to love mercy, and to walk humbly with thy God?" And it was from Micah that his figtree and none shall make them afraid; for the mouth of the Lord of hosts hath spoken it."

It seemed to many Americans that the English colonies with their heterogenous mixture of races and nationalities were the fulfillment of Micah's famous prophecy: "in the last days it shall come to pass, that the mountain of the house of the Lord shall be established in the top of the mountains. . .and the people shall flow unto it. And many nations shall come. . ."

The fact is that the passage "every man. . .under his vine and under his figtree" was the most potent expression of the colonists' determination to be *independent* whatever the cost. This did not necessarily mean *politically* independent; it meant *practically* independent, having substantial control over their own affairs. No theme was more constantly reiterated by writers and speakers in the era of the Revolution.

# 2

---

John Calvin's *Institutes of the Christian Religion* belong, in the opinion of the editor of this anthology, among the half-dozen most important books ever written. Its influence if not readily measured is generally admitted to have been enormous. The two chapters in that vast work which have the most relevance for this work are those on "Christian Freedom" and "Civil Government". Christian Freedom, Calvin points out, does not extend to license. The devout Christian is not outside the law (Antinomian). His relation to law is, indeed, subtle and complex. Certainly he cannot expect Divine favor simply as a consequence of dutifully complying with the law, ecclesiastical or civil. That is the basic message of Protestantism: salvation is not to be earned. It is a free (and mysterious) gift of the Almighty. The Christian's conscience is moreover at liberty. "Freed from the law's yoke, they willingly obey God's will." "Those who infer that we ought to sin because we are not under the law understand" Calvin writes, "that this Freedom has nothing to do with them, for its purpose is to encourage us to do good."

Also essential to the notion of Christian liberty is a freedom from "outward" or material things "that are in themselves indifferent . . . . The knowledge of this Freedom is very necessary for us; for if it is lacking, our consciences will have repose."

Of special importance is Calvin's careful distinction between temporal and spiritual laws. Having made the distinction in his chapter on "Christian Freedom," Calvin goes on to argue the case of temporal or civil law in chapter 20 of his fourth Book. The devout Christian cannot dismiss "the whole nature of government as a thing polluted . . . " The world is, after all, a place of preparation for life eternal; and civil government has as its appointed end, so long as we live among men, to cherish and support the outward worship of God, to defend sound doctrine of piety and the position of the church, to adjust our life to the society of men . . . and to promote general peace and tranquility . . ." These lines read like a charter for the Puritans of the Massachusetts Bay Company. There is, in fact, an apparent contradiction in Calvin's belief that the state should "defend the piety and position of the Church" while at the same time, stating: "I do not allow men to make laws respecting religion and the worship of God . . . ."

The Puritans took seriously both injunctions. They wished the civil government (the state) to defend and protect the Church, suppress blasphemy, etc.; but they also resisted the notion that the civil government could pass any laws regarding religious doctrine. They went so far as to forbid ministers from running for political office.

It is worth noting Calvin's argument that the civil magistrate is a legatee of God, and all his actions lie under Divine judgment.

In his discussion of the forms of government — monarchy, aristocracy, and democracy, Calvin follows a long tradition in political theory that went back to Plato the philosopher and Polybius the historian. Calvin also asserts that either aristocracy or a combination of aristocracy and democracy are the best forms of government and pure democracy the worst. He adds a most interesting point in favor of the democratic element in government: "men's fault or failing causes it to be safer and more bearable for a number to exercise government, so that they may help one another, teach and admonish one another; and that if one asserts himself unfairly, there may be a number of censors and masters to restrain his willfulness." As we will see later in this work, Calvin's conception of human depravity (not just Calvin's but a conception rooted in Christian dogma) underlay the thinking of most of those Americans responsible for framing the Federal Constitution and establishing a new nation as well as the thinking of their constituents. The rationale of the theorists of the French Revolution for popular government, on the other hand, was based on the idea of the natural goodness of man uncorrupted by decadent institutions and a superstitious church. Thus Calvin wished government, though mixed, to have a democratic base because man was by nature "desperately wicked and deceitful" (i.e. "fallen"), and no individual or group could thus be trusted with unchecked power, while the other great "democratic" revolution of the century wished to place authority in the hands of the people because they were "good".

Especially striking is Calvin's injunction to the faithful that they must "obey and suffer" even under the rule of tyrants who abuse their office. Such "insolent kings" may, indeed, be instruments of Divine punishment. But there is *one* circumstance in which the Christian not only may but is required to resist tyranny; that is, quite simply where the actions of the king seduce the faithful from their ultimate allegiance which is to God. Thus whenever it is clear that the impositions of a ruler work an effect contrary to the true interests of the Almighty, it is the duty of the Christian to oppose him whatever the risk.

While these selections from the *Institutes* are lengthy, they were (and remain) two of the most important reflections on the nature of government in the whole body of political writings.

[The text is taken from John Calvin, "Christian Freedom," *Calvin: Institutes of the Christian Religion,* ed. by John T. McNeill and trans. by Ford Lewis Battles, (Philadelphia: Westminster Press, 1960), Book III, Chapter XIX, pp. 833-49.]

## Christian Freedom

*(Necessity of a doctrine of Christian freedom, which has three parts, the first seen in Gal., chs. 1 to 3)*

*1. Need for a right understanding of the Christian doctrine of freedom*

We must now discuss Christian freedom. He who proposes to summarize gospel teaching ought by no means to omit an explanation of this topic. For it is a thing of prime necessity, and apart from a knowledge of it consciences dare undertake almost nothing without doubting; they hesitate and recoil from many things; they constantly waver and are afraid. But freedom is especially an appendage of justification and is of no little avail in understanding its power. Indeed, those who seriously fear God will enjoy the incomparable benefit of this doctrine, one that impious and Lucianic men humorously satirize with their witicisms. For in the spiritual drunkenness that has laid hold upon them every sort of impudence is lawful. Accordingly, here is the right place to introduce this topic. It was profitable to put off a fuller discussion of it to this place, although we have lightly touched upon it several times before.

For, as soon as Christian freedom is mentioned, either passions boil or wild tumults rise unless these wanton spirits are opposed in time, who otherwise most wickedly corrupt the best things. Some, on the pretext of this freedom, shake off all obedience toward God and break out into unbridled license. Others disdain it, thinking that it takes away all moderation, order, and choice of things. What should we do here, hedged about with such perplexities? Shall we say good-by to Christian freedom, thus cutting off occasion for such dangers? But, as we have said, unless this freedom be comprehended, neither Christ nor gospel truth, nor inner peace of soul, can be rightly known. Rather, we must take care that so necessary a part of doctrine be not suppressed, yet at the same time that those absurd objections which are wont to arise be met.

*2. Freedom from the law*

Christian freedom, in my opinion, consists of three parts. The first: that the consciences of believers, in seeking assurance of their justification before God, should rise above and advance beyond the law, forgetting all law righteousness. For since, as we have elsewhere shown, the law leaves no one righteous, either it excludes us from all hope of justification or we ought to be freed from it, and in such a way, indeed, that no account is taken of works. For he who thinks that in order to obtain righteousness he ought to bring some trifle of works is incapable of determining their measure and limit but makes himself debtor to the whole law. Removing, then, mention of law, and laying aside all consideration of works, we should, when justification is being discussed, embrace God's mercy alone, turn our attention from ourselves, and look only to Christ. For there the question is not how we may become righteous but how, being unrighteous and unworthy, we may be reckoned righteous. If consciences wish to attain any certainty in this matter, they ought to give no place to the law.

Nor can any man rightly infer from this that the law is superfluous for believers, since it does not stop teaching and exhorting and urging them to good, even though before God's judgment seat it has no place in their consciences. For, inasmuch as these two things are very different, we must rightly and conscientiously distinguish them. The whole life of Christians ought to be a sort of practice of godliness, for we have been called to sanctification [I Thess. 4:7; cf. Eph. 1:4; I Thess. 4:3]. Here it is the function of the law, by warning men of their duty, to arouse them to a zeal for holiness and innocence. But where consciences are worried how to render God favorable, what they will reply, and with what assurance they will stand should they be called to his judgment, there we are not to reckon what the law requires, but Christ alone, who surpasses all perfection of the law, must be set forth as righteousness.

### 3. The argument of Galatians

Almost the entire argument of the letter to the Galations hinges upon this point. For those who teach that Paul in this contends for freedom of ceremonies alone are absurd interpreters, as can be proved from the passages adduced in the argument. Such passages are these: That Christ "became a curse for us" to "redeem us from the curse of the law" [Gal. 3:13]. Likewise: "Stand fast in the freedom wherewith Christ has set you free, and do not submit again to the yoke of slavery. Now I, Paul, say . . . that if you receive circumcision, Christ will become of no advantage to you. . . . And every man who receives circumcision is a debtor to the whole law. For any of you who are justified by the law, Christ has become of no advantage; you have fallen away from grace" [Gal. 5:1-4p.]. These passages surely contain something loftier than freedom of ceremonies! Of course I admit that Paul is there discussing ceremonies, for his quarrel is with false apostles who were trying to reintroduce into the Christian church the old shadows of the law that had been abolished by Christ's coming. But for the discussion of this question, the higher topics upon which the whole controversy rested had to be considered. First, because the clarity of the gospel was obscured by those Jewish shadows, Paul showed that we have in Christ a perfect disclosure of all those things which were foreshadowed in the Mosaic ceremonies. Further, because those imposters imbued the common people with the very wicked notion that this obedience obviously availed to deserve God's grace, Paul here strongly insists that believers should not suppose they can obtain righteousness before God by any works of the law, still less by those paltry rudiments! And at the same time he teaches that through the cross of Christ they are free from the condemnation of the law, which otherwise hangs over all men [Gal. 4:5], so that they may rest with full assurance in Christ alone. This topic properly pertains to our argument. Finally, he claims for the consciences of believers their freedom, that they may not be obligated in things unnecessary.

*(The second, freedom of conscience willingly obeying without compulsion of the law, 4-6)*

*4. Freedom from the constraint of the law establishes the true obedience of believers*

The second part, dependent upon the first, is that consciences observe the law, not as if constrained by the necessity of the law, but that freed from the law's yoke they willingly obey God's will. For since they dwell in perpetual dread so long as they remain under the sway of the law, they will never be disposed with eager readiness to obey God unless they have already been given this sort of freedom. By an example we shall more briefly and clearly arrive at the meaning of this. The precept of the law is that "we love our God with all our heart, with all our soul, and with all our strength" [Deut. 6:5]. To bring this about, our soul must first be emptied of all other feeling and thought, our heart cleansed of all desires, and our powers gathered and concentrated upon this one point. They who have progressed farther than all others on the Lord's way are yet far distant from that goal. For even though they love God deeply and with sincere affection of heart, they have a great part of their heart and soul still occupied with fleshly desires, by which they are drawn back and prevented from hastening forward to God. Indeed, they struggle with much effort, but the flesh partly weakens their powers, partly draws them to itself. What are they to do here, while they feel that there is nothing they are less able to do than to fulfill the law? They will, they aspire, they try, but they do nothing with the required perfection. If they look upon the law, whatever work they attempt or intend they see to be accursed. And there is no reason for any man to deceive himself by concluding that his work is not entirely evil because it is imperfect, and that God nonetheless finds acceptable what is good in it. For unless its rigor be mitigated, the law in requiring perfect love condemns all imperfection. Let him therefore ponder his own work, which he wished to be adjudged in part good, and by that very act he will find it, just because it is imperfect, to be a transgression of the law.

*5. Freedom from constraint makes us capable of joyous obedience*

See how all our works are under the curse of the law if they are measured by the standard of the law! But how, then, would unhappy souls gird themselves eagerly for a work for which they might expect to receive only a curse? But if, freed from this severe requirement of the law, or rather from the entire rigor of the law, they hear themselves called with fatherly gentleness by God, they will cheerfully and with great eagerness answer, and follow his leading. To sum up: Those bound by the yoke of the law are like servants assigned certain tasks for each day by their masters. These servants think they have accomplished nothing, and dare not appear before their masters unless they have fulfilled the exact measure of their tasks. But sons, who are more generously and candidly treated by their fathers, do not hesitate to offer them incomplete and half-done and even defective works, trusting that their obedience and readiness of mind will be accepted by their fathers, even though they have not quite achieved what their fathers intended. Such children ought we to be, firmly trusting that our services will be approved by our most merciful Father, however small, rude, and imperfect these may be. Thus also he assures us through the prophet: "I will spare them as a man spares his son who serves him" [Mal. 3:17]. The word "spare" is clearly here used in the sense of "to be indulgent or compassionately to overlook faults," while also mention is made of "service." And we need this assurance in no slight degree, for without it we attempt everything in vain. For God considers that he is revered by no work of ours unless we truly do it in reverence toward him. But how can this be done amidst all this dread, where one doubts whether God is offended or honored by our works?

### 6. Emancipated by grace, believers need not fear the remnants of sin

And this is the reason why the author of The Letter to the Hebrews refers to faith all the good works of which we read as being done among the holy fathers, and judges them by faith alone [Heb. 11:2 ff.; 11:17; etc. ]. In the letter to the Romans, there is a famous passage on this freedom, wherein Paul reasons that sin ought not to rule us [Rom. 6:12 and 6:14, conflated], for we are not under the law but under grace [Rom. 6:14]. For he had exhorted believers not to let "sin reign in" their "mortal bodies" [Rom. 6:12], nor to "yield" their "members to sin as weapons of iniquity," but to "give" themselves "to God as those who have come to life from the dead, and" their "members to God as weapons of righteousness" [Rom. 6:13]. On the other hand, they might object that they still bore with them their flesh, full of lusts, and that sin dwelt in them. Paul adds this consolation, in freedom from the law. It is as if he said: "Even though they do not yet clearly feel that sin has been destroyed or that righteousness dwells in them, there is still no reason to be afraid and cast down in mind as if God were continually offended by the remnants of sin, seeing that they have been emancipated from the law by grace, so that their works are not to be measured according to its rules. Let those who infer that we ought to sin because we are not under the law understand that this freedom has nothing to do with them. For its purpose is to encourage us to good.

### 7. Freedom in "things indifferent" with proofs from Romans, 7-9

The third part of Christian freedom lies in this: regarding outward things that are of themselves "indifferent," we are not bound before God by any religious obligation preventing us from sometimes using them and other times not using them, indifferently. And the knowledge of this freedom is very necessary for us, for if it is lacking, our consciences will have no repose and there will be no end to superstitions. Today we seem to many to be unreasonable because we stir up discussion over the restricted eating of meat, use of holidays and of vestments and such things, which seem to them vain frivolties.

But these matters are not more important than is commonly believed. For when consciences once ensnare themselves, they enter a long and inextricable maze, not easy to get out of. If a man begins to doubt whether he may use linen for sheets, shirts, handkerchiefs, and napkins, he will afterward be uncertain also about hemp; finally, doubt will ever arise over tow. For he will turn over in his mind whether he can sup without napkins, or go without a handkerchief. If any man should consider daintier food unlawful, in the end he will not be at peace before God, when he eats either black bread or common victuals, while it occurs to him that he could sustain his body on even coarser foods. If he boggles at sweet wine, he will not with clear conscience drink even flat wine, and finally he will not dare touch water if sweeter and cleaner than other water. To sum up, he will come to the point of considering it wrong to step upon a straw across his path, as the saying goes.

Here begins a weighty controversy, for what is in debate is whether God, whose will ought to precede all our plans and actions, wishes us to use these things or those. As a consequence, some, in despair, are of necessity cast into a pit of confusion; others, despising God and abandoning fear of him, must make their own way in destruction, where they have none ready-made. For all those entangled in such doubts, wherever they turn, see offense of conscience everywhere present.

*8. Freedom in the use of God's gifts for his purposes*

"I know," says Paul,"that nothing is common" (taking "common" in the sense of "profane"), "but it is common for anyone who thinks it common" [Rom. 14:14p.]. With these words Paul subjects all outward things to our freedom, provided our minds are assured that the basis for such freedom stands before God. But if any superstitious opinion poses a stumbling block for us, things of their own nature pure are for us corrupt. For this reason, he adds: "Happy is he who does not judge himself in what he approves. But he who judges, if he eats, is condemned, because he does not eat of faith. For whatever is not of faith is sin" [Rom. 14:22-23p.].

Amidst such perplexities, do not those who show themselves rather bold by daring all things confidently, nonetheless to this extent turn away from God? But they who are deeply moved in any fear of God, when they are compelled to commit many things against their conscience, are overwhelmed and fall down with fright. All such persons receive none of God's gifts with thanksgiving, yet Paul testifies that by this alone all things are sanctified for our use [I Tim. 4:4-5]. Now I mean that thanksgiving which proceeds from a mind that recognizes in his gifts the kindness and goodness of God. For many of them, indeed, understand them as good things of God which they use, and praise God in his works; but inasmuch as they have not been persuaded that these good things have been given to them, how can they thank God as the giver?

To sum up, we see whither this freedom tends: namely, that we should use God's gifts for the purpose for which he gave them to us, with no scruple of conscience, no trouble of mind. With such confidence our minds will be at peace with him, and will recognize his liberality toward us. For here are included all ceremonies whose observance is optional, that our consciences may not be constrained by any necessity to observe them but may remember that by God's beneficence their use is for edification made subject to him.

*9. Against the abuse of Christian freedom for gluttony and luxury!*

But we must carefully note that Christian freedom is, in all its parts, a spiritual thing. Its whole force consists in quieting frightened consciences before God — that are perhaps disturbed and troubled over forgiveness of sins, or anxious whether unfinished works, corrupted by the faults of our flesh, are pleasing to God, or tormented about the use of things indifferent. Accordingly, it is perversely interpreted both by those who allege it as an excuse for their desires that they may abuse God's good gifts to their own lust and by those who think that freedom does not exist unless it is used before men, and consequently, in using it have no regard for weaker brethren.

Today men sin to a greater degree in the first way. There is almost no one whose resources permit him to be extravagant who does not delight in lavish and ostentatious banquets, bodily apparel, and domestic architecture; who does not wish to outstrip his neighbors in all sorts of elegance; who does not wonderfully flatter himself in his opulence. And all these things are defended under the pretext of Christian freedom. They say that these are things indifferent. I admit it, provided they are used indifferently. But when they are coveted too greedily, when they are proudly boasted of, when they are lavishly squandered, things that were of themselves otherwise lawful are certainly defiled by these vices.

Paul's statement best distinguishes among things indifferent: "To the clean all things are clean, but to the corrupt and unbelieving nothing is clean, inasmuch as their minds and consciences are corrupted"[Titus 1:15, cf. Vg.]. For why are the rich cursed, who have their consolation, who are full, who laugh now [Luke 6:24-25], who sleep on ivory couches [Amos 6:4], "who join field to field" [Isa. 5:8], whose feasts have harp, lyre, timbrel, and wine [Isa. 5:12]? Surely ivory and gold and riches are good creations of God, permitted, indeed appointed, for men's use by God's providence. And we have never been forbidden to laugh, or to be filled, or to join new possessions to old or ancestral ones, or to delight in musical harmony, or to drink wine. True indeed. But where there is plenty, to wallow in delights, to gorge oneself, to intoxicate mind and heart with present pleasures and be always panting after new ones — such are very far removed from a lawful use of God's gifts.

Away, then, with uncontrolled desire, away with immoderate prodigality, away with vanity and arrogance — in order that men may with a clean conscience cleanly use God's gifts. Where the heart is tempered to this soberness they will have a rule for lawful use of such blessings. But should this moderation be lacking, even base and common pleasures are too much. It is a true saying that under coarse and rude attire there often dwells a heart of purple, while sometimes under silk and purple is hid a simple humility. Thus let every man live in his station, whether slenderly, or moderately, or plentifully, so that all may remember God nourishes them to live, not to luxuriate. And let them regard this as the law of Christian freedom; to have learned with Paul, in whatever state they are, to be content; to know how to be humble and exalted; to have been taught, in any and all circumstances, to be filled and to hunger, to abound and to suffer want [Phil. 4:11-12].

*(Relation of Christian freedom to the weak and to the question of offenses, 10-13)*
*10. Against the abuse of Christian freedom to the injury of the weak!*

In this respect also many err; they use their freedom indiscriminately and unwisely, as though it were not sound and safe if men did not witness it. By this heedless use, they very often offend weak brothers. You can see some persons today who reckon their freedom does not exist unless they take possession of it by eating meat on Fridays. I do not blame them for eating meat, but this false notion must be driven from their minds. For they ought to think that from their freedom they obtain nothing new in men's sight but before God, and that it consists as much in abstaining as in using. If they understand that it makes no difference in God's sight whether they eat meat or eggs, wear red or black clothes, this is enough and more. The conscience, to which the benefit of such freedom was due, is now set free. Consequently, even if men thereafter abstain from meat throughout life, and ever wear clothes of one color, they are not less free. Indeed, because they are free, they abstain with a free conscience. But in having no regard for their brothers' weakness they slip most disastrously, for we ought so to bear with it that we do not heedlessly allow what would do them the slightest harm.

But it is sometimes important for our freedom to be declared before men. This I admit. Yet we must with the greatest caution hold to this limitation, that we do not abandon the care of the weak, whom the Lord has so strongly commended to us.

### 11. On offenses

Here, then, I shall say something about offenses — how they are to be distinguished, which ones avoided, which overlooked. From this we may afterward be able to determine what place there is for our freedom among men. Now I like that common distinction between an offense given and one received, inasmuch as it has the clear support of Scripture and properly expresses what is meant.

If you do anything with unseemly levity, or wantonness, or rashness, out of its proper order or place, so as to cause the ignorant and the simple to stumble, such will be called an offense given by you, since by your fault it came about that this sort of offense arose. And, to be sure, one speaks of an offense as given in some matter when its fault arises from the doer of the thing itself.

An offense is spoken of as received when something, otherwise not wickedly or unseasonably committed, is by ill will or malicious intent of mind wrenched into occasion for offense. Here is no "given" offense, but those wicked interpreters baselessly so understand it. None but the weak is made to stumble by the first kind of offense, but the second gives offense to persons of bitter disposition and pharisaical pride. Accordingly, we shall call the one the offense of the weak, the other that of the Pharisees. Thus we shall so temper the use of our freedom as to allow for the ignorance of our weak brothers, but for the rigor of the Pahrisees, not at all!

For Paul fully shows us in many passages what must be yielded to weakness. "Receive," he says "those weak in faith." [Rom. 14:1p.]. Also: "Let us no more pass judgment upon one another, but rather not put a stumbling block or occasion to fall in the way of our brother" [Rom. 14:13p.], and many passages with the same meaning, which are more suitably sought in their place than referred to here. The sum is "We who are strong ought to bear with the infirmities of the weak, and not to please ourselves; but let each of us please his neighbor for his good, to edify him" [Rom. 15:1-2 p.; for v. 2, cf. Vg.]. In another place: "But take care lest your freedom in any way cause offense to those who are weak." [ 1 Cor. 8:9 p.] Likewise: "Eat whatever is sold in the meat market without raising any question on the ground of conscience." [ 1 Cor. 10:25] "Now I say your conscience, not another's. . . . In short, be so that you may give no offense to Jews or to Greeks or to the church of God." [ 1 Cor. 10:29, 32 p.] Also, in another passage: "You were called to freedom, brothers, only do not use your freedom as an opportunity for the flesh but through love be servants of one another." [Gal. 5:13] So indeed it is. Our freedom is not given against our feeble neighbors, for love makes us their servants in all things; rather it is given that, having peace with God in our hearts, we may also live at peace with men.

We learn from the Lord's words how much we ought to regard the offense of the Pharisees: He bids us let them alone because they are blind leaders of the blind.

[Matt. 15:14]. His disciples had warned him that the Pharisees had been offended by his talk. [Matt. 15:12] He answered that they were to be ignored and their offense disregarded.

## 12. On the right use of Christian freedom and the right renunciation of it

Still the matter will remain in doubt unless we grasp whom we are to consider weak, whom Pharisees. If this distinction is removed, I do not see what use for freedom really remains in relation to offenses, for it will always be in the greatest danger. But Paul seems to me most clearly to have defined, both by teaching and by example, how far our freedom must either be moderated or purchased at the cost of offenses. When Paul took Timothy into his company, he circumcised him. [Acts 16:3.] But he could not be brought to circumcise Titus. [Gal. 2:3.] Here was a diversity of acts but no change of purpose or mind. That is, in circumcising Timothy, although he was "free from all," he made himself "a slave to all"; and "to the Jews" he "became as a Jew" in order to win Jews; to those under the law he "became one under the law . . . that" he "might win those under the law" [ 1 Cor. 9:19-20p.]; "all things to all men that" he "might save many" [ 1 Cor. 9:22p.], as he elsewhere writes. We have due control over our freedom if it makes no difference to us to restrict it when it is fruitful to do so.

What he had in view when he stronly refused to circumcise Titus he testifies when he thus writes: "But even Titus, who was with me, was not compelled to be circumcised, though he was a Greek, but because of false brethren surreptitiously brought in, who slipped in to spy out our freedom, which we have in Christ Jesus, that they might bring us into bondage — to them we did not yield submission, even for a moment, that the truth of the gospel might be preserved among you" [Gal. 2:3-5p.]. We have need also to assert our freedom if through the unjust demands of false apostles it be endangered in weak consciences.

We must at all times seek after love and look toward the edification of our neighbor. "All things," he says elsewhere, "are lawful to me, but not all things are helpful. All things are lawful, but not all things build up. Let no one seek his own good but another's" [1 Cor. 10:23-24p.] Nothing is plainer than this rule: that we should use our freedom if it results in the edification of our neighbor, but if it does not help our neighbor, then we should forgo it. There are those who pretend a Pauline prudence in abstaining from freedom, while there is nothing to which they apply it less than to the duties of love. To protect their own repose, they wish all mention of freedom to be buried; when it is no less important sometimes to use our neighbors' freedom for their good and edification than on occasion to restrain it for their own benefit. But it is the part of a godly man to realize that free power in outward matters has been given him in order that he may be the more ready for all the duties of love.

## 13. We must not on pretext of love of neighbor offend against God

All that I have taught about avoiding offenses I mean to be referred to things intermediate and indifferent. For the things necessary to be done must not be omitted for fear of any offense. For as our freedom must be subordinated to love, so in turn ought love itself to abide under purity of faith. Surely, it is fitting here also to take love into consideration, even as far as to the altar [cf. Matt. 5:23-24 ]; that is, that for our neighbor's sake we may not offend God. We must not approve the intemperance of those who do nothing without raising a tumult and who prefer to tear into everything rather than open a matter gently. But those people also are not to be listened to who, after making themselves leaders in a thousand sorts of wickedness, pretend that they must act so as not to cause offense to their neighbors [cf. 1 Cor. 8:9]; as if they were not in the meantime building up their neighbors' consciences into evil, especially when they ever stick fast in the same mud without hope of getting out. And suave fellows are they who, whether their neighbor is to be instructed in doctrine or in example of life, say he must be fed with milk while they steep him in the worst and deadliest opinions. Paul recalls that he fed the Corinthians with milk. [1 Cor. 3:2] But if the papal Mass had then been among them would he have performed sacrifice to furnish them with milk? No, for milk is not poison. They are therefore lying when they claim to be feeding those whom they are cruelly killing under the guise of blandishments. Granted that this sort of dissimulation is to be approved for the moment — how long will they feed their children with this same milk? For if these never grow up sufficiently to be able to bear even some light food at least, it is certain that they were never brought up on milk.

Two reasons prevent me from contending with them more sharply: first, their banalities are scarcely worth refuting, since they are deservedly despised among all sane men; secondly, I do not want to do again what I have already abundantly demonstrated in special treatises. Only let my readers remember this: with whatever obstacles Satan and the world strive to turn us away from God's commands or delay us from following what he appoints, we must nonetheless vigorously go forward. Then, whatever dangers threaten, we are not free to turn aside even a fingernail's breadth from this same God's authority, and it is not lawful under any pretext for us to attempt anything but what he allows.

*(Freedom and conscience in relation to traditions, and to civil government, 14-16)*
## 14. Freedom of conscience from all human law

Now, since believers' consciences, having received the privilege of their freedom, which we previously described, have, by Christ's gift, attained to this, that they should not be entangled with any snares of observances in those matters in which the Lord has willed them to be free, we conclude that they are released from the power of all men. For Christ does not deserve to forfeit our gratitude for his great generosity — nor consciences, their profit. And we should not put a light value upon something that we see cost Christ so dear, since he valued it not with gold or silver but with his own blood [I Peter 1:18-19]. Paul does not hesitate to say that Christ's death is nullified if we put our souls under men's subjection [cf. Gal. 2:21]. For in certain chapters of the letter to the Galatians, Paul is solely trying to show how to us Christ is obscured, or rather extinguished, unless our consciences stand firm in their freedom. They have surely fallen away from it if they can, at men's good pleasure, be ensnared by the bonds of laws and constitutions [cf. Gal. 5:1,4]. But as this is something very much worth knowing, so it needs a longer and clearer explanation. For immediately a word is uttered concerning the abrogating of human constitutions, huge troubles are stirred up, partly by the seditious, partly by slanderers — as if all human obedience were at the same time removed and cast down.

## 15. The two kingdoms

Therefore, in order that none of us may stumble on that stone, let us first consider that there is a twofold government in man: one aspect is spiritual, whereby the conscience is instructed in piety and in reverencing God; the second is political, whereby man is educated for the duties of humanity and citizenship that must be maintained among men. These are usually called the "spiritual" and the "temporal" jurisdiction (not improper terms) by which is meant that the former sort of government pertains to the life of the soul, while the latter has to do with the concerns of the present life — not only food and clothing but with laying down laws whereby a man may live his life among other men holily, honorably, and temperately. For the former resides in the inner mind, while the latter regulates only outward behavior. The one we may call the spiritual kingdom, the other, the political kingdom. Now these two, as we have divided them, must always be examined separately; and while one is being considered, we must call away and turn aside the mind from thinking about the other. There are in man, so to speak, two worlds, over which different kings and different laws lave authority.

Through this distinction it comes about that we are not to misapply to the political order the gospel teaching on spiritual freedom, as if Christians were less subject, as concerns outward government, to human laws, because their consciences have been set free in God's sight; as if they were released from all bodily servitude because they are free according to the spirit.

Then, becuase there can be some delusion in the constitutions that seem to apply to the spiritual kingdom, among these also we should discern what must be considered lawful, as consonant with God's word, and on the other hand what ought to have no place among the godly. Of civil government we shall speak in another place. Concerning church laws also I forbear to speak for the present, for a fuller treatment will more appropriately come in the fourth book, where the power of the church will be discussed.

Let this be the conclusion of the present discussion. The question, as I have said, is not of itself very obscure or involved. However, it troubles many because they do not sharply enough distinguish the outer forum, as it is called, and the forum of conscience. Moreover, the difficulty is increased by the fact that Paul enjoins obedience toward the magistrate, not only for fear of punishment, but for conscience' sake [Rom. 13:1,5]. From this it follows that consciences are also bound by civil laws. But if this were so, all that we said a little while ago and are now going to say about spiritual government would fall.

To resolve this difficulty it first behooves us to comprehend what conscience is; we must seek the definition from the derivation of the word. For just as when through the mind and understanding men grasp a knowledge of things, and from this are said "to know," this is the source of the word "knowledge," so also when they have a sense of divine judgment, as a witness joined to them, which does not allow them to hide their sins from being accused before the Judge's tribunal, this sense is called "conscience." For it is a certain mean between God and man, because it does not allow man to suppress within himself what he knows, but pursues him to the point of convicting him. This is what Paul understands when he teaches that conscience also testifies to men, where their thought either accuses or excuses them in God's judgment [Rom. 2:15-16]. A simple knowledge could reside, so to speak, closed up in man. Therefore this awareness which hales man before God's judgment is a sort of guardian appointed for man to note and spy out all his secrets that nothing may remain buried in darkness. Whence that ancient proverb: "Conscience is a thousand witnesses." For the same reason, Peter also put "the response of a good conscience to God" [1 Peter 3:21] as equivalent to peace of mind, when, convinced of Christ's grace, we fearlessly present ourselves before God. And when the author of The Letter to the Hebrews states that we "no longer have any consciousness of sin" [Heb. 10:2], he means that we are held to be freed or acquitted, so that sin may no longer accuse us.

### 16. Bondage and freedom of conscience

Therefore, as works have regard to men, so conscience refers to God. A good conscience, then, is nothing but inward integrity of heart. In this sense, Paul writes that the fulfillment of the law is love from a clear conscience and sincere faith [cf. 1 Tim. 1:5]. Afterward, also, in the same chapter, he shows how much it differs understanding, stating that "certain persons made shipwreck of their faith" [ 1 Tim. 1:19 ] because they had forsaken good conscience. By these words he signifies a lively inclination to serve God and a sincere effort to live piously and holily.

Sometimes, indeed, it is also extended to men, as when the same Paul, accoring to Luke, declares that he "took pains" to walk "with a clear conscience toward God and men" [Acts 24:16]. But this was said because the fruit of a good conscience flows forth and comes even to men. But properly speaking, as I have already said, it has respect to God alone.

Hence it comes about that a law is said to bind the conscience when it simply binds a man without regard to other men, or without taking them into account. For example: God not only bids us keep our minds pure and undefiled from all lust but also forbids all obscenity of speech and outward licentiousness. My conscience is subject to the observance of this law, even if no man lived on earth. So he who conducts himself intemperately not only sins because he gives a bad example to his brothers but has a conscience bound by guilt before God.

In things of themselves indifferent there is another consideration. For we ought to abstain from anything that might cause offense, but with a free conscience. Thus Paul speaks concerning meat consecrated to idols. "If anyone," he says, "raises a scruple, do not touch it, for conscience' sake. Now I mean the other man's conscience — not yours." [ 1 Cor. 10:28-29p.] A believer who, though previousiy warned, nonetheless ate meat of this sort would sin. But however necessary it may be with respect to his brother for him to abstain from it, as God enjoins, he still does not cease to keep freedom of conscience. We see how this law, while binding outward actions, leaves the conscience free.

# B

[The text is taken from John Calvin, "Civil Government," *Calvin: Institutes of the Christian Religion,* ed. by John T. McNeill and trans. by Ford Lewis Battles, (Philadelphia: Westminster Press, 1960), Book IV, Chapter XX.]

## Civil Government

*(How civil and spiritual government are related, 1-2)*
*1. Differences between spiritual and civil government*
Now, since we have established above that man is under a twofold government, and since we have elsewhere discussed at sufficient length the kind that resides in the soul or inner man and pertains to eternal life, this is the place to say something also about the other kind, which pertains only to the establishment of civil justice and outward morality.

For although this topic seems by nature alien to the spiritual doctrine of faith which I have undertaken to discuss, what follows will show that I am right in joining them, in fact, that necessity compels me to do so. This is especially true since, from one side, insane and barbarous men furiously strive to overturn this divinely established order; while, on the other side, the flatterers of princes, immoderately praising their power, do not hesitate to set them against the rule of God himself. Unless both these evils are checked, purity of faith will perish. Besides, it is of no slight importance to us to know how livingly God has provided in this respect for mankind, the greater zeal for piety may flourish in us to attest our gratefulness.

First, before we enter into the matter itself, we must keep in mind that distinction which we previously laid down so that we do not (as commonly happens) unwisely mingle these two, which have a completely different nature. For certain men, when they hear that the gospel promises a freedom that acknowledges no king and no magistrate among men, but looks to Christ alone, think that they cannot benefit by their freedom so long as they see any power set up over them. They therefore think that nothing will be safe unless the whole world is reshaped to a new form where there are neither courts, nor laws, nor magistrates, nor anything which in their opinion restricts their freedom. But whoever knows how to distinguish between body and soul, between this present fleeting life and that future eternal life, will without difficulty know that Christ's spiritual Kingdom and the civil jurisdiction are things completely distinct. Since, then, it is a Jewish vanity to seek and enclose Christ's Kingdom within the elements of this world, let us rather ponder that what Scripture clearly teaches is a spiritual fruit, which we gather from Christ's grace; and let us remember to keep within its own limits all that freedom which is promised and offered to us in him. For why is it that the same apostle who bids us stand and not submit to the "yoke of bondage" [Gal. 5:1] elsewhere forbids slaves to be anxious about their state [ 1 Cor. 7:21], unless it be that spiritual freedom can perfectly well exist along with civil bondage?

These statements of his must also be taken in the same sense: In the Kingdom of God "there is neither Jew nor Greek, neither male nor female, neither slave nor free" [Gal. 3:28, Vg.; order changed]. And again, "there is not Jew nor Greek, uncircumcised and circumcised, barbarian, Scythian, slave, freeman; but Christ is all in all" [Col. 3:11 p.]. By these statements he means that it makes no difference what your condition among men may be or under what nation's laws you live, since the Kingdom of Christ does not at all consist in these things.

### 2. The two "governments" are not antithetical

Yet this distinction does not lead us to consider the whole nature of government a thing polluted, which has nothing to do with Christian men. That is what, indeed, certain fanatics who delight in unbridled license shout and boast: after we have died through Christ to the elements of this world [Col. 2:20], are transported to God's Kingdom, and sit among heavenly beings, it is a thing unworthy of us and set far beneath our excellence to be occupied with those vile and worldly cares which have to do with business foreign to a Christian man. To what purpose, they ask, are there laws without trials and tribunals? But what has a Christian man to do with trials themselves? Indeed, if it is not lawful to kill, why do we have laws and trials? But as we have just now pointed out that this kind of government is distinct from that spiritual and inward Kingdom of Christ, so we must know that they are not at variance. For spiritual government, indeed, is already initiating in us upon earth certain beginnings of the Heavenly Kingdom, and in this mortal and fleeting life affords a certain forecast of an immortal and incorruptible blessedness. Yet civil government has as its appointed end, so long as we live among men, to cherish and protect the outward worship of God, to defend sound doctrine of piety and the position of the church, to adjust our life to the society of men, to form our social behavior to civil righteousness, to reconcile us with one another, and to promote general peace and tranquillity. All of this I admit to be superfluous, if God's Kingdom, such as it is now among us, wipes out the present life. But if it is God's will that we go as pilgrims upon the earth while we aspire to the true fatherland, and if the pilgrimage requires such helps, those who take these from man deprive him of his very humanity. Our adversaries claim that there ought to be such great perfection in the church of God that its government should suffice for law. But they stupidly imagine such a perfection as can never be found in a community of men. For since the insolence of evil men is so great, their wickedness so stubborn, that it can scarcely be restrained by extrememly severe laws, what do we expect them to do if they see that their depravity can go scot-free — when no power can force them to cease from doing evil?

### (Necessity and divine sanction of civil government, 3-7)
### 3. The chief tasks and burdens of civil government

But there will be a more appropriate place to speak of the practice of civil government. Now we only wish it to be understood that to think of doing away with it is outrageous barbarity. Its function among men is no less than that of bread, water, sun, and air; indeed, its place of honor is far more excellent. For it does not merely see to it, as all these serve to do, that men breathe, eat, drink, and are kept warm, even though it surely embraces all these activities when it provides for their living together. It does not, I repeat, look to this only, but also prevents idolatry, sacrilege against God's name, blasphemies against his truth, and other public offenses against religion from arising and spreading among the people; it prevents the public peace from being disturbed; it provides that each man may keep his property safe and sound; that men may carry on blameless intercourse among themselves; that honesty and modesty may be preserved among men. In short, it provides that a public manifestation of religion may exist among Christians, and that humanity be maintained among men.

Let no man be disturbed that I now commit to civil government the duty of rightly establishing religion, which I seem above to have put outside of human decision. For, when I approve of a civil administration that aims to prevent the true religion which is contained in God's law from being openly and with public sacrilege violated and defiled with impunity, I do not here, any more than before, allow men to make laws according to their own decision concerning religion and the worship of God.

But my readers, assisted by the very clarity of the arrangement, will better understand what is to be thought of the whole subject of civil government if we discuss its parts separately. These are three: the magistrate, who is the protector and guardian of the laws, according to which he governs; the people, who are governed by the laws and obey the magistrate.

Let us, then, first look at the office of the magistrate, noting whether it is a lawful calling approved of God; the nature of the office; the extent of its power; then, with what laws a Christian government ought to be governed; and finally, how the laws benefit the people, and what obedience is owed to the magistrate.

### 4. The magistracy is ordained by God

The Lord has not only testified that the office of magistrate is approved by and acceptable to him, but he also sets out its dignity with the most honorable titles and marvelously commends it to us. To mention a few: Since those who serve as magistrate are called "gods" [Ex. 22:8, Vg.: Ps. 82:1,6], let no one think that their being so-called is of slight importance. For it signifies that they have a mandate from God, have been invested with divine authority, and are wholly God's representatives, in a manner, acting as his vicegerents. This is no subtlety of mine, but Christ's explanation. "If Scripture," he says, "called them gods to whom the word of God came . . . " [John 10:35.] What is this, except that God has entrusted to them the business of serving him in their office, and (as Moses and Jehoshaphat said to the judges whom they appointed in every city of Judah) of exercising judgment not for man but for God [Deut. 1:16-17; II Chron. 19:6]? To the same purpose is what God's wisdom affirms through Solomon's mouth, that it is his doing "that kings reign, and counselors decree what is just, that princes exercise dominion, and all benevolent judges of the earth" [Prov. 8:14-16]. This amounts to the same thing as to say: it has not come about by human perversity that the authority over all things on earth is in the hands of kings and other rulers, but by divine providence and holy ordinance. For God was please so to rule the affairs of men, inasmuch as he is present with them and also presides over the making of laws and the exercising of equity in courts of justice. Paul also plainly teaches this when he lists "ruling" among God's gifts [Rom. 12:8, KJV or RV], which, variously distributed according to the diversity of grace, ought to be sued though Paul is there speaking specifically of a council of sober men, who were appointed in the primitive church to preside over the ordering of public discipline (which office is called in the letter to the Corinthians, "governments" [I Cor. 12:28]), yet because we see the civil power serving the same end, there is no doubt that he commends to us every kind of just rule.

But Paul speaks much more clearly when he undertakes a just discussion of this matter. For he states both that power is an ordinance of God [Rom. 13:2], and that there are no powers except those ordained by God [Rom. 13:1]. Further, that princes are ministers of God, for those doing good unto praise; for those doing evil, avengers unto wrath [Rom. 13:3-4]. To this may be added the examples of holy men, of whom some possessed kingdoms, as David, Josiah, and Hezekiah; others, lordships, as Joseph and Daniel; others, civil rule among a free people, as Moses, Joshua, and the judges. The Lord has declared his approval of their offices. Accordingly, no one ought to doubt that civil authority is a calling, not only holy and lawful before God, but also the most sacred and by far the most honorable of all callings in the whole life of mortal men.

## 5. Against the "Christian" denial or rejection of magistracy

Those who desire to usher in anarchy object that, although in antiquity kings and judges ruled over ignorant folk, yet that servile kind of governing is wholly incompatible today with the perfection which Christ brought with his gospel. In this they betray not only their ignorance but devilish arrogance, when they claim a perfection of which not even a hundredth part is seen in them. But whatever kind of men they may be, the refutation is easy. For where David urges all kings and rulers to kiss the Son of God [Ps. 2:12], he does not bid them lay aside their authority and retire to private life, but submit to Christ the power with which they have been invested, that he alone may tower over all. Similarly, Isaiah, when he promises that kings shall be foster fathers of the church, and queens its nurses [Isa. 49:23], does not deprive them of their honor. Rather, by a noble title he makes them defenders of God's pious worshipers; for that prophecy looks to the coming of Christ. I knowingly pass over very many passages which occur frequently, and especially in the psalms, in which the right of rulers is asserted for them all [Ps. 21; 22; 45; 72; 89; 110; 132]. But most notable of all is the passage of Paul where, admonishing Timothy that prayers be offered for kings in public assembly, he immediately adds the reason: "That we may lead a peaceful life under them with all godliness and honesty" [ I Tim. 2:2]. By these words he entrusts the condition of the church to their protection and care.

## 6. Magistrates should be faithful as God's deputies

This consideration ought continually to occupy the magistrates themselves, since it can greatly spur them to exercise their office and bring them remarkable comfort to mitigate the difficulties of their task, which are indeed many and burdensome. For what great zeal for uprightness, for prudence, gentleness, self-control, and for innocence ought to be required of themselves by those who know that they have been ordained ministers of divine justice? How will they have the brazenness to admit injustice to their judgment seat, which they are told is the throne of the living God? How will they have the boldness to pronounce an unjust sentence, by that mouth which they know has been appointed an instrument of divine truth? With what conscience will they sign wicked decrees by that hand which they know has been appointed to record the acts of God? To sum up, if they remember that they are vicars of God, they should watch with all care, earnestness, and diligence, to represent in themselves to men some image of divine providence, protection, goodness, benevolence, and justice. And they should perpetually set before themselves the thought that "if all are cursed who carry out in deceit the work of God's vengeance" [Jer. 48:10], much more gravely cursed are they who deceitfully conduct themselves in a righteous calling. Therefore, when Moses and Jehoshaphat wished to urge their judges to do their duty, they had nothing more effective to persuade them than what we have previously mentioned [Deut. 1:16]: "Consider what you do, for there is no perversity with the Lord our God" [II Chron. 19:6-7p.]. And in another place it is said: "God, stood in the assembly of the gods, and holds judgment in the midst of the gods" [Ps. 82:1]. This is to hearten them for their task when they learn that they are deputies of God, to whom they must hereafter render account of the administration of their charge. And this admonition deserves to have great weight with them. For if they commit some fault, they are not only wrongdoers to men whom they wickedly trouble, but are also insulting toward God himself, whose most holy judgments they defile [cf. Isa. 3:14-15]. Again, they have the means to comfort themselves greatly when they ponder in themselves that they are occupied not with profane affairs or those alien to a servant of God, but with a most holy office, since they are serving as God's deputies.

### 7. The coercive character of magistracy does not hinder its recognition

Those who, unmoved by so many testimonies of Scripture, dare rail against this holy ministry as a thing abhorrent to Christian religion and piety — what else do they do but revile God himself, whose ministry cannot be reproached without dishonor to himself? And these folk do not just reject the magistrates, but cast off God that he may not reign over them. For if the Lord truly said this of the people of Israel because they refused Samuel's rule [ I Sam. 8:7], why will it less truly be said today of these who let themselves rage against all governments ordained by God? The Lord said to his disciples that the kings of the Gentiles exercise lordship over Gentiles, but it is not so among the disciples, where he who is first ought to become the least [Luke 22:25-26]; by this saying, they tell us, all Christians are forbidden to take kingdoms or governments. O skillful interpreters! There arose a contention among the disciples over which one would excel the others. To silence this vain ambition, the Lord taught them that their ministry is not like kingdoms, in which one is pre-eminent above the rest. What dishonor, I ask you, does this comparison do to the kingly dignity? Indeed, what does it prove at all, except that the kingly office is not the ministry of an apostle? Moreover, among magistrates themselves, although there is a variety of forms, there is no difference in this respect, that we must regard all of them as ordained of God. For Paul also lumps them all together when he says that there is no power except from God [Rom. 13:1]. And that which is the least pleasant of all has been especially commended above the rest, that is, the power of one. This, because it brings with it the common bondage of all (except that one man to whose will it subjects all things), in ancient times could not be acceptable to heroic and nobler natures. But to forestall their unjust judgments, Scripture expressly affirms that it is the providence of God's wisdom that kings reign [cf. Prov. 8:15], and particularly commands us to honor the king [Prov. 24:21; I Peter 2:17].

*(Forms of government, and duties of magistrates. Issues of war and taxation, 8-13)*

*8. The diversity of forms of government*

Obviously, it would be an idle pastime for men in private life, who are disqualified from deliberating on the organization of any commonwealth, to dispute over what would be the best kind of government in that place where they live. Also this question admits of no simple solution but requires deliberation, since the nature of the discussion depends largely upon the circumstances. And if you compare the forms of government among themselves apart from the circumstances, it is not easy to distinguish which one of them excels in usefulness, for they contend on such equal terms. The fall from kingdom to tyranny is easy; but it is not much more difficult to fall from the rule of the best men to the faction of a few; yet it is easiest of all to fall from popular rule to sedition. For if the three forms of government which the philosophers discuss be considered in themselves, I will not deny that aristocracy, or a system compounded of aristocracy and democracy, far excels all others: not indeed of itself, but because it is very rare for kings so to control themselves that their will never disagrees with what is just and right; or for them to have been endowed with such great keenness and prudence, that each knows how much is enough. Therefore, men's fault or failing causes it to be safer and more bearable for a number to exercise government, so that they may help one another, teach and admonish one another; and, if one asserts himself unfairly, there may be a number of censors and masters to restrain his willfulness. This has both been proved by experience, and also the Lord confirmed it by his authority when he ordained among the Israelites an aristocracy bordering on democracy, since he willed to keep them in best condition [Ex. 18:13-26; Deut. 1:9-17] until he should bring forward the image of Christ in David. And, as I freely admit that no kind of government is more happy than one where freedom is regulated with becoming moderation and is properly established on a durable basis, so also I reckon most happy those permitted to enjoy this state; and if they stoutly and constantly labor to preserve and retain it, I grant that they are doing nothing alien to this office. Indeed, the magistrates ought to apply themselves with the highest diligence to prevent the freedom (whose guardians they have been appointed) from being in any respect diminished, far less be violated. If they are not sufficiently alert and careful, they are faithless in office, and traitors to their country.

But if those to whom the Lord has appointed another form of government should transfer this very function to themselves, being moved to desire a change of government — even to think of such a move will not only be foolish and superfluous, but altogether harmful. However, as you will surely find if you fix your eyes not on one city alone, but look around and glance at the world as a whole, or at least cast your sight upon regions farther off, divine providence has wisely arranged that various countries should be ruled by various kinds of government. For as elements cohere only in unequal proportion, so countries are best held together according to their own particular inequality. However, all these things are needlessly spoken to those for whom the will of the Lord is enough. For if it has seemed good to him to set kings over kingdoms, senates or municipal officers over free cities, it is our duty to show ourselves compliant and obedient to whomever he sets over the places where we live.

*9. Concern for both Tables of the Law*

Now in this place we ought to explain in passing the office of the magistrates, how it is described in the Word of God and the things in which it consists. If Scripture did not teach that it extends to both Tables of the Law, we could learn this from secular writers: for no one has discussed the office of magistrates, the making of laws, and public welfare, without beginning at religion and divine worship. And thus all have confessed that no government can be happily established unless piety is the first concern; and that those laws are preposterous which neglect God's right and provide only for men. Since, therefore, among all philosophers religion takes first place, and since this fact has always been observed by universal consent of all nations, let Christian princes and magistrates be ashamed of their negligence if they do not apply themselves to this concern. And we have already shown that these duties are especially enjoined upon them by God; and it is fitting that they should labor to protect and assert the honor of him whose representatives they are, and by whose grace they govern.

Also, holy kings are greatly praised in Scripture because they restored the worship of God when it was corrupted or destroyed, or took care of religion that under them it might flourish pure and unblemished. But on the contrary, the Sacred History places anarchies among things evil: because there was no king in Israel, each man did as he pleased [Judg. 21:25].

This proves the folly of those who would neglect the concern for God and would give attention only to rendering justice among men. As if God appointed rulers in his name to decide earthly controversies but overlooked what was of far greater importance — that he himself should be purely worshiped according to the prescription of his law. But the passion to alter everything with impunity drives turbulent men to the point of wanting all vindicators of violated piety removed from their midst.

As far as the Second Table is concerned, Jeremiah admonishes kings to "do justice and righteousness," to "deliver him who has been oppressed by force from the hand of the oppressor," not to "grieve or wrong the alien, the widow, and the fatherless" or "shed innocent blood" [Jer.22:3, cf. Vg.]. The exhortation which we read in Ps. 82 has the same purpose: that they should "give justice to the poor and needy, rescue the destitute and needy, and deliver the poor and and needy from the hand of the oppressor" [Ps. 82:3-4]. And Moses commands the leaders whom he had appointed as his representatives to "hear the cases between their brethren, and judge . . . between a man and his brother, and the alien" and "not recognize faces in judgment, and hear small and great alike, and be afraid of no man, for the judgment is God's" [Deut. 1:16-17p.]. But I pass over such statements as these: that kings should not multiply horses for themselves; nor set their mind upon avarice; nor be lifted up above their brethren; that they should be constant in meditation upon the law of the Lord all the days of their life [Deut. 17:16-19]; that judges should not lean to one side or take bribes [Deut. 16:19] — and like passages which we read here and there in Scripture. For in explaining here the office of magistrates, it is not so much my purpose to instruct the magistrates themselves as to teach others what magistrates are and to what end God has appointed them. We see, therefore, that they are ordained protectors and vindicators of public innocence, modesty, decency, and tranquillity, and that their sole endeavor should be to provide for the common safety and peace of all. Of these virtues David professes that he will be a pattern: when he has been elevated to the royal throne, he will not consent to any crimes, but will detest the impious, slanderers, and the proud, and will seek out from everywhere upright and faithful counselors [Ps. 101, esp. vs. 4, 5, 7, 6].

But since they cannot perform this unless they defend good men from the wrongs of the wicked, and give aid and protection to the oppressed, they have also been armed with power with which severely to coerce the open malefactors and criminals by whose wickedness the public peace is troubled or disturbed [cf. Rom. 13:3]. For from experience we thoroughly agree with the statement of Solon that all commonwealths are maintained by reward and punishment; take these away and the whole discipline of cities collapses and is dissolved. For the care of equity and justice grows cold in the minds of many, unless due honor has been prepared for virtue; and the lust of wicked men cannot be restrained except by severity and the infliction of penalties. And the prophet has included these two functions, when he bids kings and other rulers execute judgment and justice [Jer. 22:3; cf. ch. 21:12]. Justice, indeed, is to receive into safekeeping, to embrace, to protect, vindicate, and free the innocent. But judgment is to withstand the boldness of the impious, to repress their violence, to punish their misdeeds.

*10. The magistrates' exercise of force is compatible with piety*

But here a seemingly hard and difficult question arises: if the law of God forbids all Christians to kill [Ex. 20:13; Deut 5:17; Matt. 5:21], and the prophet prophesies concerning God's holy mountain (the church) that in it men shall not afflict or hurt [Isa. 11:9; 65:25] — how can magistrates be pious men and shedders of blood at the same time?

Yet if we understand that the magistrate in administering punishments does nothing by himself, but carries out the very judgments of God, we shall not be hampered by this scruple. The law of the Lord forbids killing; but, that murders may not go unpunished, the Lawgiver himself puts into the hand of his ministers a sword to be drawn against all murderers. It is not for the pious to afflict and hurt; yet to avenge, at the Lord's command, the afflictions of the pious is not to hurt or to afflict. Would that this were ever before our minds — that nothing is done here from men's rashness, but all things are done on the authority of God who commands it; and while his authority goes before us, we never wander from the straight path! Unless perhaps restraint is laid upon God's justice, that it may not punish misdeeds. But if it is not right to impose any law upon him, why should we try to reproach his ministers? They do not bear the sword in vain, says Paul, for they are ministers of God to execute his wrath, avengers of wrongdoers [Rom. 13:4]. Therefore, if princes and other rulers recognize that nothing is more acceptable to the Lord than their obedience, let them apply themselves to this ministry, if, indeed, they are intent on having their piety, righteousness, and uprightness approved of God [cf. II Tim. 2:15].

Moses was impelled by this desire when, realizing that he had been destined by the Lord's power to be the liberator of his poeple, he laid his hand upon the Egyptian [Ex. 2:12; Acts 7:24]. This was the case again, when, by slaying three thousand men in one day, he took vengeance upon the people's sacrilege [Ex. 32:27-28]. David also, when at the end of his life he ordered his son Solomon to kill Joab and Shimei [ I Kings 2:5-6, 8-9]. Accordingly, he also includes this among kingly virtues: to destroy the wicked of the land that all evildoers may be driven out of the city of God [ Ps. 101:8]. To this also pertains the praise which is given to Solomon: "You have loved righteousness and hated iniquity" [Ps. 45:7; 44:8; Vg.].

How does Moses' gentle and peaceable nature flame up into such savageness that, sprinkled and dripping with the blood of his brethren, he dashes through the camp to new carnage? How can David, a man of such great gentleness throughout life, as he breathes his last, make that bloody testament, that his son should not allow the hoary heads of Joab and Shimei to go in peace to the grave [I Kings 2:5-6, 8-9]? But both men, by executing the vengeance ordained of God, hallowed by cruelty their hands, which by sparing they would have defiled. "It is an abomination among kings," says Solomon, "to do iniquity, for the throne is established in righteousness." [Prov. 16:12]. Again: "A king who sits on the throne of judgment casts his eyes upon every evildoer" [Prov. 20:8p.]. Again: "A wise king scatters the evildoers and turns them upon the wheel" [Prov. 20:26p.]. Again: "Remove the dross from the silver, and a from the king's sight, and his throne will be established in righteousness" [Prov. 25:4-5, cf. Geneva]. Again: "He who justifies the wicked and he who condemns the righteous are both alike an abomination to the Lord" [Prov. 17:15]. Again: "A rebel seeks evil for himself, and a cruel messenger is sent to him" [Prov. 17:11p.]. Again: "He who says to the wicked, 'You are righteous,' will be cursed by peoples . . . and nations" [Prov. 24:24p.]. Now if their true righteousness is to pursue the guilty and the impious with drawn sword, should they sheathe their sword and keep their hands clean of blood while abandoned men wickedly range about with slaughter and massacre, they will become guilty of the greatest impiety, far indeed from winning praise for their goodness and righteousness thereby!

Begone, now, with that abrupt and savage harshness, and that tribunal which is rightly called the reef of accused men! For I am not one either to favor undue cruelty or think that a fair judgment can be pronounced unless clemency, that best counselor of kings and surest keeper of the kingly throne (as Solomon declares) [Prov. 20:28] is always present — clemency, which by a certain writer of antiquity was truly called the chief gift of princes.

Yet it is necessary for the magistrate to pay attention to both, lest by excessive severity he either harm more than heal; or, by superstitious affectation of clemency, fall into the cruelest gentleness, if he should (with a soft and dissolute kindness) abandon many to their destruction. For during the reign of Nerva it was not without reason said: it is indeed bad to live under a prince with whom nothing is permitted; but much worse under one by whom everything is allowed.

*11. On the right of the government to wage war*
But kings and people must sometimes take up arms to execute such public vengeance. On this basis we may judge wars lawful which are so undertaken. For if power has been given them to preserve the tranquillity of their dominion, to restrain the seditious stirrings of restless men, to help those forcibly oppressed, to punish evil deeds — can they use it more opportunely than to check the fury of one who disturbs both the repose of private individuals and the common tranquillity of all, who raises seditious tumults, and by whom violent oppressions and vile misdeeds are perpetrated? If they ought to be the guardians and defenders of the laws, they should also overthrow the efforts of all whose offenses corrupt the

discipline of the laws. Indeed, if they rightly punish those robbers whose harmful acts have affected only a few, will they allow a whole country to be afflicted and devastated by robberies with impunity? For it makes no difference whether it be a king or the lowest of the common folk who invades a foreign country in which he has no right, and harries it as an enemy. All such must, equally, be considered as robbers and punished accordingly. Therefore, both natural equity and the nature of the office dictate that princes must be armed not only to restrain the misdeeds of private individuals by judicial punishment, but also to defend by war the dominions entrusted to their safekeeping, if at any time they are under enemy attack. And the Holy Spirit declares such wars to be lawful by many testimonies of Scripture.

## 12. Restraint and humanity in war

But if anyone object against me that in the New Testament there exists no testimony or example which teaches that war is a thing lawful for Christians, I answer first that the reason for waging war which existed of old still persists today; and that, on the other hand, there is no reason that bars magistrates from defending their subjects. Secondly, I say that an express declaration of this matter is not to be sought in the writings of the apostles; for their purpose is not to fashion a civil government, but to establish the spiritual Kingdom of Christ. Finally, that it is there shown in passing that Christ by his coming has changed nothing in this respect. For if Christian doctrine (to use Augustine's words) condemned all wars, the soldiers asking counsel concerning salvation should rather have been advised to cast away their weapons and withdraw completely from military service. But they were told: "Strike no man, do no man wrong, be content with your wages" [Luke 3:14 p.]. When he taught them to be content with their wages, he certainly did not forbid them to bear arms.

But it is the duty of all magistrates here to guard particularly against giving vent to their passions even in the slightest degree. Rather, if they have to punish, let them not be carried away with headlong anger, or be seized with hatred, or burn with implacable severity. Let them also (as Augustine says) have pity on the common nature in the one whose special fault they are punishing. Or, if they must arm themselves against the enemy, that is, the armed robber, let them not lightly seek occasion to do so; indeed, let them not accept the occasion when offered, unless they are driven to it by extreme necessity. For if we must perform much more than the heathen philosopher required when he wanted war to seem a seeking of peace, surely everything else ought to be tried before recourse is had to arms. Lastly, in both situations let them not allow themselves to be swayed by any private affection, but be led by concern for the people alone. Otherwise, they very wickedly abuse their power, which has been given them not for their own advantage, but for the benefit and service of others.

Moreover, this same right to wage war furnishes the reason for garrisons, leagues, and other civil defenses. Now, I call "garrisons," those troops which are stationed among the cities to defend the boundaries of a country; "leagues," those pacts which are made by neighboring princes to the end that if any trouble should happen in their lands, they may come to one another's aid, and join forces to put down the common enemies of mankind. I call "civil defenses," things used in the art of war.

*13. Concerning the right of the government to levy tribute*

· Lastly, I also wish to add this, that tributes and taxes are the lawful revenues of princes, which they may chiefly use to meet the public expenses of their office; yet they may similarly use them for the magnificence of their household, which is joined, so to speak, with the dignity of the authority they exercise. As we see, David, Hezekiah, Josiah, Jehoshaphat, and other holy kings, also Joseph and Daniel (according to the dignity of their office) were, without offending piety, lavish at public expense, and we read in Ezekiel that a very large portion of the land was assigned to the kings [Ezek. 48:21]. There, although the prophet portrays the spiritual Kingdom of Christ, he seeks the pattern for his picture from a lawful human kingdom.

But he does so in such a way that princes themselves will in turn remember that their revenues are not so much their private chests as the treasuries of the entire people (for Paul so testifies [Rom. 13:6]), which cannot be squandered or despoiled without manifest injustice. Or rather, that these are almost the very blood of the people, which it would be the harshest inhumanity not to spare. Moreover, let them consider that their imposts and levies, and other kinds of tributes are nothing but supports of public necessity; but that to impose them upon the common folk without cause is tyrannical extortion.

These considerations do not encourage princes to waste and expensive luxury, as there is surely no need to add fuel to their cupidity, already too much kindled of itself. But as it is very necessary that, whatever they venture, they should venture with a pure conscience before God, they must be taught how much is lawful for them, that they may not in impious self-confidence come under God's displeasure. And this doctrine is not superfluous for private individuals in order that they should not let themselves rashly and shamelessly decry any expenses of princes, even if these exceed the common expenditures of the citizens.

*(Public law and judicial procedures, as related to Christian duty, 14-21)*
*14. Old Testament law and the laws of nations*

Next to the magistracy in the civil state come the laws, stoutest sinews of the commonwealth, or, as Cicero, after Plato, calls them, the souls, without which the magistracy cannot stand, even as they themselves have no force apart from the magistracy. Accordingly, nothing truer could be said than that the law is a silent magistrate, a living law.

But because I have undertaken to say with what laws a Christian state ought to be governed, this is no reason why anyone should expect a long discourse concerning the best kind of laws. This would be endless and would not pertain to the present purpose and place. I shall in but a few words, and as in passing, note what laws can piously be used before God, and be rightly administered among men.

I would have preferred to pass over this matter in utter silence if I were not aware that here many dangerously go astray. For there are some who deny that a commonwealth is duly framed which neglects the political system of Moses, and is ruled by the common laws of nations. Let other men consider how perilous and seditious this notion is; it will be enough for me to have proved it false and foolish.

We must bear in mind that common division of the whole law of God published by Moses into moral, ceremonial, and judicial laws. And we must consider each of these parts, that we may understand what there is in them that pertains to us, and what does not. In the meantime, let no one be concerned over the small point that ceremonial and judicial laws pertain also to morals. For the ancient writers who taught this division, although they were not ignorant that these two latter parts had some bearing upon morals, still, because these could be changed or abrogated while morals remained untouched, did not call them moral laws. They applied this name only to the first part, without which the true holiness of morals cannot stand, nor an unchangeable rule of right living.

### 15. Moral, ceremonial, and judicial law distinguished

The moral law (to begin first with it) is contained under two heads, one of which simply commands us to worship God with pure faith and piety; the other, to embrace men with sincere affection. Accordingly, it is the true and eternal rule of righteousness, prescribed for men of all nations and times, who wish to conform their lives to God's will. For it is his eternal and unchangeable will that he himself indeed be worshiped by us all, and that we love one another.

The ceremonial law was the tutelage of the Jews, with which it seemed good to the Lord to train this people, as it were, in their childhood, until the fullness of time should come [Gal.4:3-4; cf. ch. 3:23-24], in order that he might fully manifest his wisdom to the nations, and show the truth of those things which then were foreshadowed in figures.

The judicial law, given to them for civil government, imparted certain formulas of equity and justice, by which they might live together blamelessly and peaceably.

Those ceremonial practices indeed properly belonged to the doctrine of piety, inasmuch as they kept the church of the Jews in service and reverence to God, and yet could be distinguished from piety itself. In like manner, the form of their judicial laws, although it had no other intent than how best to preserve that very love which is enjoined by God's eternal law, has something distinct from that precept of love. Therefore, as ceremonial laws could be abrogated while piety remained safe and unharmed, so too, when these judicial laws were taken away, the perpetual duties and precepts of love could still remain.

But if this is true, surely every nation is left free to make such laws as it foresees to be profitable for itself. Yet these must be in conformity to that perpetual rule of love, so that they indeed vary in form but have the same purpose. For I do not think that those barbarous and savage laws such as gave honor to thieves, permitted promiscuous intercourse, and others both more filthy and more abusrd, are to be regarded as laws. For they are abhorrent not only to all justice, but also to all humanity and gentleness.

### 16. Unity and diversity of laws

What I have said will become plain if in all laws we examine, as we should, these two things: the constitution of the law, and the equity on which its constitution is itself founded and rests. Equity, because it is natural, cannot but be the same for all, and therefore, this same purpose ought to apply to all laws, whatever their object. Constitutions have certain circumstances upon which they in part depend. It therefore does not matter that they are different, provided all equally press toward the same goal of equity.

It is a fact that the law of God which we call the moral law is nothing else than a testimony of natural law and of that conscience which God has engraved upon the minds of men. Consequently, the entire scheme of this equity of which we are now speaking has been prescribed in it. Hence, this equity alone must be the goal and rule and limit of all laws.

Whatever laws shall be framed to that rule, directed to that goal, bound by that limit, there is no reason why we should disapprove of them, howsoever they may differ from the Jewish law, or among themselves.

God's law forbids stealing. The penalties meted out to thieves in the Jewish state are to be seen in Exodus [Ex. 22:1-4]. The very ancient laws of other nations punished theft with double restitution; the laws which followed these distinguished between theft, manifest and not manifest. Some proceeded to banishment, others to flogging, others finally to capital punishment. False testimony was punished by damages similar and equal to injury among the Jews [Deut. 19:18-21]; elsewhere, only by deep disgrace; in some nations, by hanging; in others, by the cross. All codes equally avenge murder with blood, but with different kinds of death. Against adulterers some nations levy severer, others, lighter punishments. Yet we see how, with such diversity, all laws tend to the same end. For, together with one voice, they pronounce punishment against those crimes which God's eternal law has condemned, namely, murder, theft, adultery, and false witness. But they do not agree on the manner of punishment. Nor is this either necessary or expedient. There are countries which, unless they deal cruelly with murderers by way of horrible examples, must immediately perish from slaughters and robberies. There are ages that demand increasingly harsh penalties. If any disturbance occurs in a commonwealth, the evils that usually arise from it must be corrected by new ordinances. In time of war, in the clatter of arms, all humaneness would disappear unless some uncommon fear of punishment were introduced. In drought, in pestilence, unless greater severity is used, everything will go to ruin. There are nations inclined to a particular vice, unless it be most sharply repressed. How malicious and hateful toward public welfare would a man be who is offended by such diversity, which is perfectly adapted to maintain the observance of God's law?

For the statement of some, that the law of God given through Moses is dishonored when it is abrogated and new laws preferred to it, is utterly vain. For others are not preferred to it when they are more approved, not by a simple comparison, but with regard to the condition of times, place, and nation; or when that law is abrogated which was never enacted for us. For the Lord through the hand of Moses did not give that law to be proclaimed among all nations and to be in force everywhere; but when he had taken the Jewish nation into his safekeeping, defense, and protection, he also willed to be a lawgiver especially to it; and — as became a wise lawgiver — he had special concern for it in making its laws.

*17. Christians may use the law courts, but without hatred and revenge*

It now remains for us to examine what we had set in the last place: what usefulness the laws, judgments, and magistrates have for the common society of Christians. To this is also joined another question: how much deference private individuals ought to yield to their magistrates, and how far their obedience ought to go. To very many the office of magistrate seems superfluous among Christians, because they cannot piously call upon them for help, inasmuch as it is forbidden to them to take revenge, to sue before a court, or to go to law. But Paul clearly testifies to the contrary that the magistrate is minister of God for our good [Rom. 13:4]. By this we understand that he has been so ordained of God, that, defended by his hand and support against the wrongdoing and injustices of evil men, we may live a quiet and serene life [I Tim. 2:2]. But if it is to no purpose that he has been given by the Lord for our defense unless we are allowed to enjoy such benefit, it is clear enough that the magistrate may without impiety be called upon and also appealed to.

But here I have to deal with two kinds of men. There are very many who so boil with a rage for litigation that they are never at peace with themselves unless they are quarreling with others. And they carry on these lawsuits with bitter and deadly hatred, and an insane passion to revenge and hurt and they pursue them with implacable obstinacy even to the ruin of their adversaries. Meanwhile, to avoid being thought as doing something wrong, they defend such perversity on the pretense of legal procedure. But if one is permitted to go to law with a brother, one is not therewith allowed to hate him, or be seized with a mad desire to harm him, or hound him relentlessly.

## 18. The Christian's motives in litigation

Such men should therefore understand that lawsuits are permissable if rightly used. There is right use, both for the plaintiff in suing and for the accused in defending himself, if the defendant presents himself on the appointed day and with such exception, as he can, defends himself without bitterness, but only with this intent, to defend what is his by right, and if on the other hand, the plaintiff, undeservedly oppressed either in his person or in his property, puts himself in the care of the magistrate, makes his complaint, and seeks what is fair and good. But he should be far from all passion to harm or take revenge, far from harshness and hatred, far from burning desire for contention. He should rather be prepared to yield his own and suffer anything than be carried away with enmity toward his adversary. On the other hand, where hearts are filled with malice, corrupted by envy, inflamed with wrath, breathing revenge, finally so inflamed with desire for contention, that love is somewhat impaired in them, the whole court action of even the most just cause cannot but be impious. For this must be a set principle for all Christians: that a lawsuit, however just, can never be rightly prosecuted by any man, unless he treat his adversary with the same love and good will as if the business under controversy were already amicably settled and composed. Perhaps someone will interpose here that such moderation is so uniformly absent from any lawsuit that it would be a miracle if any such were found. Indeed, I admit that, as the customs of these times go, an example of an upright litigant is rare; but the thing itself, when not corrupted by the addition of anything evil, does not cease to be good and pure. But when we hear that the help of the magistrate is a holy gift of God, we must more diligently guard against its becoming polluted by our fault.

## 19. Against the rejection of the judicial process

As for those who strictly condemn all legal contentions, let them realize that they therewith repudiate God's holy ordinance, and one of the class of gifts that can be clean to the clean [Titus 1:15]; unless, perchance, they wish to accuse Paul of a shameful act, since he both repelled the slanders of his accusers, exposing at the same time their craft and malice [Acts 24:12ff.], and in court claimed for himself the privilege of Roman citizenship [Acts 16:37; 22:1, 25], and, when there was need, appealed from the unjust judge to the judgment seat of Caesar [Acts 25:10-11].

This does not contradict the fact that all Christians are forbidden to desire revenge, which we banish far away from Christian courts [Lev. 19:18; Matt. 5:39; Deut. 32:35; Rom. 12:19]. For if it is a civil case, a man does not take the right path unless he commits his cause, with innocent simplicity, to the judge as public protector; and he should think not at all of returning evil for evil [Rom. 12:17], which is the passion for revenge. If, however, the action is brought for some capital or serious offense, we require that the accuser be one who comes into court without a burning desire for revenge or resentment over private injury, but having in mind only to prevent the efforts of a destructive man from doing harm to society. For if you remove a vengeful mind, that command which forbids revenge to Christians is not broken.

But, some will object, not only are they forbidden to desire revenge, but they are also bidden to wait upon the hand of the Lord, who promises that he will be present to avenge the oppressed and afflicted [Rom. 12:19]; while those who seek aid from the magistrate, either for themselves or for others, anticipate all the vengeance of the Heavenly Protector. Not at all! For we must consider that the magistrate's revenge is not man's but God's, which he extends and exercises, as Paul says [Rom. 13:4], through the ministry of man for our good.

*20. The Christian endures insults, but with amity and equity defends the public interest*

We are not in any more disagreement with Christ's words in which he forbids us to resist evil, and commands us to turn the right cheek to him who has struck the left, and to give our cloak to him who has taken away our coat [Matt. 5:39-40]. He indeed wills that the hearts of his people so utterly recoil from any desire to retaliate that they should rather allow double injury to be done them than desire to pay it back. And we are not leading them away from this forbearance. For truly, Christians ought to be a kind of men born to bear slanders and injuries, open to the malice, deceits, and mockeries of wicked men. And not that only, but they ought to bear patiently all these evils. That is, they should have such complete spiritual composure that, having received one offense, they make ready for another, promising themselves throughout life nothing but the bearing of a perpetual cross. Meanwhile, let them also do good to those who do them harm, and bless those who curse them [Luke 6:28; cf. Matt. 5:44], and (this is their only victory) strive to conquer evil with good [Rom. 12:21]. So minded, they will not seek an eye for an eye, a tooth for a tooth, as the Pharisees taught their disciples to desire revenge, but, as we are instructed by Christ, they will so suffer their body to be maimed, and their possessions to be maliciously seized, that they will forgive and voluntarily pardon those wrongs as soon as they have been inflicted upon them [Matt. 5:38 ff.].

Yet this equity and moderateness of their minds will not prevent them from using the help of the magistrate in preserving their own possessions, while maintaining friendliness toward their enemies; or zealous for public welfare, from demanding the punishment of a guilty and pestilent man, who, they know, can be changed only by death. For Augustine truly interprets the purpose of all these precepts. The righteous and godly man should be ready patiently to bear the malice of those whom he desires to become good, in order to increase the number of good men — not to add himself to the number of the bad by a malice like theirs. Secondly, these precepts pertain more to the preparation of the heart which is within than to the work which is done in the open, in order that patience of mind and good will be kept in secret, but that we may openly do what we see may benefit those whom we ought to wish well.

*21. Paul condemns a litigious spirit, but not all litigation*

But the usual objection — that Paul has condemned lawsuits altogether — is also false [I Cor. 6:5-8]. It can easily be understood from his words that there was an immoderate rage for litigation in the church of the Corinthians — even to the point that they exposed to the scoffing and evilspeaking of the impious the gospel of Christ and the whole religion they professed. Paul first criticized them for disgracing the gospel among believers by the intemperateness of their quarrels. Secondly, he rebuked them also for contending in this way among themselves, brethren with brethren. For they were so far from bearing wrongs that they greedily panted after one another's possessions, and without cause assailed and inflicted loss upon one another. Therefore, Paul inveighs against that mad lust to go to law, not simply against all controversies.

But he brands it a fault or weakness for them not to accept the loss of their goods, rather than to endeavor to keep them, even to the point of strife. That is, when they were so easily aroused by every loss, and dashed to the court and to lawsuits over the least causes, he speaks of this as proof that their minds are too prone to anger, and not enough disposed to patience. Christians ought indeed so to conduct themselves that they always prefer to yield their own right rather than go into a court, from which they can scarcely get away without a heart stirred and kindled to hatred of their brother. But when any man sees that without loss of love he can defend his own property, the loss of which would be a heavy expense to him, he does not offend against this statement of Paul, if he has recourse to law. To sum up (as we said at the beginning), love will give every man the best counsel. Everything undertaken apart from love and all disputes that go beyond it, we regard as incontrovertibly unjust and impious.

*(Obedience, with reverence, due even unjust rulers, 22-29)*
*22. Deference*

The first duty of subjects toward their magistrates is to think most honorably of their office, which they recognize as a jurisdiction bestowed by God, and on that account to esteem and reverence them as ministers and representatives of God. For you may find some who very respectfully yield themselves to their magistrates and desire somebody whom they can obey, because they know that such is expedient for public welfare; nevertheless they regard magistrates only as a kind of necessary evil. But Peter requires something more of us when he commands that the king be honored [I Peter 2:17]; as does Solomon when he teaches that God and king are to be feared [Prov. 24:21]. For Peter, in the word "to honor" includes a sincere and candid opinion of the king. Solomon, yoking the king with god, shows that the king is full of a holy reverence and dignity. There is also that famous saying in Paul: that we should obey "not only because of wrath, but because of conscience" [Rom. 13:5, cf. Vg.]. By this he means that subjects should be led not by fear alone of princes and rulers to remain in subjection under them (as they commonly yield to an armed enemy who sees that vengeance is promptly taken if they resist), but because they are showing obedience to God himself when they give it to them; since the rulers' power is from God.

I am not discussing the men themselves, as if a mask of dignity covered foolishness, or sloth, or cruelty, as well as wicked morals full of infamous deeds, and thus acquired for vices the praise of virtues; but I say that the order itself is worthy of such honor and reverence that those who are rulers are esteemed among us, and receive reverence out of respect for their lordship.

I am not discussing the men themselves, as if a mask of dignity covered foolishness, or sloth, or cruelty, as well as wicked morals full of infamous deeds, and thus acquired for vices the priase of virtues; but I say that the order itself is worthy of such honor and reverence that those who are rulers are esteemed among us, and receive reverence out of respect for their lordship.

### 23. Obedience

From this also something else follows: that, with hearts inclined to reverence their rulers, the subjects should prove their obedience toward them, whether by obeying their proclamations, or by paying taxes, or by undertaking public offices and burdens which pertain to the common defense, or by executing any other commands of theirs. "Let every soul," says Paul, "be subject to the higher powers. . . . For he who resists authority, resists what God has ordained." [Rom. 13:1-2, Vg.] "Remind them," he writes to Titus, "to be subject to principalities and powers, to obey magistrates, to be ready for every good work." [Titus 3:1, cf. Vg.] And Peter says, "Be subject to every human creature (or rather, as I translate it, ordinance) for the Lord's sake, whether it be to the king, as supreme, or unto governors who are sent through him to punish evildoers, but to praise doers of good." [I Peter 2:13-14.] Now, in order that they may prove that they are not pretending subjection, but are sincerely and heartily subjects, Paul adds that they should commend to God the safety and prosperity of those under whom they live. "I urge," he says, "that supplications, prayers, intercessions, and thanksgivings be made for all men, for kings, and all that are in authority, that we may lead a quiet and peaceable life, with all godliness and honesty."[ I Tim.2:1-2, cf. Vg.]

Let no man deceive himself here. For since the magistrate cannot be resisted without God being resisted at the same time, even though it seems that an unarmed magistrate can be despised with impunity, still God is armed to avenge mightily this contempt toward himself.

Moreover, under this obedience I include the restraint which private citizens ought to bid themselves keep in public, that they may not deliberately intrude in public affairs, or pointlessly invade the magistrate's office, or undertake anything at all politically. If anything in a public ordinance requires amendment, let them not raise a tumult, or put their hands to the task — all of them ought to keep their hands bound in this respect — but let them commit the matter to the judgment of the magistrate, whose hand alone here is free. I mean, let them not venture on anything without a command. For when the ruler gives his command, private citizens receive public authority. For as the counselors are commonly called the ears and eyes of the prince, so may one reasonably speak of those whom he has appointed by his command to do things, as the hands of the prince.

### 24. Obedience is also due the unjust magistrate

But since we have so far been describing a magistrate who truly is what he is called, that is, a father of his country, and, as the poet expresses it, shepherd of his people, guardian of peace, protector of righteousness, and avenger of innocence — he who does not approve of such government must rightly be regarded as insane.

But it is the example of nearly all ages that some princes are careless about all those things to which they ought to have given heed, and, far from all care, lazily take their pleasure. Others, intent upon their own business, put up for sale laws, privileges, judgments, and letters of favor. Others drain the common people of their money, and afterward lavish it on insane largesse. Still others exercise sheer robbery, plundering houses, raping virgins and matrons, and slaughtering the innocent.

Consequently, many cannot be persuaded that they ought to recognize these as princes and to obey their authority as far as possible. For in such great disgrace, and among such crimes, so alien to the office not only of a magistrate but also of a man, they discern no appearance of the image of God which ought to have shone in the magistrate; while they see no trace of that minister of God, who had been appointed to praise the good, and to punish the evil [cf. I Peter 2:14, Vg.]. Thus, they also do not recognize as ruler him whose dignity and authority Scripture commends to us. Indeed, this inborn feeling has always been in the minds of men to hate and curse tyrants as much as to love and venerate lawful kings.

*25. The wicked ruler a judgment of God*

But if we look to God's Word, it will lead us farther. We are not only subject to the authority of princes who perform their office toward us uprightly and faithfully as they ought, but also to the authority of all who, by whatever means, have got control of affairs, even though they perform not a whit of the princes' office. For despite the Lord's testimony that the magistrate's office is the highest gift of his beneficence to preserve the safety of men, and despite his appointment of bounds to the magistrates — he still declares at the same time that whoever they may be, they have their authority solely from him. Indeed, he says that those who rule for the public benefit are true patterns and evidences of this beneficence of his; that they who rule unjustly and incompetently have been raised up by him to punish the wickedness of the people; that all equally have been endowed with that holy majesty with which he has invested lawful power.

I shall proceed no farther until I have added some sure testimonies of this thing. Yet, we need not labor to prove that a wicked king is the Lord's wrath upon the earth [Job 34:30, Vg;, Hos. 13:11; Isa. 3:4; 10:5; Deut. 28:29], for I believe no man will contradict me; and thus nothing more would be said of a king than of a robber who seizes your possessions, of an adulterer who pollutes your marriage bed, or of a murderer who seeks to kill you. For Scripture reckons all such calamities among God's curses.

But let us, rather, pause here to prove this, which does not so easily settle in men's minds. In a very wicked man utterly unworthy of all honor, provided he has the public power in his hands, that noble and divine power resides which the Lord has by his Word given to the ministers of his justice and judgment. Accordingly, he should be held in the same reverence and esteem by his subjects, in so far as public obedience is concerned, in which they would hold the best of kings if he were given to them.

*26. Obedience to bad kings required in Scripture*

First, I should like my readers to note and carefully observe that providence of God, which, the Scriptures with good reason so often recall to us, and its special operation in distributing kingdoms and appointing what kings he pleases. In Daniel, the Lord changes times and successions of times, removes kings and sets them up [Dan. 2:21, 37]. Likewise: "to the end that the living may know that the Most High rules the kingdom of men, and gives it to whom he will" [Dan. 4:17; cf. ch. 4:14, Vg.]. Although Scripture everywhere abounds with such passages, this prophecy particularly swarms with them. Now it is well enough known what kind of king Nebuchadnezzar was, who conquered Jerusalem — a strong invader and destroyer of others. Nevertheless, the Lord declares in Ezekiel that He has given him the land of Egypt for the service he had done him in devastating it [Ezek. 29:19-20]. And Daniel said to him: "You, O king, are a king of kings, to whom the God of heaven has given the kingdom, powerful, mighty, and glorious; to you, I say, he has given also all lands where the sons of men dwell, beasts of the forest and birds of the air: these he has given into your hand and made you rule over them" [Dan. 2:37-38, cf. Vg.]. Again, Daniel says to Nebuchadnezzar's son Belshazzar: "The Most High God gave Nebuchadnezzar, your father, kingship and magnificence, honor and glory; and because of the magnificence that he gave him, all peoples, tribes, and tongues were trembling and fearful before him" [Dan. 5:18-19, cf. Vg.]. When we hear that a king has been ordained by God, let us at once call to mind those heavenly edicts with regard to honoring and fearing a king; then we shall not hesitate to hold a most wicked tyrant in the place where the Lord has deigned to set him. Samuel, when he warned the people of Israel what sort of things they would suffer from their kings, said: "This shall be the right of the king that will reign over you: he will take your sons and put them to his chariot to make them his horsemen and to plow his fields and reap his harvest, and make his weapons. He will take your daughters to be perfumers and cooks and bakers. Finally, he will take your fields, your vineyards, and your best olive trees and will give them to his servants. He will take the tenth of your grain and of your vineyards, and will give it to his eunuchs and servants. He will take your menservants, maidservants, and asses and set them to his work. He will take the tenth of your flocks and you will be his servants" [I Sam. 8:11-17, with ommissions; cf. Hebrew]. Surely the kings would not do this by legal right, since the law trained them to all restraint [Deut. 17:16ff.]. But it was called a right in relation to the people, for they had to obey it and were not allowed to resist. It is as if Samuel had said: The willfulness of kings will run to excess, but it will not be your part to restrain it; you will have only this left to you: to obey their commands and hearken to their word.

*27. The case of Nebuchadnezzar in Jer., ch. 27*

But in Jeremiah, especially, there is a memorable passage, which (although rather long) it will not trouble me to quote because it very clearly defines this whole question. "I have made the earth and men, says the Lord, and the animals which are upon the face of the earth, with my great strength and outstretched arm; and I give it to him who is pleasing in my eyes. Now, therefore, I have given all these lands into the hand of Nebuchadnezzar . . . my servant. . . . All the nations and great kings shall serve him . . . , until the time of his own land comes. . . . And it shall be that any nation and kingdom that will not serve the king of Babylon, I shall visit that nation with sword, famine, and pestilence. . . . Therefore, serve the king of Babylon and live."[Jer. 27:5-8, 17, cf. Vg.] We see how much obedience the Lord willed to be paid to that abominable and cruel tyrant for no other reason than that he possessed the kingship. But it was by heavenly decree that he had been set upon the throne of the kingdom and assumed into kingly majesty, which it would be unlawful to violate. If we have continually present to our minds and before our eyes the fact that even the most worthless kings are appointed by the same decree by which the authority of all kings is established, those seditious thoughts will never enter our minds that a king should be treated according to his merits, and that it is unfair that we should show ourselves subjects to him who, on his part, does not show himself a king to us.

*28. General testimonies of Scripture on the sanctity of the royal person*
It is vain for anyone to object that that command was peculiar to the Israelites. For we must note with what reason the Lord confirms it: "I have given," he says, "the kingdom to Nebuchadnezzar" [Jer. 27:6, cf. Vg.]. "Therefore, serve him and live." [Jer. 27:17, cf. Vg.]. Let us not doubt that we ought to serve him to whom it is evident that the kingdom has been given. And when once the Lord advances any man to kingly rank, he attests to us his determination that he would have him reign. For there are general testimonies of Scripture concerning this, Solomon, in the twenty-eighth chapter of The Proverbs, says: "Because of the iniquity of the land there are many princes" [Prov. 28:2 p.]. Likewise, the twelfth chapter of Job: "He takes away subjection from kings, and girds them again with a girdle" [Job. 12:18p.]. Once this has been admitted, nothing remains but that we should serve and live.

In Jeremiah the prophet, there is also another command of the Lord by which he enjoins his people to seek the peace of Babylon, where they have been sent as captives, and to pray to the Lord on its behalf, for in its peace will be their peace [Jer. 29:7]. Behold, the Israelites, divested of all their possessions, driven from their homes, led away into exile, and cast into pitiable bondage, are commanded to pray for the prosperity of their conqueror — not as we are commanded in other passages to pray for our persecutors [cf. Matt. 5:44], but in order that his kingdom may be preserved safe and peaceful, that under him they too may prosper. So David, already designated king by God's ordination and anointed with his holy oil, when he was persecuted by Saul without deserving it, still regarded the head of his assailant as inviolable, because the Lord had sanctified it with the honor of the kingdom. "The Lord forbid," he said, "that I should do this thing before the Lord, to my lord, the Lord's anointed, to put forth my hand against him, since he is the Lord's anointed" [I Sam. 24:6 cf.Vg.]. Again: "My soul has spared you; and I have said, 'I shall not put forth my hand against my lord, for he is the Lord's anointed'" [I Sam. 24:11, cf. Vg.]. Again: 'Who will put forth his hand against the anointed of the Lord and be innocent? . . . The Lord lives; unless the Lord strike him, or the day come for him to die, or he fall in battle, the Lord forbid that I should put forth my hand against the Lord's anointed" [I Sam. 26:9-11, cf. Vg.].

*29. It is not the part of subjects but of God to vindicate the right*
We owe this attitude of reverence and therefore of piety toward all our rulers in the highest degree, whatever they may be like. I therefore the more often repeat this: that we should learn not to examine the men themselves, but take it as enough

that they bear, by the Lord's will, a character upon which he has imprinted and engraved an inviolable majesty.

But (you will say) rulers owe responsibilities in turn to their subjects. This I have already admitted. But if you conclude from this that service ought to be rendered only to just governors, you are reasoning foolishly. For husbands are also bound to their wives, and parents to their children, by mutual responsibilities. Suppose parents and husbands depart from their duty. Suppose parents show themselves so hard and intractable to their children, whom they are forbidden to provoke to anger [Eph. 6:4], that by their rigor they tire them beyond measure. Suppose husbands most despitefully use their wives, whom they are commanded to love [Eph. 5:25] and to spare as weaker vessels [I Peter 3:7]. Shall either children be less obedient to their parents or wives to their husbands? They are still subject even to those who are wicked and undutiful.

Indeed, all ought to try not to "look at the bag hanging from their back," that is, not to inquire about another's duties, but every man should keep in mind that one duty which is his own. This ought particularly to apply to those who have been put under the power of others. Therefore, if we are cruelly tormented by a savage prince, if we are greedily despoiled by one who is avaricious or wanton, if we are neglected by a slothful one, if finally we are vexed for piety's sake by one who is impious and sacrilegious, let us first be mindful of our own misdeeds, which without doubt are chastised by such whips of the Lord [cf. Dan. 9:7]. By this, humility will restrain our impatience. Let us then also call this thought to mind, that it is not for us to remedy such evils; that only this remains, to implore the Lord's help, in whose hand are the hearts of kings, and the changing of kingdoms [Prov. 21:1p.]. "He is God who will stand in the assembly of the gods, and will judge in the midst of the gods." [Ps. 82:1p.]. Before His face all kings shall fall and be crushed, and all the judges of the earth, that have not kissed his anointed [Ps. 2:10-11], and all those who have written unjust laws to oppress the poor in judgment and to do violence to the cause of the lowly, to pray upon widows and rob the fatherless [Isa. 10:1-2, cf. Vg.].

*(Constitutional magistrates, however, ought to check the tyranny of kings; obedience to God comes first, 30-31)*
*30. When God intervenes, it is sometimes by unwitting agents*
Here are revealed his goodness, his power, and his providence. For sometimes he raises up open avengers from among his servants, and arms them with his command to punish the wicked government and deliver his people, oppressed in unjust ways, from miserable calamity. Sometimes he directs to this end the rage of men who intend one thing and undertake another. Thus he delivered the people of Israel from the tyranny of Pharaoh through Moses [Ex. 3:7-10]; from the violence of Chusan, king of Syria, through Othniel [Judg. 3:9]; and from other servitudes through other kings or judges. Thus he tamed the pride of Tyre by the Egyptians, the insolence of the Egyptians by the Assyrians, the fierceness of the Assyrians by the Chaldeans; the arrogance of Babylon by the Medes and Persians, after Cyrus had already subjugated the Medes. The ungratefulness of the kings of Judah and Israel and their impious obstinancy toward his many benefits, he sometimes by the Assyrians, sometimes by the Babylonians, crushed and afflicted — although not all in the same way.

For the first kind of men, when they had been sent by God's lawful calling to carry out such acts, in taking up arms against kings, did not at all violate that majesty which is implanted in kings by God's ordination; but, armed from heaven, they subdued the lesser power with the greater, just as it is lawful for kings to punish their subordinates. But the latter kind of men, although they were directed by God's hand whither he pleased, and executed his work unwittingly, yet planned in their minds to do nothing but an evil act.

*31. Constitutional defenders of the people's freedom*
But however these deeds of men are judged in themselves, still the Lord accomplished his work through them alike when he broke the bloody scepters of arrogant kings when he overturned intolerable governments. Let the princes hear and be afraid.

But we must, in the meantime, be very careful not to despise or violate that authority of magistrates, full of venerable majesty, which God has established by the weightiest decrees, even though it may reside with the most unworthy men, who defile it as much as they can with their own wickedness. For, if the correction of unbridled despotism is the Lord's to avenge, let us not at once think that it is entrusted to us, to whom no command has been given except to obey and suffer.

I am speaking all the while of private individuals. For if there are now any magistrates of the people, appointed to restrain the willfullness of kings (as in ancient times the ephors were set against the Spartan kings, or the tribunes of the people against the Roman consuls, or the demarchs against the senate of the Athenians; and perhaps, as things now are, such power as the three estates exercise in every realm when they hold their chief assemblies), I am so far from forbidding them to withstand, in accordance with their duty, the fierce licentiousness of kings, that, if they wink at kings who violently fall upon and assault the lowly common folk, I declare that their dissimulation involves nefarious perfidy, because they dishonestly betray the freedom of the people, of which they know that they have been appointed protectors by God's ordinance.

*32. Obedience to man must not become disobedience to God*
But in that obedience which we have shown to be due the authority of rulers, we are always to make this exception, indeed, to observe it as primary, that such obedience is never to lead us away from obedience to him, to whose will the desires of all kings ought to be subject, to whose decrees all their commands ought to yield, to whose majesty their scepters ought to be submitted. And how absurd would it be that in satisfying men you should incur the displeasure of him for whose sake you obey men themselves! The Lord, therefore, is the King of Kings, who, when he has opened his sacred mouth, must alone be heard, before all and above all men; next to him we are subject to those men who are in authority over us, but only in him. If they command anything against him, let it go unesteemed. And here let us not be concerned about all that dignity which the magistrates possess; for no harm is done to it when it is humbled before that singular and truly supreme power of God. On this consideration, Daniel denies that he has committed any offense against the king when he has not obeyed his impious edict [Dan. 6:22-23, Vg.]. For the king had exceeded his limits, and had not only been a wrongdoer against men, but, in lifting up his horns against God, had himself

abrogated his power. Conversely, the Israelites are condemned because they were too obedient to the wicked proclamation of the king [Hos. 5:13]. For when Jeroboam molded the golden calves, they, to please him, forsook God's Temple and turned to new superstitions [I Kings 12:30]. With the same readiness, their descendants complied with the decrees of their kings. The prophet sharply reproaches them for embracing the king's edicts [Hos. 5:11]. Far, indeed, is the pretense of modesty from deserving praise, a false modesty with which the court flatterers cloak themselves and deceive the simple, while they deny that it is lawful for them to refuse anything imposed by their kings. As if God had made over his right to mortal men, giving them the rule over mankind! Or as if earthly power were diminished when it is subjected to its Author, in whose presence even the heavenly powers tremble as suppliants! I know with what great and present peril this constancy is menaced, because kings bear defiance with the greatest displeasure, whose "wrath is a messenger of death" [Prov. 16:14], says Solomon. But since this edict has been proclaimed by the heavenly herald, Peter — "We must obey God rather than men" [Acts 5:29] — let us comfort ourselves with the thought that we are rendering that obedience which the Lord requires when we suffer anything rather than turn aside from piety. And that our courage may not grow faint, Paul pricks us with another goad: That we have been redeemed by Christ at so great a price as our redemption cost him, so that we should not enslave ourselves to the wicked desires of men — much less be subject to their impiety [I Cor. 7:23].

## GOD BE PRAISED

# 3

---

The English Civil War (1640-1660) produced the greatest ferment of radical Christian thought since the days of the early church. The Levellers, as the name suggests, believed in a radical social "levelling", in doing away with wealth and privilege and sharing the common bounty of the earth. The Diggers concentrated their efforts on the right of poor people to till the uncultivated land. The Fifth Monarchy men took their clue from the Book of Daniel and anticipated the imminent return of Christ to rule a thousand years on earth. These radical Christians stated their positions in a flood of pamphlets, most of them published in the 1640's.

*The Power of Love* begins with the challenging words: "For there is no respect of persons with God: and whoever is possest with love, judgeth no longer as a man, but god-like, as a true Christian," and goes on to inveigh against the luxury and worldliness of England where the rich indulge themselves and the poor suffer. The power of Christian love will, if faithfully practiced, transform the world and wipe out suffering and injustice.

John Lilburne in *England's Birth-Right Justified* begins his inquiry into the nature of limited, constitutional government by taking up the issue of the King's authority over the militia. From there he proceeds to a discussion of the principles of a free government and an attack upon the injustice of monopolies. (His discussion of the wool monopoly is omitted.)

Jerrard Winstanly, one of the most gifted radical pamphleteers, identified himself with the cause of the Diggers and was arrested for "digging upon George-hill in Surrey" to demonstrate that "the Land of England ought to be a free land, and a common treasury to all her children, otherwise it cannot be called a Common-Wealth."

Milton's *Areopagita . . . for the Liberty of Unlicensed Printing*, published in London in 1644, was directed specifically against a law passed by the Long Parliament establishing censorship over all published material. The *Areopagita* is possibly the most important statement on the freedom of the press ever written. It is included here because Milton was one of the most widely read authors in colonial America because his name and principles were evoked frequently during the Revolutionary crisis and because he makes a most eloquent argument for the relationship between Christianity and freedom of expression.

In summary, the relationship of the English Civil War to the American Revolution is an important problem for historians of that latter conflict. Certainly the English Civil War was by any reasonable standard a *revolution*. There was great sympathy in America for many of its ideals. The regicides who executed Charles I fled to America for refuge. Sir Henry Vane, governor of Massachusetts Bay for a brief time, returned to England to play a prominent role in the Parliamentary party, and a number of Puritan leaders traveled to England and involved themselves in one aspect or another of the struggle against the arbitrary powers of the Crown. There is no question that the principles and ideals of the Independents and some radical sects were circulated in the colonies and often evoked a warm response. Beyond that they sank into a substratum of the colonial consciousness, more particularly that of New England; and there they lay, never very far below the surface, waiting to be brought to the surface by a certain confluence of events.

[The text is taken from *The Power of Love*, printed by R. C. for *John Sweeting*, at the signe of the Angell in Popes-head Alley, London, Sept. 19, 1643.]

## To every Reader

*For there is no respect of persons with God and whosoever is possest with love, judgeth no longer as a man, but god-like, as a true Christian. What's here towards? (sayes one) sure one of the Family of love: very well! prays and still and consider: what family are you of I pray? are you of Gods family? no doubt you are? why, God is love, and if you bee one of Gods children be not ashamed of your Father, nor his family: and bee assured that in his family, he regards neither fine clothes, nor gold rings, nor stately houses, nor abundance of wealth, nor dignities, and titles of honour, nor any mans birth or calling, indeed he regards nothing among his children but love. Consider our Saviour saith, He that hath this worlds goods, and seeth his brother lack, how dwelleth the love of God in him? Judge them by this rule who are Gods family; looke about and you will finde in these woefull dayes thousands of miserable, distressed, starved, imprisoned Christians: see how pale*

*and wan they looke: how coldly, raggedly, or unwholsesomely they are cloathed?*
*live one weeke with them in their poore houses, lodge as they lodge, eate as they*
*eate, and no oftner, and bee at the same time passe to get that wretched food for a*
*sickly wife, and hunger-starved children; (if you dare doe this for feare of death or*
*diseases) then walke abroad, and observe the generall plenty of all necessaries,*
*observe the gallant bravery of multitudes of men and women abounding in all*
*things that can be imagined: observe likewise the innumerable numbers of those*
*that have more then sufficeth. Neither will I limit you to observe the inconsiderate*
*people of the world, but the whole body of religious people themselves, and in the*
*very Churches and upon solemne dayes: view them well, and see whether they have*
*not this worlds goods; their silkes, their beavers, their rings, and other divises will*
*testifie they have; I, and the wants and distresses of the poore will testifie that love*
*of God they have not. What is here aimed at? (sayes another) would you have all*
*things common? for love seeketh not her owne good, but the good of others. You*
*say very true, it is the Apostles doctrine: and you may remember the multitude of*
*beleevers had all things common: that was another of their opinions, which many*
*good people are afraid of. But (sayes another) what would you have? would you*
*have no distinction of men, nor no government? feare it not: nor flye the truth*
*because it suites not with your corrupt opinions or courses; on Gods name*
*distinguish of men and women too, as you see the love of God abound in them*
*towards their brethren, but no otherwise; And for that great mountaine (in your*
*understanding) government, 'tis but a molehill if you would handle it familiarly,*
*and bee bold with it: it is common agreement to bee so governed: and by common*
*agreement men chuse for governours, such as their virtue and wisdome make fit to*
*govern: what a huge thing this matter of trust is made of? and what cause is there*
*that men that are chosen should keepe at such distance, or those that have chosen*
*them bee so sheepish in their presence? Come, you are mightily afraid of opinions,*
*is there no other that you feare? not the* Anabaptists, Brownists, *or* Antinomians?
*Why doe you start man? have a little patience, would you truly understand what*
*kinde of people these are, and what opinions they hold? If you would; bee advised*
*by some learned man, and with him consult what hath learnedly been written of*
*the most weake and vitious amongst any of them that could bee found, and make*
*your conclusion (according to custome) that they are all such: but if you would*
*free your selves from common mistakes concerning those your brethren, then*
*acquaint your selves with them, observe their wayes, and enquire into their*
*doctrines your selfe, and so make your conclusion, or judge not of them, visit*
*them, beare them out, stand cleare from all prejudging: and then see what*
*dangerous people they are that are generally so calied: particulars being absurd*
*rules of judging; for so the Turke is misled in his judgment of Christianity: and no*
*marvaile since hee judgeth thereof by the doctrine and life of the most*
*superstitious, Idolatrous, and vitious amongst them. Well, what next are you*
*afraid of? for some men take delight to be under the spirit of bondage, an do not*
*think themselves in good estate except they be in feare: but come, feare nothing,*
*you are advised by the Apostle to try all things, and to hold fast that which is good:*
*to prove the Spirits whether they bee of God or not: 'tis your selfe must doe it, you*
*are not to trust to the authority of any man, or to any mans relation: you will finde*
*upon tryall that scarcely any opinion hath been reported truly to you: and though*
*in every one of them you may finde some things that you cannot agree unto, you*

*will yet be a gainer by discovering many excellent things that you as yet may be unsatisfied in, and by due consideration of them all perfect your owne judgement. Reade the ensuing discourse impartially, and you will finde the minde of him that hateth no man for his opinion; nor would have any man troubled for any opinion, except such, as make the bloud of Christ ineffectuall, or such as would destroy all that will not submit to their opinions; hee seemes to bee of the Apostles minde, that considered all other things in love: (and that in matters of moment too, even where some observed a day unto the Lord,& others not observed) He bids you walke in love, as Christ hath love you, and gave himselfe for you, an offering and a Sacrifice; you that love your brother so poorely, as that you cannot allow him the peaceable enjoyment of his mind and judgement would hardly lay downe your life for him; let brotherly love continue, and let every one freely speake his minde without molestation: and so there may be hope that truth may come to light, that otherwise may be obscured for particular ends: plaine truth will prove all, sufficient for vanquishing of the most artificiall, sophisticall errour that ever was in the world; give her but due and patient audience; and her perswasions are ten thousand times more powerfull to worke upon the most dull refractory minde, then all the adulterate allurements and deceivings of art. What is here publisht is out of fervent love to the Communion of Christians: that they might taste and see how good the Lord is, In whose presence there is fulnesse of joy, and at whose right hand there are pleasures for evermore Wherefore rejoyce in the Lord alwayes, and againe I say rejoyce: and let your song bee alwayes, Glory be to God on high, in earth peace, good will towards men. Let truth have her free and perfect working, and the issue will bee increase of beleevers: let faith have her perfect working, and the issue will bee increase of love: and let love have her perfect working, and the whole world will be so refined, that God will be all in all; for he that dwelleth in love, dwelleth in God, in whom, ever save you well, and bee cheerefull.*

## The Power of Love

### Tit. 2: 11, 12

*The grace (or love) of God that bringeth salvation unto all men hath appeared, teaching us to deny ungodlinesse and worldly lusts, and to live soberly, righteously, and godly in this present world.*
It is evident (though it be little regarded or considered, the more is the pity) that in naturall things all things whatsoever that are necessary for the use of mankinde, the use of them is to be understood easily with out study or difficulty: every Capacity is capable thereof; and not only so, but they are all likewise ready at hand, or easily to be had: a blessing that God hath afforded to every man, insomuch, that there is no part of the habitable world, but yeeldes sufficient of usefull things for a comfortable and pleasant sustentation of the inhabitants; as experience testifieth in all places; and Saint *Paul* witnessed that God left himselfe not without witnesse, in that he did good, gave them raine from heaven, and fruitfull seasons, feeding their hearts with foode and gladnesse: by all which it

plainely appeares that God ever intendeth unto man a pleasant and comfortable
life: you know it is said, that God made man righteous, but he fought out many
inventions: that is, he made him naturally a rationall creature, judging rightly of
all things, and desiring only what was necessary, and so being exempt from all
labour, and care of obtaining things superfluous, he passed his dayes with
aboundance of delight and contentment: until he sought out unto himselfe many
inventions: inventions of superfluous subtilities and artificiall things, which have
been multiplied with the ages of the world, every age still producing new: so now in
these lattertimes we see nothing but mens inventions in esteeme, and the newer the
more precious; if I should instance in particulars, I should or might be endlesse, as
in diet, your selves know to your costs, (for it costs you not only your monyes, but
your healths, and length of dayes) that this fruitfull nation refuseth not to furnish
scarce the meanest meale you make, but something must be had to please the
luxurious palate from forraine and farre countryes: and ever the farther the better,
and the dearer the more acceptable; you know likewise the excessive provision
that is made for entertainments and set meetings, where all groose meates (you
know my meaning) must be banished, and nothing admitted but what is rare and
fine, and full of invention, in the dresses, sauces, and manner of service: where all
the senses must be pleased to the heighth of all possible conceipt. If I should
reckon up your new inventions for buildings, and furniture for your houses, and
the common costlinesse of your apparell, and should set before you the manifold
vexations, perplexities, distractions, cares, and inconveniences that accrew unto
you by these your vain and ridiculous follies, I might be endlesse therein also, and
lose my labour; for there is no hope that I should prevaile for a reformation of
these things, when your daily experience scourges you continually therunto, in one
kind or other, and all in vaine; yet I shall take leave to tell you that in these things,
you walke not as becommeth the gospell of *Christ,* but are carnall and walke as
men, as vaine, fantasticall, inconsiderate men; such as very heathen and meere
naturall men would be ashamed of: their experience (that a life according to
nature, to be content with little, with what was ever ready, and easy to be had, was
the most pleasant life and exempt from all vexations) was instruction sufficient
unto many of them, to frame themselves thereunto, and to abandon all kindes of
superfluities, without retaining the least; & thereby obtained a freedome to apply
themselves to the consideration and practise of wisdome and vertue.

   It is a wonderfull thing to my understanding, that men should call themselves
Christians, and professe to be religious, and to be diligent readers of Scripture,
and hearers of Sermons, and yet content themselves to bee indeed in many things
carnall, and to walke as did the most indiscreete and inconsiderate Gentiles. Doth
the Scripture teach no more then nature teacheth? though it doe infinitely, yet
your practise compared with wise considerate naturall men declares it doth not;
how extreamely then (thinke you) doe you cause the name of God to be
blasphemed? Doe you thinke it is sufficient that you are not drunkards, nor
adulterers, nor usurers, nor contentious persons, nor covetous? beloved, if you
will truely deserve the name of Christians, it is not sufficient: but you are to
abandon all superfluities, all poring after vaine superfluous things, and thereby to
exempt your selves from all unnecessary cares that choake the Word, and bee at
liberty to consider, and to apply your selves freely to the continuall contemplation
of the infinte love of God, evidently and plainely set forth unto you in his blessed

word: as in the words that I have read unto you: for as it is in naturall things, so holds it in spirituall: God hath dealt abundantly well with us; there being nothing that is necessary either for the enlightning of our understandings, or the peace of our mindes, but what hee hath plainely declared and manifestly set forth in his Word: so plainely that the meanest capacity is fully capable of a right understanding thereof, and need not to doubt but that he is so, I will not say that God is not more good unto us, then we are hurtfull to ourselves, (for his goodnesse is more availeable to our welfare, then our evill can be to our misery) but wee are as evill to our selves in all things as we can be possible: and that not onely in naturall things, but likewise in spirituall and divine things too, for therein also we have our inventions; the plaine and evident places of Scripture manifestly declaring our peace and reconciliation with God, is become nauseous to us: they make salvation too easie to be understood, and tender it upon too easie tearmes, and too generall: this *Manna* that comes to us without our labour, industry, study, and watching, is two fulsome, something that hath bones in it must be found out, and will become more acceptable: every child or babe in Christs Schoole can understand these: We are full growne men in Christ, wee have spent our time in long and painefull studies, and have full knowledge in all Arts and Sciences: there is no place of Scripture too hard for us: shew us the mysteries we cannot reveale: the Parables that wee cannot clearely open: the prophesies that wee cannot interpret: a word or Syllable that wee cannot fitly apply, or the most palpable seeming contradiction that we cannot reconcile; nay it is to be doubted (wee have seene the vaine humour of man puft so high, and the world so filled and pestered with works and labours of this vaine nature) lest there are some such daring undertakers, that like as *Alexander* the great is said to have wept that there were no more worlds to conquer, so these Champions are grieved that there are no harder places for their braines to worke upon: or (which is more to bee lamented) one would feare they are much troubled that the most necessary truths are so easie to be understood: for that when they treate upon some very plaine place of Scripture, even so plaine as this which I have read unto you, yet in handling thereof they make it difficult, and darken the cleare meaning thereof with their forced and artificiall glosses: but as I wish there were no such dealers in divine things, so have I in my selfe resolved to avoid these extreame evills: for as in naturall things I am fully assured there is nothing of necessary use but what is easily understood and even ready at hand, so also doth my experience tell me, that we have no bettering of our understandings, or quieting of our mindes (the end for which God has vouchsafed his word) from any places of Scripture that hath any obscurity in them, but from such as are clearly exempt from all difficulty. You know God frequently complaines by his Prophets, saying, My people will not consider, they will not understand: and when I consider that your owne experience schooles you not sufficiently against your dotage upon the vaine superfluities of this world, wherein you know your selves to be carnall, and to walke as men, heaping unto your selves vexation upon vexation; I doe wonder that it doth not stagger the Ministers of God in their publishing of things divine to a people so qualified, so extreamely inconsiderate: indeed it would make one to suspect the doctrine that you continually heare, that it were not powerfull nor from heaven, but weake and fitted to your corrupt humours, and customes, since after so long time, it hath not subdued your worldly mindednesse. Sure I am, and I must leave to tell you, that there is utterly a fault amongst you, nay those expressions are too soft, you have almost nothing but faults amongst you, and you will not consider, which you must doe, and seriously too, or you will never reduce yourselves into such a condition, as will be really sutable to the blessed name of Christians. Beloved I have seriously considered it, and it is not your case alone, but it is the universall disease. I know not any that is not infected therewith, nor to whom it may be said, Physitian heale thyself; the milke we have suckt, and the common ayre hath beene totally corrupted: our first instructions, and all after discourse have been indulgent flatterers to our darling superfluities: and therefore he that undertakes the cure, must bee sure to bee provided of a fit and powerfull medicine, and to be diligent and faithfull in his undertaking; it is a taske that I have proposed unto my selfe, and though I should meete with the greatest discouragements, (as, the world is like enough to furnish his utmost forces to preserve his Kingdome) yet considering whose service I have undertaken, and whose works it is, I shall not despaire of successe. I am not ignorant that this worke hath often-times beene attempted, and persisted in: but with little fruit; through the universall mistake, that men are sooner perswaded from their vanities, through pressures of the law, and affrighting terrors of wrath and hell, then by the cordes of love: which yet I abundantly preferre, as you may perceive by this text which I have chosen: for when all is done, It is the love of God bringing salvation, that teacheth us to deny all ungodliness, and worldly lusts, and to live soberly, righteously, and godly in this present world. I must entreate your most earnest attention, as being full of hope that I shall doe you much more good then you conceive: for I must tell you, I cannot cure you of your earthly mindednesse, of your dotage upon superfluities, till I have furst showne you your peace and reconciliation with God, and have wroght in you (through the power of Gods word) peace of conscience and joy in the holy Ghost. You are then seriously to consider what is said, and understanding will succeed. The love of God I know is often spoken of: a theame that hath begotten abundance of bookes and discourses: yet none in no comparison like the Scriptures: most (if not all) discourses, that ever I have read or heard, doe in some sense or other, or in some measure injure and wrong those blessed discourses thereof.

The love and favour of God (saith *David)* is better then life it selfe; What man in the whole world doth not gladly heare the joyfull tydings of the love of God? . . .And to that righteous nature wherein first man was created, for in the likenesse of God created he him: and whilst you consider this, I shall advise you not to flatter your selves as the Pharisee did, saying Lord I thanke thee I am not as other men, extortioners, unjust, adulterers, drunkards, covetous, proude, or licentious; can you say you have noe sinne? if you should, the word of God would contradict you, which testifieth that he that saith he hath no sinne is a liar, and the truth is not in him; and if sinne be in every one, necessarily it followes where sinne is, there is Gods hatred; nor doeth it any whit excuse or exempt those from the hatred of God, that can say their sinnes are fewe in numbers, and of very meane condition compared to others: whosoever you are that are thus indulgent to your selves, you doe but deceive your selves, for Gods hatred, his wrath and anger, is so exact against all and every sinne, and so odious it is in his sight, that he denounceth, saying, Cursed is every one that continueth not to doe all that is written in the booke of the law: So as every mouth must be stopped, and all the world stand guilty before God; and though the sense and deepe apprehension of this woefull condition, doe worke in you the deepest of sorrow, though you should spend your dayes in weeping, and your nights in woefull lamentation, though you should repent your selves in dust and ashes, and cover your selves with sackcloathes: though you should fall your selves into palenesse, and hang downe your heads alwayes: though you should give all your goods to the poore; nay though you should offer up the fruit of your bodies, for the sinne of your soules; all this and more could be no satisfaction for the least sinne, nor bring any peace to your mindes: but you must of force cry out at last, as Saint *Paul* did, (stating this sad condition of all mankind under the law) *Oh wretched man that I am, who shall deliver me from this body of death!* Justly is it called a body of death; for man is of a fraile and weake condition at the best: a considerate man hath death alwayes before him: What joy or comfort then can hee take all his life long; being in the hatred of God, a vessel of wrath, and liable to eternall death in hell fire for ever? What can he looke upon that can give him content? Love will be as a new light in your understandings by which you will judge quite otherwise of all things, then formerly you have done: the vanities and superfluities which in the beginning of my discourse I reckoned up unto you, will seeme odious unto you, and you will no longer fashion yourselves like unto this world, but will walk as becometh the Gospel of Christ: you will no longer minde high things, but make yourselves equall to men of low degree: you will no longer value men and women according to their wealth, or outward shewes, but according to their vertue, & as the love of God appeareth in them: nay if you be studious in this worke of love, nothing will be more deare unto you then the glory of God (who hath so infinitely loved you) so as you will be most zealously opposite to whatsoever is opposite unto God, you will finde it nothing to hazzard your lives for God, in defence of his truth from errour; in defence of your brother or neighbour from oppression or tyranny: love makes you no longer your owne but Gods servants, and prompts you to doe his will in the punishment of all kinde of exorbitances, whether it be breach of oathes, breach of trust, or any kinde of injustice in whomsoever, and to be no respecter of persons; nor will any ones greatnesse over sway or daunt your resolutions, but you will be bold as Lions, not fearing the faces of men: you will when neede requires, that is, when tyrants and oppressors endeavour by might and force to pervert all Lawes, and compacts amongst men, and to pervert the truth of God into a lie, interpreting his sacred word as patron of their unjust power, as if any unjust power were of God, and were not to be resisted: I say, such insolencies as these will inflame your zeale, and set you all on fire manfully to fight the Lords battell, and to bring into subjection those abominable imaginations and ungodly courses of men: your judgements will be so well informed, as you will know these things are by God referred unto you, and you will not resigne them up to him, but willingly sacrifice your lives and fortunes, and all that is neare and deare unto you, rather then suffer his name to be so blasphemed, or your innocent brethren, or your wives and children to become a prey to wicked and bloud-thirsty men. The politicians of this world would have religious men to be fooles, not to resist, no by no meanes, lest you receive damnation: urging Gods holy Word, whilst they proceed in their damnable courses; but (beloved) they will finde that true Christians are of all men the most valiant defenders of the just liberties of their Countrey, and the most zealous preservers of true Religion: vindicating the truths of God with their lives, against all ungodlinesse and unrighteousnesse of men: making thereby the whole world to know that true Christianity hates and abhorres tyranny, oppression, perjury, cruelty, deceipt, and all kinde of filthinesse; and true Christians to be the most impartiall, and most severe punishers thereof, and of all kinde of wickednesse, of any men whatsoever.

Great is the power of love, for love makes men to bee of one mind: and what can bee too strong for men united in love? and therefore I shall warne you to marke and consider those that make divisions amongst you. I pray mistake me not, I doubt you are too apt in this case to make a wrong application: I doe not meane that you should marke those, that are different from you in judgement, with any ridiculous or reproachfull names: but my adivce is that you marke those that make divisions amongst you, and those are they that have invented a name of reproach for every particular difference in judgement: and in their publick Sermons and private discourses, endeavour might and maine to keep at the widest distance, and by odious tales and false imputations make you irreconciliable: nay make you even ready to cut one anothers throates; or by this division prepare you for your common adversaries to cut both yours and theirs too; difference in judgement there will be, untill love have a more powerfull working in our hearts: wee should therefore like wise men at least beare with one anothers infirmities: love will cover all that can bee called infirmity; but resolved malice love itselfe will punish. Such opinions as are not destructive to humane society, nor blaspheme the worke of our Redemption, may be peaceably endured, and considered in love: and in case of conspiracy against our common liberty, what a madnesse is it for men to stand in strife about petty opinions? for who are all those that are so much railed at by our common Preachers? who are they say they? why, they are the most dangerous Anabaptists, Brownists, and Separatists: that are enemies to all order and decency, that cry down all learning and all government in the Church, or Common-wealth. (Beloved) to my knowledge these things are not true of any of them: it is true, they cannot do all things so orderly and decently as they would, because they are hunted into corners, and from one corner to another, and are not free to exercise their consciences, as had they liberty they might, and would; And as for learning, as learning goes now adaies, what can any judicious man make of it, but as an Art to deceive and abuse the understandings of men, and to mislead them to their ruine? if it be not so, whence comes it that the Universities, and University men throughout the Kingdome in great numbers are opposers of the welfare of the Common-wealth, and are pleaders for absurdities in government, arguers for tyranny, and corrupt the judgements of their neighbours? no man can be so simple as to imagine that they conceive it not lawfull, or not usefull for men to understand the Hebrew, Greeke, or Latine: but withall, if they conceive there is no more matter in one language then another, nor no cause why men should be so proud for understanding of languages, as therefore to challenge to themselves the sole dealing in all spirituall matters; who (I say) can blame them for this judgement? they desire that a mans ability of judgement should be proved by the cleare expression of necessary truths, rather then by learning: and since the Scriptures are now in English, which at first were in Hebrew, Greeke, or Syriack, or what other language; why may not one that understands English onely, both understand and declare the true meaning of them as well as an English Hebrician, or Grecian, or Roman whatsoever? I, but saies some politick learned man, a man that doth not understand the Originall language, cannot so perfectly give the sense of the Scripture, as he that doth: or as one that makes it his study for ten or twenty yeares together, and hath no other employment: everyman being best skilled in his owne profession wherein he hath been bred and accustomed. I did well to say some politicke learned man might thus object: for indeed what is here but policie? for it be as such men would imply, I pray what are you the better for having the Scripture in your owne language: when it was lock'd up in the Latine tongue by the policie of *Rome,* you might have had a learned Fryar for your money at any time to have interpreted the same: and though now you have it in your owne language, you are taught not to trust your owne understanding, (have a care of your purses) you must have an University man to interpret the English, or you are in as bad a case as before but not in worse; for, for your money you may have plenty at your service, & to interpret as best shall please your fancie. Let me prevaile with you to free your selves from this bondage, and to trust to your owne considerations in any thing that is usefull for your understandings and consciences: and ajudge more charitably of your brethren, & understand what learning is, and to make those that cause divisions among you, and you shall finde that they are learned men, & not unlearned. The learned man must live upon the unlearned, and therefore when the unlearned shall presume to know as much as the learned, hath not the learned man cause to bestir his wits, and to wrangle too when his Copy-hold is in such danger? I pray what was the cause that *Demetr* and the Craftsmen cried out, great is *Diana* of the Ephesians, whom al Asia and the world worship? was it the love to the goddesse or her worship? no, we find it was their covetousnesse and particular gaine? What is it els to cry out, great is learning, great are the Universities, who shall answer an adversary? (money answereth all things) ambition covetousnesse, disdaine, pride, and luxury are the things aimed at: and if it be not so, by the fruits you shall certainly know. As for government, those that are accused are not guilty, for they are enemies onely to usurpations, and innovations, and exorbitances in government: indeed they are haters of tyranny, and all arbitrary power, but no other: and therefore those that falsely accuse them, are they that cause and foment divisions amongst you: therefore marke them, and be not deceived by their dissembled insinuations to hold you in division, whilst they have opportunity to make a prey of you. You know there are Wolves in Sheepes cloathing: be wise as Serpents, able to discover them, innocent as Doves, gently bearing with the infirmities of the weake, having nothing in more esteeme then love: thus you will answer love with love: that henceforwards your owne soules may constantly witnes to your selves (what this Scripture expresseth) *That the love of God bringing salvation to all men hath appeared, teaching you to live soberly, righteously, and godly in this present world:* Now unto him that hath loved us, and washed away our sinnes in his owne bloud, be praise and glory for ever, Amen.

# B

[The text is taken from John Liburne, *England's Birth-Right Justified Against All Arbitrary Usurpation*, (n.p.: October, 1645).]

## England's Birth-Right Justified

In the 150. *page* of the Booke called, An exact Collection of the *Parliaments* Remonstrances, Declarations, &c. published by speciall Order of the House of *Commons*, March 24. 1642. we find there a Question answered, fit for all men to take notice of in these sad times; which followeth.

Now *in our extreame distractions, when forraigne forces threaten, and probably are invited, and a malignant and Papish party at home offended, the Devill hath cast a bone, and rais'd a Contestation between the KING and PARLIAMENT touching the MILITIA. His Majestie claims the disposing of it to be in Him by the right of Law; The Parliament saith,* Rebus sic santibus, *and* nolenti Rege, *the Ordering of it is in them?*

*Ans* Which Question, may receive its solution by this distinction. That there is in Laws and equitable, and a literall sense. His Majestie (let it be granted) is intrusted by Law with the *Militia,* but it is for the good and preservation of the Republick, against Forraign Invasions or domestick Rebellions. For it cannot be supposed that the *Parliament* would ever by Law intrust the King with the *Militia* against themselves, or the Common-wealth, that intrusts them to provide for their weal, not for their woe. So that when there is certain appearance or grounded suspition, that the Letter of the Law shall be improved against the *equitie* of it (that is, the publick good, whether of the body reall or representative) then the Commander going against its *equity,* gives liberty to the commanded to refuse *obedience* to the Letter: for the Law taken abstract from its originall reason and end is made a shell without a kernell, a shadow without a substance, and a body without a soul. It is the execution of Laws according to their *equity* and *reason,* which (as I may say) is the spirit that gives life to Authority the Letter kills.

Nor need this *equity* be expressed in the Law, being so naturally implyed and supposed in all Laws that are not meerly Imperiall, from that Analogie which all bodies Politick hold with the Naturall; whence all Government and Governours borrow a proportionable respect; And therefore when the *Militia* of an Army is committed to the Generall, it is not with any expresse condition, that he shall not turn the mouthes of his Cannons against his own Souldiers, for that is so naturally and necessarily implyed, that its needlesse to be expressed, insomuch as if he did attempt or command such a thing against the nature of his trust and place, it did *ipsofacto* estate the Army in a right of Disobedience, except we think that obedience binds Men to cut their owne throats, or at least their companions.

And indeed if this distinction be not allowed, then the legall and mixt *Monarchy* is the greatest *Tyranny;* for if Laws invest the King in an absolute power, and the Letter be not controlled by the equity, then whereas other Kings that are absolute *Monarchs,* and rule by Will and not by Law are *Tyrants* perforce. Those that rule by Law, and not by Will, have hereby a *Tyranny* confer'd upon them legally, and so the very end of Laws, which is to give bounds and limits to the exorbitant wills of Princes, is by the laws themselves disappointed, for they hereby give corroboration (and much more justification) to an arbitrary *Tyranny,* by making it legall, not assumed; which Laws are ordained to cross; not countenance: and therefore is the Letter (where it seems absolute) alwayes to receive qualification from the equity, else the foresaid absurdity must follow. *So farre in Parliaments own words.*

It is confessed by all rationall men, that the *Parliament* hath a power to annull a Law, and to make a new Law, and to declare a Law, but known Laws in force & unrepealed by them, are a Rule (so long as they so remain) for all the *Commons* of *England* whereby to walk; and upon rationall grounds is conceived to be binding to the very *Parliament* themselves as well as others. And though by their legislative power they have Authority to make new Laws, yet no free-man of *England* is to take notice (or can he) of what they intend till they declare it: neither can they, as is conceived, justly punish any man for walking closely to the knowne and declared Law, though it cross some pretended Priviledge of theirs, remaining onely in their own breasts.

For where there is no Law declared, there can be no transgression; therefore it is very requisite, that the *Parliament* would declare their Priviledges to the whole *Commons of England,* that so no man may through ignorance (by the *Parliaments* default) run causelessly into the hazard of the losse of their lives, liberties, or estates: for here it is acknowledged by themselves, that their Power is limited by those that betrust them; and that they are not to doe what they list, but what they ought, namely to provide for the peoples weal, and not for their woe: so that unknown Priviledges are as dangerous as unlimited Prerogatives, being both of them secret snares, expecially for the best affected people.

It is the greatest hazard and danger that can be run unto, to disart the onely known and declared Rule; the laying aside whereof brings in nothing but Will and Power, lust and strength, and so the strongest to carry all away; for it is the known, established, declared, and unrepealed Law, that tells all the Free-men of *England,* that the Knights and Burgesses chosen according to Law, and sent to make up the *Parliament,* are those that all the *Commons* of *England* (who send and choose them) are to obey.

But take away this declared Law: and where will you find the rule of Obedience? and if there be no rule of Obedience, then it must necessarily follow, that if a greater and stronger number come to a *Parliament* sitting, and tell them that they are more and stronger then themselves, and therefore they shall not make Laws for them, but they will rather make Laws for them, must they not needs give place? undoubtedly they must.

Yea, take away the declared, unrepealed Law, and then where is *Ideum& Tuum,* and Libertie, and Propertie? But you will say, the Law declared, binds the People, but is no rule for a Parliament fitting, who are not to walke by a knowne Law. It is answered: *It cannot be imagined that ever the People would be so sottish, as to give such a Power to those whom they choose for their Servants;* for this were to give them a Power to provide for their woe, but not for their weal. . .which is contrary to their own foregoing Maxim.

From the *equity* and letter of which *Lawes,* it is desired that our learned Lawyers would Answer these insuing QUERIES.

1. *Whether the Letter and* equity *of this Law doe not binde the very Parliament themselves, during the time of their sitting, in the like cases here expressed, to the same Rules here laid downe? Which if it should be denied,* Then

2. *Whether the Parliament itself, when it is sitting, be not bound to the observation of the Letter and equity of this Law, when they have to doe with Free-men, that in all these actions and expressions have declared faithfulness to the Common-wealth? And if this be denied;* Then

3. *Whether ever God made any man law-lesse? Or whether ever the Common-wealth, when they choose the Parliament, gave them a lawlesse unlimited Power, and at their pleasure to walke contrary to their own Laws and Ordinances before they have repealed them?*

4. *Whether it be according to Law, Justice, or Equity, for the Parliament to Imprison or punish a man for doing what they command him, and by Oath injoyne him?*

5. *Whether it be legall, just or equall, that when Free-men doe endeavour according to their duty, Oath, and Protestation, to give in Information to the Parliament of Treason acted and done by* Sir John Lenthall, *against the State and Kingdome, and long since communicated to several Members of the House of* Commons, *but by them concealed and smothered; and now by God's Providence brought upon the sage againe, and during the time that Inquisition is made of it before the Committee of Examination, before any legall charge be fixed upon* Sir John Lenthall, *or be required to make any Answer or Defence, that he shall be present to out-face, discourage, and abuse the Informers and Witnesses in the face of the Committee, without any check or controll from them?*

*And sometimes, while they are sitting about the Examination of his Treason, that he shall sit down beside them with his hat on, as if he were one of them, and that he shall injoy from the Committee ten times more favour and respect, then the just, bones, and legall Informers against him; who by some of the Committees themselves, while they are sitting, are threatned, jeared, nick-named, and otherwayes most shamefully abused.*

*Yea, and the friends of the Informers for the State are kept without doores, and the friends of the accused admitted to come in alwayes without controll, and during the Examination of the Information, that the Committee shall refuse to remove the Informers out of* Sir John Lenthalls *custody of* Kings-bench, *to another Prison, although they have been truly informed, that he hath set Instruments on work to murther them, and also importuned to remove them.*

6. *Whether it be not most agreeable to Law, Justice and Equity, that seeing Sir* John Lenthall, *having so many friends in the House conectned in the businesse, that he should not rather be tried by the same Councell of Warre in London, where* Sir John Hotham *and his Sonne were, then at the Parliament, his principall crime being against the Law Marshall as theirs was?*

7. *Whether to answer to an Indictment, when a man is demanded Guilty or not Guilty, be not a criminall Interrogatory, concerning a mans selfe, and so a man not by law bound to Answer to it, especially seeing to a Consciencious man, who dare*

*not lie, it is a great snare, who if he be indicted of a thing he hath done or spoken, dare not plead, Not Guilty, for feare of lying, and if he plead guilty, he shall become a self-destroyer (contrary to the law of Nature, which teacheth a man to preserve but not destroy himself) in declaring that which per adventure all his Adversaries would never be able to prove against him.* And

*Whether it be not more suitable and agreeable to the true intent of* Magna Carta *(expressed in the 28 Chap. thereof) where it is said,* No Bailiffe from henceforth shall put any man to his open Law, not to an Oath upon his owne bare saying, without faithfull Witnesse brought in for the same, and to the time intent and meaning of the *Petition of Right,* and the Act made this present *Parliament* for the abolishing the *Star-Chamber, etc.*

*For a free-man to have a charge laid against him, and his Adversaries brought face to face to prove it, and then the Accused to have liberty to make the best defence for himself he can, which was the practise amongst the very Heathen* Romans, *who had no light but the Light of Nature to guide them,* Act. 25.16.

Yea, Christ himself, when his enemies endeavoured to catch him by *Interrogateries,* he puts them off, without an Answer. *Luke 22.67, 68, 70, Chap. 23.3.*

Yea, when the High *Priest* asked him about his Disciples, and his Doctrine, He answers, *Hee ever taught openly,* and therefore saith, he, *Why aske ye mee? aske them that heard me for they know what I said,* John 18, 20, 21.

Hence justly it is conceived, that the *Parliament* may not condemne that man for concerning their Authoritie, who refuseth to answer to Interrogatories before them the Supreme Court, who answereth to Interrogatories in the like case before an inferiour Court, but you will say, it is the usuall practice of the COMMON-LAW, the Question is whether that practise be just or no? or whether any Law in practice in the KINGDOME of *England* doth binde the Free-men thereof, but what is made and declared by Common Consent in Parliament? and whether or no is there, or ought there not to be a plaine platforme agreed on, and laid down by the Parliament concerning things of so high consequence to all the Commons of *England?* and seeing the Parliament hath taken care that the *Bible* shall be in English, that so *Laymen* (as they call them) may read it as well as the Clergy, ought they not also to be as carefull, that all the binding Lawes in *England* be in English likewise, that so every Free-man may reade it as well as Lawyers (seeing they have *Lives, Liberties* and *Estates* as well as the other) and peaceably enjoy them no longer then they continue in the observation of the *Laws* of this Kingdom; whereof they are Members: and seeing the Lawyers are so full of broyles and contentions, and grow so rich and great thereby; have not the people cause to beleeve they drive on an Interest of their owne, distructrive to the Peoples wellfare; yea juggle, and put false glosses upon the *Law* (meerly) for their own ends: Seeing so great a part of it is in an unknown tongue, (which the Commons call *Pedlers-french,* or *Heathen-Greeke,)* even as our State Clergy did in the daies of old before the Scripture was tollerated to be in English, in which dayes they could easily make the poor poeple beleeve the Poopes unwritten verities were as binding as Scripture Rules, which the *Lawyers* have given the Commons just cause to fear, is their present practise with law Cases; many of which are besides the Rule of the Statute-law, and also against Justice, Equity and Conscience, tending to no other end, but to inslave the People?

8. *Whether it be not just and equall, that seeing* Monopolisers *were blown out of the House about Foure years agoe, as infringers upon the Common right of all the free-men of* England, *in setting up Pattents of* Soape, Salt, Lether, &c. *why should not those be partakers of the same justice now, that have been chief sticklers in setting up greater Patentees then ever the former were?*

As first the Patent of ingrossing the Preaching of the Word only to such men as weare Black and rough garments *to deceive, Zech. 13. 4.* and have had a Cannonicall Ordination from the Bishops, and so from the Pope, and consequently from the Divell, although the Spirit of God doth command every man that hath received a gift *to minister the same one to another, as good Stewards of the manifold grace of God,* 1 Pet. 4.10, 11.

And although ignorance and blindnesse be so universall all over the Kingdome, experience teaching, that where that most abounds they draw their swords soonest against the Parliament and Common-wealth (and so consequently against themselves, and continue the longest in their Rebellion, as now wee have woefull experience, yet these grand Monopolizers will neither goe amongst them themselves, nor suffer others without severe punishment to instruct and teach them the Principles of Christianity,or Morallity, by means of which they become destroyers and murderers of soules and bodies, and enemies to the very Civill societies of Mankind. . . .

The third *Monopoly,* is that insufferable, unjust and tyrannical Monopoly of Printing, whereby a great company of the very same Malignant fellows that *Canterbury* and his Malignant party engaged in their Arbitrary *Designes,* against both the Peoples and *Parliaments* just Priviledges (who turning with every winde, doe endeavour by all possible means, as well now as then, to sell and betray the Kingdome for their own gaine,) are invested with an Arbitrary unlimmitted *Power,* even by a generall Ordinance of Parliament, to print, divulge and disperse whatsoever Books, Pamphlets and Libells they please, though they be full of *Lyes,* and tend to the poysoning of the Kingdom with unjust and Tyrannicall *Principles.*

And not only so, but most violently (even now in Parliament time, which should be like a cryed *Faire,* and each one free to make the best use of their *Ware,* both for the publick and their own private good) to suppresse every thing which hath any true Declaration of the just Rights and liberties of the free-borne people of this Nation, and to brand and traduce all such Writers and Writings with the odious termes Sedition, Conspiracie and Treason, but to countenance and authorize such as shall calumniate them, and so both accept & reward such men far better then their most faithfull servants and best advancers, just as the Bishops formerly did against both the *Scots,* and the Parliament themselves.

They doe not rest here neither, but are yet further authorized with a generall Ordinance of this very Parliament, contrary to all law, justice, equity and reason, under pretence of searching for scandalous Books, to call numbers of debays men with Smiths and Constables, yea and the trained Bands also (when they please) to assist them, and in most bold and tumultuous manner to break open and rifle, even the Parliaments owne (in all their greatest dangers, troubles & distresses) most faithfull friends Houses, Chests, Truncks and Drawers; and from thence to rob, steale, and felloniously to carry away such of the Possessors proper goods, choice Linnens, and best things, as they please, as well as Books new and old, after they have put the owners themselves out of doores, and commanded Constables to carry them before a Committee, and thence to Prison. . . .

The next *Monopoly,* it is to be feared will be upon *Bread* and *Beere,* for as justly may there be a Monopoly upon them, as upon the former.

Oh *Englishmen!* Where is your freedoms? and what is become of your *Liberties* and *Priviledges* that you have been fighting for all this while, to the large expense of your *Bloods* and *Estates,* which was hoped would have procured your *Liberties* and *freedoms?* but rather, as some great ones Order it, ties you faster in bondage and slavery, then before; therefore look about you betimes, before it be too late, and give not occasion to your Children yet unborne to curse you, for making them slaves by your covetousnesse, cowardly basenesse, and faint-heartednesse; therefore up as one man, and in a just and legall way call those to account, that endeavour to destroy you, and betray your Liberties and Freedomes. . . .

# C

[The text is taken from Jerrard Winstanly, *A Watch-Word to the City of London and the Armie* . . ., (London: Giles Calvert, 1649).]

# A Watch-Word to the City

*To the City of* London, *Freedome and Peace desired.*

Thou City of London, I am one of thy sons by freedome, and I do truly love thy peace; while I had an estate in thee, I was free to offer my Mite into thy publike Treasury Guild-hall, for a preservation to thee and the whole Land; but by thy cheating sons in the theeving art of buying and selling, and by the burdens of, and for the Souldiery in the beginning of the war, I was beaten out both of estate and trade, and forced to accept of the good will of friends crediting of me, to live a Countrey-life, and there likewise by the burthen of Taxes and much Freequarter, my weak back found the burthen heavier then I could bear, yet in all the passages of these eight yeers troubles I have been willing to lay out what my Talent was, to procure Englands peace inward and outward, and yet all along I have found such as in words have professed the same cause, to be enemies to me. Not a full yeere since, being quiet at my work, my heart was filled with sweet thoughts, and many things were revealed to me which I never read in books, nor heard from the mouth of any flesh, and when I began to speak of them, some people could not bear my words, and amongst those revelations this was one, *That the earth shall be made a common Treasury of livelihood to whole mankind, without respect of persons;* and I had a voice within me bad me declare it all abroad, which I did obey, for I declared it by word of mouth wheresoever I came, then I was made to write a little book called *The new Law of righteousnesse,* and therein I declared it; yet my mind was not at rest, because nothing was acted, and thoughts run in me, that words and writings were all nothing, and must die, for action is the life of all, and if thou dost not act, thou dost nothing. Within a little time I was made obedient to the word in that particular likewise; for I tooke my spade and went and broke the ground upon *George-hill* in Surrey, thereby declaring freedome to the Creation, and that the earth must be set free from intanglements of Lords and Landlords, and that it shall become a common Treasury to all, as it was first made and given to the sonnes of men: For which doing the Dragon presently casts a flood of water to drown the manchild, even that freedom that now is declared for the old Norman Prerogative Lord of that Mannour M *Drake,* causes me to be arrested for a trespasse against him, in digging upon that barren Heath, and the unrighteous proceedings of Kingstone Court in the businesse I have here declared to thee, and to the whole land, that you may consider the case that England is in; all men have stood for freedome thou hast kept fasting daies, and prayed in morning exercises for freedome thou hast given thanks for victories, because hopes of freedome; plenty of Petitions and promises thereupon have been made for freedome, and now the common enemy is gone, you are all like men in a mist, seeking for freedom, and know not where, nor what it is: and those of the richer sort of you that see it, are ashamed and afraid to owne it, because it comes clothed in a clownish garment, and open to the best language that scoffing *Ishmael* can afford, or that railing *Rabsheka* can speak, or furious *Pharaoh* can act against him; for freedom is the man that will turn the world upside downe, therefore, no wonder he hath enemies.

And assure your selves, if you pitch not right now upon the right point of freedome in action, as your Covenant hath it in words, you will wrap up your children in greater slavery than ever you were in: the Word of God is Love, and when all thy actions are done in love to the whole Creation, then thou advancest freedome, and freedome is Christ in you, and Christ among you; bondage is Satan in you, and Satan among you: no true freedom can be established for Englands peace, or prove you faithfull in Covenant, but such a one as hath respect to the poor, as well as the rich; for if thou consent to freedom to the rich in the City and givest freedome to the Freeholders in the Countrey, and to Priests and Lawyers, and Lords of Mannours, and Impropriators, and yet allowest the poor no freedome, thou art then a declared hypocrite, and all thy prayers, fasts, and thanksgivings are, and will be proved an abomination to the Lord, and freedome himselfe will be the poors portion, when thou shalt lie groaning in bondage.

I have declared this truth to the Army and Parliament, and now I have declared it to thee likewise, that none of you that are the fleshly strength of this Land may be left without excuse, for now you have been all spoken to, and because I have obeyed the voice of the Lord in this thing, therefore doe the Free-holders and Lords of Mannours seek to oppresse me in the outward livelihood of the world, but I am in peace. And London, nay England look to thy freedom, I'le assure thee, thou art very neere to be cheated of it, and if thou lose it now after all thy boasting, truly thy posterity will curse thee, for thy unfaithfulnesse to them: every one talks of freedome, but there are but few that act for freedome, and the actors for freedome are oppressed by the talkers and verball professors of freedome; if thou wouldst know what true freedome be read over this and other my writings, and thou shalt see it lies in the community in spirit, and community in the earthly treasury, and this is Christ the true manchild spread abroad in the Creation,

restoring all things into himselfe; and so I leave thee,
August 26. 1649.
Being a free Denizon of thee, and a true lover of thy peace,
Jerrard Winstanly,

## WATCH-WORD TO THE CITY OF LONDON, AND THE ARMY.

Whereas we *Henry Bickerstaffe, Thomas Star,* and *Jerrard Winstanly,* were arrested into Kingstone Court, by *Thomas Wenman, Ralph Verny,* and *Richard Winwood,* for a trespasse in digging upon George-hill in Surrey, being the rights of Mr. *Drake* the Lord of that Mannour, as they say, we all three did appear the first Court day of our arrest and demanded of the Court, what was laid to our Charge, and to give answer thereunto our selves: But the answer of your Court was this, that you would not tell us what the Trespasse was, unlesse we would fee an Attorney to speak for us; we told them we were to plead our own cause, for we knew no Lawyer that we could trust with this businesse: we desired a copie of the Declaration, and profered to pay for it; and still you denied us, unlesse we would fee an Attorney. But in conclusion, the Recorder of your Court told us, the cause was not entred; we appeared two Court daies after this, and desired to see the Declaration, and still you denied us, unlesse we will fee an Attorney; so greedy are these Attorneys after money, more then to justifie a righteous cause: we told them we could not fee any, unlesse we would willfully break our Nationall Covenant, which both Parliament and people have taken joyntly together to endeavour a Reformation. And unlesse we would be professed Traytors to this Nation and Common-wealth of England, by upholding the old Norman tyrannicall and destructive Lawes, when they are to be cast out of equity, and reason be the Moderator.

Then seeing you would not suffer us to speak, one of us brought this following writing into your Court, that you might read our answer because we would acknowledge all righteous proceedings in Law, though some slander us, and say we deny all Law, because we deny the corruption in Law, and endeavour a Reformation in our place and calling according to that Nationall Covenant: and we know if your Lawes be built upon equity and reason, you ought both to have heard us speak and read our answer; for that is no righteous Law, whereby to keep a Common-wealth in peace, when one sort shall be suffered to speak, and not another, as you deal with us, to passe sentence and execution upon us before both sides be heard to speak.

This principle in the forehead of your Laws, foretells destruction to this Common-wealth: for it declares that the Laws that follow such refusall, are selfish and theevish, and full of murder, protecting all that get money by their Laws, and crushing all others.

The writer hereof does require Mr. *Drake,* as he is a Parliament man; therefore a man counted able to speak rationally, to plead this cause of digging with me, and if he shew a just and rationall title, that Lords of Mannours have to the Commons, and that they have a just power from God, to call it their right, shutting out others; then I will write as much against it, as ever I writ for this cause. But if I shew by the Law of Righteousnesse, that the poorest man hath as true a title and just right to the Land, as the richest man, and that undeniably the earth ought to be a common treasury of livelihood for all, without respecting persons: Then I shall require no more of Mr. *Drake,* but that he would justifie our cause of digging, and declare abroad, that the Commons ought to be free to all sorts, and that it is a great trespasse before the Lord God Almighty, for one to hinder another of his liberty to dig the earth, that he might feed and cloath himself with the fruits of his labor therefrom freely, without owning any Landlord, or paying any rent to any person of his own kind.

I sent this following answer to the Arrest, in writing into Kingstone Court: In foure passages, your Court hath gone contrary to the righteousnesse of your own Statute Laws: for first it is mentioned in 36 *Ed.* 3, 15, that no Processe, Warrant, or Arrest should be served, till after the cause was recorded and entred; but your Bailiffe either could not, or would not tell us the cause when he arrested us, and Mr. *Rogers* your Recorder told us the first Court day we appeared, that our cause was not entred.

Secondly, we appeared two other Court daies, and desired a copy of the Declaration, and profered to pay for it, and you denied us. This is contrary to equity and reason, which is the foundation your Lawes are, or should be built upon, if you would have England to be a Common-wealth and stand in peace.

Thirdly, we desired to plead our own cause, and you denied us, but told us we must fee an Attorney to speak for us, or els you would mark us for default in not appearance. This is contrary to your own Laws likewise, for in 28. *Ed.* 1. 11 chap. there is freedome given to a man to speak for himself, or els he may choose his father, friend or neighbor to plead for him, without the help of any other Lawyer.

Fourthly, you have granted a judgement against us, and are proceeding to an execution, and this is contrary likewise to your own Laws, which say, that no plaint ought to be received, or judgement passed, till the cause be heard, and witnesses present, to testifie the plaint to be true as Sir *Edward Cook 2.part of Institutes* upon the 29. chap. of *Magna Charta,* fol. 51. 52. 53. The *Mirror of Justice.*

But that all men may see, we are neither ashamed nor afraid, to justifie that cause we are arrested for, neither to refuse to answer to it in a righteous way, therefore we have here delivered this up in writing, and we leave it in your hands, disavowing the proceedings of your Court, because you uphold Prerogative oppression, though the Kingly office be taken away, and the Parliament hath declared England a Common-Wealth; so that Prerogative Laws cannot be in force, unlesse you be besotted by your covetousnesse and envy.

We deny that we have trespassed against those three men, or Mr. *Drake* either, or that we should trespasse against any, if we should dig up, or plow for a livelihood, upon any the wast Land in England, for thereby we break no particular Law made by any Act of Parliament, but only an ancient custome, bred in strength of Kingly Prerogative, which is that old Law or custome, by which Lords of Mannours lay claime to the Commons, which is of no force now to bind the people of England, since the Kingly power and office was cast out; and the common people, who have cast out the oppressor, by their purse and person, have not authorized any as yet, to give away from them their purchased freedome; and if any assume a power to give away or withhold this purchased freedome, they are Traytors to this Common-Wealth of England: and if they imprison, oppresse, or put to death any for standing to maintaine the purchased freedome, they are murderers and thieves, and no just rulers.

Therefore in the light of reason and equity, and in the light of the Nationall Covenant, which Parliament and people have taken, with joynt consent: all such Prerogative customes, which by experience we have found to burden the Nation, ought to be cast out, with the Kingly office, and the Land of England now ought to be a free Land, and a common treasury to all her children, otherwise it cannot properly be called a Common-Wealth.

Therefore we justifie our act of digging upon that hill, to make the earth a common treasurie. First, because the earth was made by Almighty God, to be a common treasury of livelihood for whole mankind in all his branches, without respect of persons; and that not any one according to the Word of God (which is love) the pure Law of righteousnesse ought to be Lord or landlord over another, but whole mankind was made equall, and knit into one body by one spirit of love, which is Christ in you the hope of glory, even all the members of mans body, called the little world, are united into equality of love, to preserve the whole body.

But since the fall of man there from, which came in by the rising up of covetousnesse in the heart of mankind (to which Serpent the man consented) and from thence mankind was called *A-dam:* for this covetousnesse makes mankind to be a stoppage of freedome in the creation and by this covetous power, one branch of mankind began to lift up himself above another, as *Cain* lifted up himself, and killed his brother *Abel:* and so one branch did kill and steal away the comfortable use of the earth from another, as it is now: the elder brother lives in a continuall theevery, stealing the Land from the younger brother. And the plain truth is, theeves and murderers upheld by preaching witches and deceivers, rule the Nations: and for the present, the Laws and Government of the world, are Laws of darknesse, and the divells Kingdome, for covetousnesse rules all. And the power of the sword over brethren in Armies, in Arrests, in Prisons, in gallows, and in other inferiour torments, indicted by some upon others, as the oppression of Lords of Mannours, hindring the poore from the use of the common Land, is *Adam* fallen, or *Cain* killing *Abel* to this very day.

And these Prerogative oppressors, are the Adamites & Cainites that walk contrary to the Word of God (which is love) by upholding murder and theft, by Laws which their Fathers made, and which they now justifie; for in the conquests that Kings got, their Ancestors did murder and kill, and steal away the earth, and removed the Land mark from the conquered, and made Laws to imprison, torment, or put to death, all that would adventure to take the Land from them againe, and left both that stoln Land, and murdering Laws to their children, the Lords of Mannours, and Freeholders, who now with violence, do justifie their Fathers wickednesse by holding fast, that which was left them by succession.

For what are all the Laws of the Nations, in this corrupt covetous Government, lifting up one branch of *Adam* mankind above another, the Conqueror, above the conquered, or those that have power above them that are weak, I say what are they, but Laws of murder and theft, yea enmity itself, against the Law of righteousnesse, which is love, which makes people do, as they would be done unto?

And so all Kingly power, (in one or many mens hands) raigning by the sword, giving the use of the earth to some of mankind (called by him his Gentry) and denying the free use of the Earth to others, called the younger brothers, or common people, is no other but *Cain* lifted up above *Abel;* the Prerogative Lawes is *Belzebub*, for they are the strength of covetousnesse and bondage in the creation, lifting up one, and casting down another: the Atturneys, and Priests, and Lawyers, and Bayliffs are servants to *Belzebub*, and are Devils; their Prisons, Whips, and Gallows are the torments of this Hell, or government of darknesse; for mind it all along, and you shall see, that covetousnesse and bitter envie gets freedome by these Lawes; But the sincere and meek in spirit, is trod underfoot.

And this is that power, that hath made such havock in the Creation, it is that murderer and Devill that is to be cast out: this power of covetousnesse, is he that does countenance murder and theft in them that maintaines his Kingdom by the sword of Iron, and punishes it in other; and so that which is called a sin in the Common people, if they act such things, is counted no sin in the action of Kings, because the have they [*sic*] power of the sword in their hands, the fear whereof makes people to feare them.

But since this Kingly Office by the Parliament, is cast out of *England,* and *England* by them is declared to be a free State or Common-wealth, we are in the first place thereby set free from those bonds and ties that the Kings laid upon us: Therefore this Tyranny of one over another, as of Lords of Mannors over the Common people, and for people to be forced to hire Lawyers to plead their causes for them, when they are able to plead themselves, ought to be taken away with the Kingly Office, because they are the strength of the Ancient Prerogative custom.

Secondly we justifie our digging upon *George's* hill to make the Earth a common Treasury, because all sorts of people have lent assistance of purse and person to cast out the Kingly Office, as being a burden *England* groaned under; therefore those from whom money and blood was received, ought to obtain freedom in the Land to themselves and Posterity, by the Law of contract between Parliament and People.

But all sorts, poor as well as rich, Tenant as well as Landlord, have paid Taxes, Free-quarter, Excise, or adventured their lives, to cast out that Kingly Office.

Therefore, all sorts of people ought to have freedom in the Land of this their nativity, without respecting persons, now the Kingly Office is cast out, by their joynt assistance. And those that doe imprison, oppresse and take away the livelihood of those that rise up to take Possession of this purchased freedome, are Traitors to this Nation, and Enemies to righteousnesse: And of this number are those men that have arrested, or that may arrest the Diggers, that endeavour to advance freedome, therefore I say all sorts ought to have their freedom.

And that in regard they have not only joyned persons and purses together, but in regard likewise, they took the Nationall Covenant, with joynt consent together, which the Parliament did make, of whom Mr. *Drake* that caused us to be arrested was one; which Covenant likewise the Ministers in their Sermons, most vehemently prest upon the people to take the intent whereof was this, That every one in his severall place and calling, should endeavor the peace, safety and freedom of *England* and that the Parliament should assist the people, and the people the Parliament, and every one that had taken it, should assist those that had taken it, while they were in pursuit thereof, as in the sixth Article of the Nationall Covenant.

But now Mr. *Drake* that was one that made this Covenant, and the *Surrey* Ministers that took it with great zeal at *Kingstone,* which I was eye witnesse to, and shall be of their hypocrisie therein, have set up a Lecturer at *Cobham* one purpose to drive off the Diggers to forsake the persuit of their Covenant are the most vehement to break Covenant and to hinder them that would keep it, neither entring into peace themselves, nor suffering them that are entring in to enter.

But in regard some of us did dig upon *George's* Hill, thereby to take Possession of that freedom we have recovered out of the hands of the Kingly Office, and thereby endeavour a Reformation in our place and calling according to the Word of God (which is Love:) And while we are in persuit of this our Covenant, we expect both Parliament that made the Covenant, and the Officers of this Court, and Parish Ministers, and Lords of Mannors themselves, and especially Mr. *Drake,* to assist us herein, against all that shall oppose us in this righteous work of making the Earth a common Treasury; and not to beat us, imprison us, or take away our estates or lives, unlesse they will wilfully break Covenant with God and man, to please their own covetous froward heart, and thereby declare themselves to be the worst of Devils.

Therefore, in that we doe dig upon that Hill, we do not thereby take away other mens rights, neither do we demand of this Court, or from the Parliament, what is theirs and not ours: But we demand our own to be set free to us and them out of the Tyranicall oppression of ancient custome of Kingly Prerogative; and let us have no more gods to rule over us, but the King of righteousnesse only.

Therefore as the Free-holders claime a quietnesse and freedom in their inclosures, as it is fit they should have, so we that are younger brothers, or the poore oppressed, we claime our freedome in the Commons, that so elder and younger brother may live quietly and in peace, together freed from the straits of poverty and oppression, in this Land of our nativitie.

Thus we have in writing declared in effect, what we should say, if we had liberty to speak before you, declaring withall, that your Court cannot end this Controversie in that equity and reason of it, which wee stand to maintaine: Therefore we have appealed to the Parliament, who have received our Appeal and promised an Answer, and we wait for it; And we leave this with you, and let Reason and righteousnesse be our Iudge; therefore we hope you will do nothing rashly, but seriously consider of this cause before you proceed to execution upon us.

You say God will blast our work, and you say, you are in the right, and we are in the wrong: Now if you be Christians, as you say you are; Then do you act love to us, as we doe to you; and let both sides waite with patience on the Lord, to see who he blesses; but if you oppose by violence, arrest us, judge, condemn and execute us, and yet will not suffer us to speak for our selves, but you will force us to give money to our Enemies to speak for us, surely you cannot say your cause is right; but hereby you justifie our cause to be right, because you are the Persecutors of a loving meek spirited people, and so declare that the God you say that will blast us, is covetousnesse, whom you serve by your persecuting power.

*Covetous might may overcome rationall right for a time,*
*But rationall right must conquer covetous might, and that's the life of mine.*

*The Law is righteous, just and good, when Reason is the rule,*
*But who so rules by the fleshly will, declares himself a foole.*

Well, this same writing was delivered into their Court, but they cast it away and would not read it, and all was because I would not fee an Atturney; and then the next Court day following, before there was any tryall of our cause, for there was none suffered to speak but the Plaintiffe, they passed a Iudgement, and after that an Execution.

Now their Iury was made of rich Free-holders, and such as stand strongly for the Norman power: And though our digging upon that barren Common hath done the Common good, yet this Jury brings in damages of ten pounds a man, and the charges of the Plaintiffe in their Court, twenty-nine shillings and a peny; and this was their sentence and the passing of the Execution upon us.

And 2 dayes after (for in this case they can end a cause speedily in their Court; but when the Atturney and Lawyers get money they keep a cause depending seven yeares, to the utter undoing of the parties, so unrighteous is the Law, and Lawyers) I say, two dayes after they sent to execute the execution, and they put *Henry Beckarstaffe* in prison, but after three dayes, Mr. *Drake* released him again, *Beckarstaffe* not knowing of it till the release came; They seek after *Thomas Star* to imprison his body who is a poore man not worth ten pounds.

Then they came privately by day to *Gerrard Winstanleys* house, and drove away foure Cowes; I not knowing of it and some of the Lords Tenants rode to the next Town shouting the diggers were conquered, the diggers were conquered. Truly it is an easie thing to beat a man, and cry conquest over him after his hands are tied, as they tyed ours. But if their cause be so good, why will they not suffer us to speak, and let reason and equity, the foundation of righteous Lawes, judge them and us. But strangers made rescue of those Cowes, and drove them astray out of the Bailiffes hands, so that the Bailiffes lost them; but before the Bailiffes had lost the Cowes, I hearing of it went to them and said here is my body, take me that I may come to speak to those *Normans* that have stolne our land from us; and let the Cowes go, for they are none of mine; and after some time, they telling me that they had nothing against my body, it was my goods they were to have; then said I, take my goods, for the Cowes are not mine; and so I went away and left them, being quiet in my heart, and filled with comfort within my self, that the King of righteousnesse would cause this to work for the advancing of his own Cause, which I prefer above estate or livelyhood,

Saying within my heart as I went along, that if I could not get meat to eat, I would feed upon bread, milk and cheese; and if they take the Cowes, that I cannot feed on this, or hereby make a breach between me and him that owns the Cowes, then Ile feed upon bread and beere, till the King of righteousnesse clear up my innocency, and the justice of his own cause: and if this be taken from me for maintaining his Cause, Ile stand still and see what he will doe with me, for as yet I know not.

Saying likewise within my heart as I was walking along, O thou King of righteousnesse shew thy power, and do thy work thy self, and free thy people now from under this heavy bondage of miserie, *Pharaoh* the covetous power. And the answer in my heart was satisfactory, and full of sweet joy and peace: and so I said Father, do what thou wilt, this cause is thine, and thou knowest that the love to righteousnesse makes me do what I do.

I was made to appeal to the Father of life in the speakings of my heart likewise thus: Father thou knowest that what I have writ or spoken, concerning this light, that the earth should be restored and become a common Treasurie for all mankind, without respect of persons, was thy free revelation to me, I never read it in any book, I heard it from no mouth of flesh till I understood it from thy teaching first within me. I did not study nor imagine the conceit of it; self-love to my own particular body does not carry me along in the mannaging of this businesse; but the power of love flowing forth to the liberty and peace of thy whole Creation, to enemies as well as friends: nay towards those that oppresse me, endeavouring to make me a beggar to them. And since I did obey thy voice, to speak and act this truth, I am hated, reproached, and oppressed on evere side. Such as make profession of thee, yet revile me. And though they see I cannot fight with fleshly weapons, yet they will strive with me by that power. And so I see Father, that *England* yet does choose rather to fight with the Sword of Iron, and covetousnesse, then by the Sword of the Spirit which is love: and what thy purpose is with this land, or with my body, I know not; but establish thy power in me, and then do what pleases thee.

These and such like sweet thoughts dwelt upon my heart as I went along, and I feel my self now like a man in a storm, standing under shelter upon a hill in peace, waiting till the storm be over to see the end of it, and of many other things that my eye is fixed upon: But I will let this passe,

And return again to the Dragons Den, or Hornets nest, the selfish murdering fleshly Lawes of this Nation, which hangs some for stealing, and protects others in stealing; Lords of Mannours stole the land from their fellow creatures formerly in the conquests of Kings, and now they have made Lawes to imprison and hang all those that seek to recover the land again out of their thieving murdering hands.

They took away the Cowes which were my livelyhood, and beat them with their clubs, that the Cowes heads and sides did swell, which grieved tender hearts to see: and yet these Cowes never were upon *George* Hill, nor never digged upon that ground, and yet the poore beasts must suffer because they gave milk to feed me, but they were driven away out of those Devills hands the Bailiffes, and were delivered out of hell at that time.

And thus Lords of Mannours, their Bailiffes the true upholders of the *Norman* power, and some Freeholders that doe oppose this publick work, are such as the countrey knowes have beene no friends to that Cause the Parliament declared for, but to the Kingly power; and now if they get the foot fast in the stirrup, they will lift themselves again into the *Norman* saddle; and they do it secretly; for they keep up the *Norman* Lawes, and thereby Traytours to freedome, get into places of Law and power, and by that will enslave *England* more then it was under the Kingly power.

Therefore *England* beware; thou art in danger of being brought under the *Norman* power more then ever. The King *Charles* that was successour to *William* the Conquerour thou hast cast out: and though thy Parliament have declared against the Kingly office, and cast it out, and proclaimed *England* a Common wealth, that is to be a free land for the liberty and livelyhood of all her children;

Yet *William* the Conquerours Army begins to gather into head againe and the old *Norman* Prerogative Law is the place of their randezvous: for though their chief Captain *Charles* be gone, yet his Colonells, which are Lords of Mannours, his Councellours and Divines, which are our Lawyers and Priests, his inferiour officers and Souldiers, which are the Freeholders and Land-lords, all which did steal away our Land from us when they killed and murdered our Fathers in that *Norman* conquest: And the Bailiffes that are slaves to their covetous lusts and all the ignorant bawling women, against our digging for freedome, are the snapsack boyes and the ammunition sluts that follow the *Norman* Camp.

These are all striving to get into a body againe, that they may set up a new *Norman* slaverie over us; and the place of their randezvous, Prerogative power is fenced already about, with a Line of Communication. An act made by a piece of the Parliament to maintain the old Lawes, which if once this Camp be fortified in his full strength , it will cost many a sighing heart, and burdened spirit before it is taken.

And this *Norman* Camp are got into so numerous a body already, that they have appointed their Sutlers to drive away the Cowes which were my livelyhood, and some of them they would sell to make money of to pay the Atturney, *Gilder,* and Lawyers their fees, for denying the diggers our privilege to plead our own cause; for as it is clearly seen that if we be suffered to speak we shall batter to pieces all the old Lawes, and prove the maintainers of them hypocrites and Traitours to this Common wealth of *England,* and then the Atturneys and Lawyers Trade goes down, and Lords of Mannours must be reckoned equall to other men. And this covetous flesh and blood cannot endure.

And other of the Cows were to be killed to victuall the Camp, that is, to feed those *Normans, Will Star & Ned Sutton,* both Freeholders & others the snapsack boyes, and ammunition drabs that helped to drive away the Cows that they might be encouraged by a belly full of stoln goods to stick the closer to the businesse another time. Or else the price of these Cowes were to pay for the sack and Tobacco which the *Norman* officers of Knights, Gentlemen, and rich Freeholders did spend at the White Lion at *Cobham,* when they met the 24. of *August* 1649, to advise together what course they should take to subdue the diggers; for say they, if the cause of the diggers stand, we shall lose all our honour and titles, and we that have had the glory of the earth shall be of no more account then those slaves our servants and yonger brothers that have been footstools to us and our Fathers ever since the *Norman William* our beloved Generall took this land (not by love) but by a sharp sword, the power by which we stand: and though we own Christ by name, yet we will not do as he did to save enemies, but by our sword we will destroy our enemies, and do we not deserve the price of some of the diggers Cows to pay us for this our good service? And doe not our reverend Ministers tell us that *William* the Conquerour, and the succeeding Kings were Gods anointed? And do not they say that our inclosures which were got by that murdering sword, and given by *William* the Conquerour to our Fathers, and so successively, from them, the land is our inheritance, and that God gave it us, and shall these broken fellows, and beggarly rogues take our rights from us, and have the use of the land equall with us? Thus do these *Norman* Gentlemen comfort their hearts, and support themselves with broken reeds, when they meet together in their Counsels.

But stay you *Norman* Gentlemen, let me put in a word amongst you, doth the murderers sword make any man to be Gods anointed? Surely, Iesus Christ was called Gods annointed not because he conquered with a Sword of iron, but because he conquered by love, and the spirit of patience: therefore your Generall was not Gods annointed, as Christ was.

And then the Earth was not made to be the successive inheritance of children of murderers, that had the strongest arm of flesh, and the best sword, that can tread others under foot with a bold brasen forehead under colour of the Law of justice as the *Norman* power does; But it was made for all by the Law of righteousnesse, and he gives the whole Earth to be the inheritance of every single branch of mankind without respect of persons, and he that is filled with the love of this righteous King, doing as he would be done by is a true annointed one.

Therefore, that god whom you serve, and which did intitle you Lords, Knights Gentlemen, and Landlords, is covetousnesse, the god of this world, which alwayes was a murderer, a devil and father of lies, under whose dark governing power, both you and all the nations of the world for the present are under. But the King of righteousnesse or God of love whom I serve, did not call the earth your inheritance, shutting out others, but gave the earth to be a common treasurie to whole mankind (who is the Lord of it) without respect of person.

This power of love, is the King of righteousnesse, the Lord God Almighty that rules the whole Creation in peace, that is the Seed that breaks covetousnesse the Serpents head; he is the restoring power, that is now rising up to change all things into his own nature, he will be your Iudge, for vengance is his; and for any wrong you have done me, as I can tell you of many, yet I have given all matters of judgment and vengance into his hand, and I am sure he will doe right, and discover him that is the true Trespasser, that takes away my rights from me.

And take notice of this, you Lords of Mannors, and Norman Gentry, though you should kill my body or starve me in prison, yet know, that and more you strive, the more troubles you hearts shall be filled with and doe the worst you can to hinder publick freedom, you shall come off losers in the later end, I meane you shall lose your Kingdom of darknesse, though I lose my livelihood, he [*sic*] poor Cowes that is my living, and should be imprisoned; you have been told this 12 Months ago, that you should lose ground by striving, and will you not take warning will you needs shame your selves, to let the poore Diggers take away your Kingdome from you? surely, the power that is in them, will take the rule and government from you, and give it a people that will make better use of it.

Alas! you poor blind earth mouls, you strive to take away my livelihood, and the liberty of this poor weak frame my body of flesh, which is my house I dwell in for a time; but I strive to cast down your kingdom of darknesse, and to open Hell gates, and to break the Devils bands asunder, wherewith you are tied, that you my Enemies may live in peace, and that is all the harm I would have you to have.

Therefore you Lords of Mannors, you Free-holders, you Norman-Clergy, oppressing Tith-mungers, and you of the Parliament men, that have plaid fast and loose with this poor Nation, for what is past let it goe; hereafter advance freedom and liberty, and pluck up bondage; and sinne no more by Lording it over your Lords and Masters, that set you upon those Parliament Seats, lest worse things befall you then yet hath.

But to return again to Mr. *Gilders* advice, the Atturney of *Kingstone* Court, and the proceeding of that Court with the Cowes; you heare how they did judge, condemn and execute me, not suffering me to speak; and though those four Cowes were rescued out of their hands by strangers, not by me; and so by their own Law, they should have looked after the Rescuers, yet contrary to their own Law, they came againe to *Winstanleys* dwelling a fortnight after, and drove away seven Cowes and a Bull in the night time, some of the Cowes being Neighbour's that had hired pasture; and yet the damage which their Norman Iury, and their covetous besotted ignorant Atturney Mr. *Gilder,* had judged me to pay for a Trespasse in digging upon that barren *George's* Hill, was but eleven pound nine shillings and a penney charges & all, which they are like never to have of me, for an empty carrier will dance and sing before these Norman theeves and pick-purses: And thus you see they judged and passed sentence upon me but once at their prerogative pleasure, which they call *Englands* Law: but they executed me twice, that they might be sure to kill me. But yet these Cowes likewise are brought home againe, and the heart of my Enemies is put into the pound of vexation because the Cowes are set free. Surely, these Lords of Mannors and the Atturney Mr. *Gilder,* that gave advice to Arrest us for digging, have burned their Bibles long agoe, because they have so quite and clean forgotten that Petition in the Lords prayer, *forgive us our trespasses as we forgive them*; for they make this a trespasse against them, for digging upon the wast land of our mother the Land of *England* for a livelihood, when as their Law it self saith, *That the Commons and wasts belong to the poore.*

So that you see the Norman Camp is grown very numerous and big, that they want much beeffe to vituall them, and they are such hungry ones, that they will eat poor lean Cowes, that are little better then skin & bone; and poor Cowes if I keep them in the winter, they are like to be poorer for want of Hay; for before the report of our digging was much known, I bought three Acres of grasse of a Lord of a Mannor, whom I will not here name, because I know the councel of others made him prove fals to me; for when the time came to Mow, I brought mony to pay him before hand; but he answered me, I should not have it, but sold it to another before my face; this was because his Parish Priest, and the *Surrey* Ministers, and sorry ones too they are that have set up a Lecturer at *Cobham* for a little time, to preach down the Diggers, have bid the people neither to buy nor sell with us, but to beat us, imprison us, or banish us; and thereby they prove themselves to be members of the Beast that had two horns, like a Lamb, and yet speak like a Dragon, & so they fulfill that Scripture in *Rev.* 13.16. *that no man might buy and sell, save he that had the mark of the Beast.* Or else surely, they do it on purpose to quicken us to our work, and to drive us to Plant the Commons with all speed as may be.

But though the Cowes were poor, yet they care not, so the skins will but pay the Lawyers and Atturneys *Gilder* his Fees, and the flesh to feed the snapsack boyes, either to eat and make merry with, or else to sell to make money of, to pay those that drive away the Cowes for their paines or charges they have been at, in this 18 weeks striving to beat the Diggers off their work: But the bones will serve the Bailiffs to pick, because their action will be both proved thievery in stealing another mans cattell, and their trespasse very great against the same man, in opening all the Gates round about the ground, where *Winstanley* dwells, and let Hogs and common Cattell into the standing barly and other corn, which the right owner will seek satisfaction for.

So that the fury of this Norman Camp against the Diggers is so great, that they would not only drive away all the Cowes upon the ground, but spoyl the corn too, and when they had done this mischief, the Bayliff and the other Norman snapsack boyes went hollowing and shooting, as if they were dancing at a whitson Ale; so glad they are to do mischief to the Diggers, that they might hinder the work of freedome.

And why are they so furious against us? but because we endeavour to dig up their Tythes, their Lawyers Fees, their Prisons, and all that Art and Trade of darknesse, whereby they get money under couller of Law and to plant the plesant fruit trees of freedom, in the room of that cursed thornbush, the power of the murdering sword; for they say, they doe all they do by the Law of the Land which the Parliament hath confirmed in them by an Act: And if so, Then Souldiers where is the price of your blood? and Countrey-men, and Citizens, Where is the price of your Law and Free-quarter? If this be the freedom, you are like to have, to be beaten and not be suffered to say why doe you so, and shall have no remedy, unlesse you will Fee a Lawyer (an Enemy) to plead for you, when you are able to plea your own cause better your self, and save that charge, and have your cause ended sooner and with more peace and quietnesse.

And you zealous Preachers, and professors of the City of *London* and you great Officers and Souldiery of the Army, where are all your Victories over the Cavaliers, that you made such a blaze in the Land, in giving God thanks for, and which you begged in your Fasting dayes, and morning Exercises; Are they all sunck into the Norman power again, and must the old Prerogative Laws stand; what freedom then did you give thanks for? Surely, that you had killed him that rid upon you, that you may get up into his saddle to ride upon others; O thou City, thou Hypocriticall City! thou blindfold drowsie *England,* that sleps and snores in the bed of covetousnesse, awake, awake, the Enemies is upon thy back, he is ready to scale the walls and enter Possession, and wilt thou not look out.

Does not the streames of bondage run in the same river that it did, and with a bigger stream of Norman power; so that if you awaken not betimes, the flood of the Norman Prerogative power, will drown you all; here's more rivers comes into the maine stream, since the storm fell and the waters of fury rises very high, banked in by Laws; and while you are talking and disputing about words, the Norman Souldiers are secretly working among you to advance their power again; and so will take away the benefit of all your victories by a subtile act of intricate Lawes, which the sword in the field could not do against you: and when you have lost that freedom, which you boasted of that you will leave to your posterity, then who must give thanks, you that vapoured in words, or they that lay close in action, waiting to trip up your heels by pollicy, when the sword could not do it.

I tell thee thou *England,* thy battells now are all spirituall. Dragon against the Lamb, and the power of love against the power of covetousnesse; therefore all that will be Souldiers for Christ, the Law of righteousnesse joyn to the Lamb. He that takes the iron sword now shall perish with it, and would you be a strong Land and flourish in beauty, then fight the Lambs battels, and his strength shall be thy walls and bulwarks.

You Knights, Gentlemen, and Freeholders, that sat is councell at the Lion in *Cobham* to find out who are our backers, and who stirs us up to dig the Commons, Ile tel you plainly who it is, it is love, the love of righteousnes ruling in our hearts, that makes us thus to act that the creation may be set at liberty, and now I have answered your inquirie, do what you can to him and us his servants: And we require you in his name, to let our cause have a publick triall, and do not work any longer in darknesse, set not your Bailiffs and slaves to come by night to steal away the Cowes of poore men under colour of justice, when as the cause was never yet heard in open Court.

He that backs you, and that sets you to work, to deny to us our younger brother the use of the common land, is covetousnesse, which is Beelzebub the greatest, devil so that there is the 2 generalls known, which you & we fight under, the 2 great

Princes of light and darkness, bondage and freedom, that does Act all flesh in the great controversies of the world. *These* are the 2 men that stir in this busines, that is, the wicked man that councels, & backs you to be so envious and furious against us, and the righteous man Christ, that backs and councells us to love you our enemies. And do we not see that *Gebal, Ammon* and *Amaleck,* and all the rabble of the nations, Lords, Knights, Gentlemen, Lawyers, Bailiffes, Priests, and all the *Norman* snapsack boyes, and ammunition women to the old *Norman* Camp do all combine together in the art of unrighteous fury, to drive the poore diggers off from their work, that the name of community and freedome which is Christ, may not be known in earth. Thus I have dealt plainly with you all, and I have not flattered Parliament, Army, City, nor Countrey, but have declared in this, and other writings the whole light of that truth revealed to me by the word of the Lord: and I shall now wait to see his hand to do his own work in what time, and by what instruments he pleases. And I see the poore must first be picked out, and honoured in this work, for they begin to receive the word of righteousnesse, but the rich generally are enemies to true freedome.

> *The work of digging still goes on, and stops not for a rest:*
> *The Cowes were gone, but are return'd, and we are all at rest.*
> *No money's paid, nor never shall, to Lawyer or his man*
> *To plead our cause, for therein wee'll do the best we can.*
> *In* Cobham *on the little Heath our digging there goes on.*
> *And all our friends, they live in love, as if they were but one.*

Thus you Gentlemen, that will have no Law to rule over you, but your Prerogative will must be above Law, and above us that are the yonger brothes [*sic*] in the Land; but if you say, no, your wil shal be subject to Law: then I demand of you Mr. *Drake,* Mr. *Gilder,* and other Bailiffes and Officers of *Kingston* Court, why will you arrest us, and trouble us, and say we trespasse against you, and though we came in answer to your arrest, and to plead our own cause, yet contrary to the equity, nay contrary to the bare letter that the Law, as I shewed you before, you denyed me that priviledge, but went on and did condemne and execute a forceable power upon body and goods, is not your will here, above Law? do you not hereby uphold the *Norman* conquest?

Mr. *Drake*, you are a Parliament man, and was not the beginning of the quarrel between King *Charles* and your House? This the King pleaded to uphold Prerogative, and you were against it, and yet must a Parliament man be the first man to uphold Prerogative, who are but servants to the Nation for the peace and liberty of every one, not conquering Kings to make their wil a Law? did you not promise liberty to the whole Nation, in case the Cavalier party were cast out? and why now will you seek liberty to your self and Gentry, with the deniall of just liberty and freedome to the common people, that have born the greatest burden?

You have arrested us for digging upon the common Land, you have executed your unrighteous power, in distraining cattel, imprisoning our bodies, and yet our cause was never publickly heard, neither can it be proved that we have broke any Law, that is built upon equity and reason, therefore we wonder where you had your power to rule over us by will, more then we to rule over you by our will. We request you before you go too far, not to let covetousnesse be your Master, trample not others under your feet, under colour of Law, as if none knew equity of Law but you; for we and our estates shall be horns in your eyes, and pricks in your sides, and you may curse that Councell bid you beg our estates, or imprison our persons. But this we request that you would let us have a fair open triall, and do not carry on the course of Law in secret like *Nicodemus* that is afraid to have his businesse come to light; therefore I challenge you once more, seeing you professe your selves Christians, to let us be brought to a trial of our cause; let your ministers plead with us in the scriptures, & let your Lawyers plead with us in the equity and reason of your own Law; and if you prove us transgressours, then we shall lay down our work and acknowledge we have trespassed against you in digging upon the Commons, & then punish us. But if we prove by Scripture & reason, that undeniably the land belongs to one as well as another, then you shal own our work, justifie our cause, & declare that you have done wrong to Christ, who you say is your Lord and master, in abusing us his servants, & your fellow creatures, while we are doing his task. Therefore I knowing you to be men of moderation in outward shew, I desire that your actions towards your fellow creatures may not be like one beast to another, but carry your selves, like man to man; for your proceeding in your pretence of law hitherto against us, is both unrighteous, beastly & divelish, and nothing of the spirit of man seen in it, You Atturnies and Lawyers, you say you are ministers of justice, & we know that equity and reason is, or ought to be the foundation of Law; if so, then plead not for mony altogether but stand for universall justice & equity, then you will have peace; otherwise both you with the corrupt Clergy will be cast out as unsavoury salt.

# D

[The text is taken from John Milton, *Areopagitica for the Liberty of Unlicensed Printing*, 1644. ed. by Edward Arber (London: 1869).]

## Areopagitica for the Liberty of Unlicensed Printing

"This is true liberty, when free-born men
Having to advise the public, may speak free,
Which he who can, and will, deserves high praise;
Who neither can, nor will, may hold his peace:
What can be juster in a state than this?" — *Euripid. Hicetid.*

They, who to states and governors of the commonwealth direct their speech, high court of parliament! or wanting such access in a private condition, write that which they foresee may advance the public good; I suppose them, as at the beginning of no mean endeavour not a little altered and moved inwardly in their minds; some with doubt of what will be the success, others with fear of what will be the censure; some with hope, others with confidence of what they have to speak. And me perhaps each of these dispositions, as the subject was whereon I entered, may have at other times variously affected; and likely might in these foremost expressions now also disclose which of them swayed most, but that the very attempt of this address thus made, and the thought of whom it hath recourse to, hath got the power within me to a passion, far more welcome than incidental to a preface.

Which though I stay not to confess ere any ask, I shall be blameless, if it be no other than the joy and gratulation which it brings to all who wish to promote their country's liberty; whereof this whole discourse proposed will be a certain testimony, if not a trophy. For this is not the liberty which we can hope, that no grievance ever should arise in the commonwealth: that let no man in this world expect; but when complaints are freely heard, deeply considered, and speedily reformed, then is the utmost bound of civil liberty obtained that wise men look for. To which if I now manifest, by the very sound of this which I shall utter, that we are already in good part arrived, and yet from such a steep disadvantage of tyranny and superstition grounded into our principles, as was beyond the manhood of a Roman recovery, it will be attributed first, as is most due, to the strong assistance of God, our deliverer; next, to your faithful guidance and undaunted wisdom, lords and commons of England! Neither is it in God's esteem, the diminution of his glory, when honourable things are spoken of good men, and worthy magistrates; which if I now first should begin to do, after so fair a progress of your laudable deeds, and such a long obligement upon the whole realm to your indefatigable virtues, I might be justly reckoned among the tardiest and the unwillingest of them that praise ye.

Nevertheless there being three principal things, without which all praising is but courtship and flattery: first, when that only is praised which is solidly worth praise; next, when greatest likelihoods are brought, that such things are truly and really in those persons to whom they are ascribed; the other, when he who praises, by shewing that such his actual persuasion is of whom he writes, can demonstrate that he flatters not; the former two of these I have heretofore endeavoured, rescuing the employment from him who went about to impair your merits with a trivial and malignant encomium; the latter as belonging chiefly to mine own acquittal, that whom I so extolled I did not flatter, hath been reserved opportunely to this occasion. For he who freely magnifies what hath been nobly done, and fears not to declare as freely what might be done better, gives ye the best covenant of his fidelity; and that his loyalest affection and his hope waits on your proceedings. His highest praising is not flattery, and his plainest advice is a kind of praising; for though I should affirm and hold by argument, that it would fare better with truth, with learning, and the commonwealth, if one of your published orders, which I should name, were called in; yet at the same time it could not but much redound to the lustre of your mild and equal government, whenas private persons are hereby animated to think ye better pleased with public advice than other statists have been delighted heretofore with public flattery. And men will then see what difference there is between the magnanimity of a triennial parliament, and that jealous haughtiness of prelates and cabin counsellors that usurped of late, whenas they shall observe ye in the midst of your victories and successes more gently brooking written exceptions against a voted order, than other courts, which have produced nothing worth memory but the weak ostentation of wealth, would have endured the least signified dislike at any sudden proclamation.

If I should thus far presume upon the meek demeanour of your civil and gentle greatness, lords and commons! as what your published order hath directly said, that to gainsay, I might defend myself with ease, if any should accuse me of being new or insolent, did they but know how much better I find ye esteem it to imitate the old and elegant humanity of Greece, than the barbaric pride of a Hunnish and Norwegian stateliness. And out of those ages, to whose polite wisdom and letters we owe that we are not yet Goths and Jutlanders, I could name him who from his private house wrote that discourse to the parliament of Athens, that persuades them to change the form of democracy which was then established. Such honour was done in those days to men who professed the study of wisdom and eloquence, not only in their own country, but in other lands, that cities and signiories heard them gladly and with great respect, if they had aught in public to admonish the state. Thus did Dion Prusæus, a stranger and a private orator, counsel the Rhodians against a former edict; and I abound with other like examples, which to set here would be superfluous. But if from the industry of a life wholly dedicated to studious labours, and those natural endowments haply not the worst for two and fifty degrees of northern latitude, so much must be derogated, as to count me not equal to any of those who had this privilege, I would obtain to be thought not so inferior, as yourselves are superior to the most of them who received their counsel; and how far you excel them, be assured, lords and commons! there can no greater testimony appear, than when your prudent spirit acknowledges and obeys the voice of reason, from what quarter soever it be heard speaking; and renders ye as willing to repeal any act of your own setting forth, as any set forth by your predecessors.

If ye be thus resolved, as it were injury to think ye were not, I know not what should withhold me from presenting ye with a fit instance wherein to show both that love of truth which ye eminently profess, and that uprightness of your judgment which is not wont to be partial to yourselves; by judging over again that order which ye have ordained "to regulate printing: that no book, pamphlet, or paper shall be henceforth printed, unless the same be first approved and licensed by such, or at least one of such, as shall be thereto appointed." For that part which preserves justly every man's copy to himself, or provides for the poor, I touch not; only wish they be not made pretences to abuse and persecute honest and painful men, who offend not in either of these particulars. But that other clause of licensing books, which we thought had died with his brother quadragesimal and matrimonial when the prelates expired, I shall now attend with such a homily, as shall lay before ye, first, the inventors of it to be those whom ye will be loath to own; next, what is to be thought in general of reading, whatever sort the books be; and that this order avails nothing to the suppressing of scandalous, seditious, and libellous books, which were mainly intended to be suppressed. Last, that it will be primely to the discouragement of all learning, and the stop of truth, not only by disexercising and blunting our abilities, in what we know already, but by hindering and cropping the discovery that might be yet further made, both in religious and civil wisdom.

I deny not, but that it is of greatest concernment in the church and commonwealth, to have a vigilant eye how books demean themselves, as well as men; and thereafter to confine, imprison, and do sharpest justice on them as malefactors; for books are not absolutely dead things, but do contain a progeny of life in them to be as active as that soul was whose progeny they are; nay, they do preserve as in a vial the purest efficacy and extraction of that living intellect that bred them. I know they are as lively, and as vigorously productive, as those fabulous dragon's teeth: and being sown up and down, may chance to spring up armed men. And yet, on the other hand, unless wariness be used, as good almost kill a man as kill a good book: who kills a man kills a reasonable creature, God's image; but he who destroys a good book, kills reason itself, kills the image of God, as it were, in the eye. Many a man lives a burden to the earth; but a good book is the precious life-blood of a master-spirit, embalmed and treasured up on purpose to a life beyond life. It is true, no age can restore a life, whereof, perhaps, there is no great loss; and revolutions of ages do not oft recover the loss of a rejected truth, for the want of which whole nations fare the worse. We should be wary, therefore, what persecution we raise against the living labours of public men, how we spill that seasoned life of man, preserved and stored up in books; since we see a kind of homicide may be thus committed, sometimes a martyrdom; and if it extend to the whole impression, a kind of massacre, whereof the execution ends not in the slaying of an elemental life, but strikes at the ethereal and fifth essence, the breath of reason itself; slays an immortality rather than a life. But lest I should be condemned of introducing licence, while I oppose licensing, I refuse not the pains to be so much historical, as will serve to shew what hath been done by ancient and famous commonwealths, against this disorder, till the very time that this project of licensing crept out of the inquisition, was catched up by our prelates, and hath caught some of our presbyters.

In Athens, where books and wits were ever busier than in any other part of Greece, I find but only two sorts of writings which the magistrate cared to take notice of; those either blasphemous and atheistical, or libellous. Thus the books of Protagoras were by the judges of Areopagus, commanded to be burnt, and himself banished the territory for a discourse, begun with his confessing not to know "whether there were gods, or whether not." And against defaming, it was agreed that none should be traduced by name, as was the manner of Vetus Comœdia, whereby we may guess how they censured libelling; and this course what quick enough, as Cicero writes, to quell both the desperate wits of other atheists, and the open way of defaming, as the event showed. Of other sects and opinions, though tending to voluptuousness, and the denying of divine Providence, they took no heed. Therefore we do not read that either Epicurus, or that libertine school of Cyrene, or what the Cynic impudence uttered, was ever questioned by the laws. Neither is it recorded that the writings of those old comedians were suppressed, though the acting of them were forbid; and that Plato commended the reading of Aristophanes, the loosest of them all, to his royal scholar, Dionysius, is commonly known, and may be excused, if holy Chrysostom, as is reported, nightly studied so much the same author, and had the art to cleanse a scurrilous vehemence into the style of a rousing sermon.

That other leading city of Greece, Lacedæmon, considering that Lycurgus their lawgiver was so addicted to elegant learning, as to have been the first that brought out of Ionia the scattered works of Homer, and sent the poet Tales from Crete, to prepare and mollify the Spartan surliness with his smooth songs and odes, the better to plant among them law and civility; it is to be wondered how museless and unbookish they were, minding nought but the feats of war. There needed no licensing of books among them, for they disliked all but their own laconic apophthegms, and took a slight occasion to chase Archilochus out of their city, perhaps for composing in a higher strain than their own soldiery ballads and roundels could reach to; or if it were for his broad verses, they were not therein so cautious, but they were as dissolute in their promiscuous conversing; whence Euripides affirms, in Andromache, that their women were all unchaste.

This much may give us light after what sort of books were prohibited among the Greeks. The Romans also for many ages trained up only to a military roughness, resembling most the Lacedæmonian guise, knew of learning little but what their twelve tables and the pontific college with their augurs and flamens taught them in religion and law; so unacquainted with other learning, that when Carneades and Critolaus, with the stoic Diogenes, coming ambassadors to Rome, took thereby occasion to give the city a taste of their philosophy, they were suspected for seducers by no less a man than Cato the Censor, who moved it in the senate to dismiss them speedily, and to banish all such Attic babblers out of Italy. But Scipio and others of the noblest senators withstood him and his old Sabine austerity; honoured and admired the men; and the censor himself at last, in his old age, fell to the study of that whereof before he was so scrupulous. And yet, at the same time, Nævius and Plautus, the first Latin comedians, had filled the city with all the borrowed scenes of Menander and Philemon. Then began to be considered there also what was to be done to libellous books and authors; for Nævius was quickly cast into prison for his unbridled pen, and released by the tribunes upon his recantation: we read also that libels were burnt, and the makers punished, by Augustus.

The like severity, no doubt, was used, if aught were impiously written against their esteemed gods. Except in these two points, how the world went in books, the magistrate kept no reckoning. And therefore Lucretius, without impeachment, versifies his Epicurism to Memmius, and had the honour to be set forth the second time by Cicero, so great a father of the commonwealth; although himself disputes against that opinion in his own writings. Nor was the satirical sharpness or naked plainness of Lucilius, or Catullus, or Flaccus, by any order prohibited. And for matters of state, the story of Titus Livius, though it extolled that part which Pompey held, was not therefore suppressed by Octavius Cæsar, of the other faction. But that Naso was by him banished in his old age, for the wanton poems of his youth, was but a mere covert of state over some secret cause; and besides, the books were neither banished nor called in. From hence we shall meet with little else but tyranny in the Roman empire, that we may not marvel, if not so often bad as good books were silenced. I shall therefore deem to have been large enough, in producing what among the ancients was punishable to write, save only which, all other arguments were free to treat on.

By this time the emperors were become Christians, whose discipline in this point I do not find to have been more severe than what was formerly in practice. The books of those whom they took to be grand heretics were examined, refuted, and condemned in the general councils; and not till then were prohibited, or burnt, by authority of the emperor. As for the writings of heathen authors, unless they were plain invectives against Christianity, as those of Porphyrius and Proclus, they met with no interdict that can be cited, till about the year 400, in a Carthaginian council, wherein bishops themselves were forbid to read the books of Gentiles, but heresies they might read; while others long before them, on the contrary, scrupled more the books of heretics, than of Gentiles. And that the primitive councils and bishops were wont only to declare what books were not commendable, passing no further, but leaving it to each one's conscience to read or to lay by, till after the year 800, is observed already by Padre Paolo, the great unmasker of the Trentine council. After which time the popes of Rome, engrossing what they pleased of political rule into their own hands, extended their dominion over men's eyes, as they had before over their judgments, burning and prohibiting to be read what they fancied not; yet sparing in their censures, and the books not many which they so dealt with; till Martin the Fifth, by his bull, not only prohibited, but was the first that excommunicated the reading of heretical books; for about that time Wickliffe and Husse growing terrible, were they who first drove the papal court to a stricter policy of prohibiting. Which course Leo the Tenth and his successors followed, until the council of Trent and the Spanish inquisition, engendering together, brought forth or perfected those catalogues and expurging indexes, that rake through the entrails of many an old good author, with a violation worse than any could be offered to his tomb.

Nor did they stay in matters heretical, but any subject that was not to their palate, they either condemned in a prohibition, or had it straight into the new purgatory of an index. To fill up the measure of encroachment, their last invention was to ordain that no book, pamphlet, or paper should be printed (as if St. Peter had bequeathed them the keys of the press also as well as of Paradise) unless it were approved and licensed under the hands of two or three gluttonous friars. For example: —

"I have seen this present work, and find nothing athwart the catholic faith and good manners: in witness whereof I have given, &c.
"Nicolo Cini, Chancellor of Florence."
"Attending the precedent relation, it is allowed that this present work of Davanzati may be printed.
"Vincent Rabbata," &c.
"It may be printed, July 15.
"Friar Simon Mompei d'Amelia, Chancellor of the Holy Office in Florence."

Sure they have a conceit, if he of the bottomless pit had not long since broke prison, that this quadruple exorcism would bar him down. I fear their design will be to get into their custody the licensing of that which they say Claudius intended, but went not through with. Vouchsafe to see another of their forms, the Roman stamp: —

"Imprimatur, If it seem good to the reverend master of the Holy Palace.
"Belcastro, Vicegerent."
"Imprimatur,
"Friar Nicholo Rodolphi, Master of the Holy Palace."

Sometimes five imprimaturs are seen together, dialogue wise, in the piazza of one titlepage, complimenting and ducking each to other with their shaven reverences, whether the author, who stands by in perplexity at the foot of his epistle, shall to the press or to the spunge. These are the pretty responsories, these are the dear antiphonies, that so bewitched of late our prelates and their chaplains, with the goodly echo they made; and besotted us to the gay imitation of a lordly imprimatur, one from Lambeth-house, another from the west end of Paul's; so apishly romanizing, that the word of command still was set down in Latin; as if the learned grammatical pen that wrote it would cast no ink without Latin; or perhaps, as they thought, because no vulgar tongue was worthy to express the pure conceit of an imprimatur; but rather, as I hope, for that our English, the language of men ever famous and foremost in the achievements of liberty, will not easily find servile letters enow to spell such a dictatory presumption Englished.

And thus ye have the inventors and the original of book licensing ripped up and drawn as lineally as any pedigree. We have it not, that can be heard of, from any ancient state, or polity, or church, nor by any statute left us by our ancestors elder or later; nor from the modern custom of any reformed city or church abroad; but from the most antichristian council, and the most tyrannous inquisition that ever inquired. Till then books were ever as freely admitted into the world as any other birth; the issue of the brain was no more stifled than the issue of the womb: no envious Juno sat cross-legged over the nativity of any man's intellectual offspring; but if it proved a monster, who denies but that it was justly burnt, or sunk into the sea? But that a book, in worse condition than a peccant soul, should be to stand before a jury ere it be born to the world, and undergo yet in darkness the judgment of Radamanth and his colleagues, ere it can pass the ferry backward into light, was never heard before, till that mysterious iniquity provoked and troubled at the first entrance of reformation, sought out new limboes and new hells wherein they might include our books also within the number of their damned. And this was the rare morsel so officiously snatched up, and so illfavouredly imitated by our inquisiturient bishops, and the attendant minorities, their chaplains. That ye like not now these most certain authors of this licensing order, and that all sinister intention was far distant from your thoughts, when ye were importuned the passing it, all men who know the integrity of your actions, and how ye honour truth, will clear ye readily.

But some will say, what though the inventors were bad, the thing for all that may be good. It may so; yet if that thing be no such deep invention, but obvious and easy for any man to light on, and yet best and wisest commonwealths through all ages and occasions have forborne to use it, and falsest seducers and oppressors of men were the first who took it up, and to no other purpose but to obstruct and hinder the first approach of reformation; I am of those who believe, it will be a harder alchymy than Lullius ever knew, to sublimate any good use out of such an invention. Yet this only is what I request to gain from this reason, that it may be held a dangerous and suspicious fruit, as certainly it deserves, for the tree that bore it, until I can dissect one by one the properties it has. But I have first to finish, as was propounded, what is to be thought in general of reading books, whatever sort they be, and whether be more the benefit or the harm that thence proceeds.

Not to insist upon the examples of Moses, Daniel, and Paul, who were skilful in all the learning of the Egyptians, Chaldeans, and Greeks, which could not probably be without reading their books of all sorts, in Paul especially, who thought it no defilement to insert into holy scripture the sentences of three Greek poets, and one of them a tragedian; the question was notwithstanding sometimes controverted among the primitive doctors, but with great odds on that side which affirmed it both lawful and profitable, as was then evidently perceived, when Julian the Apostate, and subtlest enemy to our faith, made a decree forbidding Christians the study of heathen learning; for, said he, they wound us with our own weapons, and with our own arts and sciences they overcome us. And indeed the Christians were put so to their hifts by his crafty means, and so much in danger to decline into all ignorance, that the two Appollinarii were fain, as a man may say, to coin all the seven liberal sciences out of the Bible, reducing it into divers forms of orations, poems, dialogues, even to the calculating of a new Christian grammar.

But, saith the historian, Socrates, the providence of God provided better than the industry of Appollinarius and his son, by taking away that illiterate law with the life of him who devised it. So great an injury they then held it to be deprived of Hellenic learning; and thought it a persecution more undermining, and secretly decaying the church, than the open cruelty of Decius or Diocletian. And perhaps it was with the same politic drift that the devil whipped St. Jerome in a lenten dream, for reading Cicero; or else it was a phantasm, bred by the fever which had then seized him. For had an angel been his discipliner, unless it were for dwelling too much on Ciceronianisms, and had chastised the reading, not the vanity, it had been plainly partial, first, to correct him for grave Cicero, and not for scurril Plautus, whom he confesses to have been reading not long before; next to correct him only, and let so many more ancient fathers wax old in those pleasant and florid studies, without the lash of such a tutoring apparition; insomuch that Basil teaches how some good use may be made of Margites, a sportful poem, not now extant, writ by Homer; and why not then of Morgante, an Italian romance much to the same purpose?

But if it be agreed we shall be tried by visions, there is a vision recorded by Eusebius, far ancienter than this tale of Jerome, to the nun Eustochium, and besides, has nothing of a fever in it. Dionysius Alexandrinus was, about the year 240, a person of great name in the church, for piety and learning, who had wont to avail himself much against heretics, by being coversant in their books; until a certain presbyter laid it scrupulously to his conscience, how he durst venture himself among those defiling volumes. The worthy man, loath to give offence, fell into a new debate with himself, what was to be thought; when suddenly a vision sent from God (it is his own epistle that so avers it) confirmed him in these words: "Read any books whatever come to thy hands, for thou art sufficient both to judge aright, and to examine each matter." To this revelation he assented the sooner, as he confesses, because it was answerable to that of the apostle to the Thessalonians: "Prove all things, hold fast that which is good."

And he might have added another remarkable saying of the same author: "To the pure, all things are pure;" not only meats and drinks, but all kind of knowledge, whether of good or evil: the knowledge cannot defile, nor consequently the books, if the will and conscience be not defiled. For books are as meats and viands are; some of good, some of evil substance; and yet God in that unapocryphal vision said without exception, "Rise, Peter, kill and eat;" leaving the choice to each man's discretion. Wholesome meats to a vitiated stomach differ little or nothing from unwholesome; and best books to a naughty mind are not unapplicable to occasions of evil. Bad meats will scarce breed good nourishment in the healthiest concoction; but herein the difference is of bad books, that they to a discreet and judicious reader serve in many respects to discover, to confute, to forewarn, and to illustrate. Whereof what better witness can ye expect I should produce, than one of your own now sitting in parliament, the chief of learned men reputed in this land, Mr. Selden; whose volume of natural and national laws proves, not only by great authorities brought together, but by exquisite reasons and theorems almost mathematically demonstrative, that all opinions, yea, errors, known, read, and collated, are of main service and assistance toward the speedy attainment of what is truest.

I conceive, therefore, that when God did enlarge the universal diet of man's body, (saving ever the rules of temperance,) he then also, as before, left arbitrary the dieting and repasting of our minds; as wherein every mature man might have to exercise his own leading capacity. How great a virtue is temperance, how much of moment through the whole life of man! Yet God commits the managing so great a trust, without particular law or prescription, wholly to the demeanour of every grown man. And therefore when he himself tabled the Jews from heaven, that omer, which was every man's daily portion of manna, is computed to have been more than might have well sufficed the heartiest feeder thrice as many meals. For those actions which enter into a man, rather than issue out of him, and therefore defile not, God uses not to captivate under a perpetual childhood of prescription, but trusts him with the gift of reason to be his own chooser; there were but little work left for preaching, if law and compulsion should grow so fast upon those things which heretofore were governed only by exhortation. Solomon informs us, that much reading is a weariness to the flesh; but neither he, nor other inspired author, tells us that such or such reading is unlawful; yet certainly had God thought good to limit us herein, it had been much more expedient to have told us what was unlawful, than what was wearisome.

As for the burning of those Ephesian books by St. Paul's converts; it is replied, the books were magic, the Syriac so renders them. It was a private act, a voluntary act, and leaves us to a voluntary imitation: the men in remorse burnt those books which were their own; the magistrate by this example is not appointed; these men practised the books, another might perhaps have read them in some sort usefully. Good and evil we know in the field of this world grow up together almost inseparably; and the knowledge of good is so involved and interwoven with the knowledge of evil, and in so many cunning resemblances hardly to be discerned, that those confused seeds which were imposed upon Psyche as an incessant labour to cull out, and sort asunder, were not more intermixed. It was from out the rind of one apple tasted, that the knowledge of good and evil, as two twins cleaving together, leaped forth into the world. And perhaps this is that doom which Adam fell into of knowing good and evil, that is to say, of knowing good by evil.

As therefore the state of man now is; what wisdom can there be to choose, what continence to forbear, without the knowledge of evil? He that can apprehend and consider vice with all her baits and seeming pleasures, and yet abstain, and yet distinguish, and yet prefer that which is truly better, he is the true warfaring Christian. I cannot praise a fugitive and cloistered virtue unexercised and unbreathed, that never sallies out and seeks her adversary, but slinks out of the race, where that immortal garland is to be run for, not without dust and heat. Assuredly we bring not innocence into the world, we bring impurity much rather; that which purifies us is trial, and trial is by what is contrary. That virtue therefore which is but a youngling in the contemplation of evil, and knows not the utmost that vice promises to her followers, and rejects it, is but a blank virtue, not a pure; her whiteness is but an excremental whiteness; which was the reason why our sage and serious poet Spenser, (whom I dare be known to think a better teacher than Scotus or Aquinas,) describing true temperance under the person of Guion, brings him in with his palmer through the cave of Mammon, and the bower of earthly bliss, that he might see and know, and yet abstain.

Since therefore the knowledge and survey of vice is in this world so necessary to the constituting of human virtue, and the scanning of error to the confirmation of truth, how can we more safely, and with less danger, scout into the regions of sin and falsity, than by reading all manner of tractates, and hearing all manner of reason? And this is the benefit which may be had of books promiscuously read. But of the harm that may result hence, three kinds are usually reckoned. First, is feared the infection that may spread; but then, all human learning and controversy in religious points must remove out of the word, yea, the Bible itself; for that ofttimes relates blasphemy not nicely, it describes the carnal sense of wicked men not unelegantly, it brings in holiest men passionately murmuring against Providence through all the arguments of Epicurus: in other great disputes it answers dubiously and darkly to the common reader; and ask a Talmudist what ails the modestly of his marginal Keri, that Moses and all the prophets cannot persuade him to pronounce the textual Chetiv. For these causes we all know the Bible itself put by the papist into the first rank of prohibited books. The ancientest fathers must be next removed, as Clement of Alexandria, and that Eusebian book of evangelic preparation, transmitting our ears through a hoard of heathenish obscenities to receive the gospel. Who finds not that Irenæus, Epiphanius, Jerome, and others discover more heresies than they well confute, and that oft for heresy which is the truer opinion?

Nor boots it to say for these, and all the heathen writers of greatest infection, if it must be thought so, with whom is bound up the life of human learning, that they wrote in an unknown tongue, so long as we are sure those languages are known as well to the worst of men, who are both most able and most diligent to instil the poison they suck, first into the courts of princes, acquainting them with the choicest delights, and criticisms of sin. As perhaps did that Petronius, whom Nero called his arbiter, the master of his revels; and that notorious ribald of Arezzo, dreaded and yet dear to the Italian courtiers. I name not him, for posterity's sake, whom Henry the Eighth named in merriment his vicar of hell. By which compendious way all the contagion that foreign books can infuse will find a passage to the people far easier and shorter than an Indian voyage, though it could be sailed either by the north of Cataio eastward, or of Canada westward, while our Spanish licensing gags the English press never so severely.

But, on the other side, that infection which is from books of controversy in religion, is more doubtful and dangerous to the learned than to the ignorant; and yet those books must be permitted untouched by the licenser. It will be hard to instance where any ignorant man hath been ever seduced by any papistical book in English, unless it were commended and expounded to him by some of that clergy;

and indeed all such tractates, whether false or true, are as the prophecy of Isaiah was to the eunuch, not to be "understood without a guide." But of our priests and doctors how many have been corrupted by studying the comments of Jesuits and Sorbonists, and how fast they could transfuse that corruption into the people, our experience is both late and sad. It is not forgot, since the acute and distinct Arminius was perverted merely by the perusing of a nameless discourse written at Delft, which at first he took in hand to confute.

Seeing therefore that those books, and those in great abundance, which are likeliest to taint both life and doctrine, cannot be suppressed without the fall of learning, and of all ability in disputation, and that these books of either sort are most and soonest catching to the learned, (from whom to the common people whatever is heretical or dissolute may quickly be conveyed), and that evil manners are as perfectly learnt without books a thousand other ways which cannot be stopped, and evil doctrine not with books can propagate, except a teacher guide, which he might also do without writing, and so beyond prohibiting; I am not unable to unfold, how this cautelous enterprise of licensing can be exempted from the number of vain and impossible attempts. And he who were pleasantly disposed, could not well avoid to liken it to the exploit of that gallant man, who thought to pound up the crows by shutting his park gate.

Besides another inconvenience, if learned men be the first receivers out of books, and dispreaders both of vice and error, how shall the licensers themselves be confided in, unless we can confer upon them, or they assume to themselves, above all others in the land, the grace of infallibility and uncorruptedness? And again, if it be true, that a wise man, like a good refiner, can gather gold out of the drossiest volume, and that a fool will be a fool with the best book, yea, or without book; there is no reason that we should deprive a wise man of any advantage to his wisdom, while we seek to restrain from a fool that which being restrained will be no hinderance to his folly. For if there should be so much exactness always used to keep that from him which is unfit for his reading, we should in the judgment of Aristotle not only, but of Solomon, and of our Saviour, not vouchsafe him good precepts, and by consequence not willingly admit him to good books; as being certain that a wise man will make better use of an idle pamphlet, than a fool will do of sacred scripture.

It is next alleged, we must not expose ourselves to temptations without necessity, and next to that, not employ our time in vain things. To both these objections one answer will serve, out of the grounds already laid, that to all men such books are not temptations, nor vanities; but useful drugs and materials wherewith to temper and compose effective and strong medicines, which man's life cannot want. The rest, as children and childish men, who have not the art to qualify and prepare these working minerals, well may be exhorted to forbear; but hindered forcibly they cannot be, by all the licensing that sainted inquisition could ever yet contrive; which is what I promised to deliver next: that this order of licensing conduces nothing to the end for which it was framed; and hath almost prevented me by being clear already while thus much hath been explaining. See the ingenuity of truth, who, when she gets a free and willing hand, opens herself faster than the pace of method and discourse can overtake her. It was the task which I began with, to shew that no nation, or well instituted state, if they valued books at all, did ever use this way of licensing; and it might be answered, that this is a piece of prudence lately discovered.

To which I return, that as it was a thing slight and obvious to think on, so if it had been difficult to find out, there wanted not among them long since, who suggested such a course; which they not following, leave us a pattern of their judgment that it was not the not knowing, but the not approving, which was the cause of their not using it. Plato, a man of high authority indeed, but least of all for his Commonwealth, in the book of his laws, which no city ever yet received, fed his fancy with making many edicts to his airy burgomasters, which they who otherwise admire him, wish had been rather buried and excused in the genial cups of an academic night sitting. By which laws he seems to tolerate no kind of learning, but by unalterable decree, consisting most of practical traditions, to the attainment whereof a library of smaller bulk than his own dialogues would be abundant. And there also enacts, that no poet should so much as read to any private man what he had written, until the judges and law keepers had seen it, and allowed it; but that Plato meant this law peculiarly to that commonwealth which he had imagined, and to no other, is evident. Why was he not else a lawgiver to himself, but a transgressor, and to be expelled by his own magistrates, both for the wanton epigrams and dialogues which he made, and his perpetual reading of Sophron Mimus and Aristophanes, books of grossest infamy; and also for commending the latter of them, though he were the malicious libeller of his chief friends, to be read by the tyrant Dionysius, who had little need of such trash to spend his time on? But that he knew this licensing of poems had reference and dependence to many other provisoes there set down in his fancied republic, which in this world could have no place; and so neither he himself, nor any magistrate or city, ever imitated that course, which, taken apart from those other collateral injunctions, must needs be vain and fruitless.

For if they fell upon one kind of strictness, unless their care were equal to regulate all other things of like aptness to corrupt the mind, that single endeavour they knew would be but a fond labour; to shut and fortify one gate against corruption, and be necessitated to leave others round about wide open. If we think to regulate printing, thereby to rectify manners, we must regulate all recreations and pastimes, all that is delightful to man. No music must be heard, no song be set or sung, but what is grave and doric. There must be licensing dancers, that no gesture, motion, or deportment be taught our youth, but what by their allowance shall be thought honest; for such Plato was provided of. It will ask more than the work of twenty licensers to examine all the lutes, the violins, and the guitars in every house; they must not be suffered to prattle as they do, but must be licensed what they may say. And who shall silence all the airs and madrigals that whisper softness in chambers? The windows also, and the balconies, must be thought on; these are shrewd books, with dangerous frontispieces, set to sale: who shall prohibit them, shall twenty licensers? The villages also must have their visitors to inquire what lectures the bagpipe and the rebec reads, even to the ballatry and the gamut of every municipal fiddler; for these are the countryman's Arcadias, and his Monte Mayors.

Next, what more national corruption, for which England hears ill abroad, than household gluttony? Who shall be the rectors of our daily rioting? And what shall be done to inhibit the multitudes that frequent those houses where drunkenness is sold and harboured? Our garments also should be referred to the licensing of some more sober work-masters, to see them cut into a less wanton garb. Who shall regulate all the mixed conversation of our youth, male and female together, as is the fashion of this country? Who shall still appoint what shall be discoursed, what presumed, and no further? Lastly, who shall forbid and separate all idle resort, all evil company? These things will be, and must be; but how they shall be least hurtful, how least enticing, herein consists the grave and governing wisdom of a state.

To sequester out of the world into Atlantic and Utopian politics, which never can be drawn into use, will not mend our condition; but to ordain wisely as in this world of evil, in the midst whereof God hath placed us unavoidably. Nor is it Plato's licensing of books will do this, which necessarily pulls along with it so many other kinds of licensing, as will make us all both ridiculous and weary, and yet frustrate; but those unwritten, or at least unconstraining laws of virtuous education, religious and civil nurture, which Plato there mentions, as the bonds and ligaments of the commonwealth, the pillars and the sustainers of every written statute; these they be, which will bear chief sway in such matters as these, when all licensing will be easily eluded. Impunity and remissness for certain are the bane of a commonwealth; but here the great art lies, to discern in what the law is to bid restraint and punishment, and in what things persuasion only is to work. If every action which is good or evil in man at ripe years were to be under pittance, prescription, and compulsion, what were virtue but a name, what praise could be then due to well doing, what gramercy to be sober, just, or continent?

Many there be that complain of divine Providence for suffering Adam to transgress. Foolish tongues! when God gave him reason, he gave him freedom to choose, for reason is but choosing; he had been else a mere artificial Adam, such an Adam as he is in the motions. We ourselves esteem not of that obedience, or love, or gift, which is of force; God therefore left him free, set before him a provoking object ever almost in his eyes; herein consisted his merit, herein the right of his reward, the praise of his abstinence. Wherefore did he create passions within us, pleasures round about us, but that these rightly tempered are the very ingredients of virtue? They are not skilful considerers of human things, who imagine to remove sin, by removing the matter of sin; for, besides that it is a huge heap increasing under the very act of diminishing, though some part of it may for a time be withdrawn from some persons, it cannot from all, in such a universal thing as books are; and when this is done, yet the sin remains entire. Though ye take from a covetous man all his treasure, he has yet one jewel left, ye cannot bereave him of his covetousness. Banish all objects of lust, shut up all youth into the severest discipline that can be exercised in any hermitage, ye cannot make them chaste, that came not thither so: such great care and wisdom is required to the right managing of this point.

Suppose we could expel sin by this means; look how much we thus expel of sin, so much we expel of virtue: for the matter of them both is the same: remove that, and ye remove them both alike. This justifies the high providence of God, who, though he commands us temperance, justice, continence, yet pours out before us even to a profuseness all desirable things, and gives us minds that can wander beyond all limit and satiety. Why should we then affect a rigour contrary to the manner of God and of nature, by abridging or scanting those means, which books freely permitted, are both to the trial of virtue, and the exercise of truth?

It would be better done, to learn that the law must needs be frivolous, which goes to restrain things, uncertainly and yet equally working to good and to evil.

And were I the chooser, a dram of well-doing should be preferred before many times as much the forcible hinderance of evil doing. For God sure esteems the growth and completing of one virtuous person, more than the restraint of ten vicious. And albeit, whatever thing we hear or see, sitting, walking, travelling, or conversing, may be fitly called our book, and is of the same effect that writings are; yet grant the thing to be prohibited were only books, it appears that this order hitherto is far insufficient to the end which it intends. Do we not see, not once or oftener, but weekly, that continued court-libel against the parliament and city, printed, as the wet sheets can witness, and dispersed among us for all that licensing can do? Yet this is the prime service a man would think wherein this order should give proof of itself. If it were executed, you will say. But certain, if execution be remiss or blindfold now, and in this particular, what will it be hereafter, and in other books?

If then the order shall not be vain and frustrate, behold a new labour, lords and commons, ye must repeal and proscribe all scandalous and unlicensed books already printed and divulged; after ye have drawn them up into a list, that all may know which are condemned, and which not; and ordain that no foreign books be delivered out of custody, till they have been read over. This office will require the whole time of not a few overseers, and those no vulgar men. There be also books which are partly useful and excellent, partly culpable and pernicious; this work will ask as many more officials, to make expurgations and expunctions, that the commonwealth of learning be not damnified. In fine, when the multitude of books increase upon their hands, ye must be fain to catalogue all those printers who are found frequently offending, and forbid the importation of their whole suspected typography. In a word, that this your order may be exact, and not deficient, ye must reform it perfectly, according to the model of Trent and Sevil, which I know ye abhor to do.

Yet though ye should condescend to this, which God forbid, the order still would be but fruitless and defective to that end whereto ye meant it. If to prevent sects and schisms, who is so unread or uncatechised in story, that hath not heard of many sects refusing books as a hinderance, and preserving their doctrine unmixed for many ages, only by unwritten traditions? The Christian faith (for that was once a schism!) is not unknown to have spread all over Asia, ere any gospel or epistle was seen in writing. If the amendment of manners be aimed at, look into Italy and Spain, whether those places be one scruple the better, the honester, the wiser, the chaster, since all the inquisitional rigour that hath been executed upon books.

Another reason, whereby to make it plain that this order will miss the end it seeks, consider by the quality which ought to be in every licenser. It cannot be denied, but that he who is made judge to sit upon the birth or death of books, whether they may be wafted into this world or not, had need to be a man above the common measure, both studious, learned, and judicious; there may be else no mean mistakes in the censure of what is passable or not; which is also no mean injury. If he be of such worth as behoves him, there cannot be a more tedious and unpleasing journeywork, a greater loss of time levied upon his head, than to be made the perpetual reader of unchosen books and pamphlets, ofttimes huge volumes. There is no book that is acceptable, unless at certain seasons; but to be enjoined the reading of that at all times, and in a hand scarce legible, whereof three pages would not down at any time in the fairest print, is an imposition I cannot believe how he that values time, and his own studies, or is but of a sensible nostril, should be able to endure. In this one thing I crave leave of the present licensers to be pardoned for so thinking: who doubtless took this office up, looking on it through their obedience to the parliament, whose command perhaps made all things seem easy and unlaborious to them; but that this short trial hath wearied them out already, their own expressions and excuses to them who make so many journeys to solicit their licence, are testimony enough. Seeing therefore those, who now possess the employment, by all evident signs wish themselves well rid of it, and that no man of worth, none that is not a plain unthrift of this own hours, is ever likely to succeed them, except he mean to put himself to the salary of a press corrector, we may easily foresee what kind of licensers we are to expect hereafter, either ignorant, imperious, and remiss, or basely pecuniary. This is what I had to show, wherein this order cannot conduce to that end whereof it bears the intention.

I lastly proceed from the no good it can do, to the manifest hurt it causes, in being first the greatest discouragement and affront that can be offered to learning and to learned men. It was the complaint and lamentation of prelates, upon every least of a motion to remove pluralities, and distribute more equally church revenues, that then all learning would be for ever dashed and discouraged. But as for that opinion, I never found cause to think that the tenth part of learning stood or fell with the clergy: nor could I ever but hold it for a sordid and unworthy speech of any churchman, who had a competency left him. If therefore ye be loath to dishearten utterly and discontent, not the mercenary crew of false pretenders to learning, but the free and ingenuous sort of such as evidently were born to study and love learning for itself, not for lucre, or any other end, but the service of God and of truth, and perhaps that lasting fame and perpetuity of praise, which God and good men have consented shall be the reward of those whose published labours advance the good of mankind: then know, that so far to distrust the judgment and the honesty of one who hath but a common repute in learning, and never yet offended, as not to count him fit to print his mind without a tutor and examiner, lest he should drop a schism, or something of corruption, is the greatest displeasure and indignity to a free and knowing spirit that can be put upon him.

What advantage is it to be a man, over it is to be a boy at school, if we have only escaped the ferula, to come under the fescue of an imprimatur? if serious and elaborate writings, as if they were no more than the theme of a grammar-lad under his pedagogue, must not be uttered without the cursory eyes of a temporizing and extemporizing licenser? He who is not trusted with his own actions, his drift not being known to be evil, and standing to the hazard of law and penalty, has no great argument to think himself reputed in the commonwealth wherein he was born for other than a fool or a foreigner. When a man writes to the world, he summons up all his reason and deliberation to assist him; he searches, meditates, is industrious, and likely consults and confers with his judicious friends; after all which done, he takes himself to be informed in what he writes, as well as any that wrote before him; if in this, the most consummate act of his fidelity and ripeness, no years, no industry, no former proof of his abilities, can bring him to that state of maturity, as not to be still mistrusted and suspected, unless he carry all his considerate diligence, all his midnight watchings, and expense of Palladian oil, to the hasty view of an unleisured licenser, perhaps much his younger, perhaps far his inferior in judgment, perhaps one who never knew the labour of bookwriting; and if he be not repulsed, or slighted, must appear in print like a puny with his guardian, and his censor's hand on the back of his title to be his bail and surety, that he is no idiot or seducer; it cannot be but a dishonour and derogation to the author, to the book, to the privilege and dignity of learning.

And what if the author shall be one so copious of fancy, as to have many things well worth the adding, come into his mind after licensing, while the book is yet under the press, which not seldom happens to the best and diligentest writers; and that perhaps a dozen times in one book. The printer dares not go beyond his licensed copy; so often then must the author trudge to his leave-giver, that those his new insertions may be viewed; and many a jaunt will be made, ere that licenser, for it must be the same man, can either be found, or found at leisure; meanwhile either the press must stand still, which is no small damage, or the author lose his accuratest thoughts, and send the book forth worse than he had made it, which to a diligent writer is the greatest melancholy and vexation that can befall.

And how can a man teach with authority, which is the life of teaching; how can he be a doctor in his book, as he ought to be, or else had better be silent, whenas all he teaches, all he delivers, is but under the tuition, under the correction of his patriarchal licenser, to blot or alter what precisely accords not with the hide-bound humour which he calls his judgment? When every acute reader, upon the first sight of a pedantic licence, will be ready with these like words to ding the book a quoit's distance from him: — "I hate a pupil teacher; I endure not an instructor that comes to me under the wardship of an overseeing fist. I know nothing of the licenser, but that I have his own hand here for his arrogance; who shall warrant me his judgment?" "The state, sir," replies the stationer: but has a quick return: — "The state shall be my governors, but not my critics; they may be mistaken in the choice of a licenser, as easily as this licenser may be mistaken in an author. This is some common stuff:" and he might add from Sir Francis Bacon, that "such authorized books are but the language of the times." For though a licenser should happen to be judicious more than ordinary, which will be a great jeopardy of the next succession, yet his very office and his commission enjoins him to let pass nothing but what is vulgarly received already.

Nay, which is more lamentable, if the work of any deceased author, though never so famous in his lifetime, and even to this day, comes to their hands for licence to be printed, or reprinted, if there be found in his book one sentence of a venturous edge, uttered in the height of zeal, (and who knows whether it might not be the dictate of a divine spirit?) yet, not suiting with every low decrepit humour of their own, though it were Knox himself, the reformer of a kingdom, that spake it, they will not pardon him their dash; the sense of that great man shall to all posterity be lost, for the fearfulness, or the presumptuous rashness of a perfunctory licenser. And to what an author this violence hath been lately done, and in what book, of greatest consequence to be faithfully published, I could now instance, but shall forbear till a more convenient season. Yet if these things be not resented seriously and timely by them who have the remedy in their power, but that such iron moulds as these shall have authority to gnaw out the choicest periods of exquisitest books, and to commit such a treacherous fraud against the orphan remainders of worthiest men after death, the more sorrow will belong to that hapless race of men, whose misfortune it is to have understanding.

Henceforth let no man care to learn, or care to be more than worldly wise; for certainly in higher matters to be ignorant and slothful, to be a common steadfast dunce, will be the only pleasant life, and only in request.

And as it is a particular disesteem of every knowing person alive, and most injurious to the written labours and monuments of the dead, so to me it seems an undervaluing and vilifying of the whole nation. I cannot set so light by all the invention, the art, the wit, the grave and solid judgment which is in England, as that it can be comprehended in any twenty capacities, how good soever; much less that it should not pass except their superintendence be over it, except it be sifted and strained with their strainers, that it should be uncurrent without their manual stamp. Truth and understanding are not such wares as to be monopolized and traded in by tickets, and statutes, and standards. We must not think to make a staple commodity of all the knowledge in the land, to mark and license it like our broad-cloth and our woolpacks. What is it but a servitude like that imposed by the Philistines, not to be allowed the sharpening of our own axes and coulters, but we must repair from all quarters to twenty licensing forges?

Had any one written and divulged erroneous things and scandalous to honest life, misusing and forfeiting the esteem had of his reason among men, if after conviction this only censure were adjudged him, that he should never henceforth write, but what were first examined by an appointed officer, whose hand should be annexed to pass his credit for him, that now he might be safely read; it could not be apprehended less than a disgraceful punishment. Whence to include the whole nation, and those that never yet thus offended, under such a diffident and suspectful prohibition, may plainly be understood what a disparagement it is. So much the more whenas debtors and delinquents may walk abroad without a keeper, but unoffensive books must not stir forth without a visible jailor in their title. Nor is it to the common people less than a reproach; for if we be so jealous over them, as that we dare not trust them with an English pamphlet, what do we but censure them for a giddy, vicious, and ungrounded people; in such a sick and weak state of faith and discretion, as to be able to take nothing down but through the pipe of a licenser? That this is care or love of them, we cannot pretend, whenas in those popish places, where the laity are most hated and despised, the same strictness is used over them. Wisdom we cannot call it, because it stops but one breach of licence, nor that neither: whenas those corruptions, which it seeks to prevent, break in faster at other doors, which cannot be shut.

And in conclusion it reflects to the disrepute of our ministers also, of whose labours we should hope better, and of their proficiency which their flock reaps by them, than that after all this light of the gospel which is, and is to be, and all this continual preaching, they should be still frequented with such an unprincipled, unedified, and laic rabble, as that the whiff of every new pamphlet should stagger them out of their catechism and Christian walking. This may have much reason to discourage the ministers, when such a low conceit is had of all their exhortations, and the benefiting of their hearers, as that they are not thought fit to be turned loose to three sheets of paper without a licenser; that all the sermons, all the lectures preached, printed, vended in such numbers, and such volumes, as have now well-nigh made all other books unsaleable, should not be armour enough against one single Enchiridion, without the castle of St. Angelo of an imprimatur.

And lest some should persuade ye, lords and commons, that these arguments of learned men's discouragement at this your order are mere flourishes, and not real,

I could recount what I have seen and heard in other countries, where this kind of inquisition tyrannizes; when I have sat among their learned men, (for that honour I had,) and been counted happy to be born in such a place of philosophic freedom, as they supposed England was, while themselves did nothing but bemoan the servile condition into which learning amongst them was brought; that this was it which had damped the glory of Italian wits; that nothing had been there written now these many years but flattery and fustian. There it was that I found and visited the famous Galileo, grown old, a prisoner to the inquisition, for thinking in astronomy otherwise than the Franciscan and Dominican licensers thought. And though I knew that England then was groaning loudest under the prelatical yoke, nevertheless I took it as a pledge of future happiness, that other nations were so persuaded of her liberty.

Yet was it beyond my hope, that those worthies were then breathing in her air, who should be her leaders to such a deliverance, as shall never be forgotten by any revolution of time that this world hath to finish. When that was once begun, it was as little in my fear, that what words of complaint I heard among learned men of other parts uttered against the inquisition, the same I should hear, by as learned men at home, uttered in time of parliament against an order of licensing; and that so generally, that when I had disclosed myself a companion of their discontent, I might say, if without envy, that he whom an honest quæstorship has endeared to the Sicilians, was not more by them importuned against Verres, than the favourable opinion which I had among many who honour ye, and are known and respected by ye, loaded me with entreaties and persuasions, that I would not despair to lay together that which just reason should bring into my mind, towards the removal of an undeserved thraldom upon learning.

That this is not therefore the disburdening of a particular fancy, but the common grievance of all those who had prepared their minds and studies above the vulgar pitch, to advance truth in others, and from others to entertain it, thus much may satisfy. And in their name I shall for neither friend nor foe conceal what the general murmur is; that if it come to inquisitioning again, and licensing, and that we are so timorous of ourselves, and suspicious of all men, as to fear each book, and the shaking of each leaf, before we know what the contents are; if some who but of late were little better than silenced from preaching, shall come now to silence us from reading, except what they please, it cannot be guessed what is intended by some but a second tyranny over learning: and will soon put it out of controversy, that bishops and presbyters are the same to us, both name and thing.

That those evils of prelaty which before from five or six and twenty sees were distributively charged upon the whole people will now light wholly upon learning, is not obscure to us: whenas now the pastor of a small unlearned parish, on the sudden shall be exalted archbishop over a large diocess of books, and yet not remove, but keep his other cure too, a mystical pluralist. He who but of late cried down the sole ordination of every novice bachelor of art, and denied sole jurisdiction over the simplest parishioner, shall now at home in his private chair, assume both these over worthiest and excellentest books, and ablest authors that write them. This is not the covenants and protestations that we have made! This is not to put down prelacy; this is but to chop an episcopacy; this is but to translate the palace metropolitan from one kind of dominion into another; this is but an old canonical sleight of commuting our penance. To startle thus betimes at a mere unlicensed pamphlet, will, after a while, be afraid of every conventicle, and a while after will make a conventicle of every Christian meeting.

But I am certain, that a state governed by the rules of justice and fortitude, or a church built and founded upon the rock of faith and true knowledge, cannot be so pusillanimous. While things are yet not constituted in religion, that freedom of writing should be restrained by a discipline imitated from the prelates, and learned by them from the inquisition to shut us up all again into the breast of a licenser, must needs give cause of doubt and discouragement to all learned and religious men; who cannot but discern the fineness of this politic drift, and who are the contrivers; that while bishops were to be baited down, then all presses might be open; it was the people's birthright and privilege in time of parliament, it was the breaking forth of light.

But now the bishops abrogated and voided out of the church, as if our reformation sought no more, but to make room for others into their seats under another name; the episcopal arts begin to bud again; the cruise of truth must run no more oil; liberty of printing must be enthralled again, under a prelatical commission of twenty; the privilege of the people nullified; and, which is worse, the freedom of learning must groan again, and to her old fetters: all this the parliament yet sitting. Although their own late arguments and defences against the prelates might remember them, that this obstructing violence meets for the most part with an event utterly opposite to the end which it drives at: instead of suppressing sects and schisms, it raises them and invests them with a reputation: "The punishing of wits enhances their authority," saith the Viscount St. Albans; "and a forbidden writing is thought to be a certain spark of truth, that flies up in the faces of them who seek to tread it out." This order, therefore, may prove a nursing mother to sects, but I shall easily shew how it will be stepdame to truth: and first, by disenabling us to the maintenance of what is known already.

Well knows he who uses to consider, that our faith and knowledge thrives by exercise, as well as our limbs and complexion. Truth is compared in scripture to a streaming fountain; if her waters flow not in a perpetual progression, they sicken into a muddy pool of conformity and tradition. A man may be a heretic in the truth; and if he believes things only because his pastor says so, or the assemby so determines, without knowing other reason, though his belief be true, yet the very truth he holds becomes his heresy. There is not any burden that some would gladlier post off to another, than the charge and care of their religion. There be, who knows not that there be? of protestants and professors, who live and die in as errant and implicit faith, as any lay papist of Loretto.

A wealthy man, addicted to his pleasure and to his profits, finds religion to be a traffic so entangled, and of so many piddling accounts, that of all mysteries he cannot skill to keep a stock going upon that trade. What should he do? Fain he would have the name to be religious, fain he would bear up with his neighbours in that. What does he therefore, but resolves to give over toiling, and to find himself out some factor, to whose care and credit he may commit the whole managing of his religious affairs; some divine of note and estimation that must be. To him he adheres, resigns the whole warehouse of his religion, with all the locks and keys, into his custody; and indeed makes the very person of that man his religion; esteems his associating with him a sufficient evidence and commendatory of his own piety. So that a man may say his religion is now no more within himself, but is become a dividual moveable, and goes and comes near him, according as that good man frequents the house. He entertains him, gives him gifts, feasts him, lodges him; his religion comes home at night, prays, is liberally supped, and sumptuously laid to sleep; rises, is saluted, and after the malmsey, or some well-spiced bruage, and better breakfasted, than He whose morning appetite would have gladly fed on green figs between Bethany and Jerusalem, his religion walks abroad at eight, and leaves his kind entertainer in the shop trading all day without his religion.

Another sort there be, who when they hear that all things shall be ordered, all things regulated and settled; nothing written but what passes through the custom-house of certain publicans that have the tonnaging and poundaging of all free-spoken truth, will straight give themselves up into your hands, make them and cut them out what religion ye please: there be delights, there be recreations and jolly pastimes, that will fetch the day about from sun to sun, and rock the tedious year as in a delightful dream. What need they torture their heads with that which others have taken so strictly, and so unalterably into their own purveying? These are the fruits which a dull ease and cessation of our knowledge will bring forth among the people. How goodly, and how to be wished were such an obedient unanimity as this! What a fine conformity would it starch us all into! Doubtless a staunch and solid piece of framework, as any January could freeze together.

Nor much better will be the consequence even among the clergy themselves: it is no new thing never heard of before, for a parochial minister, who has his reward, and is at his Hercules' pillars in a warm benefice, to be easily inclinable, if he have nothing else that may rouse up his studies, to finish his circuit in an English Concordance and a topic folio, the gatherings and savings of a sober graduateship, a Harmony and a Catena, treading the constant round of certain common doctrinal heads, attended with their uses, motives, marks and means; out of which, as out of an alphabet or sol-fa, by forming and transforming, joining and disjoining variously, a little bookcraft, and two hours' meditation, might furnish him unspeakably to the performance of more than a weekly charge of sermoning: not to reckon up the infinite helps of interliniaries, breviaries, synopses, and other loitering gear. But as for the multitude of sermons ready printed and piled up, on every text that is not difficult, our London trading St. Thomas in his vestry, and add to boot St. Martin and St. Hugh, have not within their hallowed limits more vendible ware of all sorts ready made: so that penury he never need fear of pulpit provision, having where so plenteously to refresh his magazine. But if his rear and flanks be not impaled, if his back door be not secured by the rigid licenser, but that a bold book may now and then issue forth, and give the assault to some of his old collections in their trenches, it will concern him then to keep waking, to stand in watch, to set good guards and sentinels about his received opinions, to walk the round and counterround with his fellow-inspectors, fearing lest any of his flock be seduced who also then would be better instructed, better exercised, and disciplined. And God send that the fear of this diligence, which must then be used, do not make us affect the laziness of a licensing church!

For if we be sure we are in the right, and do not hold the truth guiltily, which becomes not, if we ourselves condemn not our own weak and frivolous teaching, and the people for an untaught and irreligious gadding route; what can be more fair, than when a man judicious, learned, and of a conscience, for aught we know, as good as theirs that taught us what we know, shall not privily from house to house, which is more dangerous, but openly by writing, publish to the world what his opinion is, what his reasons, and wherefore that which is now thought cannot be sound? Christ urged it as wherewith to justify himself, that he preached in public; yet writing is more public than preaching; and more easy to refutation if need be, there being so many whose business and profession merely it is to be the champions of truth; which if they neglect, what can be imputed but their sloth or inability?

Thus much we are hindered and disinured by this course of licensing towards the new knowledge of what we seem to know. For how much it hurts and hinders the licensers themselves in the calling of their ministry, more than any secular employment, if they will discharge that office as they ought, so that of necessity they must neglect either the one duty or the other, I insist not, because it is a particular, but leave it to their own conscience, how they will decide it there.

There is yet behind of what I purposed to lay open, the incredible loss and detriment that this plot of licensing puts us to, more than if some enemy at sea should stop up all our havens, and ports, and creeks; it hinders and retards the importation of our richest merchandise, — truth: nay, it was first established and put in practice by anti-christian malice and mystery, or set purpose to extinguish, if it were possible, the light of reformation, and to settle falsehood; little differing from that policy wherewith the Turk upholds his Alcoran, by the prohibiting of printing. It is not denied, but gladly confessed, we are to send our thanks and vows to heaven, louder than most of nations, for that great measure of truth which we enjoy, especially in those main points between us and the pope, with his appurtenances the prelates: but he who thinks we are to pitch our tent here, and have attained the utmost prospect of reformation that the mortal glass wherein we contemplate can shew us, till we come to beatific vision, that man by this very opinion declares that he is yet far short of truth.

Truth indeed came once into the world with her divine master, and was a perfect shape most glorious to look on: but when he ascended, and his apostles after him were laid asleep, then straight arose a wicked race of deceivers, who, as that story goes of the Egyptian Typhon with his conspirators, how they dealt with the good Osiris, took the virgin Truth, hewed her lovely form into a thousand pieces, and scattered them to the four winds. From that time ever since, the sad friends of Truth, such as durst appear, imitating the careful search that Isis made for the mangled body of Osiris, went up and down gathering up limb by limb still as they could find them. We have not yet found them all, lords and commons, nor ever shall do, till her Master's second coming; he shall bring together every joint and member, and shall mould them into an immortal feature of loveliness and perfection. Suffer not these licensing prohibitions to stand at every place of opportunity forbidding and disturbing them that continue seeking, that continue to do our obsequies to the torn body of our martyred saint.

We boast our light; but if we look not wisely on the sun itself, it smites us into darkness. Who can discern those planets that are oft combust, and those stars of brightest magnitude that rise and set with the sun, until the opposite motion of their orbs bring them to such a place in the firmament, where they may be seen evening or morning? The light which we have gained was given us, not to be ever staring on, but by it to discover onward things more remote from our knowledge. It is not the unfrocking of a priest, the unmitring of a bishop, and the removing him from off the presbyterian shoulders, that will make us a happy nation: no; if other things as great in the church, and in the rule of life both economical and political, be not looked into and reformed, we have looked so long upon the blaze that Zuinglius and Calvin have beaconed up to us, that we are stark blind.

There be who perpetually complain of schisms and sects, and make it such a calamity that any man dissents from their maxims. It is their own pride and ignorance which causes the disturbing, who neither will hear with meekness, nor can convince, yet all must be suppressed which is not found in their Syntagma. They are the troublers, they are the dividers of unity, who neglect and permit not others to unite those disservered pieces, which are yet wanting to the body of truth. To be still searching what we know not, by what we know, still closing up truth to truth as we find it, (for all her body is homogeneal, and proportional,) this is the golden rule in theology as well as in arithmetic, and makes up the best harmony in a church; not the forced and outward union of cold, and neutral, and inwardly divided minds.

Lords and commons of England! consider what nation it is whereof ye are, and whereof ye are the governors: a nation now slow and dull, but of a quick, ingenious, and piercing spirit; acute to invent, subtile and sinewy to discourse, not beneath the reach of any point the highest that human capacity can soar to. Therefore the studies of learning in her deepest sciences have been so ancient, and so eminent among us, that writers of good antiquity and able judgment have been persuaded, that even the school of Pythagoras, and the Persian wisdom, took beginning from the old philosophy of this island. And that wise and civil Roman, Julius Agricola, who governed once here for Cæsar, preferred the natural wits of Britain before the laboured studies of the French.

Nor is it for nothing that the grave and frugal Transylvanian sends out yearly from as far as the mountainous borders of Russia, and beyond the Hercynian wilderness, not their youth, but their staid men, to learn our language and our theological arts. Yet that which is above all this, the favour and the love of Heaven, we have great argument to think in a peculiar manner propitious and propending towards us. Why else was this nation chosen before any other, that out of her, as out of Sion, should be proclaimed and sounded forth the first tidings and trumpet of reformation to all Europe? And had it not been the obstinate perverseness of our prelates against the divine and admirable spirit of Wickliffe, to suppress him as a schismatic and innovator, perhaps neither the Bohemian Husse and Jerome, no, nor the name of Luther or of Calvin, had been ever known: the glory of reforming all our neighbours had been completely ours. But now, as our obdurate clergy have with violence demeaned the matter, we are become hitherto the latest and the backwardest scholars, of whom God offered to have made us the teachers.

Now once again by all concurrence of signs, and by the general instinct of holy and devout men, as they daily and solemnly express their thoughts, God is decreeing to begin some new and great period in his church, even to the reforming of reformation itself; what does he then but reveal himself to his servants, and as his manner is, first to his Englishmen? I say, as his manner is, first to us, though we mark not the method of his counsels, and are unworthy. Behold now this vast city, a city of refuge, the mansion-house of liberty, encompassed and surrounded with his protection; the shop of war hath not there more anvils and hammers working, to fashion out the plates and instruments of armed justice in defence of beleagured truth, than there be pens and heads there, sitting by their studious lamps, musing, searching, revolving new notions and ideas wherewith to present, as with their homage and their fealty, the approaching reformation: others as fast reading, trying all things, assenting to the force of reason and convincement.

What could a man require more from a nation so pliant and so prone to seek after knowledge? What wants there to such a towardly and pregnant soil, but wise and faithful labourers, to make a knowing people, a nation of prophets, of sages, and of worthies? We reckon more than five months yet to harvest; there need not be five weeks, had we but eyes to lift up, the fields are white already. Where there is much desire to learn, there of necessity will be much arguing, much writing, many opinions; for opinion in good men is but knowledge in the making. Under these fantastic terrors of sect and schism, we wrong the earnest and zealous thirst after knowledge and understanding, which God hath stirred up in this city. What some lament of, we rather should rejoice at, should rather praise this pious forwardness among men, to reassume the ill-deputed care of their religion into their own hands again. A little generous prudence, a little forbearance of one another, and some grain of charity might win all these diligencies to join and unite into one general and brotherly search after truth; could we but forego this prelatical tradition of crowding free consciences and Christian liberties into canons and precepts of men. I doubt not, if some great and worthy stranger should come among us, wise to discern the mould and temper of a people, and how to govern it, observing the high hopes and aims, the diligent alacrity of our extended thoughts and reasonings in the pursuance of truth and freedom, but that he would cry out as Pyrrhus did, admiring the Roman docility and courage, "If such were my Epirots, I would not despair the greatest design that could be attempted to make a church or kingdom happy."

Yet these are the men cried out against for schismatics and sectaries, as if, while the temple of the Lord was building, some cutting, some squaring the marble, others hewing the cedars, there should be a sort of irrational men, who could not consider there must be many schisms and many dissections made in the quarry and in the timber ere the house of God can be built. And when every stone is laid artfully together, it cannot be united into a continuity, it can but be contiguous in this world: neither can every piece of the building be of one form; nay, rather the perfection consists in this, that out of many moderate varieties and brotherly dissimilitudes that are not vastly disproportional, arises the goodly and the graceful symmetry than commends the whole pile and structure.

Let us therefore be more considerate builders, more wise in spiritual architecture, when great reformation is expected. For now the time seems come, wherein Moses, the great prophet, may sit in heaven rejoicing to see that memorable and glorious wish of his fulfilled, when not only our seventy elders, but all the Lord's people, are become prophets. No marvel then though some men, and some good men too perhaps, but young in goodness, as Joshua then was, envy them. They fret, and out of their own weakness are in agony, lest these divisions and subdivisions will undo us. The adversary again applauds, and waits the hour: when they have branched themselves out, saith he, small enough into parties and partitions, then will be our time. Fool! he sees not the firm root, out of which we all grow, though into branches; nor will beware, until he see our small divided maniples cutting through at every angle of his ill-united and unwieldy brigade.

And that we are to hope better of all these supposed sects and schisms, and that we shall not need that solicitude, honest perhaps, though overtimorous, of them that vex in this behalf, but shall laugh in the end at those malicious applauders of our differences, I have these reasons to persuade me.

First, when a city shall be as it were besieged and blocked about, her navigable river infested, inroads and incursions round, defiance and battle oft rumoured to be marching up, even to her walls and suburb trenches; that then the people, or the greater part, more than at other times, wholly taken up with the study of highest and most important matters to be reformed, should be disputing, reasoning, reading, inventing, discoursing, even to a rarity and admiration, things not before discoursed or written of, argues first a singular good will, contentedness, and confidence in your prudent foresight, and safe government, lords and commons; and from thence derives itself to a gallant bravery and well-grounded contempt of their enemies, as if there were no small number of as great spirits among us, as his was who, when Rome was nigh besieged by Hannibal, being in the city, bought that piece of ground at no cheap rate whereon Hannibal himself encamped his own regiment.

Next, it is a lively and cheerful presage of our happy success and victory. For as in a body when the blood is fresh, the spirits pure and vigorous, not only to vital, but to rational faculties, and those in the acutest and the pertest operations of wit and subtlety, it argues in what good plight and constitution the body is; so when the cheerfulness of the people is so sprightly up, as that it has not only wherewith to guard well its own freedom and safety, but to spare, and to bestow upon the solidest and sublimest points of controversy and new invention, it betokens us not degenerated, nor drooping to a fatal decay, by casting off the old and wrinkled skin of corruption to outlive these pangs, and wax young again, entering the glorious ways of truth and prosperous virtue, destined to become great and honourable in these latter ages. Methinks I see in my mind a noble and puissant nation rousing herself like a strong man after sleep, and shaking her invincible locks: methinks I see her as an eagle mewing her mighty youth, and kindling her undazzled eyes at the full midday beam; purging and unscaling her long-abused sight at the fountain itself of heavenly radiance; while the whole noise of timorous and flocking birds, with those also that love the twilight, flutter about, amazed at what she means, and in their envious gabble would prognosticate a year of sects and schisms.

What should ye do then, should ye suppress all this flowery crop of knowledge and new light sprung up and yet springing daily in this city? Should ye set an oligarchy of twenty engrossers over it, to bring a famine upon our minds again, when we shall know nothing but what is measured to us by their bushel? Believe it, lords and commons! they who counsel ye to such a suppressing, do as good as bid ye suppress yourselves; and I will soon show how. If it be desired to know the immediate cause of all this free writing and free speaking, there cannot be assigned a truer than your own mild, and free, and humane government; it is the liberty, lords and commons, which your own valorous and happy counsels have purchased us; liberty which is the nurse of all great wits: this is that which hath rarified and enlightened our spirits like the influence of heaven: this is that which hath enfranchised, enlarged, and lifted up our apprehensions degrees above themselves. Ye cannot make us now less capable, less knowing, less eagerly pursuing of the truth, unless ye first make yourselves, that made us so, less the lovers, less the founders of our true liberty. We can grow ignorant again, brutish, formal, and slavish, as ye found us; but you then must first become that which ye cannot be, oppressive, arbitrary, and tyrannous, as they were from whom ye have freed us. That our hearts are now more capacious, our thoughts more erected to the search and expectation of greatest and exactest things, is the issue of your own virtue propagated in us; ye cannot suppress that unless ye reinforce an abrogated and merciless law, that fathers may dispatch at will their own children. And who shall then stick closest to ye and excite others? Not he who takes up arms for coat and conduct, and his four nobles of Danegelt. Although I dispraise not the defence of just immunities, yet love my peace better, if that were all. Give me the liberty to know, to utter, and to argue freely according to conscience, above all liberties.

What would be best advised then, if it be found so hurtful and so unequal to suppress opinions for the newness or the unsuitableness to a customary acceptance, will not be my task to say; I shall only repeat what I have learned from one of your own honourable number, a right noble and pious lord, who had he not sacrificed his life and fortunes to the church and commonwealth, we had not now missed and bewailed a worthy and undoubted patron of this argument. Ye know him, I am sure; yet I for honour's sake, and it be eternal to him, shall name him, the Lord Brook. He writing of episcopacy, and by the way treating of sects and schisms, left ye his vote, or rather now the last words of his dying charge, which I know will ever be of dear and honoured regard with ye, so full of meekness and breathing charity, that next to His last testament, who bequeathed love and peace to his disciples, I cannot call to mind where I have read or heard words more mild and peaceful. He there exhorts us to hear with patience and humility those, however they be miscalled, that desire to live purely, in such a use of God's ordinances, as the best guidance of their conscience gives them, and to tolerate them, though in some disconformity to ourselves. The book itself will tell us more at large, being published to the world, and dedicated to the parliament by him, who both for his life and for his death deserves, that what advice he left be not laid by without perusal.

And now the time in special is, by privilege to write and speak what may help to the further discussing of matters in agitation. The temple of Janus, with his two controversial faces, might now not unsignificantly be set open. And though all the winds of doctrine were let loose to play upon the earth, so truth be in the field, we do injuriously by licensing and prohibiting to misdoubt her strength. Let her and falsehood grapple; who ever knew truth put to the worse, in a free and open encounter? Her confuting is the best and surest suppressing. He who hears what praying there is for light and clear knowledge to be sent down among us, would think of other matters to be constituted beyond the discipline of Geneva, framed and fabricated already to our hands.

Yet when the new light which we beg for shines in upon us, there be who envy and oppose, if it come not first in at their casements. What a collusion is this, whenas we are exhorted by the wise man to use diligence, "to seek for wisdom as for hidden treasures," early and late, that another order shall enjoin us, to know nothing but by statute? When a man hath been labouring the hardest labour in the deep mines of knowledge, hath furnished out his findings in all their equipage, drawn forth his reasons as it were a battle ranged, scattered and defeated all objections in his way, calls out his adversary into the plain, offers him the advantage of wind and sun, if he please, only that he may try the matter by dint of argument; for his opponents then to skulk, to lay ambushments, to keep a narrow bridge of licensing where the challenger should pass, though it be valour enough in soldiership, is but weakness and cowardice in the wars of truth. For who knows not that truth is strong, next to the Almighty; she needs no policies, nor stratagems, nor licensings to make her victorious; those are the shifts and the defences that error uses against her power: give her but room, and do not bind her when she sleeps, for then she speaks not true, as the old Proteus did, who spake oracles only when he was caught and bound, but then rather she turns herself into all shapes except her own, and perhaps tunes her voice according to the time, as Micaiah did before Ahab, until she be adjured into her own likeness.

Yet is it not impossible that she may have more shapes than one? What else is all that rank of things indifferent, wherein truth may be on this side, or on the other, without being unlike herself? What but a vain shadow else is the abolition of "those ordinances, that hand-writing nailed to the cross?" What great purchase is this Christian liberty which Paul so often boasts of? His doctrine is, that he who eats or eats not, regards a day or regards it not, may do either to the Lord. How many other things might be tolerated in peace, and left to conscience, had we but charity, and were it not the chief stronghold of our hypocrisy to be ever judging one another? I fear yet this iron yoke of outward conformity hath left a slavish print upon our necks; the ghost of a linen decency yet haunts us. We stumble, and are impatient at the least dividing of one visible congregation from another, though it be not in fundamentals; and through our forwardness to suppress, and our backwardness to recover, any enthralled piece of truth out of the gripe of custom, we care not to keep truth separated from truth, which is the fiercest rent and disunion of all. We do not see that while we still affect by all means a rigid external formality, we may as soon fall again into a gross conforming stupidity, a stark and dead congealment of "wood and hay and stubble" forced and frozen together, which is more to the sudden degenerating of a church than many subdichotomies of petty schisms.

Not that I can think well of every light separation; of that all in a church is to be expected "gold and silver, and precious stones:" it is not possible for man to sever the wheat from the tares, the good fish from the other fry; that must be the angels' ministry at the end of mortal things. Yet if all cannot be of one mind, as who looks they should be? this doubtless is more wholesome, more prudent, and more Christian, that many be tolerated rather than all compelled. I mean not tolerated popery, and open superstition, which as it extirpates all religions and civil supremacies, so itself should be extirpate, provided first that all charitable and compassionate means be used to win and regain the weak and the misled: that also which is impious or evil absolutely either against faith or manners, no law can possibly permit, that intends not to unlaw itself: but those neighbouring differences, or rather indifferences, are what I speak of, whether in some point of doctrine or of discipline, which though they may be many, yet need not interrupt the unity of spirit, if we could but find among us the bond of peace.

In the meanwhile, if any one would write, and bring his helpful hand to the slow-moving reformation which we labour under, if truth have spoken to him before others, or but seemed at least to speak, who hath so bejesuited us, that we should trouble that man with asking licence to do so worthy a deed; and not consider this, that if it come to prohibiting, there is not aught more likely to be prohibited than truth itself: whose first appearance to our eyes, bleared and dimmed with prejudice and custom, is more unsightly and unplausible than many errors; even as the person is of many a great man slight and contemptible to see to. And what do they tell us vainly of new opinions, when this very opinion of theirs, that none must be heard but whom they like, is the worst and newest opinion of all others; and is the chief cause why sects and schisms do so much abound, and true knowledge is kept at distance from us; besides yet a greater danger which is in it. For when God shakes a kingdom, with strong and healthful commotions, to a general reforming, it is not untrue that many sectaries and false teachers are then busiest in seducing.

But yet more true it is, that God then raises to his own work men of rare abilities, and more than common industry, not only to look back and revive what hath been taught heretofore, but to gain further, and to go on some new enlightened steps in the discovery of truth. For such is the order of God's enlightening his church, to dispense and deal out by degrees his beam, so as our earthly eyes may best sustain it. Neither is God appointed and confined, where and out of what place these his chosen shall be first heard to speak; for he sees not as man sees, chooses not as man chooses, lest we should devote ourselves again to set places and assemblies, and outward callings of men; planting our faith one while in the old convocation house; and another while in the chapel at Westminster; when all the faith and religion that shall be there canonized, is not sufficient without plain convincement, and the charity of patient instruction, to supple the least bruise of conscience, to edify the meanest Christian, who desires to walk in the spirit, and not in the letter of human trust, for all the number of voices that can be there made; no, though Harry the Seventh himself there, with all his liege tombs about him, should lend them voices from the dead to swell their number.

And if the men be erroneous who appear to be the leading schismatics, what wthholds us but our sloth, our self-will, and distrust in the right cause, that we do not give them gentle meetings and gentle dismissions, that we debate not and examine the matter thoroughly with liberal and frequent audience; if not for their sakes yet for our own? Seeing no man who hath tasted learning, but will confess the many ways of profiting by those who, not contented with stale receipts, are able to manage and set forth new positions to the world. And were they but as the dust and cinders of our feet, so long as in that notion they may yet serve to polish and brighten the armoury of truth, even for that respect they were not utterly to be cast away. But if they be of those whom God hath fitted for the special use of these times with eminent and ample gifts, and those perhaps neither among the priests, nor among the pharisees, and we, in the haste of a precipitant zeal, shall make no distinction, but resolve to stop their mouths, because we fear they come with new and dangerous opinions, as we commonly forejudge them ere we understand them; no less that woe to us, while, thinking thus to defend the gospel, we are found the persecutors!

There have been not a few since the beginning of this parliament, both of the presbytery and others, who by their unlicensed books to the contempt of an imprimatur first broke that triple ice clung about our hearts, and taught the people to see day; I hope that none of those were the persuaders to renew upon us this bondage, which they themselves have wrought so much good by contemning. But if neither the check that Moses gave to young Joshua, nor the countermand which our Saviour gave to young John, who was so ready to prohibit those whom he thought unlicensed, be not enough to admonish our elders how unacceptable to God their testy mood of prohibiting is; if neither their own remembrance what evil hath abounded in the church by this lett of licensing, and what good they themselves have begun by transgressing it, be not enough, but that they will persuade and execute the most Dominican part of the inquisition over us, and are already with one foot in the stirrup so active at suppressing, it would be no unequal distribution in the first place to suppress the suppressors themselves; whom the change of their condition hath puffed up, more than their late experience of harder times hath made wise.

And as for regulating the press, let no man think to have the honour of advising ye better than yourselves have done in that order published next before this, "That no book be printed, unless the printer's and the author's name, or at least the printer's be registered." Those which otherwise come forth, if they be found mischievous and libellous, the fire and the executioner will be the timeliest and the most effectual remedy than man's prevention can use. For this authentic Spanish policy of licensing books, if I have said aught, will prove the most unlicensed book itself within a short while; and was the immediate image of a star-chamber decree to that purpose made in those times when that court did the rest of those her pious works, for which she is now fallen from the stars with Lucifer. Whereby ye may guess what kind of state prudence, what love of the people, what care of religion or good manners there was at the contriving, although with singular hypocrisy it pretended to bind books to their good behavior. And how it got the upper hand of your precedent order so well constituted before, if we may believe those men whose profession gives them cause to inquire most, it may be doubted there was in it the fraud of some old patentees and monopolizers, in the trade of bookselling; who under pretence of the poor in their company not to be defrauded, and the just retaining of each man his several copy, (which God forbid should be gainsaid,) brought divers glossing colours to the house, which were indeed by colours, and serving to no end except it be to exercise a superiority over their neighbours; men who do not therefore labour in an honest profession, to which learning is indebted, that they should be made other men's vassals. Another end is thought was aimed at by some of them in procuring by petition this order, that having power in their hands, malignant books might the easier escape abroad, as the event shows. But of these sophisms and elenchs of merchandise I skill not: this I know, that errors in a good government and in a bad are equally almost incident; for what magistrate may not be misinformed, and much the sooner, if liberty of printing be reduced into the power of a few? But to redress willingly and speedily what hath been erred, and in highest authority to esteem a plain advertisement more than others have done a sumptuous bride, is a virtue (honoured lords and commons!) answerable to your highest actions, and whereof none can participate but greatest and wisest men.

# 4

Robert Browne was the principal theorist of that branch of radical Protestantism which took the name of Brownists, or Separatists. It was from this group, which rejected any compromise with the Church of England and wished to "separate" from it, that the settlers of the Plymouth Plantation (the so-called Pilgrims) were drawn.

Especially to be noted in *Reformation Without Tarrying for Any* is Browne's insistence that the true Christian cannot compromise with "the Magistrates and . . . Parliamentes." Browne revives the ancient doctrine of the two swords — one temporal and one spiritual — and, in effect, challenges the doctrine of a state church. Thus his tract contains, among other things, the seed of the separation of church and state.

Equally important is the idea of "independency": the individual congregation should be left free to go its own way — to govern itself according to its own needs and determinations (assuming always the purity of the re-formed faith). From the emphasis on the congregation came the name Congregationalists, the true name of the Brownists (Separatists) and Puritans (who, as distinguished from Separatists, refused to break entirely with the Church of England).

Browne argues that we should leave to the Magistrates — the public officials — all "outward justice", the managing of the political realm, and leave to the devout Protestant the matters of the spiritual realm . While Browne does not explicitly condone disobedience to the state, the implication is there: the spiritual realm is above the temporal; thus when spiritual and temporal clash, the Christian will know where his duty lies. He will, above all, not "tarry" while the civil realm comes to realize its spiritual duties and perform them.

[The text is taken from Robert Browne, *Reformation Without Tarrying for Any*, 1582 (Boston: Directorie of the Old South Work, 1899).]

# Reformation Without Tarrying for Any

Seeing in this Booke wee shewe the state of Christians, and haue laboured also in good conscience to liue as Christians, It is maruailed & often talked of among manie, why we should be so reuiled and troubled of manie, & also leaue our countrie. *Forsooth* (say the enimies) *there is some hiddē thing in them more thē plainly appeareth: for they beare euill will to their Princes Queene* ELIZABETH *and to their coūtrie, yea they forsake the Church of God,& cōdemne the same, and are cōdemned of all, and they also discredit & bring into cōtēpt the Preachers of the Ghospel.* To aunswere them, we say, That they are the men which trouble Israel, and seeke euill to the Prince, and not we. And that they forsake and condemne the Church and not we. First concerning our faithfulnesse to our Prince and Countrie, and what our iudgement is of the ciuill authoritie, we aunswere as appeareth in this Treatise. For their other accustations and slaunders of forsaking and condemning the Church, &c. if our doings will not stoppe their mouthes, nor this booke which followeth of the state of Christians, we purpose by the grace of God, to shewe in an other booke, which shall hereafter come foorth, whether we or they be the rebellious children and a false seede. But for the Magistrate, howe farre by their authoritie or without it, the Church must be builded and reformation made, and whether anie open wickednesse must be tollerated in the Church because of them, let this be our aunswere. For chieflie in this point they haue wrought vs great trouble, and dismayed manie weakelings from imbracing the trueth. We say therefore, and often haue taught, concerning our Soueraigne Queene Elizabeth, that neither the Pope, nor other Popeling, is to haue anie authoritie either ouer her, or ouer the Church of God, and that the Pope of Rome is Antichrist, whose kingdome ought vtterlie to be taken away. Agayne we say, that her Authoritie is ciuil, and that power she hath as highest under God within her Dominions, and that ouer all persons and causes. By that she may put to death all that deserue it by Lawe, either of the Church or common Wealth, and none may resiste Her or the Magistrates vnder her by force or wicked speaches, when they execute the lawes. Seeing we graunt and holde thus much, howe doe they charge us as euill willers to the Queene? Surelie, for that wee holde all those Preachers and teachers accursed, which will not doe the duties of Pastors and teachers till the Magistrates doe force them thereto. They saye, the time is not yet come to builde the Lordes House [Hag. 1.], they must tarie for the Magistrates and for Parliaments to do it. They want the ciuill sworde forsooth, and the Magistrates doe hinder the Lordes building and kingdome, and keepe awaye his gouernement. Are they not ashamed thus to slaunder the Magistrate? They haue runne their owne swordes vppon the Wall and broken them, and nowe woulde they snatche vnto them the Magistrates sworde. In deede can the Lordes spirituall gouernement be no waye executed but by the ciuill sworde, or is this the judgement that is written [Psal. 149.], Such honour shall be to all his Saintes? Is this to binde the Kinges in chaines, and the Nobles with Fetters of

Iron, by the highe actes of GOD in their mouthes, and a two edged sworde in their handes? Those bandes and chaines, which is the spirituall power of the Church, they haue broken from them selues, and yet woulde they haue Magistrates bounde with them, to beginne Discipline. They would make the Magistrates more then Goddes, and yet also worse then beastes. For they teache that a lawefull Pastour must giue ouer his charge at their discharging, and when they withholde the Church gouernement, it ought for to cease, though the Church goe to ruine thereby. Beholde nowe, doeth not the Lordes kingdome giue place vnto theirs? And doe they not pull downe the heade Christe Iesus [Col. 1. 18], to sett vppe the hande of the Magistrate? yea and more then this, for they firste proclaime the names and tytles of wicked Bishoppes and popishe officers, and the Lordes name after: Seeing also the Bishoppes must discharge the lawfull Preachers, and stoppe their mouthes, though the Lorde God haue giuen them a charge for to speake, and not to keepe silence. The Lorde hath exalted Christe Iesus [Phil. 2], and giuen him a name aboue euerie name, that all things should bowe and serue vnto him, and yet haue they exalted the power of wicked Bishoppes aboue him. Beholde a great and moste wholesome riuer, and yet their pudle water is preferred before it. Except the Magistrates will goe into the tempest and raine, and bee weather beaten with the haile of Gods wrath, they muste keepe vnder the roafe of Christes gouernement. They must bee vnder a Pastorall charge: They must obeye to the Scepter of Christe, if they bee Christians. Howe then shoulde the Pastor, which hath the ouersight of the Magistrate, if hee bee of his flocke, bee so ouerseene of the Magistrate, as to leaue his flocke, when the Magistrate shall uniustlie and wrongfullie discharge him. Yet these Preachers and teachers will not onelie doo so, but euen holding their charge and keeping with it, will not guide and reforme it aright, because the Magistrates doo forbidde them forsooth. But they slaunder the Magistrate, and because they dare not charge them as forbidding them their dueties, they haue gotten this shift, that they doo but tarie for the Magistrates authoritie, and then they will guide and reforme as they ought. Beholde, is not all this one thing, seeing they lift vppe the throne of the Magistrates, to thrust out the kingdome of Christe? For his gouernement or Discipline is wanting (saye they) but wee keepe it not awaye. And who then? For moste of them dare not charge the Magistrates, but onelie closelie, and with manie flatterings, that they might still be exalted by the Magistrates. They leaue their owne burthen, and crie out that it is not caried by faulte of the Magistrate. So they make them enimies, because they saye they withholde the Church gouernement: euen enimies doo they make them to the Lordes kingdome and righteousnesse: and why then do they not wage that spirituall battell against them, whiche is to cut them of from the Church? For the Scepter and kingdome of Christ is not of this worlde, to fight with dint of sworde, but it is a right Scepter, which subdueth the people vnder vs, and the Nations vnder our feete. [Psal. 47., Psal. 45.] Hee judgeth the wicked, and by the rebuke of his worde, he filleth all places with the slaine, and smiteth the Heades ouer great countries. [Psal. 110.] . . .

He that will be saued, must not tarie for this man or that: and he that putteth his hande to the plowe, and then looketh backe, is not fitt for the kingdome of God [Luke 9.] Therefore woe vnto you ye blinde guides, which cast away all by tarying for the Magistrates. The Lorde will remember this iniquitie, and visite the sinne vpon you. Ye will not haue the kingdome of God, to go forward by his spirit, but by an armie & strength for sooth [Zacha. 4.]: ye will not haue it as Leauen hidde in three peckes of meale, till it leauen all [Matt. 13.], but at once ye will haue all aloft, by ciuill power and authoritie: you are offended at the baseness and small beginnings, and because of the troubles in beginning reformation, you will doe nothing. Therefore shall Christ be that rocke of offence vnto you, and ye shall stumble and fall, and shall be broken, and shall be snared, and shal be taken. You wil be deliuered from the yoke of Antichrist, to the which you doo willinglie giue your neckes, by bowe, and by sworde, and by battell, by horses and by horssemen [Hosea 2.], that is, by ciuill power and pompe of Magistrates: by their Proclamations and Parliamentes: and the kingdome of God must come with obseruation [Luke 17.], that men may say, Loe the Parliament, or loe the Bishoppes decrees: but the kingdome of God shoulde be within you. The inwarde obedience to the outwarde preaching and gouernement of the Church with newnes of life, that is the Lordes kingdome . . .

The magistrates commaundement, must not be a rule vnto me of this and that duetie, but as I see it agree with the worde of God. So thē it is an abuse of my guifte and calling, if I cease preaching for the Magistrate, when it is my calling to preach, yea & woe unto me, if I preache not, for necessitie is laied vpon me, and if I doe it unwillinglie, yet the dispensation is committed vnto me [I. Cor. 9.]. And this dispensation did not the Magistrate giue me, but God by consent and ratifying of the Church, and therefore as the Magistrate gaue it not, so can he not take it away. In deede if God take it away for my wickednesse and euill deserte, he may remoue me from the Chruch, and withholde me from preaching: but if God doo it not, and his worde doeth approue me, as most meete for that calling, I am to preache still, except I be shut vp in prison, or otherwise with violence withhelde from my charge. For the Magistrate so vsing me cannot be a Christian, but forsaketh the Church: and howe then should my office in the Church depende on him which is none of the Church? And the welfare of the Church must be more regarded and sought, then the welfare of whole Kingdomes and Countries, as it is written [Isa. 43.]: Because thou wast precious in my sight, and thou wast honourable and I loued thee, therefore will I giue man for thee, and people for thy sake. And againe he saieth, I gaue Egypt for thy raunsome, Ethiopia and Seba for thee. The Lorde shall therefore judge these men, and cut them of both heade & tayle, braunch and rushe in one day. The auncient and the honorable men, which take on them to put downe the Lordes authoritie, and to stoppe the mouthes of his messengers, they be the heade, and the wicked teachers which exalte men aboue God, they are the tayle. They are afrayde of the face of the Magistrate, & do flatter and currie fauour with them, and they would have vs also to doo the like . . .

Goe to therefore, and the outwarde power and ciuil forcings, let vs leaue to the Magistrates: to rule the common wealth in all outwarde iustice, belongeth to them: but let the Church rule in spirituall wise, and not in worldlie maner: by a liuelie lawe preached, and not by a ciuill lawe written: by holinesse in inwarde and outwarde obedience, and not in straightnesse of the outward onelie. But these handsome Prelates, would haue the Mase and the Scepter in their handes, and then hauing safetie and assurance by a lawe on their sides, they would make a goodlie reformation.

Beholde the Lorde hath seene this their villanie, and he hath made them despised and vile in the sight of the people. They haue refused knowledge, and the

Lorde hath refused them, they shall beare no more the name of his message.
*Of their wicked aunswere, that they can not remedie things, and therefore they will tollerate.*

Beholde, the Lorde hath cast dunge on their faces, euen the dunge of their solemn feastes [Mala. 2.], as of their Christmasse, and Easter, and Whitsuntide, and of all their traditions, receyued from Baal. For in their solemne meetings, then doeth their iniquitie most woefullie appeare. And they haue saide plainlie (as in the dayes of Malachie) [Mala. 1.] the table of the Lorde is not to be regarded. For though hogges and Dogges come thereto, yet who can redresse it: or why should the Communion be counted polluted vnto vs? Thus they pollute my name saieth the Lorde, and yet they say Wherein haue we polluted thy name? In that ye suffer such wickednesse amongest you, saieth the Lorde, and say also that it is sufferable, and can no way be remedied. O goodlie teachers, which eate vp the sinne of the people, and devoure seelie soules whyle they wil tollerate forsooth: For by tolleration, they make vnlawfull things lawfull: and by a protestation they iustifie all iniquitie. In deede they be euill say they, but yee must beare with them, for there is no remedie. So not onlie they practise and vse them them selues, and drawe on others by their wicked example, but also commaunde and teache all men the like, yea hate and persecute all those which stande not with them. O notable Protestantes, whiche both witnesse euil & do the same. Darkenes hath certainlie couered vs, and grosse darkenesse hath filled vs, that we could not hitherto espie this great follie. For no wickednesse is tollerable, except for the hardnes of mennes hartes, we yeelde them vp to their wickednesse. For the Lordes way sayeth the Scripture [Isa. 35.], is holy, and no polluted shall passe by it. And again it is written [Isa. 60], That the Lordes people (he speaketh of the Church) shal be all righteous, that is, no open wickednesse shal so shew it selfe in the Church, that it shoulde be incurable. For either the parties which offende, shalbe separate, or else they shalbe reclaymed by due admonition. And therefore the Church is called the house of the liuing God, the piller and grounde of trueth [I. Tim. 3.]. For by the due order therein, Religion and holinesse is vphelde, and all heresies, euill maners, and wicked examples put awaye. If then anie open wickednesse must needes be suffered, it is suffered in those which are none of the church: as it is written [I. Cor. 5.]. What haue I to doo to iudge them which are without, doe yee not iudge them which are within? for God iudgeth them which are without. Knowe ye not (saith the Scripture) that a little leauen leaueneth the whole lumpe. Howe then shall we suffer but a little wickednesse, whiche indeede is not little if it can not be remedied. Yea Paule [I. Cor. 7.] would not bee brought into bondage of the least thing that is, and it is horrible iniquitie to be seruantes to men, that is, when we are bought for so great a price to glorifie God as his free men, that we should be made seruaunts to menne to suffer their wickednesse. Goe to therefore yee tolerating Preachers, this you get by your tolerating, to haue no name amonge the righteous, nor to be of the bodie of the Church. For Ierusalem is called a citie of trueth, and the mountaine of the Lorde, the holie mountaine [Zacha. 8.]. But ye are vnholie, in that ye saye, some pollutions can not bee clensed awaye, but muste needes be suffered among you. And this is a certaine trueth, that where anie open disorder is incurable, there is not the Lords Zion, to the which he is turned to dwell therein: that is, they are not the Lordes Church, ouer whom he doeth raigne to shewe his kingdome and gouernement. For the Lordes kingdome is not as mannes, and his rule in his church is not the rule of man. Man is not able to reforme al things, and in the common wealthes manie thinges are suffered. But in the Church, though hypocrites which are called the tares, can not bee rooted out, yet no open disorder shall so spreade it selfe, that it cannot be remedied. Else should not the Church be called the pillar and ground of trueth, the Lordes resting place, his holie habitation, his kingdome and glorious renowne. Therefore doth Paule call [I. Cor. 5.] that parte of church gouernement, which is to separate the vngodlie, the power of our Lorde Iesus Christ. For thereby are the Kings bounde with chaines, and the Nobles with fetters of yron [Psal. 149], that they may execute vppon them, the iudgement that is written, Such honor bee to all his Saintes. And in deede this is a great honour we haue, as Paule sayeth [2. Cor. 10.], that though we walke in the fleshe, yet we warre not after the fleshe. For the weapons of our warfare are not carnall, but mightie through God, to caste downe houldes, casting downe the imaginations, and euerie high thing, that is exalted against the knowledge of God, & bringing into captiuitie euerie thought to the obedience of Christ. So then there is nothing which the Lorde will not breake, if it be against his glorie, neither anie wickednes which the gouernement of his Churche is not able to put downe. For the Scepter of Christ is a right Scepter [Psal. 45.], hee will keepe in awe his people in this life, and put aparte from them the vnrulie: he shall be Iudge among the Heathen, and fill all with dead bodies, and smite the heades ouer great Countries [Psal. 110.], and after this life he hath made readie the last vengeance against all disobedience, when the obedience of his people is fulfilled. Howe then dare these menne teache vs, that anie euill thing is tolerable in the Church, as though the church gouernement could

not remedie it: yea and so tolerable, that all men
should be brought into bondage thereby: yea
into so foolishe bondage, that they should
protest a thing to be euill, and
so thinke they are excused to
practise the same.

# 5

---

Eleven years after the Pilgrims landed at what they named Plymouth, the Puritans set out for Massachusetts Bay. They were a very different body of men and women than their predecessors. While they shared the same basic Calvinistic creeds (predestination, salvation by grace not works, and a congregational polity or form of church organization) they included a number of prosperous and important persons, graduates of Cambridge, prominent ministers and substantial landowners. These men had no intention of "separating" from the Church of England. They intended, rather, to reform it. And during the forthcoming English Civil War, they came very close to doing so.

On the way to Massachusetts Bay, John Winthrop, a layman who was to govern the colony for nineteen years, delivered a speech to his fellow "undertakers" (those who had undertaken to voyage to the New World). He described the nature of their common venture and the principles on which it was founded. In *A Model of Christian Charity* can be found not only themes that were to dominate New England history for a hundred years or more but that were to play a crucial role in shaping the particular American version of that new consciousness created by the Reformation.

In our opinion, Winthrop's lay sermon belongs with the Declaration of Independence and the Federal Constitution as one of the seminal documents of American history.

[The text is taken from John Winthrop, "A Model of Christian Charity," *The American Puritans*, ed. by Perry Miller, (Garden City: Doubleday & Company, Inc., 1956), pp. 79-84.]

# A Model of Christian Charity

God Almighty in His most holy and wise providence hath so disposed of the condition of mankind as in all times some must be rich, some poor; some high and eminent in power and dignity, others mean and in subjection.

The reason hereof:

First, to hold conformity with the rest of His works, being delighted to show forth the glory of His wisdom in the variety and difference of the creatures and the glory of His power, in ordering all these differences for the preservation and good of the whole, and the glory of His greatness: that as it is the glory of princes to have many officers, so this great King will have many stewards, counting Himself more honored in dispensing His gifts to man by man than if He did it by His own immediate hand.

Secondly, that He might have the more occasion to manifest the work of His Spirit: first, upon the wicked in moderating and restraining them, so that the rich and mighty should not eat up the poor, nor the poor and despised rise up against their superiors and shake off their yoke; secondly, in the regenerate, in exercising His graces in them — as in the great ones, their love, mercy, gentleness, temperance, etc., in the poor and inferior sort, their faith, patience, obedience, etc.

Thirdly, that every man might have need of other, and from hence they might be all knit more nearly together in the bond of brotherly affection. From hence it appears plainly that no man is made more honorable than another or more wealthy, etc., out of any particular and singular respect to himself, but for the glory of his creator and the common good of the creature, man. Therefore God still reserves the property of these gifts to Himself (Ezek. 16. 17). He there calls wealth His gold and His silver, etc. (Prov. 3. 9). He claims their service as His due: "Honor the Lord with thy riches." All men being thus (by divine providence) ranked into two sorts, rich and poor, under the first are comprehended all such as are able to live comfortably by their own means duly improved, and all others are poor, according to the former distribution.

There are two rules whereby we are to walk, one towards another: justice and mercy. These are always distinguished in their act and in their object, yet may they both concur in the same subject in each respect: as sometimes there may be an occasion of showing mercy to a rich man in some sudden danger of distress, and also doing of mere justice to a poor man in regard of some particular contract.

There is likewise a double law by which we are regulated in our conversation, one towards another: in both the former respects, the law of nature and the law of grace, or the moral law or the law of the Gospel — to omit the rule of justice as not properly belonging to this purpose, otherwise than it may fall into consideration in some particular cases. By the first of these laws, man, as he was enabled so, withal [is] commanded to love his neighbor as himself; upon this ground stand all the precepts of the moral law, which concerns our dealings with men. To apply this to the works of mercy, this law requires two things: first, that every man afford his help to another in every want or distress; secondly, that he perform this out of the same affection which makes him careful of his own good according to that of our savior (Matt. 7. 12): "Whatsoever ye would that men should do to you." This was practiced by Abraham and Lot in entertaining the angels and the old man of Gibea.

The law of grace or the Gospel hath some difference from the former, as in these respects: first, the law of nature was given to man in the estate of innocency, this of the Gospel in the estate of regeneracy. Secondly, the former propounds one man to another as the same flesh and image of God, this as a brother in Christ also, and in the communion of the same spirit, and so teacheth us to put a difference between Christians and others. "Do good to all, especially to the household of faith." Upon this ground the Israelites were to put a difference between the brethren of such as were strangers though not of the Canaanites. Thirdly, the law of nature could give no rules for dealing with enemies, for all are to be considered as friends in the estate of innocency; but the Gospel commands love to an enemy. Proof: "If thine enemy hunger, feed him; love your enemies, do good to them that hate you" (Matt. 5. 44).

This law of the Gospel propounds likewise a difference of seasons and occasions. There is a time when a Christian must sell all and give to the poor as they did in the apostles' times; there is a time also when a Christian, though they give not all yet, must give beyond their ability, as they of Macedonia (II Cor. 8). Likewise, community of perils calls for extraordinary liberality, and so doth community in some special service for the church. Lastly, when there is no other means whereby our Christian brother may be relieved in this distress, we must help him beyond our ability, rather than tempt God in putting him upon help by miraculous or extraordinary means . . .

1. For the persons, we are a company professing ourselves fellow members of Christ, in which respect only, though we were absent from each other many miles, and had our employments as far distant, yet we ought to account ourselves knit together by this bond of love, and live in the exercise of it, if we would have comfort of our being in Christ. This was notorious in the practice of the Christians in former times, as is testified of the Waldenses from the mouth of one of the adversaries, Aeneas Sylvius: *Mutuo solent amare penè antequam norint* — they used to love any of their own religion even before they were acquainted with them.

2. For the work we have in hand, it is by mutual consent, through a special overruling providence and a more than an ordinary approbation of the churches of Christ, to seek out a place of cohabitation and consortship, under a due form of government both civil and ecclesiastical. In such cases as this, the care of the public must oversway all private respects by which not only conscience but mere civil policy doth bind us; for it is a true rule that particular estates cannot subsist in the ruin of the public.

3. The end is to improve our lives to do more service to the Lord, the comfort and increase of the body of Christ whereof we are members, that ourselves and posterity may be the better preserved from the common corruptions of this evil world, to serve the Lord and work out our salvation under the power and purity of His holy ordinances.

4. For the means whereby this must be effected, they are twofold: a conformity with the work and the end we aim at; these we see are extraordinary, therefore we must not content ourselves with usual ordinary means. Whatsoever we did or ought to have done when we lived in England, the same must we do, and more also where we go. That which the most in their churches maintain as a truth in profession only, we must bring into familiar and constant practice: as in this duty of love we must love brotherly without dissumulation, we must love one another with a pure heart fervently, we must bear one another's burdens, we must not look only on our own things but also on the things of our brethren. Neither must we think that the Lord will bear with such failings at our hands as He doth from those among whom we have lived . . .

Thus stands the cause between God and us: we are entered into covenant with Him for this work; we have taken out a commission, the Lord hath given us leave to draw our own articles. We have professed to enterprise these actions upon these and these ends; we have hereupon besought Him of favor and blessing. Now if the Lord shall please to hear us and bring us in peace of the place we desire, then hath He ratified this covenant and sealed our Commission, [and] will expect a strict performance of the articles contained in it. But if we shall neglect the observation of these articles which are the ends we have propounded, and dissembling with our God, shall fall to embrace this present world and prosecute our carnal intentions, seeking great things for ourselves and our posterity, the Lord will surely break out in wrath against us, be revenged of such a perjured people, and make us know the price of the breach of such a covenant.

Now the only way to avoid this shipwreck and to provide for our posterity is to follow the counsel of Micah: to do justly, to love mercy, to walk humbly with our God. For this end, we must be knit together in this work as one man. We must entertain each other in brotherly affection; we must be willing to abridge ourselves of our superfluities, for the supply of others' necessities; we must uphold a familiar commerce together in all meekness, gentleness, patience and liberality. We must delight in each other, make others' conditions our own, rejoice together, mourn together, labor and suffer together: always having before our eyes our commission and community in the work, our community as members of the same body. So shall we keep the unity of the spirit in the bond of peace, the Lord will be our God and delight to dwell among us, as His own people, and will command a blessing upon us in all our ways, so that we shall see much more of His wisdom, power, goodness, and truth than formerly we have been acquainted with. We shall find that the God of Israel is among us, when ten of us shall be able to resist a thousand of our enemies, when He shall make us a praise and glory, that men shall say of succeeding plantations: "The Lord make it like that of New England." For we must consider that we shall be as a city upon a hill, the eyes of all people are upon us. So that if we shall deal falsely with our God in this work we have undertaken, and so cause Him to withdraw His present help from us, we shall be made a story and a by-word through the world: we shall open the mouths of enemies to speak evil of the ways of God and all professors of God's sake; we shall shame the faces of many of God's worthy servants, and cause their prayers to be turned into curses upon us, till we be consumed out of the good land whither we are going.

And to shut up this discourse with that exhortation of Moses, that faithful servant of the Lord, in his last farewell to Israel (Deut. 30): Beloved, there is now set before us life and good, death and evil, in that we are commanded this day to love the Lord our God, and to love one another, to walk in His ways and to keep His commandments and His ordinance and His laws and the articles of our covenant with Him, that we may live and be multiplied, and that the Lord our God may bless us in the land whither we go to possess it: but if our hearts shall turn away so that we will not obey, but shall be seduced and worship . . . other gods, our pleasures and profits, and serve them, it is propounded unto us this day, we shall surely perish out of the good land whither we pass over this vast sea to possess it.

Therefore, let us choose life,
that we, and our seed,
may live; by obeying His
voice and cleaving to Him,
for He is our life and
our prosperity.

# 6

---

At the center of the Puritan experience in America lay the idea of a "covenant" or compact. Winthrop has already described the nature of this compact or covenant in his *Model of Christian Charity* .It was such agreements, in most instances written out and jealously guarded, which established the vast majority of the "covenanted communities" of New England. (They were not, of course, confined to New England, though they were most prominent there).

John Cotton was a graduate of Emmanuel College, Cambridge and a prominent Puritan leader and preacher who had been vicar of St. Botolph's Church in Boston, England for twenty years prior to his 1633 migration to Boston, Massachusetts. His essay on the "Limitations of Government" is the most effective statement of the Puritan covenant concept.

[The text is taken from John Cotton, "Limitations of Government," *The American Puritans*, ed. by Perry Miller, (Garden City: Doubleday & Company, Inc., 1956), pp. 85-88.]

## Limitations of Government

This may serve to teach us the danger of allowing to any mortal man an inordinate measure of power to speak great things: to allow to any man uncontrollableness of speech; you see the desperate danger of it.

Let all the world learn to give mortal men no greater power than they are content they shall use — for use it they will. And unless they be better taught of God, they will use it ever and anon: it may be, make it the passage of their proceeding to speak what they will. And they that have liberty to speak great things, you will find it to be true, they will speak great blasphemies. No man would think what desperate deceit and wickedness there is in the hearts of men. And that was the reason why the beast did speak such great things; he might speak and nobody might control him: "What," saith the Lord (in Jer. 3. 5), "thou hast spoken and done evil things as thou couldst." If a church or head of a church could have done worse, he would have done it. This is one of the strains of nature: it affects boundless liberty, and to run to the utmost extent. Whatever power he hath received, he hath a corrupt nature that will improve it in one thing or other; if he have liberty, he will think why may he not use it?

Set up the Pope as Lord Paramount over kings and princes, and they shall know that he hath power over them; he will take liberty to depose one and set up another. Give him power to make laws, and he will approve and disapprove as he list: what he approves is canonical, what he disapproves is rejected. Give him that power, and he will so order it at length, he will make such a state of religion, that he that so lives and dies shall never be saved; and all this springs from the vast power that is given to him and from the deep depravation of nature. He will open his mouth: "His tongue is his own, who is Lord over him" (Psal. 12. 3,4).

It is therefore most wholesome for magistrates and officers in church and commonwealth never to affect more liberty and authority than will do them good, and the people good: for whatever transcendent power is given will certainly overrun those that give it and those that receive it. There is a strain in a man's heart that will sometime or other run out to excess, unless the Lord restrain it; but it is not good to venture it.

It is necessary, therefore, that all power that is on earth be limited, church-power or other. If there be power given to speak great things, then look for great blasphemies, look for a licentious abuse of it. It is counted a matter of danger to the state to limit prerogatives; but it is a further danger not to have them limited: they will be like a tempest if they be not limited. A prince himself cannot tell where he will confine himself, nor can the people tell; but if he have liberty to speak great things, then he will make and unmake, say and unsay, and undertake such things as are neither for his own honor nor for the safety of the state.

It is therefore fit for every man to be studious of the bounds which the Lord hath set: and for the people, in whom fundamentally all power lies, to give as much power as God in His word gives to men. And it is meet that magistrates in the commonwealth, and so officers in churches, should desire to know the utmost bounds of their own power, and it is safe for both. All intrenchment upon the bounds which God hath not given, they are not enlargements, but burdens and snares; they will certainly lead the spirit of a man out of his way, sooner or later.

It is wholesome and safe to be dealt withal as God deals with the vast sea: "Hitherto shalt thou come, but there shalt thou stay thy proud waves." And therefore if they be but banks of simple sand, they will be good enough to check the vast, roaring sea. And so for imperial monarchies: it is safe to know how far their power extends; and then if it be but banks of sand, which is most slippery, it will serve as well as any brazen wall. If you pinch the sea of its liberty, though it be walls of stone or brass, it will beat them down. So it is with magistrates: stint them where God hath not stinted them, and if they were walls of brass, they would beat them down, and it is meet they should; but give them the liberty God allows, and if it be but a wall of sand it will keep them.

As this liquid air in which we breathe, God hath set it for the waters of the clouds to the earth; it is a firmament, it is the clouds, yet it stands firm enough; because it keeps the climate where they are, it shall stand like walls of brass. So let there be due bounds set — and I may apply it to families: it is good for the wife to acknowledge all power and authority to the husband, and for the husband to acknowledge honor to the wife; but still give them that which God hath given them, and no more nor less. Give them the full latitude that God hath given, else you will find you dig pits, and lay snares, and cumber their spirits, if you give them less; there is never peace where full liberty is not given, nor never stable peace where more than full liberty is granted. Let them be duly observed, and give men no more liberty than God doth, nor women, for they will abuse it. The devil will draw them, and God's providence lead them thereunto; therefore give them no more than God gives.

And so for children and servants, or any others you are to deal with: give them the liberty and authority you would have them use, and beyond that stretch not the tether; it will not tend to their good nor yours. And also, from hence gather and go home with this meditation: that certainly here is this distemper in our natures, that we cannot tell how to use liberty, but we shall very readily corrupt ourselves. Oh, the bottomless depth of sandy earth! of a corrupt spirit, that breaks over all bounds, and loves inordinate vastness! That is it we ought to be careful of.

# 7

---

The Puritans gave a great deal of thought to the problems of government and, in a broader sense, to man's common social life. In the selection that follows, William Hubbard, who graduated in the first class at Harvard College in 1642 and lived at Ipswich studying both medicine and theology, describes that order which he and his fellow-Puritans believed was an essential part of God's plan for human society. The notion of an order, typically hierarchial, was a very old one. It was given its modern form by Newton and became a commonplace of political thought in the seventeenth and eighteenth centuries. At the time of the Revolution it was, as we shall see, frequently and eloquently stated. It underlay all the assumptions of the Revolutionary generation and the Founding Fathers about the nature of government.

# A

[The text is taken from William Hubbard, "The Happiness of a People in the Wisdome of Their Rulers Directing and in the Obedience of Their Brethren Attending," election sermon of May 3, 1676, *The American Puritans.* ed. by Perry Miller. (Garden City: Doubleday & Company, Inc., 1956), pp. 117-121]

## The Happiness of a People

It was order that gave beauty to this goodly fabric of the world, which before was but a confused chaos, without form and void. Therefore when Job — when he would set out the terribleness of the grave and dismal state of death — he calls it the land of darkness, and the shadow of death without any order (Job 10. 22). For order is as the soul of the universe, the life and health of things natural, the beauty and strength of things artificial.

The better to understand this we may consider what order is. The schools tell us it is: *parium impariumque; sua cuique; tribuens loca, opta disposito* — such a disposition of things in themselves equal and unequal as gives to every one their due and proper place. It suited the wisdom of the infinite and omnipotent creator to make the world of differing parts, which necessarily supposes that there must be differing places for those differing things to be disposed into, which is order. The like is necessary to be observed in the rational and political world, where persons of differing endowments and qualifications need differing stations to be disposed into, the keeping of which is both the beauty and strength of such a society. Naturalists tell us that beauty in the body arises from an exact symmetry or proportion of contrary humors, equally mixed one with another: so doth an orderly and artificial distribution of diverse materials make a comely building, while homogeneous bodies (as the depths of waters in the sea, and heaps of sand on the shore) run into confused heaps, as bodies incapable to maintain an order in themselves. So that it appears: whoever is for a parity in any society will in the issue reduce things into an heap of confusion. That God, who assumes to Himself the title of being the God of glory, is the God of peace or order, and not of confusion (I Cor. 14. 33 compared with verse 40). He is so in His palace of the world as well as in His temple of His church: in both may be observed a sweet subordination of persons and things, each unto other.

Look we into the third heavens, the high and holy place, as a royal pavilion pitched by the Almighty for the residence of His glory: although it be furnished with inhabitants suitable to the nature of that celestial throne, yet are they not all of one rank and order; there are cherubims as well as seraphims, archangels as well as angels, thrones and dominions as well as principalities and powers. There are also, as in a middle rank, the spirits of just men made perfect: though no unclean thing may enter in, yet have they not attained their perfection in glory, but do yet expect an addition of glory. But in the outward court, as there are diversity of gifts, so there are of places and order some that are to rule and go before, others that are to be subject and to follow.

If we shall but descend and take notice of the firmament — the pavement of that glorious mansion place, although it be the roof of this lower world — may we not there see one star differing from another in glory? There is placed the sun, the lord and ruler of the day, as well as the moon that rules the night, together with the stars as the common people of that upper region, who yet do immediately veil their glory and withdraw their light when their bridegroom cometh forth of his chamber. In the firmament of the air, may we not see the lofty eagle in his flight far surmounting the little choristers of the valleys? The like disproportion, who observes not amongst those creatures that take their pastime in the deep waters, or that range upon the high mountains, hunting for their prey?

And hath not the same Almighty Creator and Disposer of all things made some of the sons of men as far differing in height of body one from the other, as Saul from the rest of the people? And are not some advanced as high above others in dignity and power as much as the cedars of Lebanon the low shrubs of the valley? It is not then the result of time or chance that some are mounted on horseback while others are left to travel on foot, that some have with the Centurion power to command while others are required to obey. The poor and the rich meet together, the Lord is the maker of them both. The Almighty hath appointed her that sits behind the mill, as well as him that ruleth on the throne. And herein hath He as well consulted the good of human nature as the glory of His own wisdom and power, those of the superior rank but making a supply of what is wanting in the other. Otherwise might not the foolish and ignorant be like to lose themselves in the wilderness if others were not as eyes to them? The fearful and the weak might be destroyed if others more strong and valiant did not protect and defend them. The poor and needy might starve with hunger and cold, were they not fed with the morsels and warmed with the fleece of the wealthy. Is it not found by experience that the greatest part of mankind are but as tools and instruments for others to work by, rather than any proper agents to effect any thing of themselves? In peace, how would most people destroy themselves by slothfulness and security? In war, they would be destroyed by others were it not for the wisdom and courage of the valiant. If the virtue and valor of the good did not interpose by their authority to prevent and save, the vice of the bad would bring mischief enough upon places to ruin both. Else why is it so frequently intimated in the latter end of the Book of Judges that in those days, when there was no king in Israel, but every man was left to do what seemed right in his own eyes, that these and those enormities break forth that violated all laws, and offered violence even unto nature itself? . . .

Thus if order were taken away, soon would confusion follow, and every evil work (James 3. 16). Nothing therefore can be imagined more remote either from right reason or true religion than to think that, because we were all once equal at our birth and shall be again at our death, therefore we should be so in the whole course of our lives. In fine, a body would not be more monstrous and deformed without an head, nor a ship more dangerous at sea without a pilot, nor a flock of sheep more ready to be devoured without a shepherd, than would human society be without an head and leader in time of danger . . .

In a curious piece of architecture that which first offers itself to the view of the beholder is the beauty of the structure, the proportion that one piece bears to another, wherein the skill of the architect most shows itself. But that which is most admirable in sensitive and rationable beings is that inward principle, seated in some one part, able to guide the whole and influence all the rest of the parts, with an apt and regular motion, for their mutual good and safety. The wisdom of the creation was more seen in the breath of life breathed into the nostrils of Adam, whereby he became a living soul, than in the feature and beauty of the goodly frame of his body formed out of the dust — as the Poet speaks, *Os homini sublime dedit* ["He imparted sublimity to the bone of man"]. . . .

The architect of that curious piece hath placed the head in the forefront, the highest sphere, where are lodged all the senses, as in a watchtower, ready to be improved upon all occasions, for the safety and preservation of the whole. There are placed those that look out at the windows, to foresee evil and danger approaching, accordingly to alarm all the other inferior powers, to take the signal and stand upon their guard for defense of the whole. There also is the seat of the daughters of music, ready to give audience to all reports and messages that come from abroad. If anything should occur or happen nearer home or further off, imparting either fear of evil or hope of good, their work is immediately to dispatch messages through the whole province of nature, to summon all the other members together, to come in and yield the assistance to prevent the mischief feared, or prepare for the reception of the good promised or pretended, as the nature of the case may require.

Thus are all orders wont to be dispatched and issued from the Cinque ports of the senses in and about the head, for the benefit and advantage of the whole body. Very fitly therefore in the body politic are the rulers by way of allusion, called heads. And in case of inability to discharge those functions, such societies may not undeservedly be compared to the Psalmist's idols, that have eyes but see not, and have ears but hear not. Suppose the hands be never so strong for action or the feet never so swift for motion, yet if there be not discretion in the head to discern, or judgment to determine what is meet to be done for the obviating of evil and danger, or procuring of good, it will be impossible to save such a body from ruin and destruction. If the mast be never so well strengthened, and the tackling never so well bound together, yet if there want a skillful pilot to steer and guide, especially in a rough and tempestuous sea, the lame will soon take the prey.

# B

Roger Williams has become a symbol of liberal resistance to an autocratic state (the Massachusetts Bay Colony and its ministers and magistrates.) Actually the case is more complicated than that. Williams, who came to the colony in 1631 when he was twenty-eight, was a religious zealot whose views were too radical for the leaders of the Puritan migration. As minister of the Salem church, he questioned the legality of the royal land grant to the settlers, demanded that the New England churches declare their separation from the Church of England and denied the authority of the magistrates themselves in matters of religion. He believed that ". . . the *Soveraigne, originall,* and *foundation of civill power* lies in the *people.. . .*A people may erect and establish what *forme* of *Government* seemes to them meete for their *civill condition. . . .*Such governments have no more *power,* nor for a longer time, then the *civill power,* of people consenting and agreeing shall betrust them with."

Again we are reminded of John Locke (whose *Second Treatise on Government* was not written until the 1680's) the radical Christians of the Interregnum like Lilburne and Winstanley, and, finally, the Declaration of Independence itself.

The selections that follow are from the preface to Williams' pamphlet *The Bloudy Tenent of Persecution* and Williams' letter on the town of Providence which he had helped to establish on liberty of conscience.

[The text is taken from Roger Williams, "The Bloudy Tenant of Persecution," 1644 *Publications of the Narragunsett Church*, ed. by Samuel L. Caldwell, (Providence, 1867) Chapter III, pp. 3 - 4.]

# The Bloudy Tenant of Persecution

First, That the blood of so many hundred thousand soules of Protestants and Papists, spilt in the Wars of present and former Ages, for their respective Consciences, is not required nor accepted by Jesus Christ the Prince of Peace.

Secondly, Pregnant Scripturs and Arguments are throughout the Worke proposed against the Doctrine of persecution for the cause of Conscience.

Thirdly, Satisfactorie Answers are given to Scriptures, and objections produced by Mr. Calvin, Beza, Mr. Cotton, and the Ministers of the New English Churches and others former and later, tending to prove the Doctrine of persecution for cause of Conscience.

Fourthly, The Doctrine of persecution for cause of Conscience, is proved guilty of all the blood of the Soules crying for vengeance under the Altar.

Fifthly, All Civill States with their Officers of justice in their respective constitutions and administrations are proved essentially Civill, and therefore not Judges, Governours or Defendours of the Spirituall or Christian state and Worship.

Sixtly, It is the will and command of God, that (since the comming of his Sonne the Lord Jesus) a permission of the most Paganish, Jewish, Turkish, or Antichristian consciences and worships, bee granted to all men in all Nations and Countries: and they are onely to bee fought against with that Sword which is only (in Soule matters) able to conquer, to wit, the Sword of Gods Spirit, the Word of God.

Seventhly, The state of the Land of Israel, the Kings and people thereof in Peace & War, is proved figurative and ceremoniall, and no patterne nor president for any Kingdome or civill state in the world to follow.

Eightly, God requireth not an uniformity of Religion to be inacted and inforced in any civill state; which inforced uniformity (sooner or later) is the greatest occasion of civill Warre, ravishing of conscience, persecution of Christ Jesus in his servants, and of the hypocrisie and destruction of millions of souls.

Ninthly, in holding an inforced uniformity of Religion in a civill state, wee must necessarily disclaime our desires and hopes of the Jewes conversion to Christ.

Tenthly, An inforced uniformity of Religion throughout a Nation or civill state, confounds the Civill and Religious, denies the principles of Christianity and civility, and that Jesus Christ is come in the Flesh.

Eleventhly, The permission of other consciences and worships then a state professeth, only can (according to God) procure a firme and lasting peace, (good assurance being taken according to the wisedome of the civill state for uniformity of civill obedience from all sorts.)

Twelfthly, lastly, true civility and Christianity may both flourish in a state or Kingdome, notwithstanding the permission of divers and contrary consciences, either of Jew or Gentile.

[*Williams' advocacy of individual liberty naturally attracted a varied company of religionists to his colony. Some were excessively contumacious in matters of dogma and others were inspired by their "divine madness" into complete anarchism. It was in answer to current denials that the government had any authority over men that he wrote the following letter in January of 1655.*]

That ever I should speak or write a tittle, that tends to such an infinite liberty of conscience, is a mistake, and which I have ever disclaimed and abhorred. To prevent such mistakes, I shall at present only propose this case: There goes many a ship to sea, with many hundred souls in one ship, whose weal and woe is common, and is a true picture of a commonwealth, or a human combination or society. It hath fallen out sometimes, that both papists and protestants, Jews and Turks, may be embarked in one ship; upon which supposal I affirm, that all the liberty of conscience, that ever I pleaded for, turns upon these two hinges — that none of the papists, protestants, Jews, or Turks, be forced to come to the ship's prayers or worship, nor compelled from their own particular prayers or worship, if they practice any. I further add, that I never denied, that notwithstanding this liberty, the commander of this ship ought to command the ship's cource, yea, and also command that justice, peace and sobriety, be kept and practiced, both among the seamen and all the passengers. If any of the seamen refuse to perform their services, or passengers to pay their freight; if any refuse to help, in person or purse, towards the common charges or defence; if any refuse to obey the common laws and orders of the ship, concerning their common peace or preservation: if any shall mutiny and rise up against their commanders and officers; if any should preach or write that there ought to be no commanders or officers, because all are equal in Christ, therefore no masters nor officers, no laws nor orders, nor corrections nor punishments; — I say, I never denied, but in such cases, whatever is pretended, the commander or commanders may judge, resist, compel and punish such transgressors, according to their deserts and merits. This if seriously and honestly minded, may, if it so please the Father of lights, let in some light to such as willingly shut not their eyes.

I remain studious of your common peace and liberty.

*Roger Williams.*

# C

As every schoolchild knows, William Penn founded Pennsylvania as a refuge for his persecuted co-religionists, the Quakers. Thus the beginnings of the colony were distinguished by the Quaker spirit of tolerance and piety, and these principles can be discerned in the colony's frame of government or "constitution" drawn up in 1701. What Roger Williams had declared as a principle (and tried valiantly, if not always successfully to practice), Penn incorporated in the Pennsylvania Charter.

[The text is taken from William Penn, "The Charter of October 28, 1701," *Federal and State Constitutions*, ed. by F. N. Thorpe, Book V, p. 3076f.

# The Charter of October 28, 1701

William Penn, Proprietary and Governor of the Province of *Pensilvania* and Territories thereunto belonging, To all to whom these Presents shall come, sendeth Greeting. Whereas King Charles *the Second*, by His Letters Patents, under the Great Seal of *England*, bearing Date the *Fourth* Day of *March*, in the Year *One Thousand Six Hundred and Eighty-one*, was graciously pleased to give and grant unto me, and my Heirs and Assigns, for ever, this Province of *Pensilvania*, with divers great Powers and Jurisdictions for the well Government thereof. . . .

KNOW YE THEREFORE, That for the further Well-being and good Government of the Said Province, and Territories and in Pursuance of the Rights and Powers before-mentioned, I the said *William Penn* do declare, grant and confirm, unto all the Freemen, Planters and Adventurers, and other Inhabitants of this Province and Territories, these following Liberties, Franchises and Privileges, so far as in me lieth, to be held, enjoyed and kept, by the Freemen, Planters and Adventurers, and other Inhabitants of and in the said Province and Territories thereunto annexed, for ever.

FIRST

BECAUSE no People can be truly happy, though under the greatest Enjoyment of Civil Liberties, if abridged of the Freedom of their Consciences, as to their Religious Profession and Worship: And Almighty God being the only Lord of Conscience, Father of Lights and Spirits; and the Author as well as Object of all divine Knowledge, Faith and Worship, who only doth enlighten the Minds, and persuade and convince the Understandings of People, I do hereby grant and declare, That no Person or Persons, inhabiting in this province or Territories, who shall confess and acknowledge *One* almighty God the Creator, Upholder and Ruler of the World; and profess him or themselves obliged to live quietly under the Civil Government, shall be in any Case molested or prejudiced, in his or their Person or Estate, because of his or their consientious Persuasion or Practice, nor be compelled to frequent or maintain any religious Worship, Place or Ministry, contrary to his or their Mind, or to do or suffer any other Act or Thing, contrary to their religious Persuasion.

AND that all Persons who also profess to believe in *Jesus Christ*, the Saviour of the World, shall be capable (notwithstanding their other Persuasions and Practices in Point of Conscience and Religion) to serve this Government in any Capacity, both legislatively and executively, he or they solemnly promising, when lawfully required, Allegiance to the King as Sovereign, and Fidelity to the

Proprietary and Governor, and taking the Attests as now established by the Law made at *New-Castle,* in the Year *One Thousand and Seven Hundred,* entitled, *An Act directing the Attests of several Officers and Ministers,* as now amended and confirmed this present Assembly.

II. For the wellgoverning of this Province and Territories, there shall be an Assembly yearly chosen, by the Freemen thereof, to consist of *Four* Persons out of each County, of most Note for Virtue, Wisdom and Ability. . . . Which Assembly shall have Power to chuse a Speaker and other their Officers; and shall be Judges of the Qualifications and Elections of their own Members; sit upon their own Adjournments; appoint Committees; prepare Bills in order to pass into Laws; impeach Criminals, and redress Grievances; and shall have all other Powers and Privileges of an Assembly, according to the Rights of the free-born Subjects of *England,* and as is usual in any of the King's Plantations in *America.* . . .

III THAT the Freemen in each respective County, at the Time and Place of Meeting for Electing their Representatives to serve in Assembly, may as often as there shall be Occasion, chuse a double Number of Persons to present to the Governor for Sheriffs and Coroners to serve for *Three* Years, if so long they behave themselves well; out of which respective Elections and Presentments, the Governor shall nominate and commissionate one for each of the said Officers, the *Third* Day after such Presentment, or else the *First* named in Such Presentment, for each Office as aforesaid, shall stand and serve in that Office for the Time before respectively limited; and in Case of Death or Default, such Vacancies shall be supplied by the Governor, to serve to the End of the said Term. . . .

AND that the Justices of the respective Counties shall or may nominate and present to the Governor *Three* Persons, to serve for Clerk of the Peace for the said County, when there is a Vacancy one of which the Governor shall commissionate within *Ten* Days after such Presentment, or else the *First* nominated shall serve in the said Office during good Behavior.

IV THAT the Laws of this Government shall be in this Stile, viz. *By the Governor with the Consent and Approbation of the Freemen in General Assembly met;* and shall be, after Confirmation by the Governor, forthwith recorded in the Rolls Office, and kept at *Philadelphia,* unless the Governor and Assembly shall agree to appoint another Place.

V THAT all Criminals shall have the same Priviledges of Witnesses and Council as their Prosecutors.

VI THAT no Person or Persons shall or may, at any Time hereafter, be obliged to answer any Complaint, Matter or Thing whatsoever, relating to Property, before the Governor and Council, or in any other Place, but in ordinary Course of Justice, unless Appeals thereunto shall be hereafter by Law appointed.

VII THAT no Person within this Government, shall be licensed by the Governor to keep an Ordinary, Tavern or House of Publick Entertainment, but such who are first recommended to him, under the Hands of the Justice of the respective Counties, signed in open Court; which Justices are and shall be hereby impowered, to suppress and forbid any Person, keeping such Publick-House as aforesaid, upon their Misbehavior, on such Penalties as the Law doth or shall direct; as to recommend others from time to time, as they shall see Occasion. . . .

VIII BUT because the Happiness of Mankind depends so much upon the Enjoying of Liberty of their Consciences as aforesaid, I do hereby solemnly declare, promise and grant, for me, my Heirs and Assigns, That the *First* Article of this Charter relating to Liberty of Conscience, and every Part and Clause therein, according to the true Intent and Meaning thereof, shall be kept and remain, without any Alteration, inviolably for ever. . . .

The *Subjects* also of these *Terrors* may lead us to make the like Judgment about them, and these are *Children, Women,* and *youngerly* Persons. Not that others han't been wrought upon. Instances there have been of *Men;* and these, both *middle-aged,* and *advanced in Years,* who have both *cried out* and *fallen down:* But 'tis among *Children, young People* and *Women,* whose Passions are soft and tender, and more easily thrown into a Commotion, that these Things chiefly prevail. I know, 'tis thus in those Places, where I have had Opportunity to make Inquiry. And from the Accounts transmitted to me from Friends, in other Places, it appears to have been so among them also. . . .

Moreover, the *Way* in which these *Terrors* spread themselves in a Circumstance, that does not much favour their *divine Origin.* They seem to be suddenly propagated, from one to another, as in a great Fright or Consternation. They often begin with a single Person, a *Child,* or *Woman,* or *Lad,* whose *Shrieks* set others a *Shrieking;* and so the Shrieks catch from one to another, 'till the whole Congregation is alarmed, and such an awful Scene, many Times, open'd as no Imagination can paint to the Life. . . .

It will, possibly, be said, I have, in saying these Things, reflected Disgrace upon the *Work of Conviction.* If I had had such a Thought of the Matter, I should have suppressed what is here offered. Those, in my Opinion, do the greatest Dishonour to the *blessed* SPIRIT, and *his Influence* upon the Hearts of Sinners, in the Business of *Conviction,* who make no Distinction between those *Fears* that are the *Effect* of *Truth duly imprest upon the Mind,* and those that arise from an *affrightned Imagination.* And to speak freely, I am clearly in the Sentiment, that the great Stress that has been laid upon *such Terrors,* as have evidently been produced by the *mechanical Influence* of *awful Words* and *frightful Gestures,* has been a great disserve to the Interest of Religion: Nay, I am not without Fear, least the tremendous Threatning of GOD have, by some, been *prophanely* made Use of, while, under the Pretense of wakening Men's consciences, they have thunder'd out *Death* and *Damnation,* in a *Manner* more fit for the *Stage* than the *sacred Desk,* and so as to astonish the *Imagination* rather than possess the *Mind* of a *reasonable* Conviction of these awful Truths of GOD. I am not against the *Preaching of Terror;* but whenever this is done, it ought to be in a way that may enlighten the Mind, as well as alarm the Passions; And I am greatly mistaken, if this has been the Practice, among some Sort of Preachers, so much as it ought to be. And to this it may be owing, that Religionn of late, has been *more* a *Commotion in the Passions,* than a *Change* in the *Temper* of the *Mind:* Not but that, I think, a lasting Change has been wrought in a Number: though I could wish I had Reason to say, it was so great a number as some pretend: Nay, I am not without Hopes, that some even of those who have been *frighten'd* into *Shrieks* and *Fits,* are *become new-Men;* but then, I have no other Thought, in the general, of the Surprise they were thrown into, than of the Surprise by a *terrible Clap of Thunder,* or the Shock of an *Earthquake:* They might hereby be awakened to Consideration, and put upon waiting upon GOD in his own Way, 'till a *Work of Grace* has been effected in them.

# D

The greatest theologian-philosopher of colonial times was undoubtedly Jonathan Edwards. In the more-than-a-century since the Puritans had established the Massachusetts Bay Colony, Congregationalism had grown away from the principles of the founders. Secularism had softened its stern injunctions, and piety had diminished to formal observances in many instances (a course familiar to most Protestant denominations). George Whitefield, the great English evangelical, and Jonathan Edwards, a graduate of Yale and minister at Northampton, led the Great Awakening, a religious revival that affected every colony and that infused the older churches with a fresh spirit of democracy. Edwards' letter to the Reverend Benjamin Colman gives vivid description of the beginnings of the Great Awakening and in doing so reveals one of the principal sources of radical Protestantism. It was not so much that radical political principles were espoused by the revivalists — sometimes the reverse was true — but that revivalism, with its hostility to the ministerial "establishment"and its emphasis on the centrality of the emotional experience of the individual (on conversion, grace, piety and itineracy) worked as a constantly democratizing influence both in the established churches and, through new denominations and sects formed, typically, as a result of the religious enthusiasm created by the revival.

From Charles Chauncey, minister of First Church in Boston and a spokesman of the ecclesiastical establishment, we get a very different perspective on the consequences of the Great Awakening.

The account of Whitefield's preaching gives us a vivid picture of Great Awakening in action.

The passages from the journal of Dr. Alexander Hamilton, a Maryland physician traveling through the colonies in the period of the Great Awakening, give us the perspective of a cynical observer.

# 1

[The text is taken from Jonathan Edwards, 'Letters" *Jonathan Edwards: Representative Selections*, ed. by C. H. Faust and T. J. Johnson, (New York: American Book Co. 1935), pp. 73 - 84.]

## Letters

May 30, 1735. Dear Sir In answer to your Desire, I here send you a Particular account of the Present Extraordinary circumstances of this Town, & the neighbouring Towns with Respect to Religion. I have observed that the Town for this several years have gradually been Reforming; There has appeared Less & Less of a party spirit, & a contentious disposition, which before had Prevail'd for many years between two Parties in the Town. The young People also have been Reforming more and more; They by degrees Left off their frolicking, and have been observably more decent in their attendance on the Publick worship. The winter before Last there appeared a strange flexibleness in the young People of the Town, and an unusual disposition to Hearken to Counsel, on this Occasion; It had been their manner of a Long Time, & for Ought I know, alwaies, to make sabbath day nights & Lecture days, to be Especially Times of diversion, & Company Keeping: I then Preach'd a sermon on the Sabbath before the Lecture, to show them the unsuitableness, & Inconvenience of the Practice, & to perswade them to Reform it; & urged it on Heads of Families that It should be a thing agreed among them to Govern their Families, & keep them in at those times. & There happen'd to be in my house the Evening after, men that belonged to the several parts of the Town, to whom I moved that they should desire the Heads of Families, in my name, to meet together in their several neighbourhoods, that they might Know Each others minds, and agree Every one to restrain his Family; which was done, & my motion Complied with throughout the Town; but the Parents found Little or no occasion for the Exercise of Government in the case; for the young People declared themselves convinced by what they had heard, and willing of themselves to Comply with the Counsel Given them; & I suppose it was almost universally complied with thenceforward. After this there began to be a Remarkeable Religious Concern among some Farm Houses, at a Place Called Pascommuck, & five or six that I hoped were savingly wrought upon there. & in April there was a very sudden and awfull death of a young man in Town, in the very Bloom of his youth, who was violently seized with a Pleurisy & taken Immediately out of his head, and died in two days; which much affected many young People in the Town. This was followed with another death of a young married woman, who was in Great Distress in the Beginning of her Illness, but was hopefully Converted before her death; so that she died full of Comfort, and in a most Earnest & moving manner, warning & counselling others, which I believe much contributed to the solemnizing of the spirits of the young People in the Town; and there began Evidently to appear more of a Religious concern upon Peoples minds. In the Fall of the year I moved to the young People that they should set up Religious meetings on Evenings after Lectures, which they complied with: this was followed with the death of an Elderly Person in the Town, which was attended with very unusual Circumstances, which much affected many People. about that Time began the Great noise that there was in this Part of the Countrey about Arminianism, which seemed strangely to be overruled for the Promoting of Religion; People seemed to be Put by it upon Enquiring with concern & Engagedness of mind, what was the way of salvation, and what were the Terms of our acceptance with God; & what was said Publickly on that occasion; however found fault with by many Elsewhere, & Ridicul'd by some, was most Evidently attended with a very Remarkeable blessing of Heaven, to the souls of the People in this Town, to the Giving of them an universal satisfaction & Engaging their minds with Respect to the thing in Question, the more Earnestly to seek salvation in the way, that had been made Evident to them; & then, a Concern about the Great things of Religion began about the Latter End of December, & the beginning of January, to Prevail abundantly in the Town, till in a very Little Time it became universal throughout the Town, among old and young, & from the highest to the Lowest; all seemed to be siezed with a deep concern about their Eternal salvation; all the Talk in all companies, & upon occasions was upon the things of Religion, and no other talk was anywhere Relished; & scarcely a single Person in the whole Town was Left unconcerned about the Great things of the Eternal World: Those that were wont to be the vainest, & Loosest Persons in Town seemed in General to be siezed with strong convictions: Those that were most disposed to contemn vital & Experimental Religion, & those that had the Greatest Conceit of their own Reason: the highest Families in the Town, & the oldest Persons in the Town, and many Little Children were affected Remarkeably; no one Family that I know of, & scarcely a person has been Exempt & the Spirit of God went on in his saving Influences, to the appearance of all Human Reason & Charity, in a truly wonderfull and astonishing manner. The news of it filled the neighbouring Towns with Talk, & there were many in them that scoffed and made a Ridicule of the Religion that appeared in Northampton; But it was observable that is was very frequent & Common that those of other Towns that came into this Town, & observed how it was here, were Greatly affected, and went home with wounded spirits, & were never more able to Shake off the Impression that it made upon them, till at Length there began to appear a General concern in several of the Towns in the County . . .

As to the nature of Persons Experiences, & the Influences of that spirit that there is amongst us, Persons when siezed with concern are brought to forsake their vices, & ill Practices; the Looser sort are brought to forsake & to dread their former Extravagances: Persons are soon brought to have done with their old Quarrels; Contention & Intermeddling with other mens matters seems to be dead amongst us. I believe there never was so much done at Confessing of faults to Each other, & making up differences, as there has Lately been: where this concern comes it Immediately Puts an End to differences between ministers & People: there was a considerable uneasiness at New Hadley between some of the People & their minister, but when this Concern came amongst them it Immediately Put an End to it, & the People are now universally united to their minister . . . They seem to have Given them a Lively Conviction of the Truth of the Gospel, & the divine authority of the Holy Scriptures; tho they cant have the Exercise of this at all Times alike, nor Indeed of any other Grace. they seem to be brought to abhor themselves for the sins of their Past Life, & to Long to be holy, & to Live holily, & to Gods Glory; but at the same time complain that they can do nothing, they are poor Impotent Creatures, utterly Insufficient to Glorify their Creatour & Redeemer. They Commonly seem to be much more sensible of their own wickedness after their Conversion then before, so that they are often Humbled by it, it seems to them that they are Really become more wicked, when at the same time they are Evidently full of a Gracious Spirit: Their Remaining sin seems to be their very Great Burthen, & many of them seem to Long after Heaven, that there they may be Rid of sin. They Generally seem to be united in dear Love, and affection one to another, & to have a Love to all mankind: I never saw the Christian spirit in Love to Enemies so Exemplified, in all my Life as I have seen it within this Half year. They commonly Express a Great Concern for others salvation; some say that they think they are far more Concern'd for others conversion, after they themselves have been Converted, than Ever they were for their own; several have thought (tho Perhaps they might be decieved in it) that they could freely die for the salvation of any soul, of the meanest of mankind, of any Indian in the woods . . . But there is a very vast variety of degrees of spiritual discoveries, that are made to those that we hope are Godly, as there is also in the steps, & method of the spirits operation in convincing & converting sinners, and the Length of Time that Persons are under conviction before they have comfort. There is an alteration made in the Town in a few months that strangers can scarcely [be] conscious of; our Church I believe was the Largest in New England before, but Persons Lately have thronged in, so that there are very few adult Persons Left out. There have been a Great multitude hopefully converted, too many, I find, for me to declare abroad with Credit to my Judgment . . .

There have been as I have heard many odd & strange stories that have been carried about the Countrey of this affair, which it is a wonder some wise men should be so Ready to Believe. Some indeed vnder Great terrours of Conscience have had Impressions on their Imagination; and also vnder the Power of the spiritual discoveries, they have had Livelily Impressed Ideas of Christ shedding blood for sinners, his blood Running from his veins, & of Christ in his Glory in Heaven & such Like things, but they are alwaies taught, & have been several times taught in Publick not to Lay the weight of their hopes on such things & many have nothing of any such Imaginations. There have been several Persons that have had their natures overborn vnder strong Convictions, have trembled, & han't been able to stand, they have had such a sense of divine wrath; But there are no new doctrines Embraced, but People have been abundantly Established in those that we account orthodox; there is no new way of worship affected. there is no oddity of Behaviour Prevails; People are no more superstitious about their Clothes, or any thing Else than they used to be: Indeed there is a Great deal of talk when they are together of one anothers Experiences, & Indeed no other is to be expected in a Town where the Concern of the soul, is so vniversally the Concern & that to so Great a degree. & doubtless some Persons vnder the strength of Impressions that are made on their minds and vnder the Power of strong affections, are Guilty of Imprudences, their zeal may need to be Regulated by more Prudence, & they may need a Guide to their assistance; as of old when the Church of Corinth had the Extraordinary Gifts of the spirit, they needed to be told by the apostle that the spirit of the Prophets were subject to the Prophets, & that their Gifts were to be exercised with Prudence, because God was not the author of Confusion but of Peace. There is no unlovely oddity in Peoples Temper Prevailing with this work, but on the contrary the face of things is much changed as to the appearance of a meek, humble, amiable behaviour. Indeed the devil has not been Idle, but his hand has Evidently appeared in several Instances Endeavoring to mimick the work of the spirit of God and to cast a slur upon it & no wonder: & there has hereby appeared the need of the watchfull Eye of skillfull Guides, & of wisdom from above to direct them . . .

Thus sir I have Given you a Particular account of this affair which satan has so much misrepresented in the Countrey. This is a true account of the matter as far as I have Opportunity to Know, & I suppose I am vnder Greater advantages to Know than any Person Living. Having been thus Long in the account, I forbear to make Reflections, or to Guess what God is about to do; I Leave this to you, and shall only say, as I desire alwaies to say from my Heart *To God be all the Glory whose*

*work alone it is;* & Let him have an Interest in your Prayers, who so much needs divine help at that day, & is your affectionate Brother & Humble servant, Northampton May 30, 1735.
*Jth Edwards.*

# 2

[The text is taken from Charles Chauncy, *Seasonable Thoughts on the State of Religion in New England*, (Boston: Rogers & Fowle, 1743).]

## Seasonable Thoughts

THERE is not a Man, in the Country, in the sober Exercise of his Understanding, but will acknowledge, that the late religious *Stir* has been attended with many *Irregularities* and *Disorders.* These, some are pleased to call, *Imprudencies, human Frailties, accidental Effects* only, such as might be expected, considering the Remains of Corruption in good Men, even among those in whom a *remarkable Work of Grace* is carrying on: Others are in the Opinion, they make a *main Part* of the *Appearance* that has been so much talk'd of, and have arisen unavoidably in the natural Course of Things, from the *Means* and *Instruments* of this *Appearance;* and that it could not reasonably be suppos'd, it should have been otherwise.

I shall particularly show what these *bad* and *dangerous* Things are: making such Remarks (as I go along) as may be thought needful to set Matters in a just and true Light.

Among the *bad* Things attending this *Work,*

I shall *first* mention *Itinerant Preaching.* This had its *Rise* (at least in these Parts) from Mr. WHITEFIELD; though I could never see, I own, upon what Warrant, either from *Scripture* or *Reason,* he went about Preaching from one *Province* and *Parish* to another, where the Gospel was already preach'd, and by Persons as well qualified for the Work, as he can pretend to be. I charitably hope, his Design herein was good: But might it not be leavened with some undesirable Mixture? Might he not, at first, take up this Practice from a mistaken Thought of some *extraordinary Mission* from GOD? Or from the undue influence of *two high an Opinion* of his own *Gifts* and *Graces?* And when he had got into this Way, might he not be too much encouraged to go on in it, from the *popular Applauses,* every where so liberally heaped on him? If he had not been under too strong a Biass from something or other of this Nature, why so fond of preaching always himself, to the Exclusion, not of his *Brethren* only, but his *Fathers,* in *Grace* and *Gifts* and *Learning,* as well as *Age?* And why so ostentatious and assuming as to alarm so many Towns, by proclaiming his Intentions, in the *publick Prints,* to preach such a Day in such a *Parish,* the next Day in such a one, and so on, as he past through the Country; and all this, without the Knowledge, either of *Pastors* or *People* in most

Places? What others may think of such Conduct I know not; but to me, it never appeared the most indubitable Expression of that Modesty, Humility, and prefering others in Love, which the *Scriptures* highly recommend as what will adorn the *Minister's,* as well as the Christian's Character. . . .

The next *Gentleman* that practised upon this *new Method* was Mr. GILBERT TENNENT, who came in the Middle of Winter, from NEW BRUNSWICK (a Journey of more than 300 Miles) to BOSTON, "to water the seed sown by Mr. WHITEFIELD;" the *Ministers* in the *Town,* though a considerable Body, being thought insufficient for that Purpose. . . .

The *next* Thing I shall take Notice of, as what I can't but think of dangerous Tendency, is that *Terror* so many have been the Subjects of; expressing it self in *strange Effects* upon the *Body,* such as *swooning away* and *falling to the Ground,* where Persons have lain, for a Time, speechless and motionless; bitter *Shriekings* and *Screamings; Convulsion-like Tremblings* and *Agitations, Struggling* and *Tumblings,* which, in some instances, have been attended with indecencies I shan't mention: None of which Effects seem to have been *accidental,* nor yet peculiar to some *particular Places* or *Constitutions* but have been common all over the Land. There are few Places, where there has been any considerable religious Stir, but it has been accompanied, more or less, with these Appearances. Numbers in a Congregation, 10, 20, 30, would be in this Condition at a Time; Nay, Hundreds in some Places, to the opening such a *horrible Scene* as can scarce be described in Words.

The Account, those, who have been under these Circumstances, give of themselves is various. Some say, they were surprized and astonished, and insensibly wrought upon, they can't tell how: Others, that they had presented to their View, at the Time, a Sight of their Sins, in all their Number and Desert: Others, that they saw Hell, as it were, naked before them, and Destruction without a Covering; and that it seemed to them as though they were just falling into it: Others, that they imagined the Devils were about them, and ready to lay hold on them, and draw them away to Hell. The more general Account is, that they were fill'd with great Anxiety and Distress, having upon their Minds an overpowering Sense of Sin, and Fear of divine Wrath.

But whatever was the Cause, these *bodily Agitations* were, at first, highly thought of by many; yea, look'd upon as *evident Signs* of the *extraordinary Presence of the* HOLY GHOST. Hence, it was common in one Congregation, to tell of these wonderful Things, as they had appear'd in another, to pray for the like Testimony of the divine Power, to give GOD Thanks when they had it, and lament it when religious Exercises were attended, and no such Effects followed: And too much Encouragement has been given People, to depend on these Things as *sufficient Tokens* of that *Sense of Sin,* which is of the *Operation* of the SPIRIT OF GOD.

I have now *Letters* by me, from different Parts of the Country, all concurring in this Account; and wrote by Persons of as good Character as most among us, and upon their own Knowledge. . . .

'Tis with me, an Objection of some Weight against the *Divinity* of these *bodily Effects,* that they have been, in all Ages, so *rare* among *sober* and *solid* Christians; while among others, of a contrary Character, they have, all along, been *common.* So it was with the MONTANISTS of old; with the GERMAN-ENTHUSIASTS, in the beginning of the Reformation; and with the FRENCH-PROPHETS, within the Memory of many now living; and so it was with the QUAKERS. They had their Name indeed from the *Trembling* and *shaking* they ordinarily fell into, as though they were all over convulsed: Nor can there be given more remarkable Instances of *Groaning* and *Foaming* and *Roaring,* than from these People; Whereas, if we turn our View to the more *sober* Part of Christians, we shall be at a loss to find *Examples* in this Kind. . .

The *Way* in which *these Fears* have been excited, in many Places, is not, in my Opinion, the best Evidence in Favour of them. People have been too much applied to, as though the Preacher rather aimed at putting their Passions into a Ferment, than filling them with such a *reasonable* Solicitude, as is the Effect of a just Exhibition of the Truths of GOD to their Understandings. I have myself been present, when an Air of Seriousness reigned visibly through a whole Congregation: They were all Silence and Attention; having their Eye fastened on the Minister, as though they would catch every Word that came from his Mouth: and yet, because they did not *cry out,* or *swoon away,* they were upbraided with their *Hardness of Heart* and rank'd among those who were *Sermon-proof, Gospel-glutted;* and every Topic made Use of, with all the *Voice* and *Action* the Speaker was Master of, to bring forward a general *Shriek* in the Assembly. . . . And 'tis too well known to need much to be said upon it, that the *Gentlemen,* whose preaching has been *most remarkably* accompanied with these *Extraordinaries,* not only use, in their Addresses to the People, all the *Terrible Words* they can get together, but in such a manner, as *naturally* tends to put *weaker* Minds out of Possession of themselves. . . .

There is yet another Thing that makes it look as though these *Terrors might* arise from a *lower Cause,* than that which is *Divine;* and that is, their happening in the Night. I don't mean, that there han't been *Out-cries* in the *Day Time;* but the *Night* is more commonly the *Season,* when these Things are to be seen, and in their greatest Perfection. They are more *frequent,* and more *general,*and rais'd to a higher *Degree,* at the *Night Meetings,* when there are but *two* or *three* Candles in the Place of Worship, or they are wholly in the dark. . . . And why should these *strange Effects* be more *frequent,* and *general,* in the *Gloominess* of the *Night,* if they were produc'd by the Agency of the Divine SPIRIT? Does he need the Advantage of the *dark* to fill Men's Hearts with Terror? This is certainly a shrew'd Sign, that there is more of the *Humane* in these Things, than some are willing to own. We know every Thing appears more dismal in the Night: Persons are more apt to be struck with Surprise and Consternation: And as this is a good Reason, it may be the true one, why a *doleful Voice,* and frightful *Managements* may take Effect more in the *Night* than at other Times.

The *Subjects* also of these *Terrors* may lead us to make the like Judgment about them, and these are *Children, Women,* and *youngerly* Persons. Not that others han't been wrought upon. Instances there have been of *Men;* and these, both *middle-aged,* and *advanced in Years,* who have both *cried out,*and *fallen down:* But 'tis among *Children, young People* and *Women,* whose Passions are soft and tender, and more easily thrown into a Commotion, that these Things chiefly prevail. I know, 'tis thus in those Places, where I have had Opportunity to make Inquiry. And from the Accounts transmitted to me from Friends, in other Places, it appears to have been so among them also. . . .

Moreover, the *Way* in which these *Terrors* spread themselves is a Circumstance, that does not much favour their *divine Origin.* They seem to be suddenly propagated, from one to another, as in a great Fright or Consternation. They often begin with a single Person, a *Child,* or *Woman,* or *Lad,* whose *Shrieks* set others a *Shrieking;* and so the Shrieks catch from one to another, 'till the whole Congregation is alarmed, and such an awful Scene, many Times, open'd as no Imagination can paint to the Life. . . .

It will, possibly, be said, I have, in saying these Things, reflected Disgrace upon the *Work of Conviction.* If I had had such a Thought of the Matter, I should have suppressed what is here offered. Those, in my Opinion, do the greatest Dishonour to the *blessed* SPIRIT, and *his Influence* upon the Hearts of Sinners, in the Business of *Conviction,* who make no Distinction between those *Fears* that are the *Effect* of *Truth duly imprest upon the Mind,* and those that arise from an *affrightned Imagnination.* And to speak freely, I am clearly in the Sentiment, that the great Stress that has been laid upon *such Terrors,* as have evidently been produced by the *mechanical Influence* of *awful Words* and *frightful Gestures,* has been a great disservice to the Interest of Religion: Nay, I am not without Fear, least the tremendous Threatning of GOD have, by some, been *prophanely* made Use of, while, under the Pretense of wakening Men's Consciences, they have thunder'd out *Death* and *Damnation,* in a *Manner* more fit for the *Stage* than the *sacred Desk,* and so as to astonish the *Imagination* rather than possess the *Mind* of a *reasonable* Conviction of these awful Truths of GOD. I am not against the *Preaching of Terror;* but whenever this is done, it ought to be in a way that may enlighten the Mind, as well as alarm the Passions; And I am greatly mistaken, if this has been the Practice, among some Sort of Preachers, so much as it ought to be. And to this it may be owing, that Religion, of late, has been *more* a *Commotion in the Passions,* than a *Change* in the *Temper* of the *Mind:* Not but that, I think, a lasting Change has been wrought in a Number: though I could wish I had Reason to say, it was so great a Number as some pretend: Nay, I am not without Hopes, that some even of those who have been *frighten'd* into *Shrieks* and *Fits,* are *become new-Men;* but then, I have no other Thought, in the general, of the Surprise they were thrown into, than of the Surprise by a *terrible Clap of Thunder,* or the Shock of an *Earthquake:* They might hereby be awakened to Consideration, and put upon waiting upon GOD in his own Way, 'till a *Work of Grace* has been effected in them.

# 3

[The text is taken from "Report on Whitefield in New York," *The New England Weekly Journal,* December 4, 1739.]

## Report on Whitefield

*The Rev.* Mr. *Whitefield* arrived at the city of *N. York* on Wednesday the 14th a little before Night. The next morning he waited on the Rev. Mr. Berry, and desired leave to preach in the English Church, but was refus'd: The Reason assigned for such Refusal was because Mr. *Whitefield* had no Licence to Preach in any Parish but that for which he was ordained; and an old Canon was read. To this Mr. *Whitefield* reply'd that that Canon was Obsolete, and had not been in Use for above 100 years, that the whole Body of the Clergy frequently preach out of the Bounds of their Parishes, without such Licence. These Arguments not prevailing some Application was made to the Rev. Dr. *Boel,* for the Use of the *New Dutch Church,* but this also was refus'd. Then Mr. *Whitefield* had the offer of the *Presbyterian Church,* but did not care at first to accept it, not being willing to give any Offence to his Brethren of the Church of *England;* but said, *He chose rather to go without the Camp, bearing his Reproach, and Preach in the Fields.* At length being informed, that in some Parts of this Country, the Meeting Houses had been alternately us'd by the Ministers of the several Communions, and very often borrowed by the Church of the Dissenters, he consented to accept the Offer for the Evening. However, in the Afternoon he preached in the Fields to many Hundreds of People.

Among the Hearers, the Person who gives this Account, was one. I fear Curiosity was the Motive that led me and many others into that assembly. I had read two or three of Mr. *Whitefield's* Sermons and part of his Journal, and from thence had obtained a settled Opinion, that he was a Good Man. Thus far was I prejudiced in his Favour. But then having heard of much Opposition, and many Clamours against him, I tho't it possible that he might have carried Matters too far — That some *Enthusiasm* might have mix'd itself with his Piety, and that his Zeal might have exceeded his Knowledge. With these Pre-possessions I went into the Fields; when I came there, I saw a great Number of People consisting of *Christians* of all Denominations, some *Jews,* and a few, I believe, that had no Religion at all. When Mr. *Whitefield* came to the Place before designed, which was a little Eminence on the side of a Hill, he stood still, and beckned with his Hand, and dispos'd the Multitude upon the Descent, before, and on each side of him. He then prayed most excellently, in the same manner (I guess) that the first Ministers of the *Christian Church* prayed, before they were shackled with Forms. The Assembly soon appeared to be divided into two Companies, the one of which I considered under the Name of GOD's *Church,* and the other the *Devil's Chappel.* The first were collected round the Minister, and were very serious and attentive. The last had placed themselves in the skirts of the Assembly, and spent most of their Time in Gigling, Scoffing, Talking and Laughing. I believe the Minister saw them, for in his Sermon, observing the Cowardice and Shamefacedness of *Christians* in Christ's Cause, he pointed towards this Assembly, and reproached the former with the boldness and Zeal with which The Devil's Vassals serve him. Towards the last Prayer, the whole Assembly appeared more united, and all became hush'd and still; a solemn Awe and Reverence appeared in the Faces of most, a mighty Energy attended the Word. I heard and felt something astonishing and surprizing, but, I confess; I was not at that Time fully rid of my Scruples. But as I tho't I saw a visible Presence of GOD with Mr. *Whitefield,* I kept my Doubts to my self.

Under this Frame of Mind, I went to hear him in the Evening at the *Presbyterian Church,* where he Expounded to above 2000 People within and without Doors. I never in my Life saw so attentive an Audience: Mr. *Whitefield* spake as one having Authority: All he said was *Demonstration, Life,* and *Power!* The Peoples Eyes and Ears hung on his Lips. They greedily devour'd every Word. I came Home astonished! Every Scruple vanished. I never saw nor heard the like, and I said within my self, *Surely God is with this Man of a Truth.* He preach'd and expounded in this manner twice every Day for four Days, and this Evening Assemblies were continually increasing. On Sunday Morning at 8 o'Clock, his Congregation consisted of about 1500 People; But at Night several Thousands came together to hear him, and the Place being too strait for them, many were forced to go away, and some (tis said) with Tears lamented their Disappointment.

# 4

[The text is taken from Dr. A. Hamilton, "Journal," *Gentleman's Progress*, (n.p., n.d.), 161-163.]

## Journal

I went home att 6 o'clock, and Deacon Green's son came to see me. He entertained me with the history of the behaviour of one Davenport, a fanatick preacher there who told his flock in one of his enthusiastic rhapsodies that in order to be saved they ought to burn all their idols. They began this conflagration with a pile of books in the public street, among which were Tillotson's Sermons, Beveridge's Thoughts, Drillincourt on Death, Sherlock and many other excellent authors, and sung psalms and hymns over the pile while it was a burning. They did not stop here, but the women made up a lofty pile of hoop petticoats, silk gown, short cloaks, cambrick caps, red heeld shoes, fans, necklaces, gloves and other such apparrell, and what was merry enough, Davenport's own idol with which he topped the pile, was a pair of old, wore out, plush breaches. But this bone fire was happily prevented by one more moderate than the rest, who found means to perswade them that making such a sacrifice was not necessary for their salvation, and so every one carried off[f] their idols, again, which was lucky for Davenport who, had fire been put to the pile, would have been obliged to strutt about bare-arsed, for the devil another pair of breeches had he but these same old plush ones which were going to be offered up as an expiatory sacrifise. Mr. Green took his leave of me att 10 o'clock, and I went to bed.

### Toll - Bridge— Connecticut River

I passed over a bridge in very bad repair for which I payed eight pence toll, which here is something more than a penny farthing sterling, and coming down to Seabrook Ferry upon Connecticut River, I waited there 3 or 4 hours att the house of one Mather before I could get passage. The wind blew so hard att northwest with an ebb tide which, the ferrymen told me, would have carried us out into the Sound had we attempted to pass.

Mather and I had some talk about the opinions lately broached here in religion. He seemed a man of some solidity and sense and condemnd Whitefield's conduct in these parts very much. After dinner there came in a rabble of clowns who fell to disputing upon points of divinity as learnedly as if they had been professed theologues. 'Tis strange to see how this humour prevails, even among the lower class of the people here. They will talk so pointedly about justification, sanctification, adoption, regeneration, repentance, free grace, reprobation, original sin, and a thousand other such pritty, chimerical knick knacks as if they had done nothing but studied divinity all their life time and perused all the lumber of the scholastic divines, and yet the fellows look as much, or rather more, like clowns than the very riff-raff of our Maryland planters. To talk in this dialect in our parts would be like Greek, Hebrew or Arabick.

# E

While the descendants of the Quakers who came to Pennsylvania in the early days of the colony grew more prosperous and worldly with each passing generation, the spirit of the founders was kept alive by Quakers like John Woolman who spent his life fighting against injustice and oppression, against war, against the exploitation of the Indians and against slavery. We see in Woolman the prototype of the Christian reformer who became so prominent in the nineteenth century. If the great majority of Quakers at the time of the Revolution remained neutral because of their pacificist principles or, in some instances, allied themselves with the Tory supporters of Crown and Parliament, men and women like John Woolman helped to shape that conscience which made the Revolution not only possible but perhaps inevitable.

[The text is taken from John Woolman, *A Journal of the Life Gospel Labours, and Christian Experiences of. . .John Woolman*, (New York: Collins and Brothers, 1845).]

## A Journal of the Life Gospel Labours

. . . About this time believing it good for me to settle, and thinking seriously about a companion, my heart was turned to the Lord, with desires that he would give me wisdom to proceed therein agreeably to his will; and he was pleased to give me a well-inclined damsel, Sarah Ellis; to whom I was married the eighteenth of the eighth month 1749.

In the fall of the year 1750 died my father, Samuel Woolman, of a fever, aged about sixty years. In his lifetime he manifested much care about us his children, that in our youth we might learn to fear the Lord; and often endeavoured to imprint in our minds the true principles of virtue, and particularly to cherish in us a spirit of tenderness, not only towards poor people, but also towards all creatures of which we had the command.

After my return from Carolina in 1746, I made some observations on keeping slaves, which sometime before his decease I showed to him; he perused the manuscript, proposed a few alterations, and appeared well satisfied that I found a concern on that account. In his last sickness, as I was watching with him one night, he being so far spent that there was no expectation of his recovery, though he had the perfect use of his understanding, he asked me concerning the manuscript, and whether I expected soon to proceed to take the advice of friends in publishing it? After some further conversation thereon, he said, "I have all along been deeply affected with the oppression of the poor negroes; and now, at last, my concern for them is as great as ever."

By his direction I had written his will in a time of health, and that night he desired me to read it to him, which I did; and he said it was agreeable to his mind. He then made mention of his end, which he believed was near; and signified that though he was sensible of many imperfections in the course of his life, yet his experience of the power of truth, and of the love and goodness of God from time to time, even till now, was such, that he had no doubt that in leaving this life, he should enter into one more happy.

The next day, his sister Elizabeth came to see him, and told him of the decease of their sister Anne, who died a few days before; he then said, "I reckon sister Anne was free to leave this world?" Elizabeth said she was. He then said, "I also am free to leave it;" and being in great weakness of body said, "I hope I shall shortly go to rest." He continued in a weighty frame of mind, and was sensible till near the last.

Second of ninth month, 1751. Feeling drawings in my mind to visit friends at the Great Meadows, in the upper part of West Jersey, with the unity of our monthly meeting, I went there, and had some searching laborious exercise amongst friends in those parts, and found inward peace therein.

Ninth month, 1753. In company with my well-esteemed friend John Sykes, and with the unity of friends, I travelled about two weeks visiting friends in Buck's County. We laboured in the love of the gospel, according to the measure received; and through the mercies of Him, who is strength to the poor who trust in Him, we found satisfaction in our visit. In the next winter, way opening to visit friends' families within the compass of our monthly meeting, partly by the labours of two friends from Pennsylvania, I joined in some part of the work, having had a desire some time that it might go forward amongst us. . . .

The manuscript before-mentioned having laid by me several years, the publication of it rested weightily upon me; and this year I offered it to the revisal of my friends, who having examined, and made some small alterations in it, directed a number of copies thereof to be published and dispersed amongst members of our society. . . .

From a disagreement between the powers of England and France, it was now a time of trouble on this continent; and an epistle to friends went forth from our general spring meeting, which I thought good to give a place in this journal.

*An Epistle from our general spring meeting of ministers and elders for Pennsylvania and New Jersey, held at Philadelphia, from the twenty-ninth of the third month, to the first of the fourth month, inclusive, 1755.*

To Friends on the Continent of America.

*Dear Friends,* In an humble sense of divine goodness, and the gracious continuation of God's love to his people, we tenderly salute you; and are at this time therein engaged in mind, that all of us who profess the truth, as held forth and published by our worthy predecessors in this latter age of the world, may keep near to that life which is the light of men, and be strengthened to hold fast the profession of our faith without wavering, that our trust may not be in man, but in the Lord alone, who ruleth in the army of heaven, and in the kingdoms of men, before whom the earth is "as the dust of the balance, and her inhabitants as grasshoppers." Isa. xl. 22.

Being convinced that the gracious design of the Almighty in sending his Son into the world, was to repair the breach made by disobedience, to finish sin and transgression, that his kingdom might come, and his will be done on earth as it is in heaven, we have found it to be our duty to cease from those national contests which are productive of misery and bloodshed, and submit our cause to Him, the Most High, whose tender love to his children exceeds the most warm affections of natural parents, and who hath promised to his seed throughout the earth, as to one individual, "I will never leave thee, nor forsake thee." Heb. xiii. 5. And we, through the gracious dealings of the Lord our God, have had experience of that work which is carried on, not by earthly might, nor by power, but by my spirit, saith the Lord of Hosts." Zech. iv. 6. By which operation, that spiritual kingdom is set up, which is to subdue and break in pieces all kingdoms that oppose it, and shall stand for ever. In a deep sense thereof, and of the safety, stability, and peace that are in it, we are desirous that all who profess the truth, may be inwardly acquainted with it, and thereby be qualified to conduct ourselves in all parts of our life, as becomes our peaceable profession: and we trust, as there is a faithful continuance to depend wholly upon the almighty arm, from one generation to another, the peaceable kingdom will gradually be extended "from sea to sea, and from the river to the ends of the earth," Zech. ix. 10. to the completion of those prophecies already begun, that "nation shall not lift up a sword against nation, nor learn war any more." Isa. ii. 4. Micah. iv. 3. . . .

And now, dear friends, with respect to the commotions and stirrings of the powers of the earth at this time near us, we are desirous that none of us may be moved thereat; but repose ourselves in the munition of that rock which all these shakings shall not move, even in the knowledge and feeling of the eternal power of God, keeping us subjectly given up to his heavenly will, and feeling it daily to mortify that which remains in any of us which is of this world; for the worldly part in any, is the changeable part, and that is up and down, full and empty, joyful and sorrowful, as things go well or ill in this world. For as the truth is but one, and many are made partakers of its spirit, so the world is but one, and many are made partakers of the spirit of it; and so many as do partake of it, so many will be straitened and perplexed with it. But they who are single to the truth, waiting daily to feel the life and virtue of it in their hearts, shall rejoice in the mindst of adversity, and have to experience with the prophet, that, "although the fig-tree shall not blossom, neither shall fruit be in the vines; the labour of the olive shall fail, and the fields shall yield no meat; the flock shall be cut off from the fold, and there shall be no herd in the stalls; yet will they rejoice in the Lord, and joy in the God of their salvation." Hab. iii. 17, 18.

If, contrary to this, we profess the truth, and not living under the power and influence if it, are producing fruits disagreeable to the purity thereof, and trust to the strength of man to support ourselves, our confidence therein will be vain. For he who removed the hedge from his vineyard, and gave it to be trodden under foot, by reason of the wild grapes it produced, (Isa. v. 6.) remains unchangeable; and if, for the chastisement of wickedness, and the further promoting of his own glory, he doth arise, even to shake terribly the earth, who then may oppose him, and prosper!

We remain, in the love of the gospel, your friends and brethren.

*Signed by fourteen friends.*

Scrupling to do writings relative to keeping slaves, has been a means of sundry small trials to me, in which I have so evidently felt my own will set aside, I think it good to mention a few of them. Tradesmen and retailers of goods, who depend on their business for a living, are naturally inclined to keep the good will of their customers; nor is it a pleasant thing for young men to be under any necessity to question the judgment or honesty of elderly men, and more especially of such as have a fair reputation. Deep-rooted customs, though wrong, are not easily altered; but it is the duty of all to be firm in that which they certainly know is right for them. A charitiable, benevolent man, well acquainted with a negro, may I believe, under some circumstances, keep him in his family as a servant, on no other motives than the negro's good; but man, as man, knows not what shall be after him, nor hath he any assurance that his children will attain to that perfection in wisdom and goodness, necessary rightly to exercise such power; hence it is clear to me, that I ought not to be the scribe where wills are drawn, in which some children are made absolute masters over others during life.

About this time, an ancient man of good esteem in the neighbourhood, came to my house to get his will written. He had young negroes; and I asked him privately how he purposed to dispose of them. He told me; I then said, I cannot write thy will without breaking my own peace; and respectfully gave him my reasons for it. He signified that he had a choice that I should have written it; but as I could not, consistently with my conscience, he did not desire it; and so he got it written by some other person. A few years after, there being great alterations in his family, he came again to get me to write his will. His negroes were yet young; and his son, to whom he intended to give them, was, since he first spoke to me, from a libertine, become a sober young man; and he supposed that I would have been free on that account to write it. We had much friendly talk on the subject, and then deferred it. A few days after he came again, and directed their freedom; and I then wrote his will. . . .

Having found drawings in my mind to visit friends on Long Island, after obtaining a certificate from our monthly meeting, I set off twelfth of fifth month, 1756. When I reached the island, I lodged the first night at the house of my dear friend Richard Hallet. The next day, being the first of the week, I was at the meeting in New Town; in which we experienced the renewed manifestations of the love of Jesus Christ, to the comfort of the honest-hearted. I went that night to Flushing; and the next day, I and my beloved friend Matthew Franklin, crossed the ferry at White Stone; were at three meetings on the main, and then returned to the island; where I spent the remainder of the week in visiting meetings. The Lord I believe hath a people in those parts, who are honestly inclined to serve him; but many, I fear, are too much clogged with the things of this life, and do not come forward bearing the cross in such faithfulness as He calls for.

My mind was deeply engaged in this visit, both in public and private; and, at several places where I was, on observing that they had slaves, I found myself under a necessity, in a friendly way, to labour with them on that subject; expressing as way opened, the inconsistency of that practice with the purity of the Christian religion, and the ill effects of it manifested amongst us.

The latter end of the week their yearly meeting began; at which were our friends John Scarborough, Jane Hoskins, and Susannah Brown, from Pennsylvania. The public meetings were large, and measurably favoured with divine goodness. The exercise of my mind, at this meeting, was chiefly on account of those who were considered as the foremost rank in the society; and in a meeting of ministers and elders, way opened for me to express in some measure what lay upon me; and when friends were met for transacting the affairs of the church, having sat a while silent, I felt a weight on my mind, and stood up; and through the gracious regard of our heavenly Father, strength was given fully to clear myself of a burden, which for some days had been increasing upon me.

Through the humbling dispensations of Divine Providence, men are sometimes fitted for his service. The messages of the prophet Jeremiah were so disagreeable to the people, and so adverse to the spirit they lived in, that he became the object of their reproach; and in the weakness of nature, he thought of desisting from his prophetic office; but saith he, "His word was in my heart as a burning fire shut up in my bones; and I was weary with forebearing, and could not stay." I saw at this time, that if I was honest in declaring that which truth opened in me, I could not please all men; and I laboured to be content in the way of my duty, however disagreeable to my own inclination. After this I went homeward, taking Woodbridge and Plainfield in my way; in both which meetings, the pure influence of divine love was manifested; in an humbling sense whereof I went home. I had been out about twenty-four days, and rode about three hundred and sixteen miles.

While I was out on this journey, my heart was much affected with a sense of the state of the churches in our southern provinces; and believing the Lord was calling me to some further labour amongst them, I was bowed in reverence before Him, with fervent desires that I might find strenght to resign myself to his heavenly will.

Until this year, 1756, I continued to retail goods, besides following my trade as a tailor; about which time I grew uneasy on account of my business growing too cumbersome. I had begun with selling trimmings for garments, and from thence proceeded to sell cloths and linens; and at length, having got a considerable shop of goods, my trade increased every year, and the way to large business appeared open; but I felt a stop in my mind.

Through the mercies of the Almighty, I had, in a good degree, learned to be content with a plain way of living. I had but a small family; and on serious consideration, believed truth did not require me to engage much in cumbering affairs. It had been my general practice to buy and sell things really useful. Things that served chiefly to please the vain mind in people, I was not easy to trade in; seldom did it; and whenever I did, I found it weaken me as a Christian.

The increase of business became my burden; for though my natural inclination was toward merchandize, yet I believed truth required me to live more free from outward cumbers; and there was now a strife in my mind between the two. In this exercise my prayers were put up to the Lord, who graciously heard me, and gave me a heart resigned to his holy will. Then I lessened my outward business; and as I had opportunity, told my customers of my intentions, that they might consider what shop to turn to; and in a while I wholly laid down merchandize, and followed my trade as a tailor by myself, having no apprentice. I also had a nursery of apple-trees; in which I employed some of my time in hoeing, grafting, trimming, and inoculating. In merchandize it is the custom, where I lived, to sell chiefly on credit, and poor people often get in debt; when payment is expected, not having wherewith to pay, their creditors often sue for it at law. Having frequently observed occurrences of this kind, I found it good for me to advise poor people to take such goods as were most useful, and not costly. . . .

Every degree of luxury hath some connexion with evil; and if those who profess to be disciples of Christ, and are looked upon as leaders of the people, have that mind in them which was also in Christ, and so stand separate from every wrong way, it is a means of help to the weaker. As I have sometimes been much spent in the heat, and have taken spirits to revive me, I have found by experience, that in such circumstances the mind is not so calm, nor so fitly disposed for divine meditation, as when all such extremes are avoided. I have felt an increasing care to attend to that holy Spirit which sets right bounds to our desires; and leads those who faithfully follow it, to apply all the gifts of Divine Providence to the purposes for which they were intended. Did those who have the care of great estates, attend with singleness of heart to this heavenly Instructor, which so opens and enlarges the mind, as to cause men to love their neighbours as themselves, they would have wisdom given them to manage their concerns, without employing some people in providing the luxuries of life, or others in labouring too hard; but for want of steadily regarding this principle of divine love, a selfish spirit takes place in the minds of people, which is attended with darkness, and manifold confusions in the world.

Though trading in things useful is an honest employ; yet through the great number of superfluities which are bought and sold, and through the corruption of the times, they who apply to merchandize for a living, have great need to be well experienced in that precept which the prophet Jeremiah laid down for his scribe; "Seekest thou great things for thyself? seek them not."

# 8

---

John Wise's *Vindication of the Government of the Churches of New England* is a landmark in the movement of American thought from Winthrop's *Model of Christian Charity* to Jefferson's Declaration of Independence. Wise argues that the way to understand the laws of nature "is by a narrow watch and accurate contemplation of our natural condition and propensions." No particular form of government is ordained by good — "that particular form of government is necessary which best suits the temper and inclination of a people."

While Winthrop proclaimed a government in which the wise and pious led and the ordinary folk dutifully followed, Wise was a warm advocate of democratic government in the churches and in civil government as well. Thus while no particular form of government is ordained by God, God has established the "law of nature as the general rule of government," so that all who wish to do so may, by the use of their reason, comprehend those basic principles of "sociableness" on which every sound government is based. It was this conviction (that God's laws, the laws of nature, could be discerned only by human reason) that gave the Americans in the Revolutionary era the courage to launch themselves on the perilous task of establishing a *new* government.

What is also notable in Wise is that he sees man not simply as weak and depraved but as possessing a "high and admirable frame and constitution". Not only is there a natural equality among men; but even when men in their natural state have formed societies, an individual's "personal liberty and equality is to be cherished and perserved to the highest degree as . . . shall be agreeable with the public good."

In another resonant sentence, Wise declares that "the first human subject and original of civil power is the people;" and at the end of his essay he writes: "The end of all good government is to cultivate humanity and promote the happiness of all, and the good of every man in his rights, liberty, estate, honor, etc., without injury or abuse done to any." Wise thus comes down emphatically on the side of democracy as the best form of government.

There is certainly a substantial amount of Locke in John Wise's *Vindication* (perhaps Calvin modified by Locke); but Wise goes well beyond Locke in his praise of equality and democracy. Here he is, one dares to say, uniquely American. Wise has absorbed the implications of the events of the preceeding century, most notably the English Civil War, the Glorious Revolution of 1689, and the writings of the great English civil libertarians like Algernon Sidney. Its principal importance is in what it reveals to us of the evolution of this American mind and consciousness of which we have so frequently spoken.

[The text is taken from John Wise, *A Vindication of the Government of New England Churches*, (Boston: John Boyles, 1772).]

# A Vindication

### CHAPTER I.

The divine establishment in providence of the forenamed [New England] churches in their order is apparently the royal assent of the supreme monarch of the churches to the grave decisions of reason in favor of man's natural state of being and original freedom. For if we should make a new survey of the constitution before named under the brightest light of nature, there is no greater example of natural wisdom in any settlement on earth, for the present and future security of human beings in all that is most valuable and grand, than in this: that it seems to me as though wise and provident nature, by the dictates of right reason, excited by the moving suggestions of humanity, and awed with the just demands of natural liberty, equity, equality and principles of self-preservation, originally drew up the scheme, and then obtained the royal approbation. And certainly it is agreeable that we attribute it to God, whether we receive it next from reason or revelation, for that each is equally an emanation of His wisdom: [Prov. 20, 27] "The spirit of man is the candle of the Lord, searching all the inward parts of the belly." There be many larger volumes in this dark recess called the belly to be read by that candle God has lit up. And I am very well assured the forenamed constitution is a transcript out of some of their pages: [John 1, 4, 9] "And the life was the light of men, which lighteth every man which cometh into the world." This admirable effect of Christ's creating power in hanging out so many lights to guide man through a dark world is as applicable to the light of reason as to that of revelation, for that the light of reason as a law and rule of right is an effect of Christ's goodness, care and creating power, as well as of revelation — though revelation is nature's law in a fairer and brighter edition. . . .

But in the further and more distinct management of this plea, I shall:

1. Lay before the reader several principles of natural knowledge;

2. Apply or improve them in ecclesiastical affairs;

3. Infer from the premises a demonstration that these churches, if not proerly formed, yet are fairly established in their present order by the law of nature.

CHAPTER II

I shall disclose several principles of natural knowledge, plainly discovering the law of nature, or the true sentiments of natural reason, with respect to man's being and government. And in this essay I shall peculiarly confine the discourse to two heads, *viz.* I. Of the natural (in distinction to the civil), and then, II. Of the civil being of man. . . .

I. I shall consider man in a state of natural being, as a freeborn subject under the crown of heaven and owing homage to none but God Himself.

It is certain, civil government in general is a very admirable result of providence and an incomparable benefit to mankind, yet must needs be acknowledged to be the effect of human free compacts and not of divine institution. It is the produce of man's reason, of human and rational combinations, and not from any direct orders of infinite wisdom in any positive law where is drawn up this or that scheme of civil government. Government, says Lord Warrington, is necessary, in that no society of men can subsist without it; and that particular form of government is necessary which best suits the temper and inclination of a people. Nothing can be God's ordinance but what He has particularly declared to be such; there is no particular form of civil government described in God's word, neither does nature prompt it. The government of the Jews was changed five times. Government is not formed by nature, as other births or productions: if it were, it would be the same in all countries, because nature keeps the same method, in the same thing, in all climates. If a commonwealth be changed into a monarchy, is it nature that forms and brings forth the monarch? Or if a royal family be wholly extinct (as in Noah's case, being not heir apparent from descent from Adam), is it nature that must go to work (with the king bees, who themselves alone preserve the royal race in that empire) to breed a monarch before the people can have a king or a government set over them? And thus we must leave kings to resolve which is their best title to their crowns, whether natural right or the constitution of government settled by human compacts, under the direction and conduct of reason.

But to proceed under the head of a state of natural being, I shall more distinctly explain the state of human nature in its original capacity, as man is placed on earth by his maker and clothed with many investitures and immunities which properly belong to man separately considered. As:

1. The prime immunity in man's state is that he is most properly the subject of the law of nature. He is the favorite animal on earth, in that this part of God's image — *viz.* reason — is congenate with his nature, wherein, by a law immutable, instamped upon his frame, God has provided a rule for men in all their actions, obliging each one to the performance of that which is right, not only as to justice but likewise as to all other moral virtues, the which is nothing but the dictate of right reason founded in the soul of man. . . .

That which is to be drawn from man's reason, flowing from the true current of that faculty — when unperverted — may be said to be the law of nature: on which account, the Holy Scriptures declare it written on men's hearts. For being endowed with a soul, you may know from yourself how and what you ought to act: [Rom.2. 14] "These having not a law, are a law in themselves." So that the meaning is: when we acknowledge the law of nature to be the dictate of right reason, we must mean that the understanding of man is endowed with such a power as to be able, from the contemplation of human condition, to discover a necessity of living agreeably with this law: and likewise to find out some principle by which the precepts of it may be clearly and solidly demonstrated. The way to discover the law of nature in our own state is by a narrow watch and accurate contemplation of our natural condition and propensions. Others say this is the way to find out the law of nature: if a man any ways doubts whether what he is going to do to another man be agreeable to the law of nature, then let him suppose himself to be in that other man's room. And by this rule effectually executed, a man must be a very dull scholar to nature not to make proficiency in the knowledge of her laws.

But more particularly, in pursuing our conditon for the discovery of the law of nature, this is very obvious to view, *viz.*

A principle of self-love and self-preservation is very predominant in every man's being;

A sociable disposition;

An affection or love to mankind in general.

And to give such sentiments the force of a law, we must suppose a God who takes care of all mankind, and has thus obliged each one, as a subject of higher principles of being than mere instincts. For that all law, properly considered, supposes a capable subject and a superior power; and the law of God which is binding is published by the dictates of right reason as other ways. "Therefore," says Plutarch, "to follow God and obey reason is the same thing."

But moreover, that God has established the law of nature as the general rule of government is further illustrable from the many sanctions in providence, and from the peace and guilt of conscience in them that either obey or violate the law of nature. But moreover, the foundation of the law of nature with relation to government may be thus discovered: man is a creature extremely desirous of his own preservation; of himself he is plainly exposed to many wants, unable to secure his own safety and maintenance without the assistance of his fellows; and he is also able of returning kindness by the furtherance of mutual good. But yet man is often found to be malicious, insolent and easily provoked, and as powerful in effecting mischief as he is ready in designing it. Now, that such a creature may be preserved, it is necessary that he be sociable — that is, that he be capable and disposed to unite himself to those of his own species, and to regulate himself towards them, that they may have no fair reason to do him harm, but rather incline to promote his interests and secure his rights and concerns. This then is a fundamental law of nature, that every man, as far as in him lies, do maintain a sociableness with others, agreeable with the main end and disposition of human nature in general. For this is very apparent, that reason and society render man the most potent of all creatures. And finally, from the principles of sociableness it follows as a fundamental law of nature that man is not so wedded to his own interest but that he can make the common good the mark of his aim. And hence he becomes capacitated to enter into a civil state by the law of nature; for without this property in nature — *viz.* sociableness, which is for cementing of parts — every government would soon moulder and dissolve.

2. The second great immunity of man is an original liberty instamped upon his rational nature. He that intrudes upon this liberty violates the law of nature. In this discourse I shall waive the consideration of man's moral turpitude, but shall view him physically as a creature which God has made and furnished essentially with many ennobling immunities which render him the most august animal in the world; and still, whatever has happened since his creation, he remains at the upper end of nature, and as such is a creature of a very noble character. For as to his dominion, the whole frame of the lower part of the universe is devoted to his use and at his command; and his liberty under the conduct of right reason is equal with his trust.

Which liberty may be briefly considered — internally, as to his mind; and externally, as to his person:

The internal native liberty of man's nature in general implies a faculty of doing or omitting things according to the direction of his judgment. But in a more special meaning, this liberty does not consist in a loose and ungovernable freedom or in an unbounded license of acting. Such license is disagreeing with the condition and dignity of man, and would make man of a lower and meaner constitution than brute creatures, who in all their liberties are kept under better and more rational government by their instincts. Therefore as Plutarch says, "Those persons only who live in obedience to reason are worthy to be accounted free; they alone live as they will who have learned what they ought to will." So that the true natural liberty of man, such as really and truly agrees to him, must be understood as he is guided and restrained by the ties of reason and laws of nature; all the rest is brutal, if not worse.

Man's external, personal, natural liberty, antecedent to all human parts or alliances, must also ᴜᴄ considered. And so every man must be conceived to be perfectly in his own power and disposal, and not to be controlled by the authority of any other. And thus every man must be acknowledged equal to every man, since all subjection and all command are equally banished on both sides; and considering all men thus at liberty, every man has a prerogative to judge for himself, *viz.* what shall be most for his behoof, happiness and well-being.

3. The third capital immunity belonging to man's nature is an equality amongst men, which is not to be denied by the law of nature till man has resigned himself with all his rights for the sake of a civil state. And then his personal liberty and equality is to be cherished, and preserved to the highest degree as will consist with all just distinctions amongst men of honor, and shall be agreeable with the public good. For man has a high valuation of himself, and the passion seems to lay its first foundation, not in pride, but really in the high and admirable frame and constitution of human nature. The word "Man," says my author, is thought to carry somewhat of dignity in its sound; and we commonly make use of this as the most proper and prevailing argument against a rude insulter, *viz.* "I am not a beast or a dog, but am a man as well as yourself." Since then human nature agrees equally with all persons, and since no one can live a sociable life with another that does not own or respect him as a man, it follows as a command of the law of nature that every man esteem and treat another as one who is naturally his equal, or who

is a man as well as he. There be many popular or plausible reasons that greatly illustrate this equality: *viz.* that we all derive our being from one stock, the same common father of [the] human race. On this consideration Boethius checks the pride of the insulting nobility: . . .

> Fondly our first descent we boast;
>     If whence at first our breath we drew,
>     The common springs of life we view,
> The airy notion soon is lost.
>
> The Almighty made us equal all;
>     But he that slavishly complies
>     To do the drudgery of vice,
> Denies his high original.

And also, that our bodies are composed of matter, frail, brittle, and liable to be destroyed by [a] thousand accidents. We all owe our existence to the same method of propagation. The noblest mortal, in his entrance onto the stage of life, is not distinguished by any pomp or of passage from the lowest of mankind; and our life hastens to the same general mark: death observes no ceremony, but knocks as loud at the barriers of the Court as at the door of the cottage.

This equality being admitted, bears a very great force in maintaining peace and friendship amongst men. For that he who would use the assistance of others, in promoting his own advantage, ought as freely to be at their service when they want his help on the like occasions. "One good turn requires another" is the common proverb; for otherwise he must need esteem others unequal to himself, who constantly demands their aid, and as constantly denies his own. And whoever is of this insolent temper cannot but highly displease those about him, and soon give occasion of the breach of the common peace. It was a manly reproof which Charactacus gave the Romans: *Num si vos omnibus,* etc., "What! because you desire to be masters of all men, does it follow therefore that all men should desire to be your slaves?" For that it is a command of natures's law that no man that has not obtained a particular and special right shall arrogate to himself a larger share than his fellows, but shall admit others to equal privileges with himself. So that the principle of equality in a natural state is peculiarly transgressed by pride, which is when a man without sufficient reason prefers himself to others. And though, as Hensius paraphrases upon Aristotle's *Politics* to this purpose, *viz.* "Nothing is more suitable to nature than that those who excel in understanding and prudence should rule and control those who are less happy in those advantages, etc.," yet we must note that there is room for an answer: that it would be the greatest absurdity to believe that nature actually invests the wise with a sovereignty over the weak, or with a right of forcing them against their wills. For that no sovereignty can be established, unless some human deed or covenant precede. Nor does natural fitness for government make a man presently governor over another: for that, as Ulpian says, "by a natural right all men are born free." And nature having set all men upon a level and made them equals, no servitude or subjection can be conceived without inequality; and this cannot be made without usurpation or force in others, or voluntary compliance in those who resign their freedom and give away their degree of natural being.

II. And thus we come to consider man in a civil state of being: wherein we shall observe the great difference between a natural and political state; for in the latter state many great disproportions appear, or at least many obvious distinctions are soon made amongst men.

Which doctrine is to be laid open under a few heads:

1. Every man considered in a natural state must be allowed to be free and at his own dispose; yet to suit man's inclinations to society — and in a peculiar manner to gratify the necessity he is in of public rule and order — he is impelled to enter into a civil community, and divests himself of his natural freedom and puts himself under government: which amongst other things comprehends the power of life and death over him, together with authority to enjoin him some things to which he has an utter aversion, and to prohibit him other things for which he may have as strong an inclination, so that he may be often, under this authority, obliged to sacrifice his private for the public good. So that, though man is inclined to society, yet he is driven to a combination by great necessity. For that the true and leading cause of forming governments, and yielding up natural liberty and throwing man's equality into a common pile to be new cast by the rules of fellowship, was really and truly to guard themselves against the injuries men were liable to interchangeably. For none so good to man as man, and yet none a greater enemy.

2. So that, the first human subject and original of civil power is the people. For as they have a power, every man over himself in a natural state, so upon a combination they can and do bequeath this power unto others, and settle it according as their united discretion shall determine. For that this is very plain: that when the subject of sovereign power is quite extinct, that power returns to the people again. And when they are free, they may set up what species of government they please; or, if they rather incline to it, they may subside into a state of natural being, if it be plainly for the best. In the Eastern country of the Mogul, we have some resemblance of the case: for upon the death of an absolute monarch, they live so many days without a civil head; but in that interregnum, those who survive the vacancy are glad to get into a civil state again, and usually they are in a very bloody condition when they return under the covert of a new monarch. This project is to endear the people to a tyranny, from the experience they have so lately had of an anarchy.

3. The formal reason of government is the will of a community, yielded up and surrendered to some other subject, either of one particular person or more, conveyed in the following manner:

Let us conceive in our mind a multitude of men, all naturally free and equal, going about voluntarily to erect themselves into a new commonwealth. Now, their condition being such, to bring themselves into a politic body they must needs enter into divers covenants.

They must interchangeably, each man, covenant to join in one lasting society, that they may be capable to concert the measures of their safety by a public vote.

A vote or decree must then nextly pass to set up some particular species of government over them. And if they are joined in their first compact upon absolute terms to stand to the decision of the first vote concerning the species of government, they all are bound by the majority to acquiesce in that particular form thereby settled, though their own private opinion incline them to some other model.

After a decree has specified the particular form of government, then there will be need of a new covenant, whereby those on whom sovereignty is conferred engage to take care of the common peace and welfare, and the subjects on the other hand to yield them faithful obedience. In which covenant is included that submission and union of wills by which a state may be conceived to be but one person. So that the most proper definition of a civil state is this: a civil state is a compound moral person whose will (united by those covenants before passed) is the will of all, to the end it may use and apply the strength and riches of private persons towards maintaining the common peace, security and well-being of all. Which may be conceived as though the whole state was now become but one man, in which the aforesaid covenants may be supposed, under God's providence, to be the divine fiat pronounced by God, "Let us make man."

And by way of resemblance,the aforesaid being may be thus anatomized:

The sovereign power is the soul infused, giving life and motion to the whole body.

Subordinate officers are the joints by which the body moves.

Wealth and riches are the strength.

Equity and laws are the reason.

Councilors the memory.

*Salus Populi,* or the happiness of the people, is the end of its being, or main business to be attended and done.

Concord amongst the members and all estates is the health.

Sedition is sickness, and civil war death.

4. The parts of sovereignty may be considered; so:

As it prescribes the rule of action, it is rightly termed legislative power.

As it determines the controversies of subjects by the standard of those rules, so is it justly termed judiciary power.

As it arms the subjects against foreigners or forbids hostility, so it's called the power of peace and war.

As it takes in ministers for the discharge of business, so it is called the right of appointing magistrates. So that all great officers and public servants must needs owe their original to the creating power of sovereignty. So that those whose right it is to create may dissolve the being of those who are created, unless they cast them into an immortal frame. And yet must needs be dissoluble if they justly forfeit their being to their creators.

The chief end of civil communities is that men thus conjoined may be secured against the injuries they are liable to from their own kind. For if every man could secure himself singly, it would be great folly for him to renounce his natural liberty, in which every man is his own king and protector.

The sovereign authority, besides that it inheres in every state as is a common and general subject, so farther, according as it resides in some one person, or in a council (consisting of some select persons or of all the members of a community) as in a proper and particular subject, so it produceth different forms of commonwealths, *viz.* such as are either simple and regular, or mixed.

The forms of a regular state are three only, which forms arise from the proper and particular subject in which the supreme power resides. As:

1. A democracy: which is when the sovereign power is lodged in a council consisting of all the members, and where every member has the privilege of a vote.

This form of government appears in the greatest part of the world to have been the most ancient. For that reason seems to show it to be most probable that when men (being originally in a condition of natural freedom and equality) had thoughts of joining in a civil body, [they] would without question be inclined to administer their common affairs by their common judgment, and so must necessarily, to gratify that inclination, establish a democracy. Neither can it be rationally imagined that fathers of families, being yet free and independent, should in a moment, or little time, take off their long delight in governing their own affairs and devolve all upon some single sovereign commander. For that it seems to have been thought more equitable that what belonged to all should be managed by all, when all had entered by compact into one community. "The original of our government," says Plato (speaking of the Athenian commonwealth), "was taken from the equality of our race. Other states there are, composed of different blood and of unequal lines, the consequences of which are disproportionable sovereignty, trynnical or oligarchical sway, under which men live in such a manner as to esteem themselves partly lords and partly slaves to each other. But we and our countrymen, being all born brethren of the same mother, do not look upon ourselves to stand under so hard a relation as that of lords and slaves; but the parity of our descent inclines us to keep up the like parity by our laws, and to yield the precedency to nothing but to superior virtue and wisdom."

And moreover, it seems very manifest that most civil communities arose at first from the union of families that were nearly allied in race and blood. And though ancient story make frequent mention of kings, yet it appears that most of them were such that had an influence rather in persuading than in any power of commanding. . . .

A democracy is then erected when a number of free persons do assemble together, in order to enter into a covenant for uniting themselves in a body. And such a preparative assembly hath some appearance already of a democracy: it is a democracy in embryo properly in this respect, that every man hath the privilege freely to deliver his opinion concerning the common affairs. Yet he who dissents from the vote of the majority is not in the least obliged by what they determine, till by a second covenant a popular form be actually established. For not before then can we call it a democratical government, *viz.* till the right of determining all matters relating to the public safety is actually placed in a general assembly of the whole people, or by their own compact and mutual agreement, determine themselves the proper subject for the exercise of sovereign power.

And to complete this state, and render it capable to exert its power to answer the end of a civil state, these conditions are necessary:

That a certain time and place be assigned for assembling.

That when the assembly be orderly met, as to time and place, that then the vote of the majority must pass for the vote of the whole body.

That magistrates be appointed to exercise the authority of the whole, for the better dispatch of business of every day's occurrence; who also may with more mature diligence search into more important affairs, and if in case any thing happens of greater consequence may report it to the assembly, and be peculiarly serviceable in putting all public decrees into execution — because a large body of people is almost useless in respect of the last service, and of many others as to the more particular application and exercise of power. Therefore it is most agreeable with the law of nature that they institute their officers to act in their name and stead.

2. The second species of regular government is an aristocracy. And this is said then to be constituted when the people or assembly, united by a first covenant and having thereby cast themselves into the first rudiments of a state, do then, by common decree, devolve the sovereign power on a council, consisting of some select members. And these, having accepted of the designation, are then properly invested with sovereign command. And then an aristocracy is formed.

3. The third species of a regular government is a monarchy, which is settled when the sovereign power is conferred on some one worthy person. . . .

An aristocracy is a dangerous constitution in the church of Christ, as it possesses the presbytery of all church power. What has been observed sufficiently evinces it. And not only so but from the nature of the constitution, for it has no more barrier to it — against the ambition, insults and arbitrary measures of men — than an absolute monarchy.

But to abbreviate: it seems most agreeable with the light of nature that if there be any of the regular government settled in the church of God, it must needs be a democracy.

This is a form of government which the light of nature does highly value, and often directs to as most agreeable to the just and natural prerogatives of human beings. This was of great account in the early times of the world. And not only so, but upon the experience of several thousand years, after the world had been tumbled and tossed from one species of government to another, at a great expense of blood and treasure, many of the wise nations of the world have sheltered themselves under it again: — or at least have blendished and balanced their governments with it.

It is certainly a great truth, that man's original liberty, after it is resigned (yet under due restrictions), ought to be cherished in all wise governments; or otherwise a man, in making himself a subject, he alters himself from a freeman into a slave, which to do is repugnant to the law of nature. Also the natural equality of men amongst men must be duly favored, in that government was never established by God or nature to give one man a prerogative to insult over another. Therefore in a civil, as well as in a natural, state of being, a just equality is to be indulged, so far as that every man is bound to honor every man, which is agreeable both with nature and religion: [I Pet. 2. 17] "Honor all men."

The end of all good government is to cultivate humanity and promote the happiness of all, and the good of every man in all his rights, his life, liberty, estate, honor, etc., without injury or abuse done to any. Then certainly it cannot easily be thought that a company of men, that shall enter into a voluntary compact, to hold all power in their own hands, thereby to use and improve their united force, wisdom, riches and strength for the common and particular good of every member, as is the nature of a democracy — I say, it cannot be that this sort of constitution will so readily furnish those in government with an appetite or disposition to prey upon each other, or embezzle the common stock, as some particular persons may be apt to do when set off and entrusted with the same power. And moreover, this appears very natural, that when the aforesaid government or power, settled in all — when they have elected certain capable persons to minister in their affairs, and the said ministers remain accountable to the assembly, these officers must needs be under the influence of many wise cautions from their own thoughts (as well as under confinement by their commission) in their whole administration. And from thence it must needs follow that they will be more apt and inclined to steer right for the main point, *viz.* the peculiar good and benefit of the whole and every particular members fairly and sincerely. And why may not these stand for very rational pleas in church order?

For certainly if Christ has settled any form of power in his church, he has done it for his church's safety and for the benefit of every member. Then he must needs be presumed to have made choice of that government as should least expose his people to hazard, either from the fraud or arbitrary measures of particular men. And it is as plain as daylight, there is no species of government like a democracy to attain this end. There is but about two steps from an aristocracy to a monarchy, and from thence but one to a tyranny. An able standing force and an ill nature *ipso facto* turn an absolute monarch into a tyrant; this is obvious among the Roman Caesars, and through the world. And all these direful transmutations are easier in church affairs (from the different qualities of things) than in civil states. For what is it that cunning and learned men can't make the world swallow as an article of their creed if they are once invested with an uncontrollable power, and are to be the standing orators to mankind in matters of faith and obedience?

# 9

---

The case of Jonathan Mayhew is markedly different from that of John Wise. Wise published his *Vindication* in 1717 and died eight years later. Mayhew, born in 1720, died a comparatively young man in 1766 at the beginning of the Revolutionary struggle. In his *Discourse Concerning Unlimited Submission*, the political implications of Wise's theoretical formulations are more clearly spelled out. Mayhew advances orthodox Calvinism when he writes that "no civil rulers are to be obeyed when they enjoin things that are inconsistent with the commands of God," adding "all such disobedience is lawful and glorious." This argument was directed specifically at the efforts of the Church of England to extend its establishment to America and make Anglican orthodoxy the 'state' religion of the English colonies; but it applied almost equally well to a number of other primarily secular issues which had, in Puritan eyes, definite religious dimensions (as indeed virtually everything did).

Mayhew was viewed by Lt. Governor Hutchinson as somewhat of a rabble-rouser for his sermons advocating resistance to unconstitutional authority; and his ideas were undoubtedly influential in Boston rational circles. However, it is interesting to note that when the Stamp Act riots broke out in Boston, Mayhew was as alarmed as Hutchinson and wrote him a letter disclaiming any sympathy with the rioters. So fearful was he of arousing the hostility of the patriots that he asked Hutchinson to burn the letter lest it fall into their hands.

[The text is taken from Jonathan Mayhew, *Discourse Concerning Unlimited Submission*, (Boston: D. Fowle, 1750).]

# Discourse Concerning Unlimited Submission

If we calmly consider the nature of the thing itself, nothing can well be imagined more directly contrary to common sense than to suppose that millions of people should be subjected to the arbitrary, precarious pleasure of one single man (who has naturally no superiority over them in point of authority), so that their estates and everything that is valuable in life, and even their lives also, shall be absolutely at his disposal, if he happens to be wanton and capricious enough to demand them. What unprejudiced man can think that God made all to be thus subservient to the lawless pleasure and frenzy of one, so that it shall always be a sin to resist him! Nothing but the most plain and express revelation from heaven could make a sober impartial man believe such a monstrous, unaccountable doctrine, and, indeed, the thing itself appears so shocking — so out of all proportion — that it may be questioned whether all the miracles that ever were wrought, could make it credible, that this doctrine really came from God. At present, there is not the least syllable in scripture which gives any countenance to it. The hereditary, indefeasible, divine right of kings, and the doctrine of non-resistance which is built upon the supposition of such a right, are altogether as fabulous and chimerical as transubstantiation or any of the most absurd reveries of ancient or modern visionaries. These notions are fetched neither from divine revelation nor human reason; and if they are derived from neither of those sources, it is not much matter from whence they come, or whither they go. Only it is a pity that such doctrines should be propagated in society, to raise factions and rebellions, as we see they have, in fact, been both in the last and in the present reign.

But then, if unlimited submission and passive obedience to the higher powers, in all possible cases, be not a duty, it will be asked, "How far are we obliged to submit? If we may innocently disobey and resist in some cases, why not in all? Where shall we stop? What is the measure of our duty? This doctrine tends to the total dissolution of civil government; and to introduce such scenes of wild anarchy and confusion, as are more fatal to society than the worst of tyranny."

After this manner, some men object; and, indeed, this is the most plausible thing that can be said in favor of such an absolute submission as they plead for. But the worst (or rather the best) of it is that there is very little strength or solidity in it. For similar difficulties may be raised with respect to almost every duty of natural and revealed religion. To instance only in two, both of which are near akin, and indeed exactly parallel, to the case before us: it is unquestionably the duty of children to submit to their parents, and of servants to their masters. But no one asserts that it is their duty to obey and submit to them in all supposable cases; or universally a sin to resist them. Now does this tend to subvert the just authority of parents and masters? Or to introduce confusion and anarchy into private families? No. How then does the same principle tend to unhinge the government of that larger family, the body politic? We know, in general, that children and servants are obliged to obey their parents and masters respectively. We know also, with equal certainty, that they are not obliged to submit to them in all things, without exception, but may, in some cases reasonably, and therefore innocently, resist them. These principles are acknowledged upon all hands, whatever difficulty there may be in fixing the exact limits of submission. Now there is at least as much difficulty in stating the measure of duty in these two cases as in the case of rulers and subjects. So that this is really no objection, at least no reasonable one, against resistance to the higher powers. Or, if it is one, it will hold equally against resistance in the other cases mentioned.

It is indeed true, that turbulent, vicious-minded men may take occasion from this principle, that their rulers may in some cases be lawfully resisted, to raise factions and disturbances in the state; and to make resistance where resistance is needless and therefore sinful. But is it not equally true that children and servants of turbulent, vicious minds, may take occasion from this principle, that parents and masters may in some cases be lawfully resisted, to resist when resistance is unnecessary and therefore criminal? Is the principle in either case false in itself, merely because it may be abused and applied to legitimate disobedience and resistance in those instances, to which it ought not to be applied? According to this way of arguing, there will be no true principles in the world; for there are none but what may be wrested and perverted to serve bad purposes, either through the weakness or wickedness of men.

A people, really oppressed to a great degree by their sovereign, cannot well be insensible when they are so oppressed. And such a people (if I may allude to an ancient fable) have, like the hesperian fruit, a dragon for their protector and guardian. Nor would they have any reason to mourn if some Hercules should appear to dispatch him. For a nation thus abused to arise unanimously, and to resist their prince, even to the dethroning him, is not criminal, but a reasonable way of vindicating their liberties and just rights; it is making use of the means, and the only means, which God has put into their power, for mutual and self-defense. And it would be highly criminal in them not to make use of this means. It would be stupid tameness and unaccountable folly for whole nations to suffer one unreasonable, ambitious and cruel man to wanton and riot in their misery. And in such a case it would, of the two, be more rational to suppose that they that did not resist, than that they who did, would receive to themselves damnation.

# 10

---

James Otis in his *Rights of the Colonists Asserted and Proved* drew together a number of important themes that we have tried to emphasize both in the general introduction to this volume and in the prefaces of many of the individual selections. Otis was reacting, in this instance, to the passage by Parliament of the Revenue Act of 1764, a measure which was intended to raise revenue by placing a tax on the importation of molasses for the manufacture of New England rum. "One single Act of Parliament," Otis wrote, "has set people a-thinking, in six months, more than they had done in their whole lives before."

The Revenue Act immediately summoned up the spectre of "taxation without representation." What lay even deeper than colonial anxiety about 'having their money taken out of their pockets without their consent' was a sudden sense of powerlessness and dependence. It was not that the duties imposed were excessively onerous (they fell primarily on the merchants who imported molasses); but the passage of the act symbolized the subordinate status of the Americans. Otis was one of the first colonists to perceive the implications of the Revenue Act and to undertake to formulate a relationship between Parliament and the colonies that would protect them from the arbitrary actions of the British government.

Otis begins by identifying the source of all governmental power: "it has an everlasting foundation in the unchangeable will of God, the author of nature, whose laws never vary." In this statement, Otis is the intellectual heir of Calvin, Wise and Mayhew. Otis then goes on to state that Parliament, like every human institution, also lies under the judgments of the Almighty. It thus follows that "Should an Act of Parliament be against His natural laws, which are immutably true, their declaration would be contrary to eternal truth, equity, and justice, and consequently void. . . ." But who was to adjudge them so? In a burst of quite unwarranted optimism, Otis expressed the view that Parliament itself would do so, once its error had been pointed out. Aware that he was standing on shakey ground, Otis declared that if Parliament failed to rectify its own mistake, it was then up to the executive courts to declare an act contrary to natural law to be null and void. In support of his argument, he pointed to several ancient and rather questionable cases where the courts in fact had done just that.

At this point it is well to stress the fact that Otis and his colonial contemporaries saw natural laws and the provisions of the Bill of Rights (drafted at the time of the Glorious Revolution and imposed on William and Mary as part of the Revolution Settlement) as more or less interchangeable: those rights protected by the Bill of Rights (and later to be incorporated in the constitutions of most of the new states and in the first ten amendments to the Constitution) were divine rights, derived from those same "immutable laws" that Otis refers to. It is also notable that Otis's essay contains in embryo the idea of the Supreme Court, perhaps the most novel aspect of the Federal Constitution.


[The text is taken from James Otis, *Rights of the British Colonists Asserted and Proved*, (Boston: Edes and Gill, 1764).]


# Rights of the British Colonists


A Vindication of the *British Colonies,* against the Aspersions of the *Halifax* Gentleman in his Letter to a *Rhode-Island* Friend

It had been long expected, that some American pen would be drawn in support of those measures, which to all thinking men must appear to be very extraordinary. Those who are above party, can peruse the speculations of a Whig or a Tory, a Quaker or a Jacobite, with the same composure of mind. Those who confine themselves within the bounds of moderation and decency, are so far respectable. All who grow outrageous, are disgustful. The head of a *tribunitian veto,* with a mob at his heels, and a grand *Asiatic* monarch, with a shoal of sycophants clinging about him, like the little wrecthes in the well known print of Hobbes's Leviathan, may be objects of equal diversion, derision and contempt. Mankind ever were, are and will be divisible, into the great and small vulgar. Both will have their respective heads. The laws of nature are uniform and invariable. The same causes will produce the same effects, from generation to generation. He that would be a great captain, must for a season exult in the honor of being a little one.

> "Bred on the mountains had *proud* Julius been,
> "He'd shone a *sturdy* wrestler on the green."

The Halifax Gentleman having discovered that governor H — pk — ns is "totally unacquainted with stile and diction," and yet "eagerly fond to pass upon the world for a man of letters," great perfection might be reasonably expected in the composition of the friendly epistle. Instead of this, are found inaccuracies in abundance, declamation and false logic without end; *verse* is retailed in the shape of *prose,* solecisms are attempted to be passed off for good grammar, and the most indelicate fustian for the fine taste. The whole performance is truly *Filmerian.* The picture is very well charged with shade and thick darkness, intermixed with here and there a ray of light; now and then a flash, and once in a while is heard a little rumbling thunder from a few distant broken clouds.

> "Some future bard may sing the present times,
> "And HE be made the hero of the song."

These two lines are crouded together in one short sentence, in a prosaic form. (page 4)

The gentleman (page 5.) has given us a portrait of the English nation. It contains but a dozen lines, and expresses or plainly implies the following wonderful group of ideas, viz. "A high pitch of glory and power, envy and admiration of surrounding slaves, holding fast the balance of Europe, a rival in arts / and arms of every period ancient and modern, impatience, jealousy, pride and folly, prodigality, particularly in laying wagers to the value of kingdoms, and a quick sensibility and consciousness of dignity, which renders plain simple truth intolerable," As the English nation expired about sixty years since, in the union of the two kingdoms, 'tis needless to enquire whether this be a just character of that once brave and generous, free and loyal people: But if this should be intended for a filial compliment to Great Britain, 'tis a very indifferent one. In the late war, America joined in the stakes: The bet was not for the safety of the colonies alone; it was for the salvation of Great-Britain, as well as the plantations, i.e. for the whole community. Cornwall raises and pays one company of dragoons, Devonshire another: Is Cornwall more obliged to Devonshire than Devonshire is to Cornwall? They are both obliged by the strongest ties of duty and loyalty, to the gracious Prince who protects and defends both: To each other they owe but love and good will.

I cannot think Mr. H — k — s, or any other of the writers who have the misfortune to fall under the sore displeasure of the Halifax Gentleman, ever really intended to encourage so groundless a claim as an independent uncontroulable Provincial legislative. Most of them 'tis well known expressly disavow such a claim. It is certain that the Parliament of Great-Britain hath a just, clear, equitable and constitutional right, power and authority, to bind the colonies, by all acts wherein they are named. Every lawyer, nay every Tyro knows this. No less certain is it that the Parliament of Great-Britain has a just and equitable right, power and authority, to *impose taxes on the colonies, internal and external, on lands, as well as on trade.* This is involved in the idea of a supreme legislative, or sovereign power of a state. It will however by no means from thence follow, that 'tis always expedient, and in all circumstances equitable for the supreme and sovereign legislative to tax the colonies, much less than 'tis reasonable this right should be practised upon without allowing the colonies an actual representation. An equal representation of the whole state is, at least in theory, of the essence of a perfect parliament, or supreme legislative.

There is not the least color of a contradiction between the passages from the "rights of the colonies," cited pages 6 and 7. It must indeed be confessed and lamented, that the last citation involves an sophism, unworthy the pen from whence it fell. But the critic with all his sagacity has not pointed where the fallacy lies. He has reduced his Honor's argument to the form of a syllogism, which is conclusive. "The people of Great-Britain have not any sort of power over the Americans;" "The house of commons have no greater authority than the people of Great-/Britain, who are their constituents;" "*ergo* the house of commons have not any sort of power over the Americans." This I take to be literally true. Yet by the following reduction, the fallacy of his Honor's argument will appear, "The common people of Great-Britain have no sovereign absolute authority over their fellow-subjects in America;" "The house of commons alone have no greater authority than the common people of Great-Britain;" "*ergo,* the British parliament, the King's Majesty, Lords and Commons, have no sovereign absolute authority over the subjects in the colonies." Who does not see the fallacy of this conclusion? The inquiry was not of the sole and separate power and authority of the house of commons, but of the authority of that august and transcendent body the parliament, which is composed of the three branches of the grand legislature of the nation, considered as united. But all this shows that the last citation at most is but an implicit, and is far from an "express, denial of the authority of parliament," and should, by that candor that is inseparable from a liberal mind, have been imputed to meer inadvertency.

We come now to the *rationale* of the epistle. "I have endeavoured (says the gentleman) to investigate the *true natural relation,* if I *may so speak,* between the colonies and their mother state, *abstracted* from *compact* or *positive Institution.*" What a parade is here? What "a solemnity" does "he give to his per-/formance?" "If I may so speak." Who would not think the world was about to be favored with some extraordinary discovery, too mighty for the powers and precision of language!

Let us attend the course of the bubble. "But here (adds he) I can find nothing satisfactory: Yet till this *relation* is clearly defined upon *rational* and *natural principles,* our *reasoning* upon the *measures* of the colonies obedience, will be *desultory* and inconclusive." "Every connection or relation in life has its reciprocal duties; we know the relation between a parent and a child, husband and wife, master and servant, and from thence are able to deduce their respective obligations." "But we have no notices of any *such* precise natural relation between a *mother state* and its colonies, and therefore cannot reason with so much certainty upon the *power* of the one, or the *duties* of the other." If, as the gentleman tells us, he could not find any thing satisfactory, he could only guess what reasoning would follow: And I leave it to his readers to determine, whether he has not proved that he guessed very rightly. He has placed the relation of master and servant among what he calls natural relations. In a state of nature, where all are equal, I believe the gentleman would be as much puzzled to find his master or servant, as others now may be to find his equal. 'Tis a little strange he should attempt to reason on a subject, of which he confesses he could find no "satisfactory notices." But/he seems determined to flounder on thro' thick and thin, be his reasonings "desultory" or conclusive.

"The ancients (says he) have *transmitted* (for handed down; 'tis a wonder it had not been *transported)* to us nothing that is applicable to the state of the modern colonies, because the *relation* between these (and their mother state should have been added) is formed by *political compact." Brave!* "And the *condition* of each variant in their original and from each other." Better and better still! If *condition* means the present state, and I think it can mean nothing else, what a delectable piece of jargon does the close of this period make! It amounts to this: "The present state of each modern colony is variant in its original, and from each other." Be this as it may; if the *relation* of modern colonies to their mother states, is founded on *political compact,* how came the gentleman to beat his brains to find out "their *natural relation abstracted from compact or positive institution?*" To what purpose he has done this, he tells us when he confesses he can find nothing "satisfactory" about it. Are not *natural* and meerly *political* or *civil relations* different things? Is it not a little jargonical and inconsistent, in one breath to talk of "investigating the *true, natural, clearly defined* relation of the colonies to their mother state, abstract from compact or positive institution;" and in the next to affirm, that so far as relates to modern/colonies, this relation depends, or "is founded on political compact?" Was there a natural relation between ancient states and their colonies, and none between the modern states and their colonies? Is not a "political compact", the same thing with a "positive institution"? Is this "freeing a subject from embarrassment"? Well might the gentleman "shun the walk of metaphysics." I wish he had not so much avoided that of logic. He every where seems to consider *power* and *duty* as correlated. Surely he should be the last man to charge his adversary with "vague and diffuse talk of" those levelling notions, "right and privileges". He bewilders himself for half a poor creeping page more, abruptly sings a *requiem* to his sweet soul, composes the surges of his "philosophically inquisitive mind," fatigued with its late flight after natural and political relations, and very gravely contents himself with considering the "colonies rights upon the footing of their charters." This foothold, by a new and bold figure in rhetoric, he calls "the only plain avenues that lead to the truth of this matter."

————*"facilis descensus Averni."*

The gentleman is at a loss (page 8) to "conceive how it comes to pass that the colonies now claim *any other or greater* rights than are expressly granted to them" by charter. Is the gentleman a British-born subject and a lawyer, and ignorant that charters from the/crown have usually been given for enlarging the liberties and privileges of the grantees, not for limiting them, much less for curtailing those essential rights which all his Majesty's subjects are entitled to, by the laws of God and nature, as well as by the common law, and by the constitution of their country?

The distinction (page 8.) between personal and political rights, is a new invention, and, as applied, has perplexed the author of it. He every where confounds the terms rights, liberties and privileges, which, in legal as well as vulgar acceptation, denote very different ideas. This is a common mistake with those who cannot see any difference between power and right, between a blind slavish submission, and a loyal, generous and rational obedience, to the supreme authority of a state.

The rights of men are, *natural* or *civil.* Both these are divisible into *absolute* and *relative.* The natural absolute personal rights of individuals, are so far from being opposed to political or civil rights, that they are the very basis of all municipal laws of any great value. "The absolute rights of individuals, regarded by the municipal laws, compose what is called *political* or *civil liberty."* "The absolute liberties of Englishmen, as frequently declared in parliament, are principally three.   1. The right of *personal* security, 2. personal *liberty,* and 3. private property." "Besides these three *primary rights,* there are others which are *secondary* and *subordinate,* (to preserve the former/from unlawful attacks). 1. The constitution or power of parliament. 2. The limitation of the King's perogative (and to vindicate them when actually violated). 3. The regular administration of justice. 4. The right of petitioning for redress of grievances. 5. The right of having and using arms for self-defence." See Mr. Blackstone's accurate and elegant analysis of the laws of England. The gentleman seems to have taken this and some other of his distinctions from that excellent treatise very ill understood. The analysis had given this general view of the *objects* of the laws of England. I. Rights of Person. II. Rights of Things. III. Private wrongs. IV. Public wrongs. Rights of persons are divided into these, 1. of natural persons; 2. of bodies politic or corporate, i.e. artificial persons, or subordinate societies. The rights of these are by the Letter-writer strangely confounded with the political and civil rights of natural persons. And because corporate rights, so far as they depend upon charter, are matters of the meer favor and grace of the donor or founder; he thence infers (page 9). That "the colonies have no rights independent of their charters," and that "they can claim no greater than those give them." This is a contradiction to what he admitted in the preceding page, viz. That "by the common law every colonist hath a right to his life, liberty and property." And he was so vulgar as to call these the "subjects birth-right"./But what is this birth-right worth, if it depends meerly upon a colony charter, that, as he says rightly enough, may be taken away by the parliament? I wish the gentleman would answer these questions. Would he think an estate worth much, that might be taken from him at the pleasure of another? Are charters from the crown usually given for enlarging the liberties and privileges of the grantees, in consideration of some special merit and services done the state, or would he have his readers consider them like the ordinances of a French monarch, for limiting and curtailing those rights which all Britons, and all British subjects, intituled to by the laws of God and nature, as well as by the common law and the constitution of their country, so admirably built on the principles of the former? By which of these laws, in contradistinction to the other, are the rights of life, liberty, and estate, personal?

The gentleman's positions and principles, that "the several New-England charters ascertain, define and limit the respective *rights* and privileges of each colony," and that "the colonies have no rights independent of their charter," and that "they can claim no greater than those give them," if true, would afford a curious train of consequences. Life, liberty and property, are, by the law of nature as well as by the common law, secured to the happy inhabitants of South-Britain, and constitute their *primary* civil or political rights. But in/the colonies, these and all other rights, according to our author, depend upon charter. Therefore those of the colonies who have no charter, have no right to life, liberty or property. And in those colonies who have charters, these invaluable blessings depend on the meer good will, grace and pleasure of the supreme power; and all their charters, and of course all their rights, even to life, liberty and property, may be taken away at pleasure. Thus every charter in England may be taken away; for they are but voluntary and gracious grants of the crown, of certain limited, local, political privileges, superadded to those of the common law. But would it be expedient to strike such a blow, without the most urgent necessity? "In all states there is (and must be) an absolute supreme power, to which the right of *legislation* belongs; and which by the singular constitution of these kingdoms is vested in the Kings, Lords, and Commons."* Now Magna Charta is but a law of their making, and they may alter it at pleasure; but does it thence follow, that it would be expedient to repeal every statute from William the Conqueror, to this time? But by the gentleman's principles, this may be done wantonly, and without any reason at all. Further, by his logic the parliament may make the monarchy absolute, or reduce it to a republic; both which would be contrary to the trust reposed in them by the constitution, which is to preserve, not destroy/it; and to this all are sworn, from the King's Majesty in his coronation oath, to the meanest subject in the oath of allegiance. Into such absurd and treasonable doctrines must the gentleman run, in order to be consistent. Nay, all the vagaries of Filmer, Manwaring and Sibthorp, and of the whole tribe of King Adam's subjects, will follow. As 1. That Adam was the first monarch of this earth. No Prince has a title to his crown but he who can prove himself to be the eldest heir male of the body of Adam. That all other Princes are usurpers and tyrants. That according to Filmer, God hath given to every father over his children, and much more to every Prince over his subjects, a power "absolute, arbitrary and unlimited, and unlimitable over the lives, liberties and estates of such children and subjects; so that they may take or alienate their estates sell, castrate or use their persons as he pleases, they being all his slaves, and the father or prince, lord proprietor of everything, and his unbounded will their law." This is the substance of one of Mr. Locke's inferences from these words of Filmer; "God hath given to the father a right or liberty to alien his power over his children to any other; whence we find the sale and gift of children to have been much in use in the beginning of the world, when men had their servants for a possession and inheritance, as well as other goods (and chattels); whereupon we find the power of *castrating,* and making eunuchs (for singing/songs like Lillibullero, &.) much in use in old times." Obs. 155. "Law is nothing else, but the will of him that hath the power of the *supreme* father."** Horrid blasphemy! The Lord omnipotent reigneth, but to whom hath he committed his supreme power and authority? The Pope claims to be but Lord Lieutenant of Heaven, and before Sir Robert none but the Devil ever had vanity or folly enough to contend for the whole power of the supreme Father. According to Filmer, and his followers, among which the Halifax gentleman is a close imitator, "they that shed innocent blood of their sons and their daughters, whom they sacrificed unto the idols of Canaan," did no more than they had a right to do. Upon such principles Pharaoh was a pious virtuous Prince. And the drowning the infants in the Nile, was as justifiable a piece of preventive policy, as seizing the ships of the French without a declaration of war. The Philistine rulers too acted very commendably in depriving the Hebrews of the use of iron, it being very certain that any of the most polite people, without the free use of this invaluable metal, would in one century return to the savage state of the Indians. "If the example of what hath been done, says Mr. Locke, be the rule of what ought to be, history would have furnished our author with instances of this absolute fatherly power in its height and/perfection, and he might have shewed us in Peru, people that begot children, on purpose to fatten and eat them." Mr. Locke has recited a story of this kind, so horrid, that I would, for

*Blackstone
**Obser. p. 225.

the honor of the human species, think it incredible, and but the meer flight of imagination in *Gracilasso de Vega;* like Swift's proposal to the people of Ireland, to fatten their children for sale in Leaden-Hall market, as almost the only branch of commerce that would give no offence to the good people of England. See the story cited by Mr. Locke in his treatise on government, Chap. II and VI. The Filmerians often preach the principles of anarchy in one breath, and those of despotism in another. The gentleman (page 9) says, "The individuals of the colonists participate of every blessing the English constitution can give them." "As corporations created by the crown, they are confined within the primitive views of their institution." "Whether therefore their *indulgence* is *liberal* or *scanty*, can be no cause of complaint; for when they accepted of their charters, they *tacitly* submitted to the terms and conditions of them." This is admirable! To be sure, a liberal indulgence could be no cause of complaint. I have heard of a scanty allowance, and it often happens in a transportation across the Atlantic: but what is a *scanty indulgence?* I am in doubt under what species of Hellenism to rank it. Is it Doric or Ionic? Attic I am sure it is not. But at present I am content it should pass as/very good English, for a poor pittance of bread, water, stinking beef and coarse clothes, instead of the roast beef of Old England, praised and sung by such authors as delight in compositions like Lillibullero. Has a servant no reason to complain that his allowance is scanty, that he is half naked, and more than half starved, while his less faithful and less loyal fellow-servant is well fed, plump, gay, and clothed in purple and scarlet and fine linen, faring sumptuously every day, upon the spoils of his neighbour? But admitting the former has no right to complain, or utter a single sigh, the forced effect of "submissive fear and mingled rage," I cannot for the heart of me conceive how he "participates of every blessing" of his fellow-servant; unless the gentleman will contend that half a loaf is equal to a whole one, and that *Martin* and *Jack* were really a couple of scoundrels, for denying that the crusts Lord Peter would have palm'd upon them, were very good Banstead-down mutton. That "the colonists do not hold their rights as a privilege granted them, nor enjoy them as a grace and favour bestowed, but possess them as an inherent, indefeasible right," as Mr. H — k — s very justly asserts, is a self-evident proposition, to every one in the least versed in the laws of nature and nations, or but moderately skilled in the common law, except the learned gentleman of Halifax. Even the King's writs are divided into those which the subject hath a right to, *ex debito justitiae*, and those which/depend upon meer grace and favor. These may be denied, the others cannot. The essential rights of British colonists stand on the same basis with those of their fellow-subjects of the same rank in any of the three kingdoms.

What the gentleman adds, viz. "that this postulatum of Mr. H — pk — s cannot be true, with regard to political rights," by which he evidently means the peculiar privileges of subordinate powers granted by charter, is (asking his pardon) meer impertinence, and, in a gentleman of his sense, could arise only from a certain set of prejudices having so far blinded him, as to make him confound the ideas of corporate subordinate privileges with essential, natural and civil rights, as is above most abundantly demonstrated, and clearly appears from his own words; (page 10). "The force of an act of parliament, over the colonies, is *predicated* upon the common law, the origin and basis of all those inherent *rights* and *privileges* which constitute the boast and felicity of a Briton." I wish he had said the justly boasted felicity of a Briton; because, in that case, I should have suspected him of a

Filmerian sneer in this place, which jealousy his dogmas elsewhere will justify. The inherent, indefeasible rights of the subject, so much derided and despised in other parts of the performance, are here admitted, in jest or in earnest: I care not which. The origin of those rights is in the law of nature and its author. This law is the grand basis of the com-/mon law, and of all other municipal laws that are worth a rush. True it is, that every act of parliament, which names the colonies, or describes them as by the words "plantations or dominions," binds them. But this is not so strictly and properly speaking by the common law, as by the law of nature, and by the constitution of a parliament, or sovereign and supreme legislative, in a state. 'Tis as true, that when the colonies are not named or described by an act of parliament, they are not bound by it.

What is the reason of all this? *Qui haeret in litera haeret in cortice.* Surely the bare naming of the colonies hath no magical charm or force in it. That the colonies should be bound by acts of parliament wherein they are named, is an exception from a general rule or maxim. What is that rule or maxim? It is, that the colonies being separate dominions, and at a distance from the realm, or mother state, and in fact unrepresented in parliament, shall be governed by laws of their own making; and unless named in acts of parliament, shall not be bound by them. *Quia non mittunt milites ad parliamentum,* says Lord Coke. Yet as a mark of, and to preserve their dependency on, and subordination to, the mother state, and to prevent *imperium in imperio,* the greatest of all political solicisms, the mother state justly asserts the right and authority to bind her colonies, where she really thinks the good of the whole requires it;/and of this she remains the supreme judge, from whose final determination there is no appeal. The mother state hath also an undoubted right to unite a colony to itself, and wholly to abrogate and annihilate all colony or subordinate legislation and administration, if such alteration shall appear for the best interest of the whole community. But should this be done needlesly and wantonly, and without allowing the colonies a representation, the exercise of the power that would otherwise be just and equitable, would cease to be distinguished by those amiable qualities. Should a mother state even think it reasonable to impose internal, as well as external taxes, on six millions of subjects in their remote dominions, without allowing them one voice, it would be matter of wonder and astonishment: But it could not be said that the supreme legislative had exceeded the bounds of their power and authority; nor would this render a petition undutiful and seditious. Those six millions must, on such an event, unless blind, see themselves reduced to the mortifying condition of meer cyphers and blanks in society. Should all this ever happen to the British colonies, which God forbid, might it not be truly and safely affirmed that the representation in the House of Commons would be very unequal? The right of a supreme power in a state to tax its colonies, is a thing that is clear and evident; and yet the mode of exercising that right may be questionable, in point of reason/and equity. It may be thought to be unequal and contrary to sound policy, to exercise the right, clear as it is, without allowing a representation to the colonies. And though representation would avail the colonies very little in this generation; yet, to posterity, it might be an invaluable blessing. It may also, in future ages, be very beneficial to Great-Britain. Is it to be believed, that when a continent, of 3000 miles in length, shall have more inhabitants than there are in this day in Great-Britain, France and Ireland, perhaps in all Europe; they will be quite content with the bare name of British subjects, and, to the end of time, supinely acquiesce in laws made, as it may happen, against their interest by an assembly 3000 miles beyond sea, and where, should they agree in the sentiments with the Halifax gentleman, it may be thought that an admission of an American member would "sully and defile the purity of the whole body?" One hundred years will give this continent more inhabitants, than there are in the three kingdoms.

Many great and good men have complained of the inequality of the representation in Great-Britain. This inequality can never be a reason for making it more so; which however is the method of reasoning adopted by the Halifax gentleman. At his rate, it would be just that half the counties and boroughs in Great-Britain, which now return members, should be curtailed of their right. If so, why not half the remainder, and so on 'till the House/of Commons will be reduced to a single member, and when he was split, one branch of the legislature would be annihilated. By a like process, the House of Lords, the second branch of the legislature, might be destroyed. This would be a shorter cut to absolute and unlimited monarchy, than ever Filmer was fortunate enough to invent. This brings us to the consideration of the maxim, that "no Englishman can be taxed but by his own consent, in person or by his representative." "This dry maxim, taken in a literal sense, and little understood *like* the song of *Lillibullero,* has made all the mischief in the colonies," says the gentleman; (page 11.) I cannot conceive how this, or any other dry maxim, or the song of Lillibullero like it, well or ill understood, can make any mischief in the colonies. What notable harm has the song of Lillibullero wrought in the colonies, or what like it has this "dry maxim" effected? "It is (says the gentleman, page 11.) the opinion of the House of Commons, and *may* be considered as a law of parliament, that they are the Representatives of every British subject wheresoever he be." *Festina lente domine*! This may be true in one sense. The supreme legislative indeed represents the whole society or community, as well the dominions as the realm; and this is the true reason why the dominions are justly bound by such acts of parliament as name them. This is implied in the idea of a supreme sovereign power; and if the parli-/ament had not such authority, the colonies would be independent, which none but rebels, fools or madmen, will contend for. God forbid these colonies should ever prove undutiful to their mother country! Whenever such a day shall come, it will be the beginning of a terrible scene. Were these colonies left to themselves, to-morrow, America would be a meer shambles of blood and confusion, before little petty states could be settled. How many millions must perish in building up great empires? How many more must be ruined by their fall? Let any man reflect on the revolutions of government, ancient and modern, and he will think himself happy in being born here in the infancy of these settlements, and from his soul deprecate their once entertaining any sentiments but those of loyalty, patience, meekness and forbearance, under any hardships that in the course of time they may be subjected to. These, as far as as may be consistent with the character of men and Christians, must be submitted to. If it is the opinion of the present honorable House of Commons, that they in *fact represent* the colonies, it is more than I know. Should this be their opinion, the gentleman may, if he pleases, "consider it is a law of parliament:" But I should rather chuse to consider it only as the very respectable opinion of one branch of the supreme legislative. The opinion of the House of Lords, and then, above all, the sanction of the King's Majesty must be superadded, and the/concurrence of both is absolutely necessary to make any opinion of the House of Commons an act or law of *parliament*. 'Tis humbly conceived, that it was not as representatives in *fact* of the colonies, that the House of Commons granted his Majesty an external tax on the colonies, in the instance of the late act: Nor if before this time an act for granting internal taxes on the colonies should be passed, could I conceive that the House of Commons are our representatives in fact. As one branch of the supreme legislative they have an undoubted right to originate any bills that by naming them shall bind the colonies when passed into an act; let it be for levying internal or external taxes, or for any other regulation that may appear needful: But I cannot find it affirmed or declared in one act of parliament, history or journal of parliamentary proceedings, nor in one English law book, that a British house of Commons are in *fact* the representatives of all the plebian subjects, without as well as within the *realm*. Lord Coke indeed says, that "the House of Commons represent all the commons of *England*, electors and non electors;" but he no where asserts that the House of Commons in *fact* represent the provincials of Ireland and other dominions out of the *realm*. He says, however, the people of Ireland are not represented in the English parliament and assigns that as the very reason why, in general, acts of parliament are confined to the realm. Though from the neces/sity of the thing, in several cases, by naming them, the provinces are bound. In the *fourth institute,* speaking of the truly high and most honorable court on earth, and never more so than in the present state of the British parliament and nation; his Lordship says, "This court consisteth of the King's Majesty, sitting there as in his royal political capacity, and of the three estates of the *realm;* viz. of the Lords Spiritual, Archbishops and Bishops, being in number 24, who sit there by succession in respect of their counties, or baronies, parcel of their bishopricks, which they hold also in their politic capacity; and every one of these, when any parliament is to be holden, ought, *ex debito justitiae,* to have a summons. The Lords Temporal, Dukes, Marquisses, Earls, Viscounts and Barons, who sit there by reason of the dignities, which they hold by descent or creation, in number at this time 106, and likewise every one of these being of full age, ought to have a writ of summons *ex debito justitiae*. The third estate is the *commons* of the *realm,* whereof there be knights of shires or counties, citizens of cities, and burgesses of burghs. All which are respectively elected by the shires or counties, cities and burghs, by force of the King's writ, *ex debito justitiae,* and none of them ought to be omitted; and *these represent all the commons of the whole realm, and trusted for them, and are in number at this time* 493." — 4. Inst. 1.

Here is not one word of the House of Commons representing or being trusted by or for the provincials of Ireland, or the colonists in America. And though, in page 4 of the same Institute, he says, *"in many cases multitudes are bound by acts of parliament which are not parties to the election of knights citizens, and burgesses, as all they that have no freehold, or have freehold in ancient demesne, and all women having freehold or no freehold, and men within the age of twenty-one years &."* — This, & may be supplied with female infants, lunatics, ideots and bedlamites in general. Yet this will not prove that these non-electors are in *fact* represented, and in *fact* trust the representatives in the House of Commons. In estimation of law they are justly deemed as represented. They have all fathers, brothers, friends or neighbours in the House of Commons, and many *ladies* have husbands there. Few of the members have any of these endearing ties to America.

We are, as to any personal knowledge they have of us, as perfect strangers to most of them, as the savages in *California*. But, according to our letter-writer, we are not only in *law* but in *deed* represented in the House of Commons. How does he support this? Why he has dreamt, that some one House of Commons, in some former reign, once thought they were in *fact* our representatives. That "the opinion of a House of Commons is a law of parliament;" Therefore "tis determined by act of parlia-/ment, that we are, and shall believe we are in *fact* represented in the House of Commons." Here is more logic. Suppose some future House of Commons should be of opinion, that they were the true and and proper representatives of all the common people upon the globe, would that make them so, and oblige all mankind to believe and submit to it? Would a fiction of the common law of England satisfy the innumerable multitudes on the face of the earth, that they were in *fact* represented, and consenting to all such taxes and tributes as might be demanded of them? Will any man's calling himself my agent, representative or trustee, make him so in fact? At this rate a House of Commons in one of the colonies have but to conceive an opinion that the represent all the common people of Great-Britain, and according to our author they would in *fact* represent them, and have a right to tax them. 'Tis strange the gentleman can see no difference between a literal sense of a fundamental principle or "dry Maxim" as he calls it and no sense at all. Does it follow, because it is "impracticable that each individual should be in *fact* represented," that therefore there should be no representation at all, or a very unequal one? Because the little insignificant isles of Jersey, Guernsey, and Man, have never obtained a representation, is it reasonable knowledge that the whole kingdom of Ireland and the plantations should be for ever excluded/from returning members to the British parliament, even should the parliament impose external and internal taxes on them, and take from them every subordinate power of local legislation? If this would be equal and rational, why might not Wales have been excluded from returning members, why may they not be excluded now, and Devonshire and Cornwall, and every other county and borough share the same fate? Matter of fact is one thing, matter of right another. The people of a state may in *fact* be very unequally represented; but few men would, like our author, in effect contend that it were best they should not be represented at all. Has the gentleman forgot the maxim, "that equity is equality?" 'Tis hoped he will not consider this as a levelling principle, as it has been more than once called. How astonishing is it, that the instances (page 12) of the unequal representation in Great-Britain, to which he might have added, those of "ten Cornish barns, and an ale-house," should be brought as an argument to prove, that "the right of being represented in parliament" is "an *Utopian privilege,"* a "phantom," a "cloud in the shape of Juno?" This is far from a fine compliment to the honourable House of Commons, of which as one of the branches of the supreme legislative, and of the privilege of sitting with them, it would have been more decent to have made a different choice of expressions. To atone for this indelicacy, the/next moment of the pendulum vibrated as far the other way.

In page 13 the parliament is represented as so pure and perfect, that *"the beauty and symmetry of this body would be destroyed, and its purity defiled by the unnatural mixture of representatives from* every part of the British dominions." "Parthians, Medes, Elamites, and the dwellers of Mesopotamia, &c. *would not, in such a case, speak the same language."* "What a heterogeneous council would this form?" "What a monster in government would it be?" Let me add, was ever insolence equal to this? Are the inhabitants of British America all a parcel of transported thieves, robbers and revels, or descended from such? Are the colonists blasted lepers, whose company would infect the whole House of Commons? There are some in the colonies who value themselves on their descent. We have the names of *Tudor* and of *Stuart,* of *Howard, Seymor,* and of *Russell;* who boast an unsullied descent from our ancient princes and nobles, or at least claim the honor of being of the same blood. Can none of these be returned as members without breeding a plague in the house. If this writer is an European, his insults upon the British colonies are quite unpardonable; if he be a native, he is an ungrateful parracide. Is he a venal hireling of a party? his employers on either side the Atlantic should discard him as a meer Sir Martyn Marplot. Depend upon / it, one such letter as his, if known to breathe the sentiments of the great, would tend more to disgust the colonies against the conduct of their superiors, than a hundred thousand such pamphlets as the author scolds at. Parliaments are not only "as ancient as our Saxon ancestors," but as old as the commonwealths of Israel, Greece and Rome*; nay, as old as the first compact for changing a simple democracy into any other form of government. "Attendance in parliament" is not therefore, as the gentleman conceives, a "duty arising from a tenure of lands, or the feudal system," but from the nature of man, of society, and of all original, just, social and civil compacts for forming a state. "So that the privilege of sitting in it, i.e. in a parliament or grand council of a nation, is not "territorial," in the sense of the letter-writer, nor in its nature confined to Great-Britain." What is there, what can be there, that should naturally and necessarily confine the privilege of returning members, to the inhabitants of Great-Britain, more than to those of London and Westminster?

The gentleman (p. 14) says, "the parliament may levy internal taxes, as well as regulate trade, there is no essential difference." By regulating trade, I suppose he means, according to the common sophism, taxing trade. Even in this sense, 'tis admitted the parliament have the same right to levy inter-/nal taxes on the colonies, as to regulate trade; and that the right of levying both, is undoubtedly in the parliament. Yet 'tis humbly conceived and hoped, that before the authority is fully exerted in either case, it will be thought to be reasonable and equitable, that the dominions should be in *fact* represented. Else it will follow, that the provincials in Europe, Asia, Africa and America, ought to all generations to content themselves with having no more share, weight, or influence, even in the provincial government of their respective countries, than the Hotentots have in that of China, or the Ethiopians in that of Great-Britain.

I should be glad to know how the gentleman came by his assurance, that "a stamp-duty is confessedly the most reasonable and equitable that can be devised." (p. 14) Some few may be of this opinion, and there never was a new invented tax or excise, but its favorers and partizans would highly extol, as the most just and equitable device imaginable. This is a trite game "at ways and means." But bold assertions will not pass for clear proofs, with "philosophically inquisitive minds." "If the shaft is sped," and the aim so good, I wonder the gentleman should even faintly pretend to "desire not to see a stamp-duty established among us," or "wish to prevent the blow." Were I convinced, as he is, that it is reasonable and best that the colonies should be taxed by parliament, with-/out being allowed a

*4. Inst. 2, 3.

representation; and that it is become not only necessary to levy internal taxes on them; but that the art of man could not devise so equitable and reasonable a tax as a stamp-duty; I should heartily pray for its establishment.

The gentleman no where discovers his temper more plainly than in his comparison of Greece and Rome, in their conduct towards their colonies. 'Tis well known the Grecians were kind, humane, just and generous towards theirs. 'Tis as notorious that the Romans were severe, cruel, brutal and barbarous towards theirs. I have ever pleased myself in thinking that Great-Britain, since the Revolution, might be justly compared to Greece, in its care and protection of its colonies. I also imagined that the French and Spaniards followed the Roman example. But our letter-writer tells us quite a different story. He compliments the nation, and comforts the colonies by declaring that these "exactly resemble those of Rome." "The *Roman Coloniae,*" says he, "did not enjoy all the rights of Roman citizens." "They only *used* the Roman laws and religion, and served in their legions; but had no right of suffrage, or bearing honours." "In these respects, adds he, our English colonies exactly resemble them." "We enjoy the English laws and religion, but not the right of suffrage, or of bearing honours in Great-Britain."

Is this enjoying the rights, liberties and privileges of British-born subjects within the realm, to all intents, constructions and purposes? I find all this confirmed to the colonists, not only by the common law, and by their charters, but by act of parliament. Where does the gentleman find it decreed that the British *"Coloniae"* "have no right of bearing honours in Great-Britain?" Has not the King's majesty, the fountain of honour, an undoubted right by his prerogative, to confer any rank he may be graciously pleased to bestow on his American subjects, as well as on those in Great-Britain? Cannot the word of a King as easily make even a Halifaxian letter-writer, or his Rhode-Island friend, a knight of the garter or thistle, as if either of them had been dropped and drawn their first breath in one of the three kingdoms?

The gentleman may in his anger wish for the laws of "Draco to be inforced on America," and, in his fierce anger, for the "iron rod of a Spanish inquisitor." These may be sudden gusts of passion, without malice prepence, that only hurts his cause, and which his employers will not thank him for. But hard, very hard, must his heart be, who could employ all his stock of learning in a deliberate attempt to reduce the rights of the colonists to the narrow bound of a bare permission, to "use the English laws and religion without a suffrage in things sacred or civil, and without a right to bear honours in Great-Bri-/tain," "except that of being shot at for sixpence a day, in her armies at home, as well as abroad." What is the English religion? Pray wherein does it differ from that of Scotland, Ireland, and the plantations? If it differs, and the colonies are obliged to *use* the religion of the metropolis, on her embracing paganism, so must the colonies. Since the Revolution, all dissenters, both at home and abroad, papists only excepted, have enjoyed a free and generous toleration. Would the gentleman deprive all protestants dissenters of this invaluable blessing? If he is an American by birth, what does he deserve of his country for attempting to realize, to this and to all future generations, the dreary prospect of confinement to the use of the laws and religion of a region 3000 miles beyond sea, in framing which laws, and in forming the modes of which religion, they shall have no voice nor suffrage; nor shall they have any preferment in church or state, tho' they shall be taxed, without their consent, to the support of both?

————— ————— aes triplex
Circa pectus erat. —————

The gentleman hath been at great pains in order to represent the merchants of America as a parcel of infamous smugglers. He says, "smuggling had well nigh become established in some of the colonies." 'Tis notoriously known who have been the great abettirs and patrons of smugglers, and who have shared the greatest parts of the profits. All the riot/at Ephesus proceeded from certain collectors of the revenues of Diana of the Ephesians; the shrine-makers and silver-smiths were but their tools. The craft was in danger, but if it had been only that of Demetrius and his journeymen, we might not have heard of that day's uproar. 'Tis a very unjust aspersion to charge the American merchants, in general, with a design to elude and evade the acts of trade. I cannot so well tell how matters have been managed at Halifax or Rhode-Island; but in some other colonies, only a few favorites have been indulged in the lucrative crime of smuggling, which, after an eminent writer, the gentleman calls a crime "against the law of nature;" 'tis a wonder it had not been recorded from some old commentator, *crimen lesae Majestatis, high treason.* The like indulgence, as far as I can learn, has, in Rhode-Island, been confined also to a few choice friends. The article of Melasses is every where to be excepted. It was known at home, that the importation of this was universally tolerated, paying about one tenth of the duties imposed by the old act. The connivance became very general.

I have perused Mr. H — k — s' book over and over, but cannot find the least reflection on Dr. Spry, nor do I think any was intended. The Doctor perhaps may thank the gentleman for bringing his name into question; but I doubt, notwithstanding the gentleman's assertions to the contrary, whether the Doctor's "appoint-/ments place him above any kind of influence." I believe he is under the influence of honor and conscience, a clear head, and a good heart, all which the gentleman seems too much a stranger to: And should the Doctor also be under that the influence, which flows from a general aversion, and contempt of flattery and falsehood, he must conceive an opinion of his Halifax neighbour, that will be very mortifying to one who hopes to make his court to the great, and to the Doctor among the rest, by abusing the colonies. The Doctor hath been in America some months, but I have not heard of one cause that has been tried before him. This is tolerable proof, either that smuggling was not so common a thing as the letter-writer asserts, or that those who used to be concerned in it, are reformed. I think it proves both.

In the 21st, and last page but one of the letter, the gentleman bethought himself, and having in a manner finished his epistle, makes an apology for not following Mr. H — k — s "with somewhat more of method." His excuse is, that "Mr. H — k — s hath not divided his argument with precision." He then formally proceeds to a curious, and, as he doubtless thought, precise division of the argument. "The dispute, says he, between Great-Britain and the colonies, consists of two parts. First, the jurisdiction of parliament: And secondly, the exercise of that jurisdiction: His Honour has blended these together, and no where marked the division between them./The first I have principally remarked upon." I know of no dispute between Great-Britain and her colonies. Who is so hardy as to dispute the Jurisdiction of the Parliament? But were there a thousand disputes between Great-Britain and the colonies; if the colonists in general were as the letter-writer represents them, "a simple, credulous, and hitherto loyal people," in danger of "having their minds embittered, and their affections alienated from Great-Britain, by a few pamphlets:" And if "from the pride of some, and ignorance of others, the cry against mother country has spread from colony to colony, and it were to be feared that prejudices and resentments were kindled among them, which it would be difficult ever thoroughly to sooth or extinguish;" all which insinuations are however very injurious; what would this prove against "The Rights of Colonies examined," or any other of the pamphlets that have been lately published in America? Mr. H — k — s, pages 10 and 11 of his book, speaking of the general concerns of the whole British empire, saith, "These, it is absolutely necessary, should have a general power to direct them; some supreme and over-ruling authority, with power to make laws, and form regulations for the good of all, and to compel their execution and observation. It being necessary some such general power should exist somewhere, every man of the least knowledge of the British constitution, will be na-/turally led to look for, and find it in the parliament of Great-Britain; that grand and august legislative body must, from the nature of their authority, and the necessity of the thing, be justly vested with this power." Is not this a very clear admission and acknowledgment of the jurisdiction, power, and authority of parliament over the colonies? What could put it into the gentleman's head to think the jurisdiction of the parliament was a matter in dispute? I have perused a pamphlet published in Connecticut relating to their rights! but can find no question made of the jurisdiction of the parliament. "The Rights of the British Colonies asserted and proved," I have also read. This was published before either Mr. H — k — s, or that from Connecticut. These, so far as I can find, are all the pamphlets that have been published in America, upon the proposed new regulations of the colonies. From the knowledge I have of the sentiments of the "head of the *tribunitian veto,*" as the gentleman is pleased to describe him, I take upon me to declare, that I have heard him in the most public manner declare his submission to the authority of parliament; and that from his soul he detests and abhors the thought of making a question of their jurisdiction.

The following passages from "The Rights of the British Colonies asserted and proved," may serve to shew how careful a hand the Halifax gentleman is at a matter of fact.

"I also lay it down as one of the first principles from whence I intend to deduce the civil rights of the British colonies, that all of them are subject to, and dependent on, Great-Britain; and that therefore, as over subordinate governments, the parliament of Great-Britain has an undoubted power and lawful authority to make acts for the general good, that by naming them, shall and ought to be equally binding, as upon the subjects of Great-Britain within the realm." "When the parliament shall think fit to allow the colonists a representation in the House of Commons, the equity of their taxing the colonies will be as clear as their power is at present of doing it without, if they please." "No such claim (i.e. of an independent legislative) was ever thought of by the colonists. They are all better men and better subjects; and many of them too well versed in the laws of nature and nations, and the law and constitution of Great-Britain, to think they have a right to more than a *provincial subordinate legislative.* All power is of GOD. Next and only subordinate to him, in the present state of the well-formed, beautiful constructed British monarchy, standing where I hope it ever will stand, for the pillars are fixed in judgment, righteousness and truth, is the King and Parliament." "From all which, it seems plain, that the reason why Ireland and the plantations are not bound unless named by an act of parliament, is, / because they are *not represented* in the British parliament. Yet, in special cases, the British parliament has an undoubted right, as well as power, to bind both by their acts. But whether this can be extended to an indefinite taxation of both, is the great question. I conceive the spirit of the British constitution must make an exception of all taxes, until it is thought fit to unite a dominion to the realm. Such taxation must be considered either as uniting the dominions to the realm, or disfranchising them. If they are united, they will be intitled to a representation, as well as Wales: If they are so taxed without a union, or representation, they are so far disfranchised." "The sum of my argument is, That civil government is of God: That the administrators of it were originally the whole people: That they might have devolved it on whom they pleased: That this devolution is fiduciary, for the good of the whole: That by the British constitution, this devolution is on the King, Lords and Commons, the supreme, sacred and uncontroulable legislative power, not only in the realm, but thro' the dominions: That by the Abdication, the original compact was broken to pieces. That by the Revolution, it was renewed, and more firmly established, and the rights and liberties of the subject, in all parts of the dominions, more fully explained and confirmed: That in consequence of this establishment, and the acts of succession and union, his Majesty George III. / is rightful king and sovereign, and, with his parliament, the supreme legislative of Great-Britain, France and Ireland, and the dominions thereto belonging: That this constitution is the most free one, and by far the best, now existing on earth: That by this constitution, every man in the dominions is a free man: that no part of his Majesty's dominions can be taxed without their consent: That every part has a right to be represented in the supreme or some subordinate legislature: That the refusal of this, would seem to be a contradiction in practice to the theory of the constitution: That the colonies are subordinate dominions, and are now in such a state, as to make it best for the good of the whole, that they should not only be continued in the enjoyment of subordinate legislation, but be also represented, in some proportion to their number and estates, in the grand legislature of the nation: That this would firmly unite all parts of the British empire in the greatest peace and prosperity, and render it invulnerable and perpetual." *Rights of the British colonies asserted and proved,* pages 32, 48, 59, 61, 64. Can the gentleman read these passages, and say they imply any question of the power and authority of parliament? Will he not blush, when he reflects, that he hath indiscriminately asserted, that these pamphlets "have a tendency to embitter the minds of a simple, credulous and hitherto loyal people, and to alienate their/affections from Great-Britain, their best friend and *alma mater?*" Can terms expressive of greater loyalty or submission to the jurisdiction and authority of parliament be conceived, than many that are to be found in those pamphlets? Yet the gentleman has the effrontery to talk of the "frequent abuse poured forth in pamphlets against the mother country," and laments that before his "not one filial pen in America had been drawn in her vindication." How grand we look! Are not his dragoons enough, but he must fight with his pen too? I believe he must be a man of parlous courage; yet he is modest withal. He says he has "no ambition of appearing in print," though he is the only loyal subject his Majesty has in his American dominions, and master of the only filial pen worth a button. If this is true, well might he call his countrymen a parcel of scoundrels, rebels, smugglers and traitors. I shall take leave of my gentleman, by desiring him to reflect, in his cooler hours, and well consider what would soon be his fate, if the Americans should treat him as he most richly deserves.

> *I too have seen, in all the pride of May,*
> *A flaunting sing-song genius toujour gay,*
> *Whose life was one short senseless pretty dream,*
> *Frisk on the margin of a mighty stream,*
> *Till circling dances seize his tender brain;*
> *He falls! he dies! alas a calf is slain\*!*

## POSTSCRIPT

Since the above sheets were finished, two or three pieces have been published in the Providence Gazette. The first of these hath furnished us with a clear and concise account of the several principal reasonings and arguments upon the subject of internal taxes to be imposed on the colonies by parliament, while they are unrepresented in the House of Commons. The sum is,

1. That it is the incontestible right of the subject in Great-Britain, not to be taxed out of parliament; and every subject within the realm is in fact or in law represented there.

2. The British colonists being British subjects, are to all intents and purposes intitled to the rights, liberties and privileges of the subjects within the realm, and ought to be represented, in fact as well as in law, in the supreme or some subordinate legislature, where they are taxed; else they will be deprived of one of the most essential rights of a British subject,/namely, that of being free from all taxes, but such as he shall, by himself or representative, grant and assess.

3. As the colonies have been erected into subordinate dominions, with subordinate powers of legislation; particularly that of levying taxes for the support of their respective subordinate governments, and at their own expence; have not only supported the civil provincial administration, but many of them have, to their utmost ability, contributed both in men and money for the common cause, as well as for their more immediate defence against his Majesty's enemies, it should seem very hard that they should be taxed also by parliament, and that before they are allowed a representation in fact, and while they are quite unable to pay such additional taxes.

4. The immense commercial advantages resulting to Great-Britain from her plantations, the revenue thence arising to the crown, the taxes we pay by the

---

\*"*Narcissus,* in contemplating his own image, was turned into a daffodil. Who can think of this, and feel no pity for the pride and weakness of *man that is born of woman?*"

> "So have I seen, on some bright summer's day,
> "A calf of genius debonnair and gay,
> "Dance on the brink, as if inspired by fame,
> "Fond of the pretty fellow in the stream."

Four lines of Dr. Young, very modestly applied to Governor H — k — s, in the 5th page of the Letter from Halifax, as above cited, with the Allusion to *Narcissus.*

comsumption of an infinity of British manufactures, may be thought a reasonable return for the protection received, as 'tis really all that at present is in our power to yield.

5. If the colonies could and ought to yield greater aids towards the national expence, yet it should seem but reasonable either to allow them, 1. To raise such further sums as may be required, by taxing themselves in the most easy way and manner their several provincial legislatures could devise. Or, 2. at least to/allow them a representation in the House of Commons. This, with some animadversions on the present state of commerce, with the extension and enlargement of the admiralty jurisdiction in America, is the substance of all that has so much incensed the Halifax gentleman. Governor H — k — s hath no where said that "the colonies have rights independent of, and not controulable by, the authority of parliament."

*See Providence Gazette, Feb.* 16.

According to the gentleman, "it will follow that we may enjoy *personal* liberty, and yet be slaves in a *political sense;* and so, *vice versa,* we may be *personally slaves,* and yet have a political right to liberty. Life, liberty and estate being personal rights, are (by the gentleman admitted to be) secured to us by the common law. I do not remember to have heard that the colonies ever contended for more; and yet (by this personal and political distinction) our estates may be taken away from us against our consent, without any violation of our personal right; and all this for want of a *political* right."

*Providence Gazette, Feb.* 16, 1765.

"The gentleman confidently maintains that acts of parliament derive their force from the common law; and for that reason he says, they are obligatory on the colonies. I ask him, how it is possible that the parliamentary power, which controuls, alters and amends the common law at will, can derive its support from the common law?"

*Providence Gazette, February* 23

The power and authority of parliament is from the constitution, and above all other laws, but those of God and nature.

"There may be a natural relation between two subjects that exist by nature; but mother country and colony exist only by policy, and may, and no doubt have a political relation to each other; but can have no natural one."

*Providence Gazette, March* 2.

This remark is ingenious, and the manner in which 'tis elucidated is diverting; but I fear 'tis not solid. There is nonsense and contradiction enough of all conscience in the Halifax gentleman's attempt to investigate the "natural relation between colonies and their mother state," without denying the existence of such a relation. Our allegiance is natural, and if this be admitted of each individual in a colony, as it must be, it would be strange to deny a natural relation between two whole bodies, between all the respective parts of which a natural relation is admitted. Society is certainly natural, and exists prior to, and independent of any form of civil policy, always excepting family societies and simple democracies. As there is a natural relation between father and son, so is there between their two families; and so is there between a mother-state or metropolis, and its colonies. The natural relation between two independent states or societies, is the basis of the law of nations; and all its obligations are thence de-/duceable. It would be strange that a natural relation should subsist between two neighbouring states, and none be between a metropolis and a colony. I can see no absurdity in supposing both natural and political relations to subsist between a mother state and its colonies, any more than supposing two qualities in one and the same subject. The same man may be choleric and humane, another is calm and inveterate. The same two men may be father and son, fellow-men, fellow-subjects, fellow-citizens, and brother-aldermen. Political relations are but modifications of those which are founded in nature, and from whence rise duties of universal obligation.

I cannot suppress all my indignation at a remark in the close of the Halifax letter, which should have been taken notice of before, but it escaped me. "It may become necessary for the supreme legislature of the nation to frame some code, (and canons might have been as properly added) and therein adjust the rights of the colonies with precision and certainty, otherwise Great-Britain will always be teazed with new claims about liverty and privileges." Page 22.

If I mistake not, there is, in the air of this period, the quintessence of a meer martial legislator; the insolence of a haughty and imperious minister; the indolence and half thought of a petit maitre; the flutter of a coxcomb; the pedantry of a quack, and the nonsense of a pettifogger. A strange galli-/maufry this: but I am not answerable for it, or for any other of the exhibitions of a monster monger. We want no foreign codes, nor canons here. The common law is our birth-right; and the rights and privileges confirmed and secured to us by the British constitution, and by act of parliament, are our best inheritance. Codes, pandects, novels, decretals of Popes, and the inventions of the D — l, may suit the cold bleak regions of Brandenburg and Prussia, or the scorching heats of Jamaica or Gambia; but we live in a more temperate climate, and shall rest content with the laws, customs and usages of our ancestors, bravely supported and defended with the monarchy, and from age to age handed down. These have, and ever will finally triumph over the whims of political and religious Enthusiasts; the extremes of which are libertinism and despotism, anarchy and tyranny, spiritual and temporal from all which may God ever preserve us. I must recommend it to the Halifax gentleman, before he publishes any more epistles, diligently to read over Swift's *Tale of a Tub,* and to take special note of Lord Peter's method of reasoning with his brethren. He will there find all the forms of syllogism, from the *sorites* to the categoric. Of the last form, he will find this, to prove that a little learning puffeth little men up.

> "Words are but wind,
> Learning is nothing but words,
> *Ergo.* Learning is nothing but wind."

Of the former kind of argumentation, he will find a species he seems to be peculiarly fond of.

"In the midst of all this clutter and revolution, in comes Lord Peter, with a file of dragoons at his heels, and gathering from all hands what was in the wind, he and his gang, after several millions of scurrilities and curses not very important here to repeat, by main force, very fairly kicks them (Martin and Jack) both out of doors, and would never let them come under his roof, from that day to this."

*Tale of a Tub.* p. 79. 104.

FINIS

# 11

While institutional Christianity condoned slavery, the principal opposition to it was carried on in the name of Christian doctrine. We have already noted John Woolman's long crusade against slavery among his Quaker brethren. On the eve of the Revolution the Reverend Samuel Hopkins, a Congregational minister from Newport, Rhode Island, addressed the following letter to Congress.

[The text is taken from Rev. Samuel Hopkins, *A Dialogue Concerning the Slavery of the Africans; Shewing it to be the Duty and Interest of the American States to Emancipate All Their African Slaves*, (Norwich: Spooner, 1776).]

## A Dialogue Concerning the Slavery

TO THE HONORABLE MEMBERS OF THE CONTINENTAL CONGRESS REPRESENTATIVES OF THE THIRTEEN UNITED AMERICAN COLONIES.

MUCH-HONORED GENTLEMEN:

As God, the great Father of the universe, has made you the fathers of these colonies, — and in answer to the prayers of his people given you counsel, and that wisdom and integrity in the exertion of which you have been such great and extensive blessings, and obtained the approbation and applause of your constituents and the respect and veneration of the nations in whose sight you have acted in the important, noble struggle for LIBERTY, — we naturally look to you in behalf of more than half a million of persons in these colonies, who are under such a degree of oppression and tyranny as to be wholly deprived of all civil and personal liberty, to which they have as good a right as any of their fellow-men, and are reduced to the most abject state of bondage and slavery without any just cause.

We have particular encouragement thus to apply to you, since you have had the honor and happiness of leading these colonies to resolve to stop the slave trade, and to buy no more slaves imported from Africa. We have the satisfaction of the best assurances that you have done this not merely from political reasons, but from a conviction of the unrighteousness and cruelty of that trade, and a regard to justice and benevolence, — deeply sensible of the inconsistence of promoting the slavery of the Africans, at the same time we are asserting our own civil liberty at the risk of our fortunes and lives. This leaves in our minds no doubt of your being sensible of the equal unrighteousness and oppression, as well as inconsistence with ourselves, in holding so many hundreds of thousands of blacks in slavery, who have an equal right to freedom with ourselves, while we are maintaining this struggle for our own and our children's liberty; and a hope and confidence that the cries and tears of these oppressed will be regarded by you, and that your wisdom and the great influence you have in these colonies will be so properly and effectually exerted as to bring about a total abolition of slavery, in such a manner as shall greatly promote the happiness of those oppressed strangers and the best interest of the public . . .

May you judge the poor of the people, save the children of the needy, relieve the oppressed, and deliver the spoiled out of the hands of the oppressor, and be the happy instruments of procuring and establishing universal liberty to white and black, to be transmitted down to the latest posterity . . .

The present situation of our public affairs and our struggle for liberty, and the abundant conversation this occasions in all companies, while the poor negroes look on and hear what an aversion we have to slavery and how much liberty is prized, they often hearing it declared publicly and in private, as the voice of all, that slavery is more to be dreaded than death, and we are resolved to live free or die, etc.; this, I say, necessarily leads them to attend to their own wretched situation more than otherwise they could. They see themselves deprived of all liberty and property, and their children after them, to the latest posterity, subject to the will of those who appear to have no feeling for their misery, and are guilty of many instances of hard-heartedness and cruelty towards them, while they think themselves very kind . . .

They see the slavery the Americans dread as worse than death is lighter than a feather compared to their heavy doom, and may be called liberty and happiness when contrasted with the most abject slavery and unutterable wretchedness to which they are subjected; and in this dark and dreadful situation they look round and find no help — no pity — no hope! And when they observe all this cry and struggle for liberty for ourselves and children, and see themselves and their children wholly overlooked by us, and behold the sons of liberty oppressing and tyrannizing over many thousands of poor blacks who have as good a claim to liberty as themselves, they are shocked with the glaring inconsistence, and wonder they themselves do not see it. You must not, therefore, lay it to the few who are pleading the cause of these friendless, distressed poor, that they are more uneasy than they used to be in a sense of their wretched state and from a desire of liberty: there is a more mighty and irresistible cause than this, viz., all that passes before them in our public struggle for liberty . . .

No wonder there are many and great difficulties in reforming an evil practice of this kind, which has got such deep root by length of time and is become so common . . . This matter ought, doubtless, to be attended to by the general assemblies, and continental and provincial congresses; and if they were as much united and engaged in devising ways and means to set at liberty these injured slaves as they are to defend themselves from tyranny, it would soon be effected. There were, without doubt, many difficulties and impediments in the way of the Jews liberating those of their brethren they had brought into bondage in the days of Jeremiah. But when they were besieged by the Chaldeans, and this their sin was laid before them, and they were threatened with desolation if they did not reform, they broke through every difficulty, and set their servants at liberty . . .

Let this iniquity be viewed in its true magnitude, and in the shocking light in which it has been set in this conversation; let the wretched case of the poor blacks be considered with proper pity and benevolence, together with the probably dreadful consequence to this land of retaining them in bondage, and all objections against liberating them would vanish. The mountains that are now raised up in the imagination of many would become a plain, and every difficulty surmounted.

. . . And why are we not as much affected with the slavery of the many thousands of blacks among ourselves whose miserable state is before our eyes? And why should we not be as much engaged to relieve them? The reason is obvious. It is because they are negroes, and fit for nothing but slaves, and we have been used to look on them in a mean, contemptible light, and our education has filled us with strong prejudices against them, and led us to consider them, not as our brethren, or in any degree on a level with us, but as quite another species of animals, made only to serve us and our children, and as happy in bondage as in any other state. This has banished all attention to the injustice that is done them, and any proper sense of their misery or the exercise of benevolence towards them. If we could only divest ourselves of these strong prejudices which have insensibly fixed on our minds, and consider them as by nature and by right on a level with our brethren and children, and those of our neighbors, and that benevolence which loves our neighbor as ourselves, and is agreeable to truth and righteousness, we should begin to feel towards them, in some measure at least, as we should towards our children and neighbors . . .

This leads me to observe, that our distresses are come upon us in such a way, and the occasion of the present war is such, as in the most clear and striking manner to point out the sin of holding our blacks in slavery, and admonish us to reform, and render us shockingly inconsistent with ourselves, and amazingly guilty if we refuse. God has raised up men to attempt to deprive us of liberty, and the evil we are threatened with is slavery. This, with our vigorous attempts to avoid it, is the ground of all our distresses, and the general voice is, "We will die in the attempt, rather than submit to slavery." . . . O, the shocking, the intolerable inconsistence! And this gross, barefaced inconsistence is an open, practical condemnation of holding these our brethren in slavery; and in these circumstances the crime of persisting in it becomes unspeakably greater and more provoking in God's sight, so that all the former unrighteousness and cruelty exercised in this practice is innocence compared with the awful guilt that is now contracted. And in allusion to the words of our Savior, it may with great truth and propriety be said, "If he had not thus come in his providence, and spoken unto us, (comparatively speaking,) we had not had sin in making bondslaves of our brethren; but now, we have no cloak for our sin."

And if we continue in this evil practice and refuse to let the oppressed go free, under all this light and admonition suited to convince and reform us, and while God is evidently correcting us for it as well as for other sins, have we any reason to expect deliverance from the calamities we are under? May we not rather look for slavery and destruction like that which came upon the obstinate, unreformed Jews? In this light I think it ought to be considered by us; and viewed thus, it affords a most forcible, formidable argument not to put off liberating our slaves to a more convenient time, but to arise, all as one man, and do it with all our might, without delay, since delaying in this case is awfully dangerous as well as unspeakably criminal . . .

# 12

---

The sermon of Samuel West which follows was preached as the Massachusetts election sermon in Boston, May 26, 1776. Like many other sermons in those perilous times, this one reviews the basis on which a Christian people may resist oppression and seeks to strengthen the members of the congregation in their resolve. The sermon is a truly representative one; the reader will recognize in it many now familiar strains reaching back to the beginnings of the Reformation and, indeed, back to the Old Testament itself.

It is not the argument of this work that sermons such as Samuel West's brought on the Revolution. Rather it was the ideas which West articulated which had already formed the consciousness of colonial Americans that, in the face of British obduracy, brought on the Revolution. The West sermon thus can be taken to record an already existing concensus about the nature and end of civil government. In a certain sense, the Revolution lay hidden in John Calvin's reflections on the nature of civil government.

[The text is taken from Samuel West, *A Sermon Preached Before the Honorable Council*, (Boston: Gill, 1776).]

## 1776 Election Sermon

[In 1 Peter 11:13, 14, we hear] "Submit yourselves to every ordinance of man," — or as the words ought to be rendered from the Greek, submit yourselves to every human creation; or human constitution, — "for the Lord's sake, whether it be to the king, or unto governors, — for the punishment of evil-doers, and for the praise of them that do well." Here we see that the apostle asserts that magistrates are of human creation that is, that magistrates have no power or authority but what they derive from the people; that this power they are to exert for the punishment of evil-doers, and for the praise of them that do well.

The only reason assigned by the apostle why magistrates should be obeyed . . . is because they punish the wicked and encourage the good; it follows, that when they punish the virtuous we have a right to refuse yielding any submission to them; whenever they act contrary to the design of their institution, they forfeit their authority to govern the people, and the reason for submitting to them immediately ceases. . . . Hence we see that the apostle, instead of being a friend to tyranny. . . , turns out to be a strong advocate for the just rights of mankind. . .

David, the man after God's own heart, makes piety a necessary qualification in a ruler: "He that ruleth over men must be just, ruling in the fear of God."

To despise government, and to speak evil of dignitaries is represented in Scripture as one of the worst of characters; and it is an injunction of Moses, "Thou shalt not speak evil of the ruler . . ." Great mischief may ensue upon reviling the character of good rulers; for the unthinking herd of mankind are very apt to give ear to scandal, and when it falls upon men in power, it brings their authority into contempt, lessens their influence, and disheartens them from doing service.

But though I would recommend to all Christians to treat rulers with proper honor and respect, none can reasonably suppose that I mean that rulers ought to be flattered in their vices, or honored and caressed while they are seeking to undermine and ruin the state; for this would be wickedly betraying our just rights, and we should be guilty of our own destruction.

It is with a particular view to the present unhappy controversy . . . that I chose to discourse upon the nature and design of government . . . so that we stand firm in our opposition to tyranny, while at the same time we pay all proper obedience to our lawful magistrates; while we are contending for liberty, may we avoid running into licentiousness . . . I acknowledge that I have undertaken a difficult task; but, it appears to me, the present state of affairs loudly calls for such a discourse. Need I upon this occasion descend to particulars? Can any one be ignorant what the things are of which we complain? . . . And, after all this wanton exertion of arbitrary power, is there any man who is not fired with a noble indignation against such merciless tyrants. . .

Let us treat our rulers with all that honor and respect which the dignity of their station requires; but let it be such an honor and respect as is worthy of the sons of freedom to give. Let us ever abhor the base arts used by fawning parasites and cringing courtiers, who by their flatteries obtain offices which they are unqualified to sustain. Oftentimes they have a greater number of places assigned them than any one person of the greatest abilities can properly fill . . . and the community becomes greatly injured . . . so many an important trust remains undischarged.

. . . In order to avoid this evil, I hope our legislators will always despise flattery as something below the dignity of a rational mind, and that they will ever scorn the man that will be corrupted . . . And let us all resolve with ourselves that no motives of interest, nor hopes of preferment, shall ever induce us to flattering men in power. Let the honor and respect which we show our superiors be simple and genuine. . . . Tyrants have been flattered in their vices, and have often had an idolatrous reverence paid them. The worst princes have been the most flattered and adored and many such, in the pagan world, assumed the title of gods, and had divine honors paid them. This idolatrous reverence has ever been the inseparable concomitant of arbitrary power and tryannical government; even Christian rulers, if they have not been adored as gods, yet the titles given them strongly savor of blasphemy, and the reverence paid them is idolatrous. What right has a poor sinful worm of the dust to claim the title of his most sacred Majesty? Most sacred certainly belongs only to God alone, — yet how common is it to see this title or ones like it given to rulers! And how often have we been told that the ruler can do no wrong! Even though he should be so foolish and wicked as hardly capable of ever being in the right, yet still it must be asserted and maintained that it is impossible for him to do wrong! The cruel, savage disposition of tyrants, and the idolatrous reverence paid them, are both most beautifully exhibited to view by the apostle John in Revelation, thirteenth chapter . . .

The apostle gives description of a horrible wild beast which he saw rise out of the sea, having seven heads and ten horns, and upon his heads the names of blasphemy. By heads are to be understood forms of government, and by blasphemy, idolatry; so that it seems implied that there will be a degree of idolatry in every form of tryannical government. This beast is represented as having the body of a leopard, the feet of a bear, and the mouth of a lion; i.e., a horrible monster, possessed of the rage and fury of the lion, the fierceness of the bear, and the swiftness of the leopard to sieze and devour its prey. Can words more strongly point out, or exhibit in more lively colors, the exceeding rage, fury, and impetuosity of tyrants, destroying amd making havoc of mankind? To this beast we find the dragon gave his power . . . , this is to denote that tyrants are the ministers of Satan.

Such a horrible monster, we should have thought, would have been abhorred and detested of all mankind, . . . that all nations would have joined their power and forces together to oppose and utterly destroy him from off the face of the earth; but, so far are they from doing this, that, on the contrary, they are represented as worshipping him (vers 8): "And all that dwell on the earth shall worship him" — all those "whose names are not written in the Lamb's book of life;" . . . Those who pay an undue and sinful veneration to tyrants are properly the servants of the devil. . . . Hence that terrible denunciation of divine wrath against the worshippers of the beast . . .: "If any man worship the beast . . . the same shall drink the wine of the wrath of God." . . . We have here set forth in the clearest manner, God's abhorrence of tyranny, tyrants, and the idolatrous reverence that their subjects are wont to pay them . . . Does it not, then, highly concern us all to stand fast in the liberty wherewith Heaven hath made us free, to strive to get the victory over the beast and his image — over every species of tyranny? Let us look upon a freedom from the power of tyrants as a blessing that cannot be purchased too dear, and let us bless God that he has delivered us from that idolatrous reverence which men are so apt to pay to arbitrary tyrants. Let not the powers of earth and hell prevail against liberty.

Honored fathers, we look up to you, in this day of calamity as the guardians of our invaded rights, and the defenders of our liberties against tyranny. You are called to save your country from ruin . . .

My reverend fathers and brethren in the ministry will remember that according to our text, it is part of the work of a gospel minister to teach his hearers the duty they owe to magistrates. Let us, then, endeavor to explain the nature of their duty faithfully, and show them the difference between liberty and licentiousness; and let us animate them to oppose tyranny and arbitrary power; and let us inculcate upon them the duty of yielding due obedience to lawful authority.

To conclude: While we are fighting for liberty, and striving against tyranny, let us remember to fight the good fight of faith, and earnestly seek to be delivered from that bondage of corruption which we are brought into by sin, and that we may be made partakers of the glorious liberty of the sons and children of God: which may the Father of Mercies grant us all, through Jesus Christ. AMEN."

# 13

So much has been written about the Declaration of Independence that our comments can be brief. Jefferson was one of the least orthodox of the Founding Fathers in his religious beliefs; but it is interesting to note how close his own rationale for resisting unlawful authority is to that of Samuäl West's specifically Christian argument. I take this to reinforce my point that Jefferson and other secular-minded Americans subscribed to certain propositions about law and authority that had their roots in the Protestant Reformation. It is a scholarly commonplace to point out how much Jefferson (and his fellow delegates to Continental Congress) were influenced by Locke. Without disputing this we would simply add that an older and deeper influence — John Calvin — was of more profound importance (or that Locke's consciousness, like Jefferson's was a consequence in large part of the Reformation).

[The text is taken from "Declaration of Independence," *Revised Statutes of the United States*, 1878 edition.]

## Declaration of Independence

*In Congress, July* 4, 1776,
THE UNANIMOUS DECLARATION OF THE
THIRTEEN UNITED STATES OF AMERICA,

When in the Course of human events, it becomes necessary for one people to dissolve the political bands which have connected them with another, and to assume among the Powers of the earth, the separate and equal station to which the

Laws of Nature and of Nature's God entitle them, a decent respect to the opinions of mankind requires that they should declare the causes which impel them to the separation.

We hold these truths to be self-evident, that all men are created equal, that they are endowed by their Creator with certain unalienable Rights, that among these are Life, Liberty and the pursuit of Happiness. That to secure these rights, Governments are instituted among Men, deriving their just powers from the consent of the governed, That whenever any Form of Government becomes destructive of these ends, it is the Right of the People to alter or to abolish it, and to institute new Government, laying its foundation on such principles and organizing its powers in such form, as to them shall seem most likely to effect their Safety and Happiness. Prudence, indeed, will dictate that Governments long established should not be changed for light and transient causes; and accordingly all experience hath shown, that mankind are more disposed to suffer, while evils are sufferable, than to right themselves by abolishing the forms to which they are accustomed. But when a long train of abuses and usurpations, pursuing invariably the same Object evinces a design to reduce them under absolute Despotism, it is their right, it is their duty, to throw off such Government, and to provide new Guards for their future security. — Such has been the patient sufferance of these Colonies; and such is now the necessity which constrains them to alter their former Systems of Government. The history of the present King of Great Britain is a history of repeated injuries and usurpations, all having in direct object the establishment of an absolute Tyranny over these States. To prove this, let Facts be submitted to a candid world.

He has refused his Assent to Laws, the most wholesome and necessary for the public good.

He has forbidden his Governors to pass Laws of immediate and pressing importance, unless suspended in their operation till his Assent should be obtained; and when so suspended, he has utterly neglected to attend to them.

He has refused to pass other Laws for the accomodation of large districts of people, unless those people would relinquish the right of Representation in the Legislature, a right inestimable to them and formidable to tyrants only.

He has called together legislative bodies at places unusual, uncomfortable, and distant from the depository of their Public Records, for the sole purpose of fatiguing them into compliance with his measures.

He has dissolved Representative Houses repeatedly, for opposing with manly firmness his invasions on the rights of the people.

He has refused for a long time, after such dissolutions, to cause others to be elected; whereby the Legislative Powers, incapable of Annihilation, have returned to the People at large for their exercise; the State remaining in the mean time exposed to all the dangers of invasion from without, and convulsions within.

He has endeavoured to prevent the population of these States; for that purpose obstructing the Laws of Naturalization of Foreigners; refusing to pass others to encourage their migration hither, and raising the conditions of new Appropriations of Lands.

He has obstructed the Administration of Justice, by refusing his Assent to Laws for establishing Judiciary Powers.

He has made Judges dependent on his Will alone, for the tenure of their offices, and the amount and payment of their salaries.

He has erected a multitude of New Offices, and sent hither swarms of Officers to harass our People, and eat out their substance.

He has kept among us, in times of peace, Standing Armies without the Consent of our legislature.

He has affected to render the Military independent of and superior to the Civil Power.

He has combined with others to subject us to a jurisdiction foreign to our constitution, and unacknowledged by our laws; giving his Assent to their acts of pretended legislation:

For quartering large bodies of armed troops among us:

For protecting them, by a mock Trial, from Punishment for any Murders which they should commit on the Inhabitants of these States:

For cutting off our Trade with all parts of the world:

For imposing taxes on us without our Consent:

For depriving us in many cases, of the benefits of Trial by Jury:

For transporting us beyond Seas to be tried for pretended offences:

For abolishing the free System of English Laws in a neighbouring Province, establishing therein an Arbitrary government, and enlarging its Boundaries so as to render it at once an example and fit instrument for introducing the same absolute rule into these Colonies:

For taking away our Charters, abolishing our most valuable Laws, and altering fundamentally the Forms of our Governments:

For suspending our own Legislature, and declaring themselves invested with Power to legislate for us in all cases whatsoever.

He has abdicated Government here, by declaring us out of his Protection and waging War against us.

He has plundered our seas, ravaged our Coasts, burnt our towns, and destroyed the lives of our people.

He is at this time transporting large armies of foreign mercenaries to compleat the works of death, desolation and tyranny, already begun with circumstances of Cruelty & perfidy scarcely paralleled in the most barbarous ages, and totally unworthy the Head of a civilized nation.

He has constrained our fellow Citizens taken Captive on the high Seas to bear Arms against their Country, to become the executioners of their friends and Brethren, or to fall themselves by their Hands.

He has excited domestic insurrections amongst us, and has endeavoured to bring on the inhabitants of our frontiers, the merciless Indian Savages, whose known rule of warfare, is an undistinguished destruction of all ages, sexes and conditions.

In every state of these Oppressions We have Petitioned for Redress in the most humble terms: Our repeated Petitions have been answered only by repeated injury. A Prince, whose character is thus marked by every act which may define a Tyrant, is unfit to be the ruler of a free People.

Nor have We been wanting in attention to our Brittish brethren. We have warned them from time to time of attempts by their legislature to extend an unwarrantable jurisdiction over us. We have reminded them of the circumstances of our emigration and settlement here. We have appealed to their native justice and magnanimity, and we have conjured them by the ties of our common kindred to disavow these usurpations, which, would inevitably interrupt our connections and correspondence. They too have been deaf to the voice of justice and of consanguinity. We must, therefore, acquiesce in the necessity, which denounces our Separation, and hold them, as we hold the rest of mankind, Enemies in War, in Peace Friends.

We, therefore, the Representatives of the united States of America, in General Congress, Assembled, appealing to the Supreme Judge of the world for the rectitude of our intentions, do, in the Name, and by Authority of the good People of these Colonies, solemnly publish and declare, That these United Colonies are, and of Right ought to be Free and Independent States; that they are absolved from all Allegiance to the British Crown, and that all political connection between them and the State of Great Britain, is and ought to be totally dissolved; and that as Free and Independent States, they have full Power to levy War, conclude Peace, contract Alliances, establish Commerce, and to do all other Acts and Things which Independent States may of right do. And for the support of this Declaration, with a firm reliance on the Protection of Divine Providence, we mutually pledge to each other our Lives, our Fortunes and our sacred Honor.

# 14

---

James Wilson, born in Scotland came to America on the event of the Revolution and apprenticed himself to John Dickinson, the famous Pennsylvania lawyer. He was a delegate to Continental Congress, one of the more democratically- inclined and active members of the Federal Convention, a justice on the first Supreme Court and Professor of Law at the College of Philadelphia. It was in this latter capacity that he delivered a series of lectures on law, the first before a distinguished audience of state and federal legislators and public officials. Portions on the Law of Nature are included here because Wilson's treatment of the relation of natural law to civil government is the most complete statement we have and one that we can be confident was shared by most members of his audience.

# A

[The text is taken from James Wilson, "Of the Law of Nature," *The Works of the Honourable James Wilson*, (Philadelphia: Lorenzo Press, 1804).]

## Of the Law of Nature

In every period of our existence, in every situation, in which we can be placed, much is to be known, much is to be done, much is to be enjoyed. But all that is to be known, all that is to be done, all that is to be enjoyed, depends upon the proper exertion and direction of our numerous powers. In this immense ocean of intelligence and action, are we left without a compass and without a chart? Is there no pole star, by which we may regulate our course? Has the all-gracious and all-wise Author of our existence formed us for such great and such good ends; and has he left us without a conductor to lead us in the way, by which those ends may be attained? Has he made us capable of observing a rule, and has he furnished us with no rule, which we ought to observe? Let us examine these questions — for they are important ones — with patience and with attention. Our labours will, in all probability, be amply repaid. We shall probably find that, to direct the more important parts of our conduct, the bountiful Governour of the universe has been graciously pleased to provide us with a law; and that, to direct the less important parts of it, he has made us capable of providing a law for ourselves.

That our Creator has a supreme right to prescribe a law for our conduct, and that we are under the most perfect obligation to obey that law, are truths established on the clearest and most solid principles.

In the course of our remarks on that part of Sir William Blackstone's definition of law, which includes the idea of a superiour as essential to it, we remarked, with particular care, that it was only with regard to human laws that we controverted the justness or propriety of that idea. It was incumbent on us to mark this distinction particularly; for with regard to laws which are divine, they truly come from a superiour — from Him who is supreme.

Between beings, who, in their nature, powers, and situation, are so perfectly equal, that nothing can be ascribed to one, which is not applicable to the other, there can be neither superiority nor dependence. With regard to such beings, no reason can be assigned, why any one should assume authority over others, which may not, with equal propriety, be assigned, why each of those others should assume authority over that one. To constitute superiority and dependence, there must be an essential difference of qualities, on which those relations may be founded.

Some allege, that the sole superiority of strength, or, as they express it, an irresistible power, is the true foundation of the right of prescribing laws. "This superiority of power gives," say they, "a right of reigning, by the impossibility, in which it places others, of resisting him, who has so great an advantage over them."

Others derive the right of prescribing laws and imposing obligations from superiour excellence of nature. "This," say they, "not only renders a being independent of those, who are of a nature inferiour to it; but leads us to believe, that the latter were made for the sake of the former." For a proof of this, they appeal to the constitution of man. "Here," they tell us, "the soul governs, as being the noblest part." "On the same foundation," they add, "the empire of man over the brute creation is built."

Others, again, say, that "properly speaking, there is only one general source of superiority and obligation. God is our creator: in him we live, and move, and have our being: from him we have received our intellectual and our moral powers: he, as master of his own work, can prescribe to it whatever rules to him shall seem meet. Hence our dependence on our Creator: hence his absolute power over us. This is the true source of all authority."

With regard to the first hypothesis, it is totally insufficient; nay, it is absolutely false. Because I cannot resist, am I obliged to obey? Because another is possessed of superiour force, am I bound to acknowledge his will as the rule of my conduct?

Every obligation supposes motives that influence the conscience and determine the will, so that we should think it wrong not to obey, even if resistance was in our power. But a person, who alleges only the law of the strongest, proposes no motive to influence the conscience, or to determine the will. Superiour force may reside with predominant malevolence. Has force, exerted for the purposes of malevolence, a right to command? Can it impose an obligation to obey? No. Resistance to such force is a right; and, if resistance can prove effectual, it is a duty also. On some occasions, all our efforts may, indeed, be useless; and an attempt to resist would frustrate its own aim: but, on such occasions, the exercise of resistance only is suspended; the right of resistance is not extinguished: we may continue, for a time, under a constraint; but we come not under an obligation: we may suffer all the external effects of superiour force; but we feel not the internal influence of superiour authority.

The second hypothesis has in it something plausible; but, on examination, it will not be found to be accurate. Wherever a being of superiour excellence is found, his excellence, as well as every other truth, ought, on proper occasions, to be acknowledged; we will go farther; it ought, as every thing excellent ought, to be esteemed. But must we go farther still? Is obedience the necessary consequence of honest acknowledgment and just esteem? Here we must make a pause: we must make some inquiries before we go forward. In what manner is this being of superiour excellence connected with us? What are his dispositions with regard to us? By what effects, if by any, will his superiour excellence be displayed? Will it be exerted for our happiness; or, as to us, will it not be exerted at all? We acknowledge — we esteem excellence; but till these questions are answered, we feel not ourselves under an obligation to obey it. If the opinion of Epicurus concerning his divinities — that they were absolutely indifferent to the happiness and interests of men — was admitted for a moment; the inference would unquestionably be — that they were not entitled to human obedience.

The third hypothesis contains a solemn truth, which ought to be examined with reverence and awe. It resolves the supreme right of prescribing laws for our conduct, and our indispensable duty of obeying those laws, into the omnipotence of the Divinity. This omnipotence let us humbly adore. Were we to suppose — but the supposition cannot be made — that infinite goodness could be disjoined from almighty power — but we cannot — must not proceed to the inference. No, it never can be drawn; for from almighty power infinite goodness can never be disjoined.

Let us join, in our weak conceptions, what are inseparable in their incomprehensible Archetype — infinite power — infinite wisdom — infinite goodness; and then we shall see, in its resplendent glory, the supreme right to rule: we shall feel the conscious sense of the perfect obligation to obey.

His infinite power enforces his laws, and carries them into full and effectual execution. His infinite wisdom knows and chooses the fittest means for accomplishing the ends which he proposes. His infinite goodness proposes such ends only as promote our felicity. By his power, he is able to remove whatever may possibly injure us, and to provide whatever is conducive to our happiness. By his wisdom, he knows our nature, our faculties, and our interests: he cannot be mistaken in the designs, which he proposes, nor in the means, which he employs to accomplish them. By his goodness, he proposes our happiness: and to that end directs the operations of his power and wisdom. Indeed, to his goodness alone we may trace the principle of his laws. Being infinitely and eternally happy in himself, his goodness alone could move him to create us, and give us the means of happiness. The same principle, that moved his creating, moves his governing power. The rule of his government we shall find to be reduced to this one paternal command — Let man pursue his own perfection and happiness.

What an enrapturing view of the moral government of the universe! Over all, goodness infinite reigns, guided by unerring wisdom, and supported by almighty power. What an instructive lesson to those who think, and are encouraged by their flatterers to think, that a portion of divine right is communicated to their rule. If this really was the case; their power ought to be subservient to their goodness, and their goodness should be employed in promoting the happiness of those, who are intrusted to their care. But princes, and the flatterers of princes, are guilty, in two respects, of the grossest errour and presumption. They claim to govern by divine institution and right. The principles of their government are repugnant to the principles of that government, which is divine. The principle of the divine government is goodness: they plume themselves with the gaudy insignia of power.

Well might nature's poet say —

> —————— Could great men thunder,
> As Jove himself does, Jove would ne'er be quiet;
> For every pelting, petty officer
> Would use his heaven for thunder;
> Nothing but thunder. Merciful heaven!
> Thou rather with thy sharp and sulphurous bolt
> Split'st the unwedgeable and gnarled oak,
> Than the soft myrtle: O, but man, proud man,
> Dressed in a little brief authority,
> Most ignorant of what he's most assured,
> His glassy substance; like an angry ape,
> Plays such fantastick tricks before high heaven,
> As make the angels weep.
> Shak. Meas. for Meas. Act II.

Where a supreme right to give laws exists, on one side, and a perfect obligation to obey them exists, on the other side; this relation, of itself, suggests the probability that laws will be made.

When we view the inanimate and irrational creation around and above us, and contemplate the beautiful order observed in all its motions and appearances; is not the supposition unnatural and improbable — that the rational and moral world should be abandoned to the frolicks of chance, or to the ravage of disorder? What would be the fate of man and of society, was every one at full liberty to do as he listed, without any fixed rule or principle of conduct, without a helm to steer him — a sport of the fierce gusts of passion, and the fluctuating billows of caprice?

To be without law is not agreeable to our nature; because, if we were without law, we should find many of our talents and powers hanging upon us like useless incumbrances. Why should we be illuminated by reason, were we only made to obey the impulse of irrational instinct? Why should we have the power of deliberating, and of balancing our determinations, if we were made to yield implicitly and unavoidably to the influence of the first impressions? Of what service to us would reflection be, if we were to be carried away irresistibly by the force of blind and impetuous appetites?

Without laws, what would be the state of society? The more ingenious and artful the twolegged animal, man, is, the more dangerous he would become to his equals: his ingenuity would degenerate into cunning; and his art would be employed for the purposes of malice. He would be deprived of all the benefits and pleasures of peaceful and social life: he would become a prey to all the distractions of licentiousness and war.

Is it probable — we repeat the question — is it probable that the Creator, infinitely wise and good, would leave his moral world in this chaos and disorder?

If we enter into ourselves, and view with attention what passes in our own breasts, we shall find, that what, at first, appeared probable, is proved, on closer examination, to be certain; we shall find, that God has not left himself without a witness, nor us without a guide . . .

Having thus stated the question — what is the efficient cause of moral obligation? — I give it this answer — the will of God. This is the supreme law. His just and full right of imposing laws, and our duty in obeying them, are the sources of our moral obligations. If I am asked — why do you obey the will of God? I answer — because it is my duty so to do. If I am asked again — how do you know this to be your duty? I answer again — because I am told so by my moral sense or conscience. If I am asked a third time — how do you know that you ought to do that, of which your conscience enjoins the performance? I can only say, I *feel* that such is my duty. Here investigation must stop; reasoning can go no farther. The science of morals, as well as other sciences, is founded on truths, that cannot be discovered or proved by reasoning. Reason is confined to the investigation of unknown truths by the means of such as are known. We cannot, therefore, begin to reason, till we are furnished, otherwise than by reason, with some truths, on which we can found our arguments. Even in mathematicks, we must be provided with axioms perceived intuitively to be true, before our demonstrations can commence. Morality, like mathematicks, has its intuitive truths, without which we cannot make a single step in our reasonings upon the subject. Such an intuitive truth is that, with which we just now closed our investigation. If a person was not possessed of the feeling before mentioned; it would not be in the power of arguments, to give him any conception of the distinction between right and wrong. These terms would be to him equally unintelligible, as the term *colour* to one who was born and has continued blind. But that there is, in human nature, such a moral principle, has been felt and acknowledged in all ages and nations.

Now that we have stated and answered the first question; let us proceed to the consideration of the second — how shall we, in particular instances, learn the dictates of our duty, and make, with accuracy, the proper distinction between right and wrong; in other words, how shall we, in particular cases, discover the will of God? We discover it by our conscience, by our reason, and by the Holy Scriptures. The law of nature and the law of revelation are both divine: they flow, though in different channels, from the same adorable source. It is, indeed, preposterous to separate them from each other. The object of both is — to discover the will of God — and both are necessary for the accomplishment of that end.

I. The power of moral perception is, indeed, a most important part of our constitution. It is an original power — a power of its own kind; and totally distinct from the ideas of utility and agreeableness. By that power, we have conceptions of merit and demerit, of duty and moral obligation. By that power, we perceive some things in human conduct to be right, and others to be wrong. We have the same reason to rely on the dictates of this faculty, as upon the determinations of our senses, or of our other natural powers. When an action is represented to us, flowing from love, humanity, gratitude, an ultimate desire of the good of others; though it happened in a country far distant, or in an age long past, we admire the lovely exhibition, and praise its author. The contrary conduct, when represented to us, raises our abhorrence and aversion. But whence this secret chain betwixt each person and mankind? If there is no moral sense, which makes benevolence appear beautiful; if all approbation be from the interest of the approver; "What's Hecuba to us, or we to Hecuba?"

The mind, which reflects on itself, and is a spectator of other minds, sees and feels the soft and the harsh, the agreeable and the disagreeable, the foul and the fair, the harmonious and the dissonant, as really and truly in the affections and actions, as in any musical numbers, or the outward forms or representations of sensible things. It cannot withhold its approbation or aversion in what relates to the former, any more than in what relates to the latter, of those subjects. To deny the sense of a sublime and beautiful and of their contraries in actions and things, will appear an affectation merely to one who duly considers and traces the subject. Even he who indulges this affectation cannot avoid the discovery of those very sentiments, which he pretends not to feel. A Lucretius or a Hobbes cannot discard the sentiments of praise and admiration respecting some moral forms, nor the sentiments of censure and detestation concerning others. Has a man gratitude, or resentment, or pride, or shame? If he has and avows it; he must have and acknowledge a sense of something benevolent, of something unjust, of something worthy, and of something mean. Thus, so long as we find men pleased or angry, proud or ashamed; we may appeal to the reality of the moral sense. A right and a wrong, an honourable and a dishonourable is plainly conceived. About these there may be mistakes; but this destroys not the inference, that the things are, and are universally acknowledged — that they are of nature's impression, and by no art can be obliterated.

This sense or apprehension of right and wrong appears early, and exists in different degrees. The qualities of love, gratitude, sympathy unfold themselves, in the first stages of life, and the approbation of those qualities accompanies the first dawn of reflection. Young people, who think the least about the distant influences of actions, are, more than others, moved with moral forms. Hence that strong inclination in children to hear such stories as paint the characters and fortunes of men. Hence that joy in the prosperity of the kind and faithful, and that sorrow upon the success of the treacherous and cruel, with which we often see infant minds strongly agitated.

There is a natural beauty in figures; and is there not a beauty as natural in actions? When the eye opens upon forms, and the ear to sounds; the beautiful is seen, and harmony is heard and acknowledged. When actions are viewed and affections are discerned, the inward eye distinguishes the beautiful, the amiable, the admirable, from the despicable, the odious, and the deformed. How is it possible not to own, that as these distinctions have their foundation in nature, so this power of discerning them is natural also?

The universality of an opinion or sentiment may be evinced by the structure of languages. Languages were not invented by philosophers, to countenance or support any artificial system. They were contrived by men in general, to express common sentiments and perceptions. The inference is satisfactory, that where all languages make a distinction, there must be a similar distinction in universal opinion or sentiment. For language is the picture of human thoughts; and, from this faithful picture, we may draw certain conclusions concerning the original. Now, a universal effect must have a universal cause. No universal cause can, with propriety, be assigned for this universal opinion, except that intuitive perception of things, which is distinguished by the name of common sense.

All languages speak of a beautiful and a deformed, a right and a wrong, an agreeable and disagreeable, a good and ill, in actions, affections, and characters. All languages, therefore, suppose a moral sense, by which those qualities are perceived and distinguished.

The whole circle of the arts of imitation proves the reality of the moral sense. They suppose, in human conduct, a sublimity, a beauty, a greatness, an excellence, independent of advantage or disadvantage, profit or loss. On him, whose heart is indelicate or hard; on him, who has no admiration of what is truly noble; on him, who has no sympathetick sense of what is melting and tender, the highest beauty of the mimick arts must make indeed, but a very faint and transient impression. If we were void of a relish for moral excellence, how frigid and uninteresting would the finest descriptions of life and manners appear! How indifferent are the finest strains of harmony, to him who has not a musical ear!

The force of the moral sense is diffused through every part of life. The luxury of the table derives its principal charms from some mixture of moral enjoyments, from communicating pleasures, and from sentiments honourable and just as well as elegant — "The feast of reason, and the flow of soul."

The chief pleasures of history, and poetry, and eloquence, and musick, and sculpture, and painting are derived from the same source. Beside the pleasures they afford by imitation, they receive a stronger charm from something moral insinuated into the performances. The principal beauties of behaviour, and even of countenance, arise from the indication of affections or qualities morally estimable.

Never was there any of the human species above the condition of an idiot, to whom all actions appeared indifferent. All feel that a certain temper, certain affections, and certain actions produce a sentiment of approbation; and that a sentiment of disapprobation is produced by the contrary temper, affections, and actions.

This power is capable of culture and improvement by habit, and by frequent and extensive exercise. A high sense of moral excellence is approved above all other intellectual talents. This high sense of excellence is accompanied with a strong desire after it, and a keen relish for it. This desire and this relish are approved as the most amiable affections, and the highest virtues.

This moral sense, from its very nature, is intended to regulate and control all our other powers. It governs our passions as well as our actions. Other principles may solicit and allure; but the conscience assumes authority, it must be obeyed. Of this dignity and commanding nature we are immediately conscious, as we are of the power itself. It estimates what it enjoins, not merely as superiour in degree, but as superiour likewise in kind, to what is recommended by our other perceptive powers. Without this controlling faculty, endowed as we are with such a variety of senses and interfering desires, we should appear a fabrick destitute of order: but possessed of it, all our powers may be harmonious and consistent; they may all combine in one uniform and regular direction.

In short; if we had not the faculty of perceiving certain things in conduct to be right, and others to be wrong; and of perceiving our obligation to do what is right, and not to do what is wrong; we should not be moral and accountable beings.

If we be, as, I hope, I have shown we are, endowed with this faculty; there must be some things, which are immediately discerned by it to be right, and others to be wrong. There must, consequently, be in morals, as in other sciences, first principles, which derive not their evidence from any antecedent principles, but which may be said to be intuitively discerned.

Moral truths may be divided into two classes; such as are selfevident, and such as, from the selfevident ones, are deduced by reasoning. If the first be not discerned without reasoning, reasoning can never discern the last. The cases that require reasoning are few, compared with those that require none; and a man may be very honest and virtuous, who cannot reason, and who knows not what demonstration means.

If the rules of virtue were left to be discovered by reasoning, even by demonstrative reasoning, unhappy would be the condition of the far greater part of men, who have not the means of cultivating the power of reasoning to any high degree. As virtue is the business of all men, the first principles of it are written on their hearts, in characters so legible, that no man can pretend ignorance of them, or of his obligation to practise them. Reason, even with experience, is too often overpowered by passion; to restrain whose impetuosity, nothing less is requisite than the vigorous and commanding principle of duty.

II. The first principles of morals, into which all moral argumentation may be resolved, are discovered in a manner more analogous to the perceptions of sense than to the conclusions of reasoning. In morality, however, as well as in other sciences, reason is usefully introduced, and performs many important services. In many instances she regulates our belief, and in many instances she regulates our conduct. She determines the proper means to any end; and she decides the preference of one end over another. She may exhibit an object to the mind, though the perception which the mind has, when once the object is exhibited, may properly belong to a sense. She may be necessary to ascertain the circumstances and determine the motives to an action; though it be the moral sense that perceives the action to be either virtuous or vicious, after its motive and its circumstances have been discovered. She discerns the tendencies of the several senses, affections, and actions, and the comparative value of objects and gratifications. She judges concerning subordinate ends; but concerning ultimate ends she is not employed. These we prosecute by some immediate determination of the mind, which, in the order of action, is prior to all reasoning; for no opinion or judgment can move to action, where there is not a previous desire of some end. — This power of comparing the several enjoyments, of which our nature is susceptible, in order to discover which are most important to our happiness, is of the highest consequence and necessity to corroborate our moral faculty, and to preserve our affections in just rank and regular order.

A magistrate knows that it is his duty to promote the good of the commonwealth, which has intrusted him with authority. But whether one particular plan or another particular plan of conduct in office, may best promote the good of the commonwealth, may, in many cases, be doubtful. His conscience or moral sense determines the end, which he ought to pursue; and he has intuitive evidence that his end is good: but the means of attaining this end must be determined by reason. To select and ascertain those means, is often a matter of very considerable difficulty. Doubts may arise; opposite interests may occur; and a preference must be given to one side from a small over-balance, and from very nice views. This is particularly the case in questions with regard to justice. If every single instance of justice, like every single instance of benevolence, were pleasing and useful to society, the case would be more simple, and would be seldom liable to great controversy. But as single instances of justice are often pernicious in their first and immediate tendency; and as the advantage to society results only from the observance of the general rule, and from the concurrence and combination of several persons in the same equitable conduct; the case here becomes more intricate and involved. The various circumstances of society, the various consequences of any practice, the various interests which may be proposed, are all, on many occasions, doubtful, and subject to much discussion and inquiry. The design of municipal law (for let us still, from every direction, open a view to our principal object) the design of municipal law is to fix all the questions which regard justice. A very accurate reason or judgment is often requisite, to give the true determination amidst intricate doubts, arising from obscure or opposite utilities.

Thus, though good and ill, right and wrong are ultimately perceived by the moral sense, yet reason assists its operations, and, in many instances, strengthens and extends its influence. We may argue concerning propriety of conduct: just reasonings on the subject will establish principles for judging of what deserves praise: but, at the same time, these reasonings must always, in the last resort, appeal to the moral sense.

Farther; reason serves to illustrate, to prove, to extend, to apply what our moral sense has already suggested to us, concerning just and unjust, proper and improper, right and wrong. A father feels that paternal tenderness is refined and confirmed, by reflecting how consonant that feeling is to the reltion between a parent and his child; how conducive it is to the happiness, not only of a single family, but, in its extension, to that of all mankind. We feel the beauty and excellence of virtue; but this sense is strengthened and improved by the lessons, which reason gives us concerning the foundations, the motives, the relations, the particular and the universal advantages flowing from this virtue, which, at first sight, appeared so beautiful.

Taste is a faculty, common, in some degree, to all men. But study, attention, comparison operate most powerfully towards its refinement. In the same manner, reason contributes to ascertain the exactness, and to discover and correct the mistakes, of the moral sense. A prejudice of education may be misapprehended for a determination of morality. 'Tis reason's province to compare and discriminate.

Reason performs an excellent service to the moral sense in another respect. It considers the relations of actions, and traces them to the remotest consequences.

We often see men, with the most honest hearts and most pure intentions, embarrassed and puzzled, when a case, delicate and complicated, comes before them. They feel what is right; they are unshaken in their general principles; but they are unaccustomed to pursue them through their different ramifications, to make the necessary distinctions and exceptions, or to modify them according to the circumstances of time and place. 'Tis the business of reason to discharge this duty; and it will discharge it the better in proportion to the care which has been employed in exercising and improving it . . .

The *ultimate* ends of human actions, can never, in any case, be accounted for by reason. They recommend themselves entirely to the sentiments and affections of men, without dependence on the intellectual faculties. Why do you take exercise? Because you desire health. Why do you desire health? Because sickness is painful. Why do you hate pain? No answer is heard. Can one be given? No. This is an ultimate end, and is not referred to any farther object.

To the second question, you may, perhaps, answer, that you desire health, because it is necessary for your improvement in your profession. Why are you anxious to make this improvement? You may, perhaps, answer again, because you wish to get money by it. Why do you wish to get money? Because, among other reasons, it is the instrument of pleasure. But why do you love pleasure? Can a reason be given for loving pleasure, any more than for hating pain? They are both ultimate objects. 'Tis impossible there can be a progress *in infinitum;* and that one thing can always be a reason, why another is hated or desired. Something must be hateful or desirable on its own account, and because of its immediate agreement or disagreement with human sentiment and affection.

Virtue and vice are ends; and are hateful or desirable on their own account. It is requisite, therefore, that there should be some sentiment, which they touch — some internal taste or sense, which distinguishes moral good and evil, and which embraces one, and rejects the other. Thus are the offices of reason and of the moral sense at last ascertained. The former conveys the knowledge of truth and falsehood: the latter, the sentiment of beauty and deformity, of vice and virtue. The standard of one, founded on the nature of things, is eternal and inflexible. The standard of the other is ultimately derived from that supreme will, which bestowed on us our peculiar nature, and arranged the several classes and orders of existence. In this manner, we return to the great principle, from which we set out. It is necessary that reason should be fortified by the moral sense: without the moral sense, a man may be prudent, but he cannot be virtuous.

Philosophers have degraded our senses below their real importance. They represent them as powers, by which we have sensations and ideas only. But this is not the whole of their office; they judge as well as inform. Not confined to the mere office of conveying impressions, they are exalted to the function of judging of the nature and evidence of the impressions they convey. If this be admitted, our moral faculty may, without impropriety, be called the *moral sense.* Its testimony, like that of the external senses, is the immediate testimony of nature, and on it we have the same reason to rely. In its dignity, it is, without doubt, far superiour to every other power of the mind.

The moral sense, like all our other powers, comes to maturity by insensible degrees. It is peculiar to human nature. It is both intellectual and active. It is evidently intended, by nature, to be the immediate guide and director of our conduct, after we arrive at the years of understanding.

III. Reason and conscience can do much; but still they stand in need of support and assistance. They are useful and excellent monitors; but, at some times, their admonitions are not sufficiently clear; at other times, they are not sufficiently powerful; at all times, their influence is not sufficiently extensive. Great and sublime truths, indeed, would appear to a few; but the world, at large, would be dark and ignorant. The mass of mankind would resemble a chaos, in which a few sparks, that would diffuse a glimmering light, would serve only to show, in a more striking manner, the thick darkness with which they are surrounded. Their weakness is strengthened, their darkness is illuminated, their influence is enlarged by that heaven-descended science, which has brought life and immortality to light. In compassion to the imperfection of our internal powers, our all-gracious Creator, Preserver, and Ruler has been pleased to discover and enforce his laws, by a revelation given to us immediately and directly from himself. This revelation is contained in the holy scriptures. The moral precepts delivered in the sacred oracles form a part of the law of nature, are of the same origin, and of the same obligation, operating universally and perpetually.

On some important subjects, those in particular, which relate to the Deity, to Providence, and to a future state, our natural knowledge is greatly improved, refined, and exalted by that which is revealed. On these subjects, one who has had the advantage of a common education in a christian country, knows more, and with more certainty, than was known by the wisest of the ancient philosophers.

One superiour advantage the precepts delivered in the sacred oracles clearly possess. They are, of all, the most explicit and the most certain. A publick minister, judging from what he knows of the interests, views, and designs of the state, which he represents, may take his resolutions and measures, in many cases, with confidence and safety, and may presume, with great probability, how the state itself would act. But if, besides this general knowledge, and these presumptions highly probable, he was furnished also with particular instructions for the regulation of his conduct; would he not naturally observe and govern himself by both rules? In cases, where his instructions are clear and positive, there would be an end of all farther deliberation. In other cases, where his instructions are silent, he would supply them by his general knowledge, and by the information, which he could collect from other quarters, concerning the counsels and systems of the commonwealth. Thus it is with regard to reason, conscience, and the holy scriptures. Where the latter give instructions, those instructions are supereminently authentick. But whoever expects to find, in them, particular directions for every moral doubt which arises, expects more than he will find. They generally presuppose a knowledge of the principles of morality; and are employed not so much in teaching new rules on this subject, as in enforcing the practice of those already known, by a greater certainty, and by new sanctions. They present the warmest recommendations and the strongest inducements in favour of virtue: they exhibit the most powerful dissuasives from vice. But the origin, the nature, and the extent of the several rights and duties they do not explain; nor do they specify in what instances one right or duty is entitled to preference over another. They are addressed to rational and moral agents, capable of previously knowing the rights of men, and the tendencies of actions; of approving what is good, and of disapproving what is evil.

These considerations show, that the scriptures support, confirm, and corroborate, but do not supercede the operations of reason and the moral sense.

The information with regard to our duties and obligations, drawn from these different sources, ought not to run in unconnected and diminished channels: it should flow in one united stream, which, by its combined force and just direction, will impel us uniformly and effectually towards our greatest good.

We have traced, with some minuteness, the efficient principle of obligation, and the several means, by which our duty may be known. It will be proper to turn our attention back to the opinions that have been held, in philosophy and jurisprudence, concerning this subject. On a review of them, we shall now find that, in general, they are defective rather than erroneous; that they have fallen short of the mark, rather than deviated from the proper course.

The fitness of things denotes their fitness to produce our happiness: their nature means that actual constitution of the world, by which some things produce happiness, and others misery. Reason is one of the means, by which we discern between those things, which produce the former, and those things, which produce the latter. The moral sense feels and operates to promote the same essential discriminations. Whatever promotes the greatest happiness of the whole, is congenial to the principles of utility and sociability: and whatever unites in it all the foregoing properties, must be agreeable to the will of God: for, as has been said once, and as ought to be said again, his will is graciously comprised in this one paternal precept — Let man pursue his happiness and perfection.

The law of nature is immutable, not by the effect of an arbitrary disposition, but because it has its foundation in the nature, constitution, and mutual relations of men and things. While these continue to be the same, it must continue to be the same also. This immutability of nature's laws has nothing in it repugnant to the supreme power of an all-perfect Being. Since he himself is the author of our constitution; he cannot but command or forbid such things as are necessarily agreeable or disagreeable to this very constitution, He is under the glorious necessity of not contradicting himself. This necessity, far from limiting or diminishing his perfections, adds to their external character, and points out their excellency.

The law of nature is universal. For it is true, not only that all men are equally subject to the command of their Maker; but it is true also, that the law of nature, having its foundation in the constitution and state of man, has an essential fitness for all mankind, and binds them without distinction.

This law, or right reason, as Cicero calls it, is thus beautifully described by that eloquent philosopher. "It is, indeed," says he, "a true law, conformable to nature, diffused among all men, unchangeable, eternal. By its commands, it calls men to their duty: by its prohibitions, it deters them from vice. To diminish, to alter, much more to abolish this law, is a vain attempt. Neither by the senate, nor by the people, can its powerful obligation be dissolved. It requires no interpreter or commentator. It is not one law at Rome, another at Athens; one law now, another hereafter: it is the same eternal and immutable law, given at all times and to all nations: for God, who is its author and promulgator, is always the sole master and sovereign of mankind."

"Man never *is,*" says the poet, in a seeming tone of complaint, "but always *to be* blest." The sentiment would certainly be more consolatory, and, I think, it would be likewise more just, if we were to say — man ever *is; for* always to be blest. That we should have more and better things before us, than all that we have yet acquired or enjoyed, is unquestionably a most desirable state. The reflection on this circumstance, far from diminishing our sense or the importance of our present attainments and advantages, produces the contrary effects. The present is gilded by the prospect of the future.

When Alexander had conquered a world, and had nothing left to conquer; what did he do? He sat down and wept. A well directed ambition that has conquered worlds, is exempted from the fate of that of Alexander the Great: it still sees before it more and better worlds as the objects of conquest.

It is the glorious destiny of man to be always progressive. Forgetting those things that are behind, it is his duty, and it is his happiness, to press on towards those that are before. In the order of Providence, as has been observed on another occasion, the progress of societies towards perfection resembles that of an individual. This progress has hitherto been but slow: by many unpropitious events, it has often been interrupted: but may we not indulge the pleasing expectation, that, in future, it will be accelerated; and will meet with fewer and less considerable interruptions?

Many circumstances seem — at least to a mind anxious to see it, and apt to believe what it is anxious to see — many circumstances seem to indicate the opening of such a glorious prospect. The principles and the practice of liberty are gaining ground, in more than one section of the world. Where liberty prevails, the arts and sciences lift up their heads and flourish. Where the arts and sciences flourish, political and moral improvements will likewise be made. All will receive from each, and each will receive from all, mutual support and assistance: mutually supported and assisted, all may be carried to a degree of perfection hitherto unknown; perhaps, hitherto not believed.

"Men," says the sagacious Hooker, "if we view them in their spring, are, at the first, without understanding or knowledge at all. Nevertheless, from this utter vacuity, they grow by degrees, till they become at length to be even as the angels themselves are. That which agreeth to the one now, the other shall attain to in the end: they are not so far disjoined and severed, but that they come at length to meet."

Our progress in virtue should certainly bear a just proportion to our progress in knowledge. Morals are undoubtedly capable of being carried to a much higher degree of excellence than the sciences, excellent as they are. Hence we may infer, that the law of nature, though immutable in its principles, will be progressive in its operations and effects. Indeed, the same immutable principles will direct this progression. In every period of his existence, the law, which the divine wisdom has approved for man, will not only be fitted, to the cotemporary degree, but will be calculated to produce, in future, a still higher degree of perfection.

A delineation of the laws of nature, has been often attempted. Books, under the appellations of institutes and systems of that law, have been often published. From what has been said concerning it, the most finished performances executed by human hands cannot be perfect. But most of them have been rude and imperfect to a very unnecessary, some, to a shameful degree.

A more perfect work than has yet appeared upon this great subject, would be a most valuable present to mankind. Even the most general outlines of it cannot, at least in these lectures, be expected from me.

# B

The Reverend William McClintock's letter to William Whipple, a delegate to the Continental Congress from New Hampshire, indicates that the clergy were often more radical than the politicians in their prescriptions for a democratic government.

[The text is taken from Rev. William McClintock, "Letter," (to William Whipple, August 2, 1776).]

## Letter

Perhaps no body of Men, in any period of time ever had objects of greater magnitude, or more various and complicated to engage their attention, than the grand American Congress have at the present day; and I believe I speak the sentiments of people in general when I add, never did men act with more wisdom, prudence, and fidelity than they have hitherto done in the discharge of the great trust committed to them by their country. I rejoice that we have such able *politicians* and true patriots at the helm in this convulsed, critical alarming state of our public affairs. The Wisdom, the Justice and public Spirit discovered in all their resolves and proceedings have acquired them the entire confidence of the people, excepting a few restless, disappointed malignant Tories, or venal wretches, bought with British gold, or the hope of making themselves great on the ruin of their Country, who are not *inactive* in propagating falsehoods and slanders to discourage people, and prejudice the common Cause. But I believe they are so few, that their influence is like to the drop of the Bucket to the *Ocean*. I will not say what a gentleman in Convention with me the other day said with some warmth, that people have a greater veneration for the resolves of the Congress than for the laws of the Almighty; but I will say, from my Observations that their resolves are observed by people in general with as much reverance as ever were the Laws of Solon or Lycurgus by the Athenians and Spartans, and much better than laws enforced by Royal Authority. People in general will be quiet and obedient so long as they see that their rulers are pursuing, the true end of the government, the good of the governed.

While some few among us are shewing their enmity to the Country in every thing they dare, it is merry to observe the conduct of some others, who seem to be in a state of suspense, waiting to see which side is like to prevail; are half whigs one day; and half tories the next, according as the events that turn up are for or against us. They are not governed by a regard to the Justice of the Cause but by a regard to consequences; in other words, by selfishness.

Sorry I am that there are any among us who drew their vital breath in America, and have all their connexion in America, so totally void of that noble and divine virtue *the love of their Country,* as to be unfriendly to the common cause. But I promise myself that the Wisdom, Justice, moderation and firmness of the Honorable Congress in their proceedings will finally silence all opposition. The eyes of all America are looking up to them, under God, as the Guardians of the Common Wealth, and reposing the greatest confidence in them that they will frame such regulations as effectually to secure her liberties against the future encroachment of Tyrants, and place them on a permanent basis.

It is said, virture is the basis of a Republic, and some express their fears that there is not publick virtue, *ever* in the Country for such a form of Government or if there is at present, it will not long be the case; that we shall soon become so corrupt that anarchy and confusion will take place, and we shall be in a worse state, than if we had remained as we were or submitted to absolute power. I hope not. As the abilities, virtue and public spirit of the Gentlemen who compose our Congress are unquestionable, so they have the advantage in framing a Constitution for America of the experiences of past ages, they know the rocks, on which other states have been shipwrecked, and I trust like good Pilots will steer clear of them. Can no regulations be made to guard more effectually against that corruption which has proved the ruin of all states that ever have existed, and to counteract the tendency of vice and in some measure to supply the want of publick virtue, to oblidge people to preserve and retain their liberties?

What do you think of the Agrarian Law to prevent subjects from engrossing too much property, and of consequence acquiring too much power and of consequence, acquiring too much power and influence, dangerous to the liberties of the people? What if a rotation Act to oblidge those who make laws, in their turn to experience the operation of them? Would it be a wise measure to oblidge the elected to clear themselves by a solemn oath when chosen, from having directly or indirectly used any influence to obtain their election, and to make outlawry and an incapacity ever to serve their Country afterwards, in any public post the punishment of perjury in such cases? Would it prevent the abuse of that power by which the British Parliament made themselves septennial, to make it an express rule of the constitutions that representatives shall be considered as reduced to a private station at the expiration of the term for which they shall be chosen, and that if they should presume to make any laws after the constitutional term of their existence such laws shall have no binding force on the people in any case whatsoever; and that such an attempt shall disqualify them from being re-elected? Can no method be found out to restrain and counteract that spirit of domination which in all ages has spread desolation and misery, in the earth and drench'd it in human blood.?

# 15

The faith that God had established, under the rubric of natural law (laws for the government of human society as definite and immutable as the laws that governed the physical universe), emboldened the American Revolutionists to undertake the framing of a new constitution of government for the new nation. The framers of the Constitution, with few if any exceptions, believed in original sin: they believed that when Adam was driven from the Garden of Eden for the sin of disobedience to God, his progeny had the sins of the father visited upon them and that there was therefore in human nature a radical propensity to sin. If they would not have entirely subscribed to Jeremiah's charge that the heart of man was "desperately wicked and deceitful above all things," they were conscious that such qualities as greed and vanity were quite generously distributed among the sons and daughters of Adam. From this belief it followed that any proper government ought to be based on a realistic assessment of man's nature. Only by so doing could they hope to devise a government that would 'accentuate the positive' aspects of human nature and confine its negative scope by wise laws and ingenious constitutional arrangements.

The selections that follow are chosen to demonstrate these convictions. We hear first from Alexander Hamilton, a leader of the conservative faction in the convention. George Mason, himself a slave-holder, gives one of the most moving indictments of slavery in our history (very plainly in the context of Christian dogma). Madison in the Tenth Federalist Paper describes the thought processes by which the framers of the Constitution analyzed the nature of human society and tried to devise a constitution based on what they had observed of social behavior. The last selection is from William Manning, a semi-literate

Massachusetts farmer who argues in *The Key to Liberty* that the natural human lust for wealth and power makes it imperative that ordinary working men join together to prevent their exploitation by those who control power. The portion printed here is from the beginning of Manning's essay.

A

[The text is taken from Alexander Hamilton, "June 22 Convention Debate."]

## June 22 Convention Debate

Federal Convention Debates June 22. Alexander Hamilton is speaking in favor of an article that would forbid persons from holding more than one public office under the federal government.

Mr. HAMILTON. "In all general questions which become the subjects of discussion, there are always some truths mixed with falsehoods. I confess there is a danger where men are capable of holding two offices. Take mankind in general, they are vicious — their passions may be operated upon. They have been taught to reprobate the danger of influence in the British Government, without duly reflecting how far it was necessary to support good government. We have taken up many ideas on trust, and at last, pleased with our own opinions, established them as undoubted truths. . . .Take mankind as they are, and what are they governed by? Their passions. There may be in every government a few choice spirits, who may act from more worthy motives. One great error is that we suppose mankind more honest than they are. Our prevailing passions are ambition and interest; and it will ever be the duty of a wise government to avail itself of those passions, in order to make them subservient to the public good — for these ever induce us to action. Perhaps a few men may act from patriotic motives, or to display their talents, or to reap the advantage of public applause, step forward; but if we adopt the clause we destroy the motive."

# B

[The text is taken from George Mason, "August 22 Convention Debate," *Debates of the Adoption of the Federal Constitution*, ed. by Jonathan Elliot, (Philadelphia: J. B. Lippincott, 1937), vol. V, p. 458.]

## August 22 Convention Debate

Art. vii, Sect. 4,[1] was resumed. Mr. SHERMAN was for leaving the clause as it stands. He disapproved of the slave trade; yet as the States were now possessed of the right to import slaves, as the public good did not require it to be taken from them, and as it was expedient to have as few objections as possible to the proposed scheme of government, he thought it best to leave the matter as we find it. He observed that the abolition of slavery seemed to be going on in the United States, and that the good sense of the several States would probably by degrees compleat it. He urged on the Convention the necessity of despatching its business.

Col. MASON. This infernal trafic originated in the avarice of British merchants. The British Government constantly checked the attempts of Virginia to put a stop to it. The present question concerns not the importing States alone but the whole Union. The evil of having slaves was experienced during the late war. Had slaves been treated as they might have been by the enemy, they would have proved dangerous instruments in their hands. But their folly dealt by the slaves, as it did by the tories. He mentioned the dangerous insurrections of the slaves in Greece and Sicily; and the instructions given by Cromwell to the Commissioners sent to Virginia, to arm the servants and slaves, in case other means of obtaining its submission should fail. Maryland and Virginia he said had already prohibited the importation of slaves expressly. North Carolina had done the same in substance. All this would be in vain if South Carolina and Georgia be at liberty to import. The western people are already calling out for slaves for their new lands, and will fill that country with slaves if they can be got thro' South Carolina and Georgia. Slavery discourages arts and manufactures. The poor despise labor when performed by slaves. They prevent the immigration of whites, who really enrich and strenghten a country. They produce the most pernicious effect on manners. Every master of slaves is born a petty tyrant. They bring the judgment of Heaven on a country. As nations cannot be rewarded or punished in the next world, they must be in this. By an inevitable chain of causes and effects, Providence punishes national sins, by national calamities. He lamented that some of our eastern brethren had from a lust of gain embarked in this nefarious traffic. As to the States being in possession of the right to import, this was the case with many other rights, now to be properly given up. He held it essential in every point of view that the General Government should have power to prevent the increase of slavery.

[1]Of the report of the Committe of Detail. Equivalent to art. i, s. ix, § I of the Constitution, without the limitation to 1808.

# C

[The text is taken from James Madison, "Tenth Federalist Paper," *The Federalist*, (New York: P. F. Collier & Son, 1901).]

## Tenth Federalist Paper

Among the numerous advantages promised by a well-constructed Union, none deserves to be more accurately developed than its tendency to break and control the violence of faction. The friend of popular governments never finds himself so much alarmed for their character and fate, as when he contemplates their propensity to this dangerous vice. He will not fail, therefore, to set a due value on any plan which, without violating the principles to which he is attached, provides a proper cure for it. The instability, injustice, and confusion introduced into the public councils, have, in truth, been the mortal diseases under which popular governments have everywhere perished; as they continue to be the favorite and fruitful topics from which the adversaries to liberty derive their most specious declamations. The valuable improvements made by the American constitutions on the popular models, both ancient and modern, cannot certainly be too much admired; but it would be an unwarrantable partiality, to contend that they have as effectually obviated the danger on this side, as was wished and expected. Complaints are everywhere heard from our most considerate and virtuous citizens, equally the friends of public and private faith, and of public and personal liberty, that our governments are too unstable, that the public good is disregarded in the conflicts of rival parties, and that measures are too often decided, not according to rules of justice and the rights of the minor party, but by the superior force of an interested and overbearing majority. However anxiously we may wish that these complaints had no foundation, the evidence of known facts will not permit us to deny that they are in some degree true. It will be found, indeed, on a candid review of our situation, that some of the distresses under which we labor have been erroneously charged on the operation of our governments; but it will be found, at the same time, that other causes will not alone account for many of our heaviest misfortunes; and, particularly, for that prevailing and increasing distrust of public engagements, and alarm for private rights, which are echoed from one end of the continent to the other. These must be chiefly, if not wholly, effects of the unsteadiness and injustice with which a factious spirit has tainted our public administrations.

By a faction, I understand a number of citizens, whether amounting to a majority or minority of the whole, who are united and actuated by some common impulse of passion, or of interest, adverse to the rights of other citizens, or to the permanent and aggregate interests of the community.

There are two methods of curing the mischiefs of faction: the one, by removing its causes; the other, by controlling its effects.

There are again two methods of removing the causes of faction: the one, by destroying the liberty which is essential to its existence; the other, by giving to every citizen the same opinions, the same passions, and the same interests.

It could never be more truly said than of the first remedy, that it was worse than the disease. Liberty is to faction what air is to fire, an aliment without which it instantly expires. But it could not be less folly to abolish liberty, which is essential to political life, because it nourishes faction, than it would be to wish the annihilation of air, which is essential to animal life, because it imparts to fire its destructive agency.

The second expedient is as impracticable as the first would be unwise. As long as the reason of man continues fallible, and he is at liberty to exercise it, different opinions will be formed. As long as the connection subsists between his reason and his self-love, his opinions and his passions will have a reciprocal influence on each other: and the former will be objects to which the latter will attach themselves. The diversity in the faculties of men, from which the rights of property originate, is not less an insuperable obstacle to a uniformity of interests. The protection of these faculties is the first object of government. From the protection of different and unequal faculties of acquiring property, the possession of different degrees and kinds of property immediately results; and from the influence of these on the sentiments and views of the respective proprietors, ensues a division of the society into different interests and parties.

The latent causes of faction are thus sown in the nature of man; and we see them everywhere brought into different degrees of activity, according to the different circumstances of civil society. A zeal for different opinions concerning religion, concerning government, and many other points, as well of speculation as of practice; an attachment to different leaders ambitiously contending for pre-eminence and power; or to persons of other descriptions whose fortunes have been interesting to the human passions, have, in turn, divided mankind into parties, inflamed them with mutual animosity, and rendered them much more disposed to vex and oppress each other than to co-operate for their common good. So strong is this propensity of mankind to fall into mutual animosities, that where no substantial occasion presents itself, the most frivolous and fanciful distinctions have been sufficient to kindle their unfriendly passions and excite their most violent conflicts. But the most common and durable source of factions has been the various and unequal distribution of property. Those who hold and those who are without property have ever formed distinct interests in society. Those who are creditors, and those who are debtors, fall under a like discrimination. A landed interest, a manufacturing interest, a mercantile interest, a moneyed interest, with many lesser interests, grow up of necessity in civilized nations, and divide them into different classes, actuated by different sentiments and views. The regulation of these various and interfering interests forms the principal task of modern legislation, and involves the spirit of party and faction in the necessary and ordinary operations of the government.

No man is allowed to be a judge in his own cause, because his interest would certainly bias his judgment, and, not improbably, corrupt his integrity. With equal, nay with greater reason, a body of men are unfit to be both judges and parties at the same time; yet what are many of the most important acts of legislation, but so many judicial determinations, not indeed concerning the rights of single persons, but concerning the rights of large bodies of citizens? And what are the different classes of legislators but advocates and parties to the causes which they determine? Is a law proposed concerning private debts? It is a question to which the creditors are parties on one side and the debtors on the other. Justice ought to hold the balance between them. Yet the parties are, and must be, themselves the judges; and the most numerous party, or, in other words, the most powerful faction must be expected to prevail. Shall domestic manufactures be encouraged, and in what degree, by restrictions on foreign manufactures? are questions which would be differently decided by the landed and the manufacturing classes, and probably by neither with a sole regard to justice and the public good. The apportionment of taxes on the various descriptions of property is an act which seems to require the most exact impartiality; yet there is, perhaps, no legislative act in which greater opportunity and temptation are given to a predominant party to trample on the rules of justice. Every shilling with which they overburden the inferior number, is a shilling saved to their own pockets.

It is in vain to say that enlightened statesmen will be able to adjust these clashing interests, and render them all subservient to the public good. Enlightened statesmen will not always be at the helm. Nor, in many cases, can such an adjustment be made at all without taking into view indirect and remote considerations, which will rarely prevail over the immediate interest which one party may find in disregarding the rights of another or the good of the whole.

The inference to which we are brought is, that the *causes* of faction cannot be removed, and that relief is only to be sought in the means of controlling its *effects*.

If a faction consists of less than a majority, relief is supplied by the republican principle, which enables the majority to defeat its sinister views by regular vote. It may clog the administration, it may convulse the society; but it will be unable to execute and mask its violence under the forms of the Constitution. When a majority is included in a faction, the form of popular government, on the other hand, enables it to sacrifice to its ruling passion or interest both the public good and the rights of other citizens. To secure the public good and private rights against the danger of such a faction, and at the same time to preserve the spirit and the form of popular government, is then the great object to which our inquiries are directed. Let me add that it is the great desideratum by which this form of government can be rescued from the opprobrium under which it has so long labored, and be recommended to the esteem and adoption of mankind.

By what means is this object attainable? Evidently by one of two only. Either the existence of the same passion or interest in a majority at the same time must be prevented, or the majority, having such coexistent passion or interest, must be rendered, by their number and local situation, unable to concert and carry into effect schemes of oppression. If the impulse and the opportunity be suffered to coincide, we well know that neither moral nor religious motives can be relied on as an adequate control. They are not found to be such on the injustice and violence of individuals, and lose their efficacy in proportion to the number combined together, that is, in proportion as their efficacy becomes needful.

From this view of the subject it may be concluded that a pure democracy, by which I mean a society consisting of a small number of citizens, who assemble and administer the government in person, can admit of no cure for the mischiefs of faction. A common passion or interest will, in almost every case, be felt by a majority of the whole; a communication and concert result from the form of government itself; and there is nothing to check the inducements to sacrifice the weaker party or an obnoxious individual. Hence it is that such democracies have ever been spectacles of turbulence and contention; have ever been found incompatible with personal security or the rights of property; and have in general been as short in their lives as they have been violent in their deaths. Theoretic politicians, who have patronized this species of government, have erroneously supposed that by reducing mankind to a perfect equality in their political rights, they would, at the same time, be perfectly equalized and assimilated in their possessions, their opinions, and their passions.

A republic, by which I mean a government in which the scheme of representation takes place, opens a different prospect, and promises the cure for which we are seeking. Let us examine the points in which it varies from pure democracy, and we shall comprehend both the nature of the cure and the efficacy which it must derive from the Union.

The two great points of difference between a democracy and a republic are: first, the delegation of the government, in the latter, to a small number of citizens elected by the rest; secondly, the greater number of citizens, and greater sphere of country, over which the latter may be extended.

The effect of the first difference is, on the one hand, to refine and enlarge the public views, by passing them through the medium of a chosen body of citizens, whose wisdom may best discern the true interest of their country, and whose patriotism and love of justice will be least likely to sacrifice it to temporary or partial considerations. Under such a regulation, it may well happen that the public voice, pronounced by the representatives of the people, will be more consonant to the public good than if pronounced by the people themselves, convened for the purpose. On the other hand, the effect may be inverted. Men of factious tempers, of local prejudices, or of sinister designs, may, by intrigue, by corruption, or by other means, first obtain the suffrages, and then betray the interests, of the people. The question resulting is, whether small or extensive republics are more favorable to the election of proper guardians of the public weal; and it is clearly decided in favor of the latter by two obvious considerations:

In the first place, it is to be remarked that, however small the republic may be, the representatives must be raised to a certain number, in order to guard against the cabals of a few; and that, however large it may be, they must be limited to a certain number, in order to guard against the confusion of a multitude. Hence, the number of representatives in the two cases not being in proportion to that of the two constituents, and being proportionally greater in the small republic, it follows that, if the proportion of fit characters be not less in the large than in the small republic, the former will present a greater option, and consequently a greater probability of a fit choice.

In the next place, as each representative will be chosen by a greater number of citizens in the large than in the small republic, it will be more difficult for unworthy candidates to practise with success the vicious arts by which elections are too often carried; and the suffrages of the people being more free, will be more likely to centre in men who possess the most attractive merit and the most diffusive and established characters.

It must be confessed that in this, as in most other cases, there is a mean, on both sides of which inconveniences will be found to lie. By enlarging too much the number of electors, you render the representative too little acquainted with all their local circumstances and lesser interests; as by reducing it too much, you render him unduly attached to these, and too little fit to comprehend and pursue great and national objects. The federal Constitution forms a happy combination in this respect; the great and aggregate interests being referred to the national, the local and particular to the State legislatures.

The other point of difference is, the greater number of citizens and extent of territory which may be brought within the compass of republican than of democratic government; and it is this circumstance principally which renders factious combinations less to be dreaded in the former than in the latter. The smaller the society, the fewer probably will be the distinct parties and interests composing it; the fewer the distinct parties and interests, the more frequently will a majority be found of the same party; and the smaller the number of individuals composing a majority, and the smaller the compass within which they are placed, the most easily will they concert and execute their plans of oppression. Extend the sphere, and you take in a greater variety of parties and interests; you make it less probable that a majority of the whole will have a common motive to invade the rights of other citizens; or if such a common motive exists, it will be more difficult for all who feel it to discover their own strength, and to act in unison with each other. Besides other impediments, it may be remarked that, where there is a consciousness of unjust or dishonorable purposes, communication is always checked by distrust in proportion to the number whose concurrence is necessary.

Hence, it clearly appears, that the same advantage which a republic has over a democracy, in controlling the effects of faction, is enjoyed by a large over a small republic, — is enjoyed by the Union over the States composing it. Does the advantage consist in the substitution of representatives whose enlightened views and virtuous sentiments render them superior to local prejudices and to schemes of injustice? It will not be denied that the representation of the Union will be most likely to possess these requisite endowments. Does it consist in the greater security afforded by a greater variety of parties, against the event of any one party being able to outnumber and oppress the rest? In an equal degree does the increased variety of parties comprised within the Union, increase this security. Does it, in fine, consist in the greater obstacles opposed to the concert and accomplishment of the secret wishes of an unjust and interested majority? Here, again, the extent of the Union gives it the most palpable advantage.

The influence of factious leaders may kindle a flame within their particular States, but will be unable to spread a general conflagration through the other States. A religious sect may degenerate into a political faction in a part of the Confederacy; but the variety of sects dispersed over the entire face of it must secure the national councils against any danger from that source. A rage for paper money, for an abolition of debts, for an equal division of property, or for any other improper or wicked project, will be less apt to pervade the whole body of the Union than a particular member of it; in the same proportion as such a malady is more likely to taint a particular county or district, than an entire State.

In the extent and proper structure of the Union, therefore, we behold a republican remedy for the diseases most incident to republican government. And according to the degree of pleasure and pride we feel in being republicans, ought to be our zeal in cherishing the spirit and supporting the character of Federalists.

# D

[The text is taken from William   Manning, *The Key of Liberty*, (Billerica: The Manning Association, 1922).]

## The Key of Liberty

*To all the Republicans, Farmers, Mecanicks, and Labourers In Amarica your Canded attention is Requested to the Sentiments of a Labourer*

### Introduction

*Learning & Knowledg is assential to the preservation of Libberty & unless we have more of it amongue us we Cannot Seporte our Libertyes Long.*

I am not a Man of Larning my selfe for I neaver had the advantage of six months schooling in my life. I am no travelor for I neaver was 50 Miles from whare I was born in no direction, & I am no grate reader of antiant history for I always followed hard labour for a living. But I always thought it My duty to search into & see for my selfe in all maters that consansed me as a member of society, & when the war began betwen Brittan & Amarica I was in the prime of Life & highly taken up with Liberty & a free Government. I See almost the first blood that was shed in Concord fite & scores of men dead, dying & wounded in the Cause of Libberty, which caused serious sencations in my mind.

But I beleived then & still believ it is a good cause which we aught to defend to the very last, & I have bin a Constant Reader of publick Newspapers & closely attended to men & measures ever sence, through the war, through the operation of paper money, framing Constitutions, makeing & constructing Laws, & seeing what selfish & contracted ideayes of interests would influence the best picked men & bodyes of men.

I have often thought it was imposable ever to seport a free Government, but firmly believing it to be the best sort & the ondly one approved off by heaven it was my unweryed study & prayers to the almighty for many years to find out the real cause & a remidy and I have for many years bin satisfyed in my own mind what the causes are & what would in a grate measure prove a reamidy provided it was carried into efect.

But I had no thoughts of publishing my sentiments on it untill the adoption of the Brittish trety in the manner it has bin done. But seeing the unweryed pains & the unjustifyable masures taken by large numbers of all ordirs of men who git a living without labour in Elections & many other things to ingure the interests of the Labourer & deprive us of the priviledges of a free government, I came to a resolution (although I have nither larning nor lasure for the purpose) to improve on my Constitutional Right & give you my sentiments on what the causes are & a remidy.

In doing which I must study bravity throughout the hole & but just touch on many things on which voloms mite be written, but hope I shall do it so as to be understood, and as I have no room for compliments & shall often make observations on sundry ordirs of men & their conduct, I beg leave once for all to observe that I am far from thinking any ordirs of men who live with out Labour are intirely needless or that they are all chargable with blame. But on the conterary I firmly believe that their is a large number in all ordirs who are true frinds to Libberty & that it is from them that Libberty always has & allways will receive its prinsaple seport. But I also beleive that a large majority of them are actuated by very different prinsaples. Also as I am not furnished with Documents & other Information that would be usefull I may represent Some things different from what they really are & so desire that they may be taken ondly as my Opinnion & belived no further than they appear Evident.

## A General Description of the Causes that Ruen Republicks

*The Causes that I shall Indeavor to Make appear are a Conceived Difference of Interests Betwen those that Labour for a Living & those that git a Living without Bodily Labour.*

This is no new docterin if I may judge from the many scraps of history I have Seen of antiant Republicks. The best information I ever had on this Subject & the gratest colection of historical accounts was by a writer who wrote ten long numbers in the Chronicle in December [17]85 & January 86 stileing himselfe a Free Republican.

In his 4 first numbers he recites a long & blody history about the fudes & animosityes, contentions & blood sheds that hapned in the antiant Republicks of Athens, Greesh & Roome & many other nations, betwen the few & Many, the Perthiens, & Plebians, Rich & poor, Dettor & Creditor, &cc. In his 5th No. he draws the dividing line betwen the few & the many as they apply to us in Amarica — amongue the few he reacons the marchent, phesition the lawyer & divine and all in the literary walkes of Life, the Juditial & Executive oficers & all the rich who could live with out bodily labour, so that the hole controvercy was betwen those that labour for a living & those who do not. Then tryes to prove that unless these few can have wait or influence in the Government according to their property & high stations in life it can not be free. Then goes on to shew how a government aught to be ballenced and proposes grate alterations in the Constitution of Masachusets — better to acomidate the Interests of the few — wishes to have the Senet represent the hole property of the State & the Representitives the persons ondly, & the Govenour to have as compleet a nagative on both as the King of Ingland has on the Parlement, which he thinks cant be so long as the people vote annully for Govenour & Senetors.

These Sentiments being urged in such a masterly manner just before the adoption of the federal Constitution, & have bin so closely followed by the administration eversence, (although they are directly contrary to the prinsaples of a free government & no dout written to destroy it) yet if they ware republished they would be of servis to the peopel in many things & convince the author (if he is yet alive) that his unweried resarches for his ten numbers ware not intirely lost any more than the doings of Josephs Brethering ware when they sold him into Egypt, & they would prove the truth of the reasons I give & the need of the Remidy I shall describe.

I have often Looked over those ten Nos. & Searched other historyes to satisfy my selfe as to the truth of his asertions, but am very far from thinking as he doth — that the destruction of free governments arises from the Licentiousness of the Many or their Representatives, but on the conterary shall indever to prove that their destruction always arises from the ungoverned dispositions & Combinations of the few, & the ignorance of the Many. Which I Shall attempt in the following Manner: — 1. Give a Description of Mankind & nesecaty of Government. 2ly. Give a Description of a free government & its administration. 3ly Shew how the few & Many differ in interests under its opperation. 4ly Shew how & by what meens the few destroy it. 5ly Elustrate by sundry remarkes on the opperations of these causes in our governments.

1. A Description of Mankind & Nesecaty of government

To search into & know our selves is of the gratest importance, & the want of it is the cause of the gratest evils suffered in Society. If we knew what alterations might be made in our Minds & Conduct by alterations in our Edication, age, Circumstances, & Conditions in this Life, we should be vastly less sensorious on others for their conduct, & more cautious of trusting them when their was no need of it.

Men are born & grow up in this world with a vast veriaty of capacityes, strength & abilityes both of Body & Mind, & have strongly implanted within them numerous pashons & lusts continually urging them to fraud violence & acts of injustis toards one another. He has implanted in him a sence of Right & Rong, so that if he would always follow the dictates of Contiance & consider the advantages of Society & mutual assistance he would need no other Law or Government. Yet as he is sentanced by the just decrees of heaven to hard Labour for a Living in this world, & has so strongly implanted in him a desire of Selfe Seporte, Selfe Defence, Selfe Love, Selfe Conceit, Selfe Importance, & Selfe agrandisement, that it Ingroses all his care and attention so that he can see nothing beyond Selfe — for Selfe (as once described by a Divine) is like an object plased before the eye that hinders the sight of every thing beyond.

This Selfishness may be deserned in all persons, let their conditions in life be what they will, & it opperates so pourfully as to disqualify them from judgeing impartially in their own cause, & a persons being raised to stations of high Honour & trust doth not clear him from this selfeishness. But on the conterary it is a solemn truth that the higher a Man is raised in stations of honour power and trust the greater are his temtations to do rong & gratify those selfeish prinsaples. Give a man honour & he wants more. Give him power & he wants more. Give him money & he wants more. In short he is neaver easy, but the more he has the more he wants.

The most comprehensive description of Man I ever saw was by a writer as followeth: — Viz — Man is a being made up of Selfe Love seeking his own hapiness to the misery of all around him, who would Damne a world to save him selfe from temporal or other punishment, & he who denyes this to be his real carrictor is ignorant of him selfe, or else is more than a man.

Many persons ware they to hear such a description of themselves would cry out as Haziel did, 'what, is thy Servent a Dog' &cc. But if they should once git into the circumstances he was in, & have the power & temtations he had, they would prove themselves to be just such a Doge as he did. Haman is annother striking evidence of the depravity & pride of the human hart, for though he could boste of the highest preferments in the gratest kindgom on Earth, the poor Divel exclamed 'all this avails me nothing so long as Mordica refuses to bow the knee.'

From this disposition of Man or the depravity of the human hart, arises not ondly the advantage but the absolute nesecaty of Sivil government — without it Mankind would be continually at war on their own spetia, stealing roving fighting with & killing one another. This all Nations on Earth have bin convinced off, and have established it in some form or other, & their soul aime in doing it is their safty & hapyness. But for want of wisdom or some plan to curb the ambition & govern those to hoom they gave power, they have often bin brought to suffer as Much under their governments as they would without any — and it still remains uncartain wheather any such plan can be found out or not.

2dly. A Description of a free Government & its administration.

Their are many sorts of governments, or rather names by which they are distinguished, Such as Dispotick, Monorcal, & Aristrocraticle. In these the power to govern is in the hands of one or a few to govern as they pleas, consiquently they are masters & not servents so, that the government is not free.

Their are also sundry names by which free governments are described, such as Democratical, Republican, Elective, all which I take to be senominus tarmes, or that all those nations who ever adopted them aimed at nearly the same thing, viz. to be governed by known Laws in which the hole nation had a Voice in making, by a full and fair Representation, & in which all the officers in every department of Government are (or aught to be) servents & not masters. Grate panes has bin taken & the wisdom of many Nations & States have bin put to the racke, to delineate the rights of the peopel & powers of government & forme Constitutions so that the blesings of government might be injoyed without being oppresed by them, and it is thought that it has bin much improved upon sence the Amarican Revolution.

The Constitution of Masachusets, although it doth not meterially differ from all the other Constitutions on the Continant, yet as it was later made & the Convention who formed it had the advantage of the others, took more time & fixed a Bill of Rights to it, it is generally thought both in Urope & Amarica to be the compleatest modle of a free government of any existing. France has immitated it in her Constitution & the Federal Constitution by a fair construction doth not meterially differ from it. Therefore I shall describe a free government prinsaply from it.

In the Bill of Rights it declares all men to be free & equel as to their rights in & under the government, as in Art. 1, & that all power lays in the peopel & all the officers of government are their servents & accountable to them, as in Art. 5. No man, Corporation, or Body of Men however high by birth riches or honour have no right by them any more than the poorest man in the government, as in Art. 6 & 7th. The people have the Sole right to reforme, alter & totally change their Constitution or Administration of government when they pleas, as In Art. 7th, And have a right to meet and deliberate on all matters of government at such times & in such places & bodyes as they pleas, provided they do it in a peasable Manner, as In Art. 19th. The people have a right to know & convey to each other their sentiments & circumstances through the medium of the press, as in Art. 16th.

A free Government is a government of laws made by the free consent of a majority of the hole people, But as it is Impossable for a hole Nation to meet to gether & deliberate, So all their laws Must be made judged & executed by men chosen & appointed for that purpose. And the Duty of all those men are to act & do in makeing judging & executing those laws just as all the people would, provided they ware all together & equilly knew what was for their interest. If any of said officers or any who are chosen to elect or appoint any person into office doth any thing conterary to the true interests of the majority of the peopel, he violates his trust and aught to be punnished for it.

In makeing laws in a free Government their cannot be two much pains or caution used to have them plain to be understood & not two numerous to this end. And as all bodyes of men are liable to the same rashness & mistakes as individuals are, it is nesecary that the Lejeslature Should be divided into two Branches, a Senet & house of Representitives (not that they have seperate interests or objects to act from as some pretend), but that they may gard against each others rashness & mistakes & to see that the laws are made plane & not too numerous. And as a further gard against unnesesary laws the Executive may have a partial negative on the pasing of laws, & in dificult cases the opinnion of the Judges may be called in (not that the Juditial or Executive powers aught to have a Voice in saying wheather a law is nesecary or not), but wheather it can be carryed in to execution or not. For their is nothing more assential in a free Government than to keep the Legeslative, Juditial & Executive powers intirely seperate, as in Art. 30, not only seperate Departments but intirely different sets of men (for reasons which I shall hereafter give).

The Bisness & Duty of the Juditial power is to hear & exammine all complaints & breaches of the law & pass sentance (not on the law wheather it is good or not) but wheather it is broken or not & in every respect according to law.

The Bisness & Duty of the Executive power is to execute all the laws according to the ordirs & precepts he receivs from the other Powers without any referrance to their being right or rong in his opinnion for that would be lejeslateing & judgeing two.

The soul end of Government is the protection of Life, Liberty & property. The poor mans shilling aught to be as much the care of government as the rich mans pound. Every person in the Nation aught to be compeled to do justis & have it dun to him promptly & without delay. All taxes for the seport of government aught to be layed equilly according to the property each person purseses & the advantages he receives from it, and the peopel aught to seport just so many persons in office as is absolutely nesecary and no more, & pay them just so much saleryes as will command sefitiant abilityes, & no more.

Also in free Government the most sacred regard must be paid to the Constitutions established by the peopel to gard their Rights. No law aught or can be made or constructed conterary to the true meening thereof without becomeing a nullity & those becomeing gilty who does it, let them be either Lejeslative Juditial or Executive officers or bodyes of men. And no parte of the Constitution can be constructed conterary to the declared Rights of the people.

In short a free Government is one In which all the laws are made judged & executed according to the will & interest of a majority of the hole peopel and not by the craft cunning & arts of the few. To seport such a government it is absolutely nesecary to have a larger degree or better meens of knowledge amongue the peopel than we now have, which I shall indevor to make appear before I close.

3dly. Shews how the Few & Many Differ in their Interests in its operation.

In the swet of thy face shall thou git thy bread untill thou return to the ground, is the erivarsable sentance of Heaven on Man for his rebellion. To be sentanced to hard Labour dureing life is very unplesent to humane Nature. Their is a grate avartion to it purceivable in all men — yet it is absolutly nesecary that a large majority of the world should labour, or we could not subsist. For Labour is the soul parrant of all property — the land yealdeth nothing without it, & their is no food, clothing, shelter, vessel, or any nesecary of life but what costs Labour & is generally esteemed valuable according to the Labour it costs. Therefore no person can posess property without labouring, unless he git it by force or craft, fraud or fortun out of the earnings of others.

But from the grate veriety of capacietyes strength & abilityes of men, their always was, & always will be, a very unequel distribution of property in the world. Many are so rich that they can live without Labour. Also the marchent, phisition, lawyer & divine, the philosipher and school master, the Juditial & Executive Officers, & many others who could honestly git a living without bodily labours. As all these professions require a considerable expence of time & property to qualify themselves therefor, & as no person after this qualifying himselfe & making a pick on a profession by which he meens to live, can desire to have it dishonourable or unproductive, so all these professions naturally unite in their skems to make their callings as honourable & lucrative as possable. Also as ease & rest from Labour are reaconed amongue the gratest pleasurs of Life, pursued by all with the greatest avidity & when attained at once creates a sense of superiority & as pride & ostentation are natural to the humain harte, these ordirs of men generally asotiate together and look down with two much contempt on those that labour.

On the other hand the Labourer being contious that it is Labour that seports the hole, & that the more there is that live without Labour & the higher they live or the grater their salleryes and fees are, so much the harder he must work, or the shorter he must live, this makes the Labourer watch the other with a jelous eye & often has reason to complain of real impositions. But before I proceed to shew how the few & many differ in money matters I will give a short description of what Money is.

Money is not property of itself but ondly the Representitive of property. Silver & Gold is not so valuable as Iron & Steel for real use, but receives all its value from the use that is made of it as a medium of trade. Money is simply this — a thing of lighter carrage than property that has an established value set upon it eyther by law or general Consent, For Instance, if a doller or a peace of paper, or a chip, would pass throughout a nation or the world for a burshel of corne or any other property to the value of said corne, then it would be the representitive of so much property.

Also Money is a thing that will go where it will fetch the most as naturally as water runs down hill, for the posessor will give it whare it will fetch the most. Also when their is an addition to the quantity or an extrodinary use of barter & credit in commerce the prices of property will rise. On the other hand if Credit is ruened & the medium made scarser the price of all kinds of property will fall in proportion. Here lays the grate shuffel between the few & many. As the interests & incomes of the few lays cheifly in money at interest, rents, salaryes, & fees that are fixed on the nominal value of money, they are interested in haveing mony scarse & the price of labour & produce as low as possable. For instance if the prices of labour & produce should fall one halfe if would be just the same to the few as if their rents fees & salleryes ware doubled, all which they would git out of the many. Besides the fall of Labour and produce & scarsety of money always brings the many Into destress & compels them into a state of dependance on the few for favours & assistance in a thousand ways.

On the other hand, if the many could rais the price of Labour, &c one halfe & have the mony circulate freely they could pay their debts, eat & drink & injoy the good of their labour with out being dependant on the few for assistance. Also high prices opperates as a bounty on industry & economy — an industrious & prudent man may presently lay up something against time of need when prices are high but if a person leaves off worke & lives high when prices are up his mony or property will last him but little while.

But the gratest dainger the Many are under in these money matters are from the Juditial & Executive Officers, espatssilly so as their incomes for a living are almost holly gotten from the follys and destresse of the Many, & they being governed by the same selfish prinsaples as other men are. They are the Most interested in the destreses of the many of any in the Nation. the scarser money is & the grater the destreses of the many are, the better for them. It not ondly doubles the nominal sume of their pay, but it doubles & thribbles their bisness, & the many are obliged to come to them cap in hand & beg for mercy patience & forbearance.

This gratifyes both their pride & covetousness, when on the other hand when money is plenty & prices high they have little or nothing to do. This is the Reason why they aught to be kept intirely from the Legislative Body & unless their can be wisdom anough in the Peopel to keep the three Departments of Government intirely seperate a free Government cant be seported. For in all these conceived differenc of interests, It is the bisness and duty of the Lejeslative Body to determine what is Justis or what is Right & Rong, & the duty of every individual in the nation to regulate his conduct according to their detisions. And if the Many ware always fully & fairly represented in the Legeslative Body they neaver would be oppresed or find fault so as to trouble the Government, but would always be zelous to seport it.

The Reasons why a free government has always failed is from the unreasonable demands & desires of the few. They cant bare to be on a leavel with their fellow cretures, or submit to the determinations of a Lejeslature whare (as they call it) the Swinish Multitude are fairly represented, but sicken at the eydea, & are ever hankering & striving after Monerca or Aristocracy whare the people have nothing to do in maters of government but to seport the few in luxery & idleness.

For these & many other reasons a large majority of those that live without Labour are ever opposed to the prinsaples & operation of a free Government, & though the hole of them do not amount to one eighth part of the people, yet by their combinations, arts & skeems have always made out to destroy it soner or later, which I shall indeavor to prove . . .

# 16

From the period of the Revolution on, there was among radical Christian political and social theorists an increasing tendency to separate themselves from institutional Christianity, in short from the established churches. Thomas Paine, the author of *Common Sense,* was in Paris observing the events of the French Revolution when he wrote his profession of religious faith. In Benjamin Franklin's and Thomas Jefferson's statements of their own religious convictions there are numerous similarities to Paine's credo.

[The text is taken from Thomas Paine, *Age of Reason: Being an Investigation of a True and Fabulous Theology,* (Boston: Thomas Hale, 1794).]

## Age of Reason

[*Credo*] It has been my intention for several years past to publish my thoughts upon Religion. I am well aware of the difficulties that attend the subject; and from that consideration had reserved it to a more advanced period of life. I intended it to be the last offering I should make to my fellow-citizens of all nations, and that at a time when the purity of the motive that induced me to it could not admit of a question, even by those who might disapprove the work.

The circumstance that has now taken place in France, of the total abolition of the whole national order of priesthood and of everything appertaining to compulsive systems of religion and compulsive articles of faith, has not only precipitated my intention, but rendered a work of this kind exceedingly necessary; lest, in the general wreck of superstition, of false systems of government, and false theology, we lose sight of morality, of humanity, and of the theology that is true.

As several of my colleagues, and others of my fellow-citizens of France, have given me the example of making their voluntary and individual profession of faith, I also will make mine; and I do this with all that sincerity and frankness with which the mind of man communicates with itself.

I believe in one God, and no more; and I hope for happiness beyond this life.

I believe in the equality of man, and I believe that religious duties consist in doing justice, loving mercy, and endeavoring to make our fellow-creatures happy.

But lest it should be supposed that I believe many other things in addition to these, I shall, in the progress of this work, declare the things I do not believe and my reasons for not believing them.

I do not believe in the creed professed by the Jewish church, by the Roman church, by the Greek church, by the Turkish church, by the Protestant church, nor by any church that I know of. My own mind is my own church.

All national institutions of church — whether Jewish, Christian, or Turkish — appear to me no other than human inventions set up to terrify and enslave mankind and monopolize power and profit.

I do not mean by this declaration to condemn those who believe otherwise. They have the same right to their belief as I have to mine. But it is necessary to the happiness of man that he be mentally faithful to himself. Infidelity does not consist in believing or in disbelieving; it consists in professing to believe what he does not believe.

It is impossible to calculate the moral mischief, if I may so express it, that mental lying has produced in society. When a man has so far corrupted and prostituted the chastity of his mind as to subscribe his professional belief to things he does not believe, he has prepared himself for the commission of every other crime. He takes up the trade of priest for the sake of gain, and in order to *qualify* himself for that trade, he begins with a perjury. Can we conceive anything more destructive to mortality than this?

Soon after I had published the pamphlet, *Common Sense,* in America, I saw the exceeding probability that a revolution in the system of government would be followed by a revolution in the system of religion. The adulterous connection of church and state, wherever it had taken place, whether Jewish, Christian, or Turkish, had so effectually prohibited, by pains and penalties, every discussion upon established creeds and upon first principles of religion, that until the system of government should be changed those subjects could not be brought fairly and openly before the world; but that whenever this should be done, a revolution in the system of religion would follow. Human inventions and priestcraft would be detected, and man would return to the pure, unmixed, and unadulterated belief of one God, and no more. . . .

[Chapter XI. Of the Theology of the Christians; and the True Theology]. As to the Christian system of faith, it appears to me as a species of atheism; a sort of religious denial of God. It professes to believe in a man rather than in God. It is a compound made up chiefly of manism, with but little deism, and is as near to atheism as twilight is to darkness. It introduces between man and his Maker an opaque body, which it calls a Redeemer, as the moon introduces her opaque self between the earth and the sun; and it produces by this means a religious or an irreligious eclipse of light. It has put the whole orb of reason into shade.

The effect of this obscurity has been that of turning everything upside down and representing it in reverse; and among the revolutions it has thus magically produced, it has made a revolution in theology.

That which is now called natural philosophy, embracing the whole circle of science of which astronomy occupies the chief place, is the study of the works of God, and of the power and wisdom of God and his works, and is the true theology.

As to the theology that is now studied in its place, it is the study of human opinions and of human fancies *concerning* God. It is not the study of God himself in the works that he has made, but in the works or writings that man has made; and it is not among the least of the mischiefs that the Christian system has done to the world that it has abandoned the original and beautiful system of theology, like a beautiful innocent, to distress and reproach, to make room for the hag of superstition.

The book of Job and the 19th Psalm, which even the church admits to be more ancient than the chronological order in which they stand in the book called the Bible, are theological orations conformable to the original system of theology. The internal evidence of those orations proves to a demonstration that the study and contemplation of the works of creation, and of the power and wisdom of God revealed and manifested in those works, make a great part of the religious devotion of the times in which they were written; and it was this devotional study and contemplation that led to the discovery of the principles upon which what are now called sciences are established; and it is to the discovery of these principles that almost all the arts that contribute to the convenience of human life owe their existence. Every principal art has some science for its parent, though the person who mechanically performs the work does not always, and but very seldom, perceive the connection.

It is a fraud of the Christian system to call the sciences *human inventions;* it is only the application of them that is human. Every science has for its basis a system of principles as fixed and unalterable as those by which the universe is regulated and governed. Man cannot make principles; he can only discover them.

For example. Every person who looks at an almanac sees an account when an eclipse will take place, and he sees also that it never fails to take place according to the account there given. This shows that man is acquainted with the laws by which the heavenly bodies move. But it would be something worse than ignorance were any church on earth to say that those laws are a human invention.

It would also be ignorance or something worse to say that the scientific principles, by the aid of which man is enabled to calculate and foreknow when an eclipse will take place, are a human invention. Man cannot invent anything that is eternal and immutable, and the scientific principles he employs for this purpose must be, and are, of necessity, as eternal and immutable as the laws by which the heavenly bodies move, or they could not be used as they are to ascertain the time when, and the manner how, an eclipse will take place. . . .

It is from the study of the true theology that all our knowledge of science is derived, and it is from that knowledge that all the arts have originated.

The Almighty lecturer, by displaying the principles of science in the structure of the universe, has invited man to study and to imitation. It is as if he had said to the inhabitants of this globe that we call ours: "I rendered the starry heavens visible, to teach him science and the arts. He can now provide for his own comfort, AND LEARN FROM MY MUNIFICENCE TO BE KIND TO EACH OTHER." . . .

[*Recapitulation*]. Having now extended the subject to a greater length than I first intended, I shall bring it to a close by abstracting a summary from the whole.

First — That the idea or belief of a word of God existing in print, or in writing, or in speech, is inconsistent in itself for the reasons already assigned. These reasons, among others, are the want of a universal language; the mutability of language; the errors to which translations are subject; the possibility of totally suppressing such a word; the probability of altering it, or of fabricating the whole, and imposing it upon the world.

Secondly — That the creation we behold is the real and ever-existing word of God in which we cannot be deceived. It proclaimeth his power, it demonstrates his wisdom, it manifests his goodness and beneficence.

Thirdly — That the moral duty of man consists in imitating the moral goodness and beneficence of God manifested in the creation towards all his creatures. That seeing, as we daily do, the goodness of God to all men, it is an example calling upon all men to practice the same towards each other; and consequently that everything of persecution and revenge between man and man, and everything of cruelty to animals is a violation of moral duty.

I trouble not myself about the manner of future existence. I content myself with believing, even to positive conviction, that the power that gave me existence is able to continue it in any form and manner he pleases, either with or without this body; and it appears more probable to me that I shall continue to exist hereafter than that I should have had existence, as I now have, before that existence began.

It is certain that in one point all nations of the earth and all religions agree. All believe in a God. The things in which they disagree are the redundancies annexed to that belief; and, therefore, if ever a universal religion should prevail, it will not be believing anything new, but in getting rid of redundancies and believing as man believed at first. Adam, if ever there was such a man, was created a Deist; but in the meantime let every man follow, as he has a right to do, the religion and the worship he prefers. . . .

# 17

The Reverend Samuel Thacher, an otherwise obscure Congregational minister, deserves our gratitude for producing one of the most eloquent paeans to the American Revolution ever penned. The English critic, Wyndham Lewis, has written of the "radical universalism" of the Revolution. Thatcher's sermon is perhaps the best expression of that "radical universalism" with its appeal to "the consequent emancipation of the world."

[The text is taken from Rev. Samuel Thacher, *An Oration . . . July 4, 1796,* (Boston: Hall, 1796).]

## 1796 Sermon

Liberty has been hunted about the earth with implacable malice; and like the dove from the ark has found no rest for the sole of her foot. Chased from one quarter of the globe to another, the heavenly goddess was ready to abandon her charge, when the enterprise of Columbus surmounted every difficulty, discovered the western world, and furnished her a more secure, a more inviting retreat.

Liberty is a pure, original emanation from the great source of life which animates the universe. Yet, so long have mankind been insulted with the idea that it is the exclusive property of a few, so long have they gazed in stupid admiration at the splendor of domination, which has shone but to scorch them, so long have force and artifice on one hand and fear and ignorance on the other, combined with the power of the all-conquering habit, that this eternal principle was almost erased from the human mind; when *America*, indignant at oppression, rose and proclaimed it with a voice which broke the spell of the confining nations, roused them from the lethargy of ages, and struck like thunder upon the ears of despots.

Interested, profligate minions of power, the worst of whom were our own treacherous governors, had the utmost success in representing us as a rebellious mob of insurgents. Petitions, the constitutional mode of seeking redress, were sometimes refused and always treated with neglect. Arbitrary institutions, unknown to the laws, were in many cases substituted for trial by jury, the great security of life, liberty and property.

In defiance of the tyranny which has so long bestrode creation, notwithstanding the debased condition to which servitude has reduced so great a part of the species — the sacred truth, the basis of American constitutions that "all men are born free and equal," is deeply engraven and dearly cherished in the hearts of those who have never bowed the knee to slavery.

The old governments of earth derive right and power from the grant of kings. These grants are founded upon usurpation, and supported by a well known principle in English law — that "kings can do no wrong," therefore are not responsible. The American constitutions acknowledge no authority superior to the laws. They rest upon very different principles that right is derived from heaven; the exercise of power from the people and law from the will of a majority. In the picture of Europe we behold a few hereditary robbers, in the most conspicuous point of light, engrossing the honor and profit of governing. In the remotest background, we can just discern the people, crouching under the weight of oppression, dependent on the nobles even for subsistence.

In *America*, government is maintained for the good of the whole, by men who scorn to derive support from any source but their own exertions. Equality inspires a spirit of independence. In Europe, the very light of heaven is taxed, the vitals of society are consumed to support the placemen, pensioners and superfluous officers, whose interest it is to darken and brutalize mankind. In America, taxes are scarce felt, and cheerfully bestowed, because devoted with strictest economy, to support a government which protects the liberties and enlightens the minds of the people.

With confidence we predict that the mad struggles of despotism will exhaust its strength. All hail! Approaching Revolutions!

*Americans, we have lived ages in a day.* Pyramids of lawless power, the work of centuries, have fallen in a moment!

The advantages of the American Revolution cannot be compressed within the compass of a few pages. Its effects are not confined to one age or country. The human mind has received a stimulus, and attained an expansion which will extend its influence beyond calculation.

Assembled, not like other nations, to celebrate feats of successful carnage, or the senseless ceremonials of superstition, but excited by the animating energy of gratitude, we commemorate the struggles of freemen, the consequent emancipation of a world.

# 18

Angelina Grimke, a Southern woman who married the New England reformer, Theodore Weld, was one of the most eloquent enemies of slavery. In 1838, she gave the following speech in Pennsylvania Hall, basing her opposition to slavery on Christian principles.

[The text is taken from Angelina Grimke, *May 16, 1838 Speech*, (n.p., n.d.).]

## May 16, 1838 Speech

Men, brethren and fathers — mothers, daughters and sisters, what came ye out for to see? A reed shaken with the wind? Is it curiosity merely, or a deep sympathy with the perishing slave, that has brought this large audience together? [A yell from the mob without the buiding.] Those voices without ought to awaken and call out our warmest sympathies. Deluded beings! "they know not what they do." They know not that they are undermining their own rights and their own happiness, temporal and eternal. Do you ask, "what has the North to do with slavery?" Hear it — hear it. Those voices without tell us that the spirit of slavery is *here*, and has been roused to wrath by our abolition speeches and conventions: for surely liberty would not foam and tear herself with rage, because her friends are multiplied daily, and meetings are held in quick succession to set forth her virtues and extend her peaceful kingdom. This opposition shows that slavery has done its deadliest work in the hearts of our citizens. Do you ask, then, "what has the North to do?" I answer, cast out first the spirit of slavery from your own hearts, and then lend your aid to convert the South. Each one present has a work to do, be his or her situation what it may, however limited their means, or insignificant their supposed influence. The great men of this country will not do this work; the church will never do it. A desire to please the world, to keep the favor of all parties and of all conditions, makes them dumb on this and every other unpopular subject. They have become worldly-wise, and therefore God, in his wisdom, employs them not to carry on his plans of reformation and salvation. He hath chosen the foolish things of the world to confound the wise, and the weak to overcome the mighty.

As a Southerner I feel that it is my duty to stand up here tonight and bear testimony against slavery. I have seen it — I have seen it. I know it has horrors that can never be described. I was brought up under its wing: I witnessed for many years its demoralizing influences, and its destructiveness to human happiness. It is admitted by some that the slave is not happy under the *worst* forms of slavery. But I have *never* seen a happy slave. I have seen him dance in his chains, it is true; but he was not happy. There is a wide difference between happiness and mirth. Man cannot enjoy the former while his manhood is destroyed, and that part of the being which is necessary to the making, and to the enjoyment of happiness, is completely blotted out. The slaves, however, may be, and sometimes are, mirthful. When hope is extinguished, they say, "let us eat and drink, for to-morrow we die." [Just then stones were thrown at the windows, — a great noise without, and commotion within] What is a mob? What would the breaking of every window be? What would the levelling of this Hall be? Any evidence that we are wrong, or that slavery is a good and wholesome institution? What if the mob should now burst in upon us, break up our meeting and commit violence upon our persons — would this be anything compared with what the slaves endure? No, no: and we do not remember them "as bound with them," if we shrink in the time of peril, or feel unwilling to sacrifice ourselves, if need be, for their sake. [Great Noise.] I thank the Lord that there is yet left life enough to feel the truth, even though it rages at it — that conscience is not so completely seared as to be unmoved by the truth of the living God.

Many persons go to the South for a season, and are hospitably entertained in the parlor and at the table of the slaveholder. They never enter the huts of the slaves; they know nothing of the dark side of the picture, and they return home with praises on their lips of the generous character of those with whom they had tarried. Or if they have witnessed the cruelties of slavery, by remaining silent spectators they have naturally become callous — an insensibility has ensued which prepares them to apologize even for barbarity. Nothing but the corrupting influence of slavery on the hearts of the Northern people can induce them to apologize for it; and much will have been done for the destruction of Southern slavery when we have so reformed the North that no one here will be willing to risk his reputation by advocating or even excusing the holding of men as property. The South know it, and acknowledge that as fast as our principles prevail, the hold of the master must be relaxed. [Another outbreak of mobocratic spirit, and some confusion in the house.]

How wonderfully constituted is the human mind! How it resists, as long as it can, all efforts made to reclaim from error! I feel that all this disturbance is but an evidence that our efforts are the best that could have been adopted, or else the friends of slavery, would not care for what we say and do. The South know what we do. I am thankful that they are reached by our efforts. Many times have I wept in the land of my birth over the system of slavery. I knew of none who sympathized in my feelings — I was unaware that any efforts were made to deliver the oppressed — no voice in the wilderness was heard calling on the people to repent and do works meet for repentance — and my heart sickened within me. Oh, how should I have rejoiced to know that such efforts as these were being made. I only wonder that I had such feelings. I wonder when I reflect under what influence I was brought up, that my heart is not harder than the nether millstone. But in the midst of temptation I was preserved, and my sympathy grew warmer, and my hatred of slavery more inveterate, until at last I have exiled myself from my native land because I could no longer endure to hear the wailing of the slave. I fled to the land of Penn; for here, thought I, sympathy for the slave will surely be found. But I found it not. The people were kind and hospitable, but the slave had no place in their thoughts. Whenever questions were put to me as to his condition, I felt that they were dictated by an idle curiosity, rather than by that deep feeling which would lead to effort for his rescue. I therefore shut up my grief in my own heart. I remembered that I was a Carolinian, from a state which framed his iniquity by law. I knew that throughout her territory was continued suffering, on the one part, and continual brutality and sin on the other. Every Southern breeze wafted to me the discordant tones of weeping and wailing, shrieks and groans, mingled with prayers and blasphemous curses. I thought there was no hope; that the wicked would go on in his wickedness, until he had destroyed both himself and his country. My heart sunk within me at the abominations in the midst of which I had been born and educated. What will it avail, cried I in bitterness of spirit, to expose to the gaze of strangers the horrors and pollutions of slavery, when there is no ear to hear nor heart to feel and pray for the slave. The language of my soul was, "Oh tell it not in Gath, publish it not in the streets of Askelon." But how different do I feel now! Animated with hope, nay, with an assurance of the triumph of liberty and good will to man, I will lift up my voice like a trumpet, and show this people their transgression, their sins of omission towards the slave, and what they can do towards affecting Southern mind, and overthrowing Southern oppression.

We may talk of occupying neutral ground, but on this subject, in its present attitude, there is no such thing as neutral ground. He that is not for us is against us, and he that gathereth not with us, scattereth abroad. If you are on what you suppose to be neutral ground, the South look upon you as on the side of the oppressor. And is there one who loves his country willing to give his influence, even indirectly, in favor of slavery — that curse of nations? God swept Egypt with the besom of destruction, and punished Judea also with a sore punishment, because of slavery. And have we any reason to believe that he is less just now? — or that he will be more favorable to us than to his own "peculiar people?" [Shoutings, stones thrown against the windows, &c.]

There is nothing to be feared from those who would stop our mouths, but they themselves should fear and tremble. The current is even now setting fast against them. If the arm of the North had not caused the Bastille of slavery to totter to its foundation, you would not hear those cries. A few years ago, and the South felt secure, and with a contemptuous sneer asked, "Who are the abolitionists? The abolitionists are nothing?" — Ay, in one sense they were nothing, and they are nothing still. But in this we rejoice, that "God has chosen things that are not to bring to nought things that are." [Mob again disturbed the meeting.]

We often hear the question asked, "What shall we do?" Here is an opportunity for doing something now. Every man and every woman present may do something by showing that we fear not a mob, and, in the midst of threatenings and revilings, by opening our mouths for the dumb and pleading the cause of those who are ready to perish.

To work as we should in this cause, we must know what Slavery is. Let me urge you then to buy the books which have been written on this subject and read them, and then lend them to your neighbors. Give your money no longer for things which pander to pride and lust, but aid in scattering "the living coals of truth" upon the naked heart of this nation, — in circulating appeals to the sympathies of Christians in behalf of the outraged and suffering slave. But, it is said by some, our "books and papers do not speak the truth." Why, then, do they not contradict what we say? They cannot. Moreover the South has entreated, nay commanded us to be silent; and what greater evidence of the truth of our publications could be desired?

Women of Philadelphia! allow me as a Southern woman, with much attachment to the land of my birth, to entreat you to come up to this work. Especially let me urge you to petition. *Men* may settle this and other questions at the ballot-box, but you have no such right; it is only through petitions that you can reach the Legislature. It is therefore peculiarly *your* duty to petition. Do you say, "It does no good?" The South already turns pale at the number sent. They have read the reports of the proceedings of Congress, and there have seen that among other petitions were very many from the women of the North on the subject of slavery. This fact has called the attention of the South to the subject. How could we expect to have done more as yet? Men who hold the rod over slaves, rule in the councils of the nation: and they deny our right to petition and to remonstrate against abuses of our sex and of our kind. We have these rights, however, from our God. Only let us exercise them: and though often turned away unanswered, let us remember the influence of importunity upon the unjust judge, and act accordingly. The fact that the South look with jealousy upon our measures shows that they are effectual. There is, therefore, no cause for doubting or despair, but rather for rejoicing.

It was remarked in England that women did much to apolish Slavery in her colonies. Nor are they now idle. Numerous petitions from them have recently been presented to the Queen, to abolish the apprenticeship with its cruelties nearly equal to those of the system whose place it supplies. One petition two miles and a quarter long has been presented. And do you think these labors will be in vain? Let the history of the past answer. When the women of these States send up to Congress such a petition, our legislators will arise as did those of England, and say, "When all the maids and matrons of the land are knocking at our doors we must legislate." Let the zeal and love, the faith and works of our English sisters quicken ours — that while the slaves continue to suffer, and when they shout deliverance, we may feel the satisfaction of *having done what we could.*

# 19

---

Henry David Thoreau revived the Revolutionary arguments of the necessity to resist unjust laws in his opposition to the Fugitive Slave Law. Like Nathan Fiske or Jonathan Mayhew before him, he refused to obey a law "which is merely contrary to the law of God."

[The text is taken from Henry David Thoreau, *The Law of God and the Law of the Land: Slavery in Massachusetts*, (Framingham: 1854).]

## The Law of God and the Law of the Land, Slavery in Massachusetts

I would remind my countrymen that they are to be men first, and Americans only at a late and convenient hour. No matter how valuable law may be to protect your property, even to keep soul and body together, if it do not keep you and humanity together.

I am sorry to say that I doubt if there is a judge in Massachusetts who is prepared to resign his office, and get his living innocently, whenever it is required of him to pass sentence under a law which is merely contrary to the law of God. I am compelled to see that they put themselves, or rather are by character, in this respect, exactly on a level with the marine who discharges his musket in any direction he is ordered to. They are just as much tools, and as little men. Certainly, they are not the more to be respected, because their master enslaves their understandings and consciences, instead of their bodies.

The judges and lawyers, — simply as such, I mean, — and all men of expediency, try this case by a very low and incompetent standard. They consider, not whether the Fugitive Slave Law is right, but whether it is what they call *constitutional*. Is virtue constitutional, or vice? Is equity constitutional, or iniquity? In important moral and vital questions, like this, it is just as impertinent to ask whether a law is constitutional or not, as to ask whether it is profitable or not. They persist in being the servants of the worst of men, and not the servants of humanity. The question is, not whether you or your grandfather, seventy years ago, did not enter into an agreement to serve the Devil, and that service is not accordingly now due; but whether you will not now, for once and at last, serve God, — inspite of your own past recreancy, or that of your ancestor, — by obeying that eternal and only just CONSTITUTION, which He, and not any Jefferson or Adams, has written in your being.

The amount of it is, if the majority vote the Devil to be God, the minority will live and behave accordingly, — and obey the successful candidate, trusting that, some time or other, by some Speaker's casting-vote, perhaps, they may reinstate God. This is the highest principle I can get out or invent for my neighbors. These men act as if they believed that they could safely slide down a hill a little way, — or a good way, — and would surely come to a place, by and by, where they could begin to slide up again. This is expediency, or choosing that course which offers the slightest obstacles to the feet, that is, a downhill one. But there is no such thing as accomplishing a righteous reform by the use of "expediency." There is no such thing as sliding up hill. In morals the only sliders are backsliders . . .

Will mankind never learn that policy is not morality, — that it never secures any moral right, but considers merely what is expedient? chooses the available candidate, — who is invariably the Devil, — and what right have his constituents to be surprised, because the Devil does not behave like an angel of light? What is wanted is men, not of policy, but of probity, — who recognize a higher law than the Constitution, or the decision of the majority. The fate of the country does not depend on how you vote at the polls, — the worst man is as strong as the best at that game; it does not depend on what kind of paper you drop into the ballot-box once a year, but on what kind of man you drop from your chamber into the street every morning.

What should concern Massachusetts is not the Nebraska Bill, nor the Fugitive Slave Bill, but her own slaveholding and servility. Let the State dissolve her union with the slaveholder. She may wriggle and hesitate, and ask leave to read the Constitution once more; but she can find no respectable law or precedent which sanctions the continuance of such a union for an instant.

Let each inhabitant of the State dissolve his union with her, as long as she delays to do her duty.

The events of the past month teach me to distrust Fame. I see that she does not finely discriminate, but coarsely hurrahs. She considers not the simple heroism of an action, but only as it is connected with its apparent consequences. She praises till she is hoarse the easy exploit of the Boston tea party, but will be comparatively silent about the braver and more disinterestedly heroic attack on the Boston Court-House, simply because it was unsuccessful!

Covered with disgrace, the State has sat down coolly to try for their lives and liberties the men who attempted to do its duty for it. And this is called *justice!* They who have shown that they can behave particularly well may perchance be put under bonds for *their good behavior.* They whom truth requires at present to plead guilty are, of all the inhabitants of the State, preeminently innocent. While the Governor, and the Mayor, and countless officers of the Commonwealth are at large, the champions of liberty are imprisoned.

Only they are guiltless who commit the crime of contempt of such a court. It behooves every man to see that his influence is on the side of justice, and let the courts make their own characters. My sympathies in this case are wholly with the accused, and wholly against their accusers and judges. Justice is sweet and musical; but injustice is harsh and discordant. The judge still sits grinding at his organ, but it yields no music, and we hear only the sound of the handle. He believes that all the music resides in the handle, and the crowd toss him their coppers the same as before.

Do you suppose that that Massachusetts which is now doing these things, — which hesitates to crown these men, some of whose lawyers, and even judges, perchance, may be driven to take refuge in some poor quibble, that they may not wholly outrage their instinctive sense of justice, — do you suppose that she is anything but base and servile? that she is the champion of liberty?

Show me a free state, and a court truly of justice, and I will fight for them, if need be; but show me Massachusetts, and I refuse her my allegiance, and express contempt for her courts.

The effect of a good government is to make life more valuable, — of a bad one, to make it less valuable. We can afford that railroad and all merely material stock should lose some of its value, for that only compels us to live more simply and economically; but suppose that the value of life itself should be diminished! How can we make a less demand on man and nature, how live more economically in respect to virtue and all noble qualities, than we do? I have lived for the last month — and I think that every man in Massachusetts capable of the sentiment of patriotism must have had a similar experience — with the sense of having suffered a vast and indefinite loss. I did not know at first what ailed me. At last it occurred to me that what I had lost was a country. I had never respected the government near to which I lived, but I had foolishly thought that I might manage to live here, minding my private affairs, and forget it. For my part, my old and worthiest pursuits have lost I cannot say how much of their attraction, and I feel that my investment in life here is worth many per cent. less since Massachusetts last deliberately sent back an innocent man, Anthony Burns, to slavery . . .

I feel that, to some extent, the State has fatally interfered with my lawful business. It has not only interrupted me in my passage through Court Street on errands of trade, but it has interrupted me and every man on his onward and upward path, on which he had trusted soon to leave Court Street far behind. What right had it to remind me of Court Street? I have found that hollow which even I had relied on for solid . . .

I walk toward one of our ponds; but what signifies the beauty of nature when men are base? We walk to lakes to see our serenity reflected in them; when we are not serene, we go not to them. Who can be serene in a country where both the rulers and the ruled are without principle? The remembrance of my country spoils my walk. My thoughts are murder to the State, and involuntarily go plotting against her.

# 20

---

Excerpts from Leonard Brown's *Iowa, Land of the Prophets* are included here because they serve as a reminder that that radical rural movement called Populism which surfaced at the end of the nineteenth century was primarily a Christian crusade against the money-changers of Wall Street who were desecrating God's Temple — America.

[The text is taken from Leonard Brown, *Iowa the Promised of the Prophets and Other Patriotic Poems*, (Des Moines: Central Printing Co., 1884).]

## The Promised of the Prophets

The few grow rich the many poor
The tramps are dogged from door to door
The millionaire would have his word
And e'en his very whisper heard
And Congress bow before his nob
And Presidents cry "Gould is God!"

When grasping greed and Avarice drown
And War and Poverty go down
Love, Equality and Peace
Shall bless for aye the human race.
True Christianity restored,
Mammon no longer is adored —
All in one common brotherhood,
The good for all, the greatest good —

# 21

---

During the nineteenth century the tradition of radical Christianity passed from the hands of men to women. In the Anti-slavery and Abolition movements, in temperance, in every area of social reform, women led the way (as, of course, in their own emancipation). Women writers and even more, women orators, exerted considerable influence of popular opinion. Perhaps the most remarkable of this band of "revolutionary" women was Victoria Woodhull. With her sister, Tennie C. Chaflin, Victoria was successively (and sometimes simultaneously) a Spiritualist, an advocate of free love, a muck-raking journalist and editor of *Chaflin and Woodhull's Weekly*, a financier, the first woman candidate for president of the United States, the founder of a labor union (which was too radical for Karl Marx, for he was offended by her espousal of free love), and an enormously successful public lecturer.

If there was a more radical 'Christian' document produced in the nineteenth century than Victoria Woodhull's *The Garden of Eden or The Paradise Lost and Found* it has not come to my attention.

[The text is from Victoria Woodhull, *The Garden of Eden or the Paradise Lost and Found*, (London: Culliford, 1890).]

## The Garden of Eden

Most of the ideas which permeate our social, religious, and political institutions of to-day arise from misconceptions of the human body. These institutions which are the outcome of civilization define laws to regulate and control the actions of *human beings;* and yet, the proper understanding of the growth and development of man individually was, and is, considered of secondary importance in adjusting these laws. My philosophy has been on the lines of Aristotle, who said, "The *nature* of everything is best seen in its smallest portions." My efforts were for the individual or ontogenic development of humanity as the only basis upon which to frame any laws — that by understanding and giving the proper attention to this the *quality* of the whole must of necessity ultimately reach a higher standard. And as the influence of woman is vital, no advance could be made until the co-operation of woman was properly understood and insisted upon as essential to any ideal society, to any true realization of religion, to any perfect government. Active not passive aid is what I demanded from woman. She must be appreciated as the architect of the human race. Men are what their mothers make them. Their intelligence or ignorance has the power to teach them to revere or desecrate womanhood. Night after night throughout the United States I pleaded for the intellectual emancipation and the redemption of womanhood from sexual slavery — insisting that social evils could only be eliminated by making your daughters the peers of your sons — that the greatness of a nation depends upon its mothers. I denounced as criminal the ignorant marriages which were filling the world with their hereditary consequences of woe, shame, and every manner of crime. The theme of my public work was that I would make it a criminal offence to allow persons to marry in ignorance of parental responsibility. I realized that the Bible was little understood, but had in it the germ of a great and divine truth — that is the redemption of the body. A part of this truth regarding the "Garden of Eden," &c., I gave in my extemporaneous lectures. It was afterwards put into consecutive biblical articles and pamphlets. I did not then give the whole truth with which my soul had become illuminated; for I knew the fulness of time was not yet. I considered the work I was then doing as a necessary part of the evolution of thought — as initiatory to my reformatory work. In a book that I am at present writing, it is my intention to give the entire truth of all Bibles, which was only partially understood by primeval religious sects through their ignorance of the phenomena of life.

V. C. W. M.,<br>
17, Hyde Park Gate, London.

"BUT IN THE DAYS OF THE VOICE OF THE SEVENTH ANGEL, WHEN HE SHALL BEGIN TO SOUND, THE MYSTERY OF GOD SHALL BE FINISHED."

Revelation x. 7.

. . . I take up this book and call your attention to it. You perhaps will say, "Oh, that is the old Bible, worn threadbare long ago. We do not wish to be fed with its dry husks. We want living food and drink." Well, that is what I am going to give you. Yes! it is an old book, a very old book. There are very few books extant that can compare with it, on the score of age, at least. Some parts of it were written over three thousand years ago; and all of it more than eighteen hundred years ago. Yes! an old book. And yet everybody seems to have one about the house. What is the matter with the old book? Why do people cling to it with such tenacity? Can any of those who have laid it on the shelf as worthless answer these questions? Why do they not burn it, so that it shall no longer cumber the house? This was a mystery to me for many years; but it is so no longer. I know the reason for its hold upon the people. It contains that, though clad in mystery, which acts upon the soul like a potent spell; like a magnet, which it is indeed. Had it no value, or had its value been wholly extracted; were there no truth in it unrevealed, it had long since ceased to exert any influence whatever over anybody. Books that are exhausted of their truth by its being transferred to the minds of the people, lose their force and die. And this is the reason that I ask you to search its hidden mystery with me; to cast aside preconceived ideas of its meaning; to commence to read it as if it were for the first time.

Religion and science admit that there was an original cause which set up in matter the motion that ultimated in man. The latter examines into the various works that preceded his appearance, and discovers that he came as a result of them all; indeed, that, except they had first existed, he could never have lived; that the omission of a single progressive step in the creative plan would have defeated the work. But science goes further than this. It not only asserts that man was the last link in a long chain of development, but it also maintains that, when the creation once began, there was no power residing anywhere that could have interposed its edicts to stay the progress, or defeat the final production of man; that he was a necessary product of creation, as fruit is of the tree, and that all the designs and purposes of the moving power were contained in and exhausted by his creation; that is, that as a fruit of the creative plan, man was the highest possibility of the universe.

Religious theory, in inquiring into the creation of man, has pursued the method precisely the reverse of this. Having found man on the earth, it assumes that he was a special creation; that is, that God, having purposed in Himself that He would create man, set Himself about to prepare a place in which he was to live; the earth, formed according to the account in Genesis, being that place. I say that this is the theory of religionists; but it is by no means certain that their account of the creation justifies any such conclusion. The biblical account of the creation is an allegorical picture of it, which, in detail, is strikingly in harmony with the real truth. "In the beginning God created the heavens and the earth, and the earth was without form, and void." There were light and darkness — day and night. There were the divisions into water and land; the vegetation, fish, fowl, beast, and man; and next, the rest from labour. In so few words, who could make a clearer statement of what we know about the creation of the earth than this?

We must remember that the Bible does not pretend to be a scientific book at all. It deals altogether with the inspirational or spirit side of the universe. St. Paul informs us that the God of the Bible "is a spirit." At least the translators have made him state it thus; but it is not exactly as he wrote it, although in the end it has the same significance, since if God is a spirit, a spirit is also God. The original Greek of this, which is what Paul meant to say, and did say, and which is the truth, religiously and scientifically also, is *Pneuma Theos* — Pneuma meaning spirit, and Theos God. According to St. Paul, then, spirit is God, and according to science, the life that is in the world is its creative cause; so both agree in their fundamental propositions, however much the priestcraft of the world may have attempted to twist St. Paul into accordance with their ideas of the personal character of God, and in placing God first in the declaration, instead of making spirit the predominant idea. The biblical Creator, then, as defined by the Apostle, is spirit: "And the Spirit of God moved upon the face of the waters" (Genesis i. 2), which was the beginning of creation. The fact, stated scientifically, would be: And the power (or the spirit) resident in matter, caused it to move, and by this motion the earth began to assume form and to be an independent existence, revolving upon its own axis as a planet, and around the sun as its centre.

But I do not purpose to enter into a detailed discussion of the relations which the Bible creation bears to the demonstrations of geology and astronomy. I desire to show merely that the Bible Creator, God, is not at all incompatible with the power which science is compelled to admit as having been the creative cause of all things.

If we take the Darwinian theory and endeavour to find where and how man came, we are led necessarily to a time when there was nothing existing higher than that type of animal by which man is connected with the brute creation, and through which he came to be man. Man is an animal; but he is something more as well. He knows good and evil, and this is to be more than an animal. There was a time, however, when man did not know good and evil. It was then that the form — the human man — was in existence; and it is easy to conceive that the whole face of the earth may have been occupied by human beings who were nothing more than animals, as it is now occupied by them being more than animals. These were the male and female whom God created according to the first chapter of Genesis. It does not mean at all that they were a single male and female. They were not Adam and Eve then. They were simple male and female man, or Adam; for in chapter v. verse 2, we are told, "Male and female created he them and called *their* name Adam;" that is, the human animals that inhabited the earth were called Adam.

Now, this is precisely the condition in which science informs us that man, at one time, must have been. He was not created at one and the same time, physically, mentally, and morally; he may have lived for ages in this animal condition. Of this, Moses tells us nothing in his history of the creation. But as there were immense periods of time — days — between the various epochs of the creation of which he tells us nothing, we must remember that with God there are no divisions of time, for all time is eternity. But there came a point in time when male and female man had developed to the condition in which the gleams of reason began to light up the horizon of the intellect, as the first rays of the morning sun lights the tallest mountains which reflect them into the valleys below.

It was at this time that the Lord God "planted a garden eastward in Eden," in which he put the man whom he had formed "to dress it and to keep it." It is sufficient here to say that it consisted of the ground that was cursed by reason of the sin that Adam and Eve committed. Nor is it essential to the argument, at this time, to consider whether this ground — this garden — was a single one, or whether there was more than one, scattered here and there among male and female men.

The probability is, however, that these names refer to *conditions* and not to individuals. Indeed, it may as well be said now, as later, that the Bible is not a history of individuals and nations at all, but rather the condition and development of universal man, sometimes, perhaps often, using historical facts by which to typify them, but for all that, intended to refer to the *interior* instead of the exterior progress of man; that is, the Bible relates to the building and progress of God's holy temple.

It is upon the consequences of the fall of man, which is therein set forth, that the necessity for a plan of redemption rests. Take away the first three chapters of Genesis and the superstructure of orthodox religion would topple and fall. So, then, it becomes necessary, since Christians have made them vital, to inquire into what these chapters mean — to inquire what was the Garden of Eden, there so graphically set forth — whether a spot of ground situated somewhere on the surface of the earth, or something altogether different — something, perhaps, that it may seldom or never have been suspected of being, and yet something that the language of these chapters plainly states it to have been; or, as may prove to be the exact truth, something other than which it is impossible to derive from the language in which the description is clothed. *For instance, if the various parts of a thing be described as parts, when the parts are put together, that which they form must be the real thing which was in the mind of its relator.* Therefore, if when we shall take the several things described by Moses and put them together, they shall be found to constitute something widely different from a spot of ground on the surface of the earth, why then we shall be forced to conclude that it was not such a spot that Moses had in view when he wrote the second chapter of Genesis; and therefore, also, that the Garden of Eden must be sought elsewhere than in a geographical location.

Indeed, I do not hesitate to say here at the outset, knowing full well the responsibility of the assertion, that I can demonstrate to you — to any minister or number of ministers — to all the theologians everywhere — that there is not a shadow of reason contained in the language used for concluding that the Garden of Eden ever was a geographical locality; but, on the contrary, without resorting to anything outside of the Bible — without any words of my own — I can show, beyond the possibility of cavil, and to the satisfaction of all who will give me their attention, that the Garden of Eden is something altogether different from a vegetable patch, or a fruit or flower garden; aye, more definite than this still — that I can demonstrate, so that there can be no manner of question about it, just what this garden was, and what it still is, with its cherubim and flaming sword defending the approach to its sacred precincts. Nor, as I said, will I go outside of the Bible to do all this, so that, when it shall be done, none can say that I have cited any irrelevant matter or any questionable authority.

The Bible has seldom, if ever — certainly never by professing Christians — been searched with the view to discover any new truth that might not be in harmony with their preconceived ideas as to what the truth ought to be; that is to say, it has never been searched fearlessly of what the truth might prove to be. The seal of mystery that is visible all over the face of the Bible, and that is clearly set forth in words within itself, has never been broken, nor the veil penetrated which hides its real significance from the minds of the people; while the attempts that have been made to interpret this significance have had their origin in a desire to verify some already entertained idea.

To want the truth for the sake of the truth — to want the truth, let it be what it may and lead where it may — has had, so far, no conspicuous following in the world, or at least so few that, practically, it may be said that there has never been any desire for the truth for its own sake. When the truth has appeared to be in antagonism with the cherished conceits of the people, they have shut their eyes and closed their hearts against it, and blocked up all avenues for its approach to them.

One of the best evidences that the full truth is soon to dawn upon the world, lies in the fact that there are now a few persons who want the truth for its own sake, and who will follow it wherever it may lead them.

For one I want the truth, the whole truth; and I will proclaim it, no matter if it be opposed to every vestige of organization extant — political, social, religious! No matter if it be revolutionary to every time-honoured institution in existence! Let creeds fall if they will; let churches topple if they must; let anarchy even reign temporarily if it cannot be avoided, but let us for once in the world have the simple, plain truth; and let us welcome it because it is the truth, and not because it may or may not be in accord with popular notions and opinions . . .

Do you not begin to see how preposterous and impossible, how contradictory and absurd, it is even to pretend to think that the Garden of Eden is a geographical locality? I challenge any clergyman — all clergymen — to impeach the truth, force, or application which I shall make of a single one of the rivers and countries of this famous garden. And I call upon them, failing to do it, to lay this whole fable open to their people as I have laid it open to you. Will they do so? If they care more for their theology than they do for the truth, No! But if they love the truth better than they do their theology, Yes!

But was there not a Garden of Eden! I think some will query in their minds. Or is this thing a bare-faced fraud upon the credulity of a simple people? Oh, yes! — There was a Garden of Eden. It is not at all a fraud. The fraud has been in the preachers, who would not look into the Bible with sufficient reason to discover a most palpable absurdity. There is where the fraud lies, and there it will, sooner or later, come to rest. I do not say that they have done this intentionally. I say only that they have done it; and the responsibility for having misled the people, year after year for centuries, rests with them. They have been the blind leading the blind; and they have both fallen into the ditch of deception.

It was necessary, before there could be a successful search to find the Garden of Eden, to clear away the last vestige of possibility upon which to conceive that it might have been a geographical locality. Have I not made it clear to you all that it was not? If I have, then we are ready to look without bias or prejudice in other directions to find it — for there was a Garden of Eden.

As introductory to this part of my subject, it is proper to say that the general misunderstanding of the real meaning of the Bible can be easily explained. The proper names have been translated from the original languages, arbitrarily, and mingled with the common usage of the new languages, in such a way as to deprive them of their original significance, unless we are familiar with the meaning of the words from which they were translated. The term Eden is a good example. If we are ignorant of the meaning of Eden, in the original language, its use signifies to us that there was a garden which bore this name simply for a designation. But if we were to use the meaning of the word, in the place of the word itself, then we should get at the meaning of the one who gave this designation to the garden. The failure to translate the Bible after this rule is one reason for its still being veiled in mystery; and this fact will become still more evident when it is remembered that, in early times, names were given to persons and things, not merely that they might have a name, but to embody their chief characteristics.

So, then, the first step to be taken is to inquire into the significance of the names that the rivers and countries of the Garden of Eden bear. I cannot explain better what I mean by this than by quoting St. Paul on this very subject. In his letter to the Galatians, beginning at the 22nd verse of the 4th chapter, he says: —

"For it is written, that Abraham had two sons; the one by a bondwoman, the other by a freewoman. But he who was of the bondwoman was born after the flesh; but he who was of the freewoman was by promise. Which things are an allegory: for these are the two covenants; the one from the Mount Sinai, which is Agar. For this Agar is Mount Sinai in Arabia, and answereth to Jerusalem, which is now in bondage with her children."

Now, suppose that Paul had not entered into any explanation about this story regarding Abraham. Of course we should have been left to suppose, conjecturing after the manner of the suppositions about the Garden of Eden, that Abraham really had these two children as described; and so he did. But Paul says it is an allegory; meaning that they represented all children born under both covenants; those of the first being children of bondage — that is, born in sin — and those of the latter being free-born, or born free from sin. This is still more evident when the last verse quoted is interpreted. Jerusalem always means woman, and to get the meaning of the verse it should be read thus: For this Agar is Mount Sinai in Arabia, and answereth to "*woman*," who is in bondage with her children. The succeeding verse demonstrates this clearly, since it reads: "But Jerusalem [woman, remember], which is above, is free, which is the mother of us all." The interpretation of the meaning of the words used in the description of the Garden of Eden will make equally as wonderful transformations of the apparent meaning as are made by Paul in this allegorical story about Abraham.

It is now generally admitted that the account of the creation contained in the first chapter of Genesis is wholly allegorical. Having admitted so much, it would be preposterous to not also conclude that the allegory extends into the second chapter, and includes the Garden of Eden. If the first chapter refers to the creation of the physical universe, it is not too much to say that it is a wonderfully correct picture of the manner in which the world was evolved. If we apply the same statement to the second chapter, then we are ready to inquire what the subject is which this allegorical picture represents . . .

This Garden of Eden is a very much despised place; and if I were not to prepare the way, and guard every word I utter about it with the most scrupulous care, some of you might be so very innocent (by innocence, you must know, I mean that kind which comes of ignorance), or so modest (by modesty, you must know, I mean that kind which is born of conscious corruption, and which blushes at everything, and thus unwittingly proclaims its own shame) — I repeat that, if I were to approach the culmination too abruptly, such innocence and such modesty as that of which I speak, should there happen to be any present, might be too severely shocked.

At the outset, I must ask you to remember that it is out of the most despised spots of the earth that the greatest blessings spring; that it is out of the most obnoxious truths that the forces are developed which move the people heavenward fastest. It is the same old question, "Can there any good thing come out of Nazareth?" It should also be remembered that Jesus was conceived at the most despised of all the places of Galilee. The Jews could not believe that a Saviour of any kind could come from such a source. The promulgators of the new truths have ever been, and probably ever will be, Nazarenes; that is, will be the despised people of the world — though the meaning of that term in the original language is, "consecrated or set apart." It was in this sense that Jesus was a Nazarene. It was in this sense that the prophets were able to foretell that he would be a Nazarene. They knew that he would be set apart to do the greatest work of the ages, and therefore that, at first, he would be despised by the great of this world. Therefore, when we shall find the Garden of Eden, we may expect that it will be among the most despised, ignored, and ostracized of all the despised things of the world.

Lo, here — or, Lo, there — is Christ! is the cry of the world, which is always looking in the wrong direction for Him. Jesus said, "The Kingdom of God is within you." Suppose we find that the Garden of Eden is also within you? If the human body be a place worthy to be, and indeed is, the Kingdom of God, it cannot be sacrilegious to say that it is also worthy to be, or to contain, the Garden of Eden. There cannot be a more holy place than the Kingdom of God; although I am well aware that too many of us have made our bodies most unholy places. Paul said, *"Know ye not that ye are the Temple of God; and that the Spirit of God dwelleth in you? If any man defile the Temple of God, him will God destroy."* Then, the human body is not only the Kingdom of God, it is the Temple of God. Suppose, I say again, it should, after all, turn out that the long-lost Garden of Eden is the human body; that these three, the Kingdom of God, the Temple of God, and the Garden of Eden, are synonymous terms and mean the same thing — are the human body? Suppose this, I say. What then? Would not the people be likely to regard it with a little more reverence than they do now? — and to treat it with a little more care? Would they not modify their pretences that, in their natural condition, any of the parts of the body can be vulgar and impure, and unfit to be discussed either in the public press or the public rostrum? Is it not fair to conclude that, with a higher conception of the body, this ought to be the result? Certainly it would be, unless the doctrine of total depravity is true in its literal sense.

I am well aware that there must be a great change in the present thoughts and ideas about the body before it can be expected that there will be any considerable difference in its general treatment. But a great change has to come, and will come. Certain parts of the body — indeed, its most important parts — are held to be so vulgar and indecent that they have been made the subject of penal laws. Nobody can speak about them without somebody imagining himself or herself to be shocked. Now, all this is very absurd, foolish, and ridiculous, since, do you not know, that this vulgarity and obscenity are not in the body, but in the associated idea in the minds of the people who make the pretence; especially in those who urge the making of, and who make these laws, and who act so foolishly as to discover their own vulgarity and obscenity to the world in this way. How long will it be before the people will begin to comprehend that Paul spoke the truth when he said, "To the pure all things are pure." He ought to be good authority to most of you, who profess him so loudly. But I must confess that I have yet to find the first professing Christian who believes a single word of that most truthful saying. I fear that the hearts of such Christians are still far away from Jesus. But give heed to the truths to which I shall call your attention, and they will help to bring you all nearer to Him both in lip and in heart.

The despised parts of the body are to become what Jesus was, the Saviour conceived at Nazareth. The despised body, and not the honoured soul, must be the stone cut out of the mountain that shall be the head of the corner, though now rejected by the builders. There can be no undefiled or unpolluted temple of God that is not built upon this corner-stone, perfectly. And until the temple shall be perfect there can be no perfect exercise by the in-dwelling spirit. "The stone which the builders disallowed, the same is made the head of the corner." — 1 Peter ii. 7. Christians have been thinking of taking care of the soul by sending it to heaven, while the body has been left to take care of itself and sink to hell, dragging its tenant with it.

"That through death he might destroy him that had the power of death, that is, the devil." — Heb. ii. 14.

"And deliver them who through fear of death were all their lifetime subject to bondage." — Heb. ii. 15.

"God hath chosen the foolish things of the world, to confound the wise; and God hath chosen the weak things of the world to confound the things which are mighty; and base things of the world, and things which are despised, hath God chosen." — 1 Cor. i. 27, 28.

"And those members of the body, which we think to be less honourable, upon them we bestow more abundant honour." — 1 Cor. xii. 23.

The last two chapters of the Revelation refer to the human body saved, and as being the dwelling place of God. The first two chapters of Genesis refer to the body, cursed by the acts of primitive man (male and female), through which acts they became ashamed and covered themselves, because they had done evil to the parts that they desired to hide. Remember, that to the pure all things are pure; and do not deceive yourselves by believing that anything which can be said about the natural functions and organs of the body can be otherwise than pure. From Genesis to the Revelation the human body is the chief subject that is considered — is the temple of God, which through long ages He has been creating to become, finally, His abiding place, when men and women shall come to love Him as He has commanded that they should; and this important thing is the basis of all revelation and all prophecy.

The objection that will be raised against accepting the evident meaning of the 2nd and 3rd chapters of Genesis will be that the things of which they really treat could never have been the subject of scriptural consideration. The degradation of the human race, following the transgression of Adam and Eve, through which purity was veiled from their own lustful gaze, and virtue shut out of the human heart, can never be removed until the world can bear to have that veil lifted, and to look upon and talk in purity about the whole body alike. It was not because they ought to have been ashamed of the nakedness they desired to hide, but because their thoughts were not pure and holy, and because their eyes could not endure the sight without engendering lust within them. So it is now. Only those are ashamed of any parts of the body whose secret thoughts are impure, and whose acts represent their thoughts whenever opportunities present themselves, or can be made.

People talk of purity without the least conception of the real meaning of the term. The people who do no evil because they have no desire to do it, are infinitely more virtuous than are they who refrain because there is a legal or any other kind of penalty attached thereto. So it is with the relations of the sexes. They are the really pure who need no law to compel them to do the right. I do not say that the law has not been useful, nor that it is not useful still. It is better to be restrained by law from doing wrong, than not to be restrained at all; but it is those who need restraint who ought to be ashamed, and not those who have grown beyond the need of law and wish for freedom from its force. In one sense, as Paul said it was, "the law was our schoolmaster;" but those who have graduated from the school, no longer need a master. Shall they, however, be compelled to have one, merely because all others have not yet graduated? Shall everybody be compelled to stay at school till everybody else has left? Think of these questions with but a grain of common sense, and you will see that they who urge the repeal of law are the best entitled to be considered pure at heart, as well as pure in act.

Jesus said, that "Whosoever looketh on a woman to lust after her, hath committed adultery with her already in his heart." Judged by this standard of purity, who are not adulterers? I will tell you who, and who only. Only those are not who can stand the test of natural virtue; and this test is never to do an act for which, under any circumstances, there is cause to be ashamed. Adam and Eve were not ashamed until they had eaten the forbidden fruit — the fruit of the tree which stood in "the midst of the garden," "whose seed is within itself;" but the moment they had done what they knew to be a wrong, when they had learned of good by knowing evil as its contrast, by reason of having done the evil, then they were ashamed and made covers for themselves. They are sexually pure and virtuous who enter into the most sacred and intimate relations of life just as they would go before their God, and by being drawn to them by the Spirit of God, which is ever present in His temple.

This is to have natural virtue. This is to have natural, in place of artificial purity. People who are pure and virtuous may be brought into intimate relations, and never have a lustful thought come into their souls. Now, this is the kind of virtue, purity, and morality that I would have established; it is the kind I advocate as the highest condition to which the race can rise. Suppose that the world were in the condition in which I speak, do you not know that it would be a thousand times more pure than it is? But do you say that all this is too far in the future to be of any use now? This plea is often made — that it ought not to be given to the people till they are ready to receive it and live it. I cannot have a more complete endorsement than to have it said that the people are not yet good enough to live the doctrines that I teach. But if they really do imagine this, I can assure them that they do not give the people credit enough for goodness. Bad as they are, they are not half so bad as some would make them out to be. Place men and women on their honour. You are all familiar with this principle, but you never think of applying it to the social relations, while it is really more applicable to them than it is to almost anything else. But, if the people are not good enough to live under the law of individual honour, then it is quite time that some one should have the courage to go before the world and begin to advocate the things that are needed to make them so.

Before leaving this part of my subject, I wish again to impress it upon you that when there is purity in the heart, it cannot be obscene to consider the natural functions of any part of the body, whether male or female. I am aware that this is a terrible truth to tell to the world, but it is a truth that the world needs to be told; one which it must fully realize before the people will give that care and attention to their creative functions which must precede the building up of a perfected humanity. Who shall dare say that the noblest works — nay, this holy temple — the kingdom of God — is obscene? Perish the vulgarity that makes such thoughts possible.

Where should the Garden of Eden be found if not within the human body? Is there any other place or thing in the universe more worthy to be called an "Eden"? Then let who may, esteeming himself a better judge than myself, condemn this garden as impure. If the gravity and grandeur of this subject were once realized you would never think meanly of, or desecrate your own body, but instead, you would do what Paul commanded (1 Corinthians vi. 20): "Glorify God in your body."

Anyone who will read the second chapter of Genesis, divorced from the idea that it relates to a spot of ground anywhere on the face of the earth, must it seems to me, come to, or near, the truth. I have shown, conclusively, that it is not a garden in the common acceptance of that term: indeed, that the Garden of Eden, according to Moses, is a physical absurdity, if it be interpreted to mean what it is held to mean by the Christian world.

The Garden of Eden is the human body; the second chapter of Genesis was written by Moses to mean the body; it cannot mean anything else. Furthermore, Moses chose the language used because it describes the functions and uses of the body better than any other that he could choose without using the plain terms. Could there have been a more poetic statement of what really does occur? What more complete idea could there be formed of Paradise than a perfect human body — such as there must have been before there had been corruption and degradation in the relation of the sexes? *"Know ye not that ye are the temple of God, and that the Spirit of God dwelleth in you? If any man defile the temple of God, him shall God destroy, for the temple of God is holy, which temple ye are."* — (1 Cor. iii. ver. 16, 17.) *"What! Know you not that your body is the temple of the Holy Ghost which is in you? Therefore glorify God in your body."* — (1 Cor. vi. ver. 19, 20.) . . .

The Garden of Eden then is the human body, and its four rivers, which have their source in the extension of the mouth, are the Pison, the blood; the Gihon, the bowels; the Hiddekel, the urinary organs; and the Euphrates, the reproductive functions. By these four rivers the whole garden is watered and fed or nourished and supported, drained of refuse matter, and its fruit produced. It was in this garden that mankind was planted by the Lord God after the same manner in which He performs all His other works — through the agency of law and order, as exemplified in evolution. It was the ground of this garden that was cursed, so that in sorrow man should "eat of it all the days of his life," and that it should bring forth "thorns and thistles," as Moses said it should, instead of the pleasant and agreeable fruit of perfect and beautiful children. Has not this allegorical picture been literally verified? Paul said he had only "the first fruits of the spirit;" that is to say, having the intellectual comprehension of the means for redemption of his body only.

"If any man defile the temple, him shall God destroy." Does He not do this? Does not death follow the defilement of the temple? In the temples that man has erected, and into which he enters on every seventh day to worship God, He does not dwell. These are the figures or the images only, as Paul said, of the true temple.

Neither in this mountain nor at Jerusalem shall man worship; but in spirit and in truth, said Jesus. The fact that there are so many temples made with hands, into which all the professedly Christian world feels it to be necessary to enter and worship, is a certain evidence that their temples, not made with hands, are not yet the abode of God. Not having consciously the kingdom of heaven within them, where God comes and dwells with them, they still go after Him; and they are so blind that they do not see their own condemnation in the act. If a person has God dwelling in him, he need not go to church to worship Him, nor by so doing to make it evident to others that he is one of God's people, to whom He has come, and with whom He has taken up His abode. Those who have to make a profession of faith to make it appear that they have God, only expose their own hypocrisy, for God's presence in any human being is self-evident proof of the fact.

Consider for a moment what would be the result if the people could come to recognize that their bodies are God's holy temples, and that their sexual organs, being the means by which His crowning work is created, ought never to be defiled by an unholy touch or thought, or ever made the instruments of selfish gratification merely. If the people should enter into these sacred relations only as if they were communing with God — with the same spirit in which really earnest and honest Christians enter into the temples made with hands, which they have falsely thought to be God's temples — and not with unbridled passion, what would become of the debauchery that now runs riot in the world? No; let the sexual act become the holiest act of life, and then the world will begin to be regenerated, and not before. Suppose that those who read the Scriptures, and pray regularly before eating, should go through the same ceremony before entering into the relations which should be the holiest of all relations, how long would the beastliness that now holds high carnival under cover of the law continue? If praying people believe the Bible — believe that their bodies are God's temple — why should they make such hot haste to defile them by their selfish lust and inordinate lasciviousness? Let these people become consistent at least, and in the most important act of life ask God's blessing to rest upon it.

But John saw that these fruits were to be fully realized in the new heaven and the new earth, meaning the new man and the new woman.

"Adorned as a bride prepared for her husband." Can there be any mistaking the significance of this figure? Can it mean anything save the perfected union of the sexes; and in the understanding that this perfection is coming to the world?

Why has God permitted His people to live in darkness and death (all die in Adam) so long, the Christian will ask; and if there is any truth in the Bible as being God's truth, why did He not make it so clear that none could misunderstand it and be lost thereby, the scientist will retort. Now, here is precisely where the reconciliation between religionists and scientists will come. The very thing that the Bible declares to be a gift of God, which is to be revealed when the mystery shall be solved, is the very thing after which all science seeks — the perfect life. The ultimate fact after which both religion and science bend their energies is the self-same thing. The Spirit — God — tells what this is inspirationally in the Bible; men delve for it among the laws of nature scientifically. At the same time that it shall be discovered to the world of what this mystery of God consists: it will be demonstrated by actual life in individuals. Inspiration and evolution mean the self-same thing, spoken from the opposite extremes of the development by which it shall come — the former being the spiritual comprehension of the truth before it is "made flesh and dwells among us," and evolution being its actualization in experience.

Interpret the arbitrary commands of the Bible by the language of natural law, by which alone God works, and the reconciliation between God and nature, between religion and science, between inspiration and evolution, is completed. Inspiration is the language of men who were permeated with Divine essence, but knew nothing about the law of cause and effect. They attributed the destruction of a city by fire or by an earthquake, in short, every visitation of painful effects upon men, as a direct and arbitrary command of God as punishment for sin; while by the light of science they are only the natural effects of immutable laws, occurring because they must occur, in the evolution of the universe. All the sins and punishments of which man has been made the subject are of the same order. It was impossible that man, being an animal, should be made a son of God, save by the very process through which he has had to pass.

That the law of evolution which makes growth the method by which intellectual altitude is reached, is also the law by which physical development goes forward; the perfected creation of man and his consequent salvation from death being physical and not moral, as has been falsely taught by almost the whole of Christendom. With a perfect physical body — man reconciled to God — all other perfections follow as its fruit, necessarily. The opposite proposition to this is the stumbling-block over which all Christians have fallen; they have given all their attention to saving the soul hereafter, when this salvation depends entirely upon saving the body here and now.

Is it not palpable how the acceptance of this fact, and the adoption of its logic as a rule of human action, would harmonize the relations of man? With this view, everything that occurs is a part, and a necessary part, of the evolution or the growth of man. *Suppose criminals were to be treated by this principle, what a reform might be inaugurated in this regard!* Suppose this precept were to be made a rule of life, the world could be at once transformed into a brotherhood. But this must also be a result of growth.

"And out of the ground (female-male) the Lord God formed every beast of the field, and every fowl of the air." The two sexes must have been comprised by each species, evidently a rib was not taken out of each male to make a corresponding female.

In the first dawn of the life-principle there was no such thing as sex. Life was a unit, that is, a homogeneous mass, gradually becoming heterogeneous until two sexes were evolved. The Biblical allegory of Adam and Eve, that the two sexes were evolved from one, accords with science. Had this a deeper meaning than even Moses comprehended? Still more curious was the supposition that the male animal was the first distinct sex; before the male animal, it was the two sexes in one of the female-male animal. And the male organs of the latter becoming gradually degenerated or suppressed the distinct female animal was evolved to correspond with the male animal.

Here we have the ideal marriage. The two unite to become as one from which the human family had its birth. Onward from the family next were formed the roving tribes which had a chosen head, who ruled the whole with arbitrary will in all respects. Next cities sprang into existence, and reaching over provinces united into nations, making their kings or queens, their rulers absolute. From this, the concentrated form of power, the sway began to re-dispose itself among the people. Through monarchs limited in rule to constitutions and republics has the power descended and now it is about to be assumed again by each and all individuals who have become a law unto themselves, into whose hearts Almighty God has put His law of love. From individuals such as these a brotherhood of man can form and live, but not from any other kind. And from a brotherhood wherein the good of each becomes the good of all, the higher and the holier family will spring into existence, whose King and Queen and Lord and Prince shall be the living God who from creation's dawn through long experience, sometimes dark but often bright, hath brought us kindly on our way to this exalted place as His abode . . .

# 22

---

Reinhold Neibuhr is the only contemporary to have a place in this work because he, almost single-handedly, revived the notion of Original Sin so central to the thinking of the Founding Fathers. It was he who, at least among American theologians, most clearly began that long, arduous, and deeply rewarding journey back through thickets of liberal theology to the radical roots of orthodox Protestant doctrine. In his writings we can perceive the faith of the Founders, and of *their* predecessors. Under his influence we began to reclaim that tradition which created such a large part of the modern consciousness.

[The text is taken from Reinhold Niebuhr, "Democracy, Secularism, and Christianity,"*Christian Realism and Political Problems*, (New York: Charles Scribner's Sons,1953) pp. 95 - 103.]

## Democracy, Secularism, and Christianity

For a long time a debate has been waged between Christian and secular leaders on the question whether democracy is the product of the Christian faith or of a secular culture. The debate has been inconclusive because, as a matter of history, both Christian and secular forces were involved in establishing the political institutions of democracy; and the cultural resources of modern free societies are jointly furnished by both Christianity and modern secularism. Furthermore there are traditional non-democratic Christian cultures to the right of free societies which prove that the Christian faith does not inevitably yield democratic historical fruits. And there are totalitarian regimes to the left of free societies which prove that secular doctrine can, under certain circumstances, furnish grist for the mills of modern tyrannies. The debate is, in short, inconclusive because the evidence for each position is mixed.

Perhaps a fair appraisal of it would lead to the conclusion that free societies are the fortunate products of the confluence of Christian and secular forces. This may be so because democracy requires, on the one hand, a view of man which forbids using him merely as an instrument of a political program or social process. This view the Christian and Jewish faiths have supplied. On the other hand, a free society requires that human ends and ambition, social forces and political powers be judged soberly and critically in order that the false sanctities and idolatries of both traditional societies and modern tyrannies be avoided. This sober and critical view is the fruit both of some types of Christianity and of the secular temper with its interest in efficient causes and in immediate, rather than ultimate, ends.

Democracy as a political institution is rooted in the principle of universal suffrage; which arms every citizen with political power and the chance to veto the actions of his rulers. It implements the thesis that governments derive their authority from the consent of the governed. Both clerical absolutism and orthodox Protestantism's principle of the divine rights of kings had to be challenged before political democracy could arise. As a matter of history the later Calvinism and the Christian sects of the seventeenth century and the rationalism of the eighteenth century, equally contributed to the challenge of religiously sanctified political authority. In our own nation, the equal contributions which were made to our political thought by New England Calvinism and Jeffersonian deism are symbolic of this confluence of Christianity and secularism in our democracy.

There is no doubt that the economic institutions of a free society rest upon secular theories and, moreover, upon some erroneous ones. What is usually now defined as "free enterprise" is a form of economic organization which rests upon a physiocratic theory, which is consistently secular and naturalistic. It erroneously assumes that the ambitions of men are contained within the bounds of what is called "nature"; it erroneously believes that the desires of men are chiefly economic and essentially ordinate and the the market place is a sufficient instrument for the coordination of all spontaneous human acticities. These are grievous errors. Some of them, being introduced into history at the precise moment when a technical civilization transmuted the static inequalities into dynamic ones, led to the early injustices of modern industrialism. But none of the errors could prevent the classical economic theory from rendering two great services to the development of a free society.

The one was to encourage the coordination of mutual services without political coercion, thereby establishing the flexibility of a democratic society. This contribution remains even after most healthy democracies have discovered that the market place is not an adequate coordinator, and have supplemented the automatic harmonies of interest with various forms of contrived balances in which the political power plays a role.

The other was to make genuinely secular (that is, non-sacred) objects and ends of human striving morally respectable. A free society encourages a multitude of activities which are not in themselves sacred; and it discourages the premature sanctities in which both traditional societies and modern forms of collectivism abound, partly because they make some center of political power into a false center of meaning. It must be noted, of course, that an explicit secularism disavowing reverence of the holy, and interest in the ultimate, may generate many false sanctities and idolatries. The idolatries of democracy, the worship of efficiency and the self-worship of the individual are religiously banal but comparatively harmless compared with the noxious idolatries of modern secular totalitarianism. The latter prove that an explicit denial of the ultimate and divine may be the basis for a religious politics which generates idolatries. On the other hand, the Reformation's principle of the sanctity of all work contributed to the vigor of a free society by giving men the assurance of serving God in ordinary, that is in secular, callings.

The ethos of a free society is even more problematical than its political and economic institutions. Obviously a democratic society requires a respect for the individual which will prevent him from being made into a mere instrument of a social or political process, and which will guard his integrity against collective power. Modern secular thought prides itself upon the idea that its optimistic view of human nature, depending upon an erroneous identification of the virtue and the dignity of man, laid the foundation of modern democracy. This is true only in the sense that a too pessimistic view of human nature, whether of a Hobbes or of a Luther, may lead to political absolutism. Democracy does indeed require some confidence in man's natural capacity for justice. But its institutions can be more easily justified as bulwarks against injustice. Indeed it is because democracy holds every public power under public scrutiny and challenges every pretension of wisdom, and balances every force with a countervailing force, that some of the injustices which characterize traditional societies, and modern tyrannies, are prevented.

Christian thought is offended by the idea that secularism is an aid in delivering traditional societies from their idolatries. Ostensibly the worship of the true God eliminates reverence for false sanctities. But Christians cannot deny that the religious theory of divine right of kings has been a powerful force in traditional societies; nor must they obscure the fact that even a true religion frequently generates false identifications of some human interest with God's will. Secularism is offended by the charge of its affinity with totalitarianism. There are in fact two secular theories of the community and only one of them obviously makes for totalitarianism; the one theory, the thesis of classical economics, was held by the middle classes. The Marxist theory was the weapon of the industrial classes. They both make faulty analysis of the human situation. But the classical theory provides for a multiplicity of powers and the Marxist theory leads to a monopoly of power. All the errors of the first theory are partially relieved by its one virtue; and all the truth in the second theory does not redeem it from this one serious error. The history of our age has no more significant development than that the uneasy conscience of sensitive spirits about the injustices which arose from disproportions of power in a liberal society has been overcome by the fact that the alternative organization of society, when carried through consistently, leads to a monopoly of power; and a monopoly of power leads to all the evils which the Russian tyranny exhibits. The so-called left opinion, whether Christian or secular, must plead guilty to its failure to foresee the perils of this development. Modern conservative opinion is mistaken, however, in insisting that an appreciation of the role of political power must lead to the monopoly of power of which the end product is tyranny. For the healthiest democracies have taken steps both to prevent the partial monopoly of economic power which obtained in the early organization of liberal society and to ward off total monopoly of economic and political power which results from a consistent application of the Marxist theory. Meanwhile the facts about human nature which make a monopoly of power dangerous and a balance of power desirable are understood in neither theory but are understood from the standpoint of the Christian faith.

The democratic wisdom which learns how to avoid and negate conflicting ideologies, based upon interest, may be, of course, the result of experience rather than of special Christian insights. But it cannot be denied that biblical faith (from which Judaism and Christianity are derived) is unique in offering three insights into the human situation which are indispensable to democracy. The first is that it assumes a source of authority from the standpoint of which the individual may defy the authorities of this world. ("We must obey God rather than man.") The second is an appreciation of the unique worth of the individual which makes it wrong to fit him into any political program as a mere instrument. A scientific humanism frequently offends the dignity of man, which it ostensibly extols, by regarding human beings as subject to manipulation and as mere instruments of some "socially approved" ends. It is this tendency of a scientific age which establishes its affinity with totalitarianism, and justifies the charge that a scientific humanism is harmless only because there is not a political program to give the elite, which its theories invariably presuppose, a monopoly of power. The third insight is the biblical insistence that the same radical freedom which makes man creative also makes him potentially destructive and dangerous, that the dignity of man and the misery of man therefore have the same root. This insight is the basis of all political realism in which secular theory, whether liberal or Marxist, is defective; it justifies the institutions of democracy more surely than any sentimentality about man, whether liberal or radical.

The simple fact is that philosophies, whether naturalistic or idealistic, fail to understand man in so far as they try to fit him into a system. The system obscures the height of his spirit, the uniqueness of his being, and the egoistic corruption of his freedom. That is why the dramatic-historical approach to human and divine reality validates itself despite the prestige of modern science. A scientific culture, despite its great achievements, exhibits a curious naivete in surveying the human scene. That is probably due to the fact that mysteries of good and evil in human nature are obscured to those who insist upon making man an object of scientific investigation and try to fit his radical freedom into some kind of system.

It will be seen that the evidence is too complex to justify either the thesis that secularism leads to totalitarianism or the contradictory idea that it is indispensable for the rise and preservation of democracy. One of the significant facts in the history of democracy as in modern history, generally, is that truth seems so often to have ridden into view on the back of error. Perhaps that is how "God maketh the wrath of man to praise Him."

It goes without saying, that democracy is not the sole or final criterion of the adequacy of a culture or truth of a religion. Catholicism, for instance, which is not productive of democratic cultures, at least not unaided, has some graces of the spirit which must be appreciated despite its lacks in relation to democracy. Secular democratic societies, on the other hand, may preserve freedom and sink into phillistinism in their preoccupation with the gadgets and goods of life. But there is a strong affinity at one point between democracy and Christianity: the toleration which democracy requires is difficult to maintain without Christian humility; and the challenges to pretensions of every kind which are furnished in the give and take of democratic life, are, on the other hand, strong external supports for the Christian grace of humility which recognizes the partial and particular character of everyone's interest and the fragmentary character of every human virtue.